Microsoft®

FrontPage® 2000
Illustrated Complete

Jessica Evans
Ann Barron
Chet Lyskawa

COURSE
TECHNOLOGY

Thomson Learning™

MICROSOFT OFFICE
USER SPECIALIST

APPROVED COURSEWARE

EXPERT

25 THOMSON PLACE, BOSTON, MA 02210

Australia • Canada • Denmark • Japan • Mexico • New Zealand • Philippines
Puerto Rico • Singapore • South Africa • Spain • United Kingdom • United States

Microsoft FrontPage 2000—Illustrated Complete is published by Course Technology

Managing Editor:	Nicole Jones Pinard
Product Manager:	Rebecca VanEsselstine
Production Editor:	Megan Cap-Renzi
Developmental Editor:	Pam Conrad
Composition House:	GEX, Inc.
QA Manuscript Reviewer:	Justin Rand, Alex White
Text Designer:	Joseph Lee, Black Fish Design
Cover Designer:	Doug Goodman, Doug Goodman Designs

Trademarks

Course Technology and the Open Book logo are registered trademarks of Course Technology.

Illustrated Projects and the Illustrated Series are trademarks of Course Technology.

Some of the product names and company names used in this book have been used for identification purposes only and may be trademarks or registered trademarks of their respective manufacturers and sellers.

For more information contact:

Course Technology
22 Thomson Place
Boston, MA 02210

Or find us on the World Wide Web at: www.course.com

Disclaimer

Course Technology reserves the right to revise this publication and make changes from time to time in its content without notice.

ISBN 0-619-01767-8

Printed in the United States of America

1 2 3 4 5 6 7 8 9 BM 05 04 03 02 01

The Illustrated Series Offers the Entire Package for your Microsoft Office 2000 Needs

Office 2000 MOUS Certification Coverage

The Illustrated Series offers a growing number of Microsoft-approved titles that cover the objectives required to pass the Office 2000 MOUS (Microsoft Office User Specialist) exams. After studying with any of the approved Illustrated titles (see list on inside cover), you will have mastered the Core and Expert skills necessary to pass any Office 2000 MOUS exam. In addition, the **Microsoft FrontPage Complete MOUS Certification Objectives** at the end of the book map to where specific MOUS skills can be found in each lesson and where students can find additional practice.

Helpful New Features

The Illustrated Series responded to Customer Feedback by adding a **Project Files List** at the back of the book for easy reference, changing the red font in the steps to green for easier reading, and adding new conceptual lessons to units to give students the extra information they need when learning Office 2000.

Enhance Any Illustrated Text with these Exciting Products!

Course CBT

Enhance your students' Office 2000 classroom learning experience with self-paced computer-based training on CD-ROM. Course CBT engages students with interactive multimedia and hands-on simulations that reinforce and complement the concepts and skills covered in the textbook. All the content is aligned with the MOUS program, making it a great preparation tool for the certification exams. Course CBT also includes extensive pre- and post-assessments that test students' mastery of skills.

SAM 2000

How well do your students really know Microsoft Office? SAM 2000 is a performance-based testing program that measures students' proficiency in Microsoft Office 2000. You can use SAM 2000 to place students into or out of courses, monitor their performance throughout a course, and help prepare them for the MOUS certification exams.

Create Your Ideal Course Package with CourseKits™

If one book doesn't offer all the coverage you need, create a course package that does. With Course Technology's CourseKits—our mix-and-match approach to selecting texts—you have the freedom to combine products from more than one series. When you choose any two or more Course Technology products for one course, we'll discount the price and package them together so your students can pick up one convenient bundle at the bookstore.

For more information about any of these offerings or other Course Technology products, contact your sales representative or visit our Web site at:

www.course.com

Preface

Welcome to *Microsoft FrontPage 2000—Illustrated Complete*. This highly visual book offers users a hands-on introduction to Microsoft FrontPage 2000 and also serves as an excellent reference for future use.

▶ Organization and Coverage

This text contains sixteen units that cover basic to advanced FrontPage 2000 skills. In these units, students learn how to create and manage Web sites and pages, create tables and frames, add graphics to Web pages and change their properties, create new Web sites on a server, integrate a database with a FrontPage Web, publish Web sites to the Personal Web Server and to a network server, and work with HTML code.

▶ About this Approach

What makes the Illustrated approach so effective at teaching software skills? It's quite simple. Each skill is presented on two facing pages, with the step-by-step instructions on the left page, and large screen illustrations on the right. Students can focus on a single skill without having to turn the page. This unique design makes information extremely accessible and easy to absorb, and provides a great reference for after the course is over. This hands-on approach also makes it ideal for both self-paced or instructor-led classes.

Each lesson, or "information display," contains the following elements:

Each 2-page spread focuses on a single skill.

Clear step-by-step directions explain how to complete the specific task, with what students are to type in green. When students follow the numbered steps, they quickly learn how each procedure is performed and what the results will be.

Concise text that introduces the basic principles discussed in the lesson. Procedures are easier to learn when concepts fit into a framework.

Modifying Table Properties

FrontPage 2000

Table properties allow you to control the appearance of the entire table. For example, you can select a background color for the table, determine the width of the border, change the alignment of the table, specify the cell padding, or indicate the cell spacing. Table F-1 defines the available table properties. Connie decides to change the color of her table and alter the space between the text of each cell and the cell border.

Steps

QuickTip
You can also select a background image for the entire table or for an individual cell in the table.

1. Right-click anywhere in the table, then select **Table Properties** from the pop-up menu
   The Table Properties dialog box appears.
2. Double-click in the **Border Size text box** and type **6**, double-click in the **Cell spacing text box** and type **8**, click the **Background Color list arrow**, then click **White**
   The settings for the Table Properties are shown in Figure F-5.
3. Click **Style**, click **Format**, then click **Font**
   The Font dialog box opens.
4. Select **Times** (or a similar font) for the Font, then click **OK** three times
   The Peripherals page appears with the settings applied to the entire table.
5. Right-click anywhere on the table and select **Table Properties**
   The Table Properties dialog box opens.
6. Double-click in the **Cell padding box**, type **8**, double-click in the **Cell spacing box** and type **2**, then click **OK**
   The space between the text and the borders of each cell increases, and the space between cells decreases.
7. Click the **Save button** on the Standard toolbar
   The table appears as shown in Figure F-6.

TABLE F-1: Table properties

table property	description
Alignment	Aligns the table to the left, right, or center of the window
Float	Determines whether text outside the table flows around the table (Left or Right) or not at all (Default)
Border size	Specifies the thickness of the lines on the outside edge of the table
Cell padding	Specifies the distance between the cell's contents and its border
Cell spacing	Specifies the thickness of the borders between cells
Minimum size Width/height	Determines the width and height of the table as either a percentage of the window width or a number of pixels
Custom background image	Determines the background image for the table
Custom background color	Determines the background color of the entire table
Custom border color	Determines the color of the table's border
Custom light border color	Determines the color of the table's top and left borders
Custom dark border color	Determines the color of the table's bottom and right borders

▶FRONTPAGE F-4 **CREATING TABLES AND FRAMES**

Hints as well as trouble-shooting advice, right where you need it – next to the step itself.

Quickly accessible summaries of key terms, toolbar buttons, or keyboard alternatives connected with the lesson material. Students can refer easily to this information when working on their own projects at a later time.

Every lesson features large-size, full-color representations of what the students' screen should look like after completing the numbered steps.

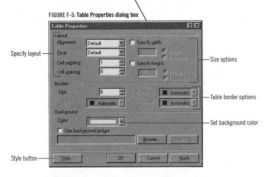

FIGURE F-5: Table Properties dialog box

Specify layout
Size options
Table border options
Set background color
Style button

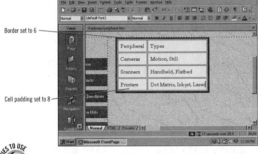

FIGURE F-6: White table with narrow border and increased cell padding.

Border set to 6

Cell padding set to 8

Peripheral	Types
Cameras	Motion, Still
Scanners	Handheld, Flatbed
Printers	Dot Matrix, Ink-jet, Laser

CLUES TO USE

Understanding cell spacing and cell padding

The differences between cell spacing and cell padding are illustrated in Figure F-7. When the Cell spacing is set to 10 and the Cell padding is 0, the text is next to the borders, but the borders are wide. In contrast, when the Cell padding is 10 and the Cell spacing is 0, substantial space separates the text and the borders.

FIGURE F-7: Cell spacing and cell padding

Cell spacing=10
Cell padding=0

Cell spacing=0
Cell padding=10

CREATING TABLES AND FRAMES FRONTPAGE F-5

FrontPage 2000

Clues to Use boxes provide concise information that either expands on one component of the major lesson skill or describes an independent task that is in some way related to the major lesson skill.

Other Features

The two-page lesson format featured in this book provides the new user with a powerful learning experience. Additionally, this book contains the following features:

▶ **MOUS Certification Coverage**
Each unit opener has a ⌐MOUS⌐ next to it to indicate where Microsoft Office User Specialist (MOUS) skills are covered. In addition, there is a MOUS appendix which contains a grid that maps to where specific MOUS skills can be found in each lesson and where students can find additional practice. This textbook prepares students for the Microsoft FrontPage 2000 MOUS exams.

▶ **Real-World Skills**
The skills used throughout the textbook are designed to be "real-world" in nature and representative of the kinds of activities that students encounter when working with FrontPage 2000. With a real-world case, the process of solving problems will be more meaningful to students.

▶ **End of Unit Material**
Each unit concludes with a Concepts Review that tests students' understanding of what they learned in the unit. The Concepts Review is followed by a Skills Review, which provides students with additional hands-on practice of the skills. The Skills Review is followed by Independent Challenges, which pose case problems for students to solve. At least one Independent Challenge in each unit asks students to use the World Wide Web to solve the problem as indicated by a Web Work icon. The Visual Workshops that follow the Independent Challenges help students develop critical thinking skills. Students are shown completed Web pages or screens and are asked to recreate them from scratch.

Instructor's Resource Kit

The Instructor's Resource Kit is Course Technology's way of putting the resources and information needed to teach and learn effectively into your hands. With an integrated array of teaching and learning tools that offers you and your students a broad range of technology-based instructional options, we believe this kit represents the highest quality and most cutting edge resources available to instructors today. Many of these resources are available at www.course.com. The resources available with this book are:

Course Test Manager Designed by Course Technology, this Windows-based testing software helps instructors design, administer, and print tests and pre-tests. A full-featured program, Course Test Manager also has an online testing component that allows students to take tests at the computer and have their exams automatically graded.

Instructor's Manual Available as an electronic file, the Instructor's Manual is quality-assurance tested and includes unit overviews, detailed lecture topics for each unit with teaching tips, an Upgrader's Guide, solutions to all lessons and end-of-unit material, and extra Independent Challenges. The Instructor's Manual is available on the Instructor's Resource Kit CD-ROM, or you can download it from **www.coursc.com**.

Course Faculty Online Companion You can browse this textbook's password-protected site to obtain the Instructor's Manual, Solution Files, Project Files, and any updates to the text. Contact your Customer Service Representative for the site address and password.

Figure Files The figures in the text are provided on the Instructor's Resource Kit CD to help illustrate key topics or concepts. Instructors can create traditional overhead transparencies by printing the figure files. Or they can create electronic slide shows by using the figures in a presentation program such as PowerPoint.

Solution Files Solution Files contain every file students are asked to create or modify in the lessons and end-of-unit material. A Help file on the Instructor's Resource Kit includes information for using the Solution Files.

Student Online Companion This book features its own Online Companion where students can go to access Web sites that will help them complete the WebWork Independent Challenges. Because the Web is constantly changing, the Student Online Companion will provide the reader with current updates regarding links referenced in the book.

WebCT WebCT is a tool used to create Web-based educational environments and also uses WWW browsers as the interface for the course-building environment. The site is hosted on your school campus, allowing complete control over the information. WebCT has its own internal communication system, offering internal e-mail, a Bulletin Board, and a Chat room.

Course Technology offers pre-existing supplemental information to help in your WebCT class creation, such as a suggested Syllabus, Lecture Notes, Figures in the Book / Course Presenter, Student Downloads, and Test Banks in which you can schedule an exam, create reports, and more.

Brief Contents

Exciting New Products   III
Preface   IV

FrontPage 2000	Getting Started with FrontPage 2000	FRONTPAGE A-1
	Working with Web Page Templates	FRONTPAGE B-1
	Working with Web Pages	FRONTPAGE C-1
	Enhancing Web Pages	FRONTPAGE D-1
	Adding Graphics Features to Web Pages	FRONTPAGE E-1
	Creating Tables and Frames	FRONTPAGE F-1
	Working with HTML Forms	FRONTPAGE G-1
	Enhancing and Maintaining a Web Site	FRONTPAGE H-1
	Working with Tables and Frames in a Web Site	FRONTPAGE I-1
	Using Shared Borders and Themes in a Web Site	FRONTPAGE J-1
	Publishing a Web Site	FRONTPAGE K-1
	Creating a New Web Site on a Web Server	FRONTPAGE L-1
	Using Office Components and Styles	FRONTPAGE M-1
	Integrating a Database with a FrontPage Web	FRONTPAGE N-1
	Publishing a Web on a Web Server	FRONTPAGE O-1
	Working with HTML Code	FRONTPAGE P-1

FrontPage 2000 MOUS Certification Objectives   1
Project Files   11
Glossary   16
Index   22

Contents

Exciting New Products   III
Preface   IV

FrontPage 2000

Getting Started with FrontPage 2000   FRONTPAGE A-1

Understanding Web Servers and Sites   FRONTPAGE A-2
    Using HTML (Hypertext Markup Language)   FRONTPAGE A-3
Starting FrontPage 2000   FRONTPAGE A-4
Planning a New Web Site   FRONTPAGE A-6
    Defining a Web folder hierarchy   FRONTPAGE A-7
Creating a New Web with a FrontPage 2000 Wizard   FRONTPAGE A-8
Working with the Tasks List   FRONTPAGE A-10
    Viewing Task History   FRONTPAGE A-10
Viewing the FrontPage Window   FRONTPAGE A-12
    Using ScreenTips   FRONTPAGE A-12
Creating Web Folders   FRONTPAGE A-14
Getting Help   FRONTPAGE A-16
    Getting FrontPage Web Help   FRONTPAGE A-16
Closing the Web and Exiting FrontPage 2000   FRONTPAGE A-18
    Opening an existing Web   FRONTPAGE A-19
Concepts Review   FRONTPAGE A-20
Skills Review   FRONTPAGE A-21
Independent Challenges   FRONTPAGE A-22
Visual Workshop   FRONTPAGE A-24

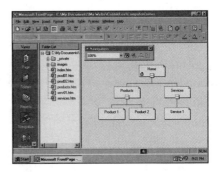

Working with Web Page Templates   FRONTPAGE B-1

Understanding FrontPage   FRONTPAGE B-2
    Planning a Web page   FRONTPAGE B-3
Opening a Web Page   FRONTPAGE B-4
    Opening existing pages   FRONTPAGE B-5
Editing a Web Page   FRONTPAGE B-6
Previewing, Saving, and Closing a Web Page   FRONTPAGE B-8
    Using the Normal, Preview, and HTML tabs   FRONTPAGE B-9
Creating a New Web Page from a Template   FRONTPAGE B-10
Adding a Banner and Navigation Bars   FRONTPAGE B-12
    Setting navigation bar properties   FRONTPAGE B-12
Creating a New Page in Navigation View   FRONTPAGE B-14
    Changing a Web theme   FRONTPAGE B-15
Using Shared Borders   FRONTPAGE B-16

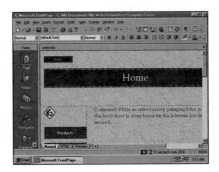

Contents

Concepts Review .... FRONTPAGE B-18
Skills Review .... FRONTPAGE B-20
Independent Challenges .... FRONTPAGE B-21
Visual Workshop .... FRONTPAGE B-24

Working with Web Pages .... FRONTPAGE C-1

Removing Shared Borders and Themes .... FRONTPAGE C-2
   Using descriptive titles for Web pages .... FRONTPAGE C-3
Setting Page Properties .... FRONTPAGE C-4
   Contrasting text and background colors .... FRONTPAGE C-5
Entering Text into a Web Page .... FRONTPAGE C-6
   Using the Thesaurus .... FRONTPAGE C-7
Formatting Text .... FRONTPAGE C-8
   Accessing the Font dialog box .... FRONTPAGE C-9
Formatting Paragraph Styles .... FRONTPAGE C-10
Printing a Web Page .... FRONTPAGE C-12
Importing a Web Page .... FRONTPAGE C-14
   Setting the download limit .... FRONTPAGE C-14
Deleting and Exporting Web Pages .... FRONTPAGE C-16
   Maintaining backups for Web pages .... FRONTPAGE C-17
Concepts Review .... FRONTPAGE C-18
Skills Review .... FRONTPAGE C-19
Independent Challenges .... FRONTPAGE C-21
Visual Workshop .... FRONTPAGE C-24

Enhancing Web Pages .... FRONTPAGE D-1

Inserting a Picture .... FRONTPAGE D-2
   Inserting a picture, text, or a hyperlink
   from a Web browser .... FRONTPAGE D-3
Editing a Picture .... FRONTPAGE D-4
   Downloading pictures .... FRONTPAGE D-5
Inserting a Horizontal Line .... FRONTPAGE D-6
Inserting a Hyperlink to a Local Web Page .... FRONTPAGE D-8
   Creating hyperlinks .... FRONTPAGE D-9
Testing a Hyperlink .... FRONTPAGE D-10
   Correcting your hyperlinks .... FRONTPAGE D-11
Creating Hyperlinks to Remote Web Pages .... FRONTPAGE D-12
   Creating a hyperlink to a new Web page .... FRONTPAGE D-12
Linking to an E-mail Address .... FRONTPAGE D-14
   Addressing E-mail .... FRONTPAGE D-15
Inserting a Hyperlink to a Bookmark .... FRONTPAGE D-16
   Inserting bookmarks .... FRONTPAGE D-16
Using a Picture for a Hyperlink .... FRONTPAGE D-18
Concepts Review .... FRONTPAGE D-20
Skills Review .... FRONTPAGE D-21
Independent Challenges .... FRONTPAGE D-22
Visual Workshop .... FRONTPAGE D-24

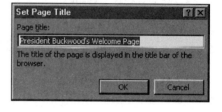

Adding Graphic Features to Web Pages

	FRONTPAGE E-1
Setting Custom Colors	FRONTPAGE E-2
Understanding color values	FRONTPAGE E-3
Using an Image for a Background	FRONTPAGE E-4
Downloading Clip Art from the Web	FRONTPAGE E-6
Using the Pictures Toolbar to Modify Images	FRONTPAGE E-8
Sizing an image	FRONTPAGE E-9
Aligning Text to an Image	FRONTPAGE E-10
Creating and Editing Hotspots	FRONTPAGE E-12
Editing hotspots	FRONTPAGE E-13
Adding a Scrolling Marquee	FRONTPAGE E-14
Adding Page Transitions and Animations	FRONTPAGE E-16
Concepts Review	FRONTPAGE E-18
Skills Review	FRONTPAGE E-20
Independent Challenges	FRONTPAGE E-22
Visual Workshop	FRONTPAGE E-24

Creating Tables and Frames

	FRONTPAGE F-1
Inserting a Table	FRONTPAGE F-2
Setting the table width	FRONTPAGE F-3
Modifying Table Properties	FRONTPAGE F-4
Understanding cell spacing and cell padding	FRONTPAGE F-5
Adding Rows, Columns, and Captions to Tables	FRONTPAGE F-6
Modifying Cell Properties	FRONTPAGE F-8
Creating a Web Page with Frames	FRONTPAGE F-10
Setting Frame Targets	FRONTPAGE F-12
Modifying Frame Properties	FRONTPAGE F-14
Exiting a Frame Page	FRONTPAGE F-16
Concepts Review	FRONTPAGE F-18
Skills Review	FRONTPAGE F-19
Independent Challenges	FRONTPAGE F-21
Visual Workshop	FRONTPAGE F-24

Working with HTML Forms

	FRONTPAGE G-1
Understanding HTML Forms	FRONTPAGE G-2
Creating an HTML Form with a Wizard	FRONTPAGE G-4
Setting Form Properties	FRONTPAGE G-6
Comparing Common Gateway Interface (CGI)	
to FrontPage Server Extensions	FRONTPAGE G-7
Adding Text Boxes	FRONTPAGE G-8
Setting Form Field Properties	FRONTPAGE G-10
Setting other field properties	FRONTPAGE G-11
Inserting Radio Buttons	FRONTPAGE G-12

Contents

Adding Check Boxes — FRONTPAGE G-14
Inserting a Drop-Down Menu — FRONTPAGE G-16
   Viewing the results file — FRONTPAGE G-17
Concepts Review — FRONTPAGE G-18
Skills Review — FRONTPAGE G-20
Independent Challenges — FRONTPAGE G-22
Visual Workshop — FRONTPAGE G-24

Enhancing and Maintaining a Web Site — FRONTPAGE H-1

Inserting a FrontPage Component — FRONTPAGE H-2
Adding a Search Form — FRONTPAGE H-4
Adding Content Listings — FRONTPAGE H-6
Inserting Hover Buttons — FRONTPAGE H-8
Inserting a Banner Ad Manager — FRONTPAGE H-10
Viewing and Verifying Hyperlinks — FRONTPAGE H-12
Working with Reports View — FRONTPAGE H-14
Publishing a Web Site — FRONTPAGE H-16
   Setting server permissions — FRONTPAGE H-16
Concepts Review — FRONTPAGE H-18
Skills Review — FRONTPAGE H-20
Independent Challenges — FRONTPAGE H-22
Visual Workshop — FRONTPAGE H-24

Working with Tables and Frames in a Web Site — FRONTPAGE I-1

Resizing a Table — FRONTPAGE I-2
Resizing a Table Cell — FRONTPAGE I-4
   Using the pop-up menu to resize table rows and columns — FRONTPAGE I-5
Centering a Picture in a Table Cell — FRONTPAGE I-6
   Centering a table on a Web page — FRONTPAGE I-7
Adding a Custom Background Color to a Table — FRONTPAGE I-8
   Using the Format Painter to format table cells — FRONTPAGE I-9
Creating a Nested Table — FRONTPAGE I-10
   Applying border colors to tables and cells — FRONTPAGE I-11
Creating a New Frame in a Frames Page — FRONTPAGE I-12
Deleting a Frame from a Frames Page — FRONTPAGE I-14
   Creating "no frames" pages for browsers that can't display frames — FRONTPAGE I-15
Printing a Frames Page in Internet Explorer — FRONTPAGE I-16
   Other printing options in Internet Explorer — FRONTPAGE I-17
Concepts Review — FRONTPAGE I-18
Skills Review — FRONTPAGE I-20
Independent Challenges — FRONTPAGE I-21
Visual Workshop — FRONTPAGE I-24

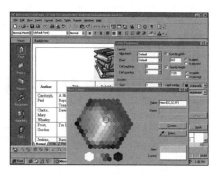

Using Shared Borders and Themes in a Web Site

Using Shared Borders and Themes in a Web Site	FRONTPAGE J-1
Creating Shared Borders in a Web Site	FRONTPAGE J-2
Adding Pages to Navigation View	FRONTPAGE J-4
Changing the Content of a Shared Border	FRONTPAGE J-6
Using FrontPage navigation bars to navigate a Web site	FRONTPAGE J-7
Turning Off a Shared Border for a Single Web Page	FRONTPAGE J-8
Examining a Web site's shared border files	FRONTPAGE J-9
Adding a Page Banner and Navigation Bar to a Web Page	FRONTPAGE J-10
Applying a Web Theme to a Web Site and Changing Its Attributes	FRONTPAGE J-12
Installing additional Web themes	FRONTPAGE J-13
Customizing a Web Site's Theme	FRONTPAGE J-14
Deleting a Web theme	FRONTPAGE J-15
Customizing a Web Theme for a Single Web Page	FRONTPAGE J-16
Changing the theme for several pages at once	FRONTPAGE J-17
Concepts Review	FRONTPAGE J-18
Skills Review	FRONTPAGE J-19
Independent Challenges	FRONTPAGE J-21
Visual Workshop	FRONTPAGE J-24

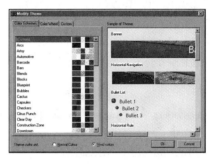

Publishing a Web Site

Publishing a Web Site	FRONTPAGE K-1
Positioning Text in a Web Page	FRONTPAGE K-2
Positioning Graphics in a Web Page	FRONTPAGE K-4
Understanding the limitations of absolute positioning	FRONTPAGE K-5
Using Drag and Drop to Move Files in Folders View	FRONTPAGE K-6
Using FrontPage for all Web site file management tasks	FRONTPAGE K-7
Changing a Filename in Folders View	FRONTPAGE K-8
Suggested naming conventions for Web pages	FRONTPAGE K-9
Finding and Replacing Text in a Web Site	FRONTPAGE K-10
Printing Navigation and Hyperlinks Views	FRONTPAGE K-12
Customizing Hyperlinks View	FRONTPAGE K-13
Publishing a Web Site on the PWS	FRONTPAGE K-14
Publishing a Web to a commercial Web server	FRONTPAGE K-15
Opening a Web Site from the PWS	FRONTPAGE K-16
Selecting an ISP to host your Web site	FRONTPAGE K-17
Concepts Review	FRONTPAGE K-18
Skills Review	FRONTPAGE K-20
Independent Challenges	FRONTPAGE K-21
Visual Workshop	FRONTPAGE K-24

Creating a New Web Site on a Web Server

Creating a New Web Site on a Web Server	FRONTPAGE L-1
Locating a Web Presence Provider	FRONTPAGE L-2
Registering and using a domain name	FRONTPAGE L-3
Using the Import Web Wizard to Create a New Web	FRONTPAGE L-4

Contents

Setting a Web Site's Page Options   FRONTPAGE L-6
Creating an Executable Web Folder   FRONTPAGE L-8
Checking Out a Web Page   FRONTPAGE L-10
Checking In a Web Page   FRONTPAGE L-12
Opening an Office Document in a Web   FRONTPAGE L-14
Troubleshooting Server Problems   FRONTPAGE L-16
Concepts Review   FRONTPAGE L-18
Skills Review   FRONTPAGE L-20
Independent Challenges   FRONTPAGE L-21
Visual Workshop   FRONTPAGE L-24

Using Office Components and Styles

    FRONTPAGE M-1
Understanding Office Components   FRONTPAGE M-2
Creating a Spreadsheet Component   FRONTPAGE M-4
Importing Data Into a Spreadsheet Component   FRONTPAGE M-6
    Why use Office components   FRONTPAGE M-7
Creating a Chart Component   FRONTPAGE M-8
    Changing a Chart component's appearance   FRONTPAGE M-9
Using a PivotTable List Component   FRONTPAGE M-10
Creating Special Styles in a Web Page   FRONTPAGE M-12
Creating a Cascading Style Sheet   FRONTPAGE M-14
    Differences between cascading style sheets and themes   FRONTPAGE M-15
Applying a Cascading Style Sheet   FRONTPAGE M-16
    Cascading style sheets and browsers   FRONTPAGE M-17
Concepts Review   FRONTPAGE M-18
Skills Review   FRONTPAGE M-19
Independent Challenges   FRONTPAGE M-21
Visual Workshop   FRONTPAGE M-24

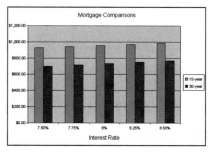

Integrating a Database with a FrontPage Web

    FRONTPAGE N-1
Reviewing Database Concepts   FRONTPAGE N-2
    More about database objects   FRONTPAGE N-3
Importing a Database into a FrontPage Web   FRONTPAGE N-4
Creating a Data Access Page   FRONTPAGE N-6
    Setting a Web page so it is not published with a Web site   FRONTPAGE N-7
Using a Data Access Page   FRONTPAGE N-8
Sending Form Results to a Database   FRONTPAGE N-10
Using an Active Server Page   FRONTPAGE N-12
Creating a Database Results Region   FRONTPAGE N-14
Creating a Search Form in a Web Page   FRONTPAGE N-16
Concepts Review   FRONTPAGE N-18
Skills Review   FRONTPAGE N-19
Independent Challenges   FRONTPAGE N-21
Visual Workshop   FRONTPAGE N-24

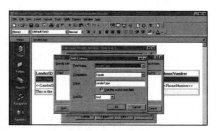

Publishing a Web on a Web Server — FRONTPAGE O-1

Assessing a Web's Overall Function and Appearance — FRONTPAGE O-2
Checking the spelling across a Web — FRONTPAGE O-3
Adding Content from an Office Document — FRONTPAGE O-4
Using Word to create a Web page — FRONTPAGE O-5
Creating Navigation Options in a Web — FRONTPAGE O-6
Recalculating and Verifying Hyperlinks — FRONTPAGE O-8
Customizing a Site Summary Report — FRONTPAGE O-10
Publishing a Web to Another Server — FRONTPAGE O-12
Checking your Web after publishing it — FRONTPAGE O-13
Securing a Web — FRONTPAGE O-14
Changing your Web's password on the server — FRONTPAGE O-15
Using a Web's Usage Logs — FRONTPAGE O-16
Submitting your Web to search engines — FRONTPAGE O-17
Concepts Review — FRONTPAGE O-18
Skills Review — FRONTPAGE O-20
Independent Challenges — FRONTPAGE O-21
Visual Workshop — FRONTPAGE O-24

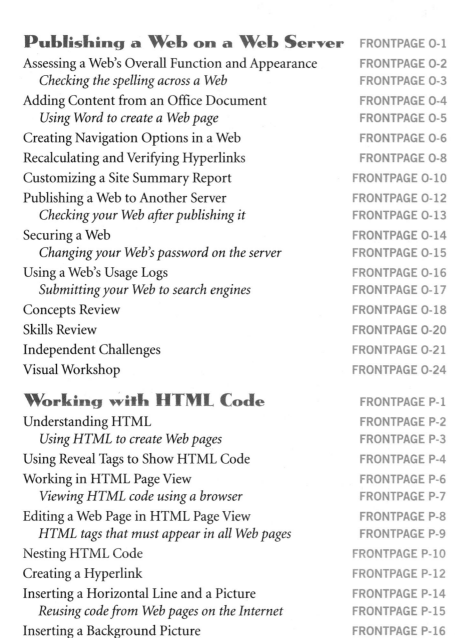

Working with HTML Code — FRONTPAGE P-1

Understanding HTML — FRONTPAGE P-2
Using HTML to create Web pages — FRONTPAGE P-3
Using Reveal Tags to Show HTML Code — FRONTPAGE P-4
Working in HTML Page View — FRONTPAGE P-6
Viewing HTML code using a browser — FRONTPAGE P-7
Editing a Web Page in HTML Page View — FRONTPAGE P-8
HTML tags that must appear in all Web pages — FRONTPAGE P-9
Nesting HTML Code — FRONTPAGE P-10
Creating a Hyperlink — FRONTPAGE P-12
Inserting a Horizontal Line and a Picture — FRONTPAGE P-14
Reusing code from Web pages on the Internet — FRONTPAGE P-15
Inserting a Background Picture — FRONTPAGE P-16
Concepts Review — FRONTPAGE P-18
Skills Review — FRONTPAGE P-19
Independent Challenges — FRONTPAGE P-21
Visual Workshop — FRONTPAGE P-24

MOUS Certification — 1
Project Files — 11
Glossary — 16
Index — 22

Read This Before You Begin

In Units A through J and Unit P of this book, you will create disk-based Webs and pages in a location of your choice; the default used in the units is C:\My Documents\My Webs\[insert your name here]\[Web folder name]. To identify Webs in a lab situation, you should create all of your disk-based Webs in the folder that contains your name (C:\My Documents\My Webs\[insert your name here]\[Web folder name]). In Units L through O, you will publish and create server-based Webs to the PWS; the default server name is *localhost*. In Unit K you will create both disk-based and server-based Webs.

Installation

The Setup program provides different options for installing FrontPage, allowing you to choose exactly how to install each feature. You can do a complete, custom, or typical installation. The default is a typical installation. As part of a typical installation, you also have three other installation options. You can:

- Set a feature to be installed the first time it is used (after a typical installation, you are automatically prompted to install a feature on first use unless you specifically choose to install the feature at the time of installation).

- Install a feature to run directly from the CD or over a network, conserving hard drive space.

- Choose not to install a feature.

Because of this added flexibility included in the Setup program, some features of FrontPage 2000 covered in the book are not installed as part of the default, typical installation on a standalone computer. These "install on first use" features include some pictures in the Clip Gallery, the Office components, and some themes. To use these features, you must insert the FrontPage 2000 CD (or the correct Office 2000 CD, if FrontPage was part of an Office 2000 installation) to install the missing feature the first time the feature is used.

To avoid needing the CD to install features on first use, make sure that your computer has a complete installation of FrontPage 2000.

Toolbars and Menus

By default, FrontPage 2000 uses personalized toolbars and menus. For the purposes of completing the exercises in this book, these features have been disabled. To disable personalized toolbars and menus, click Tools on the menu bar, click Customize, click the Options tab, then clear the following check boxes: Standard and Formatting toolbars share one row, Menus show recently used commands first, and Show full menus after a short delay. Click Close.

Installing Personal Web Server 4.0

The steps in Units H and K through O of this book are written to publish and create server-based Webs using Personal Web Server (PWS) version 4.0. To install PWS, insert the Windows 98 CD in the correct drive, open it in Windows Explorer, open the add-ons folder, then open the pws folder. Double-click setup to start the installation. Follow the instructions in the Microsoft Personal Web Server Setup dialog boxes to install the PWS and the following components: Common Program Files, Microsoft Data Access Components 1.5, and Personal Web Server (PWS). Do *not* install the FrontPage 98 Server Extensions. After installing PWS 4.0, go to **http://officeupdate.microsoft.com/frontpage/wpp/serk/inwindow.htm** to download the most current version of the FrontPage 2000 Server Extensions. Follow the instructions in this page to install and configure the Server Extensions. You must use the FrontPage 2000 Server Extensions or the steps in this book will not work correctly.

If your instructor asks you to publish and create server-based Webs on a network server, follow your instructor's directions for logging on to the server. The steps in this book will work correctly as long as the server has the FrontPage 2000 Server Extensions installed on it.

Browsers

We recommend using Microsoft Internet Explorer 5.0 or higher or Netscape Navigator 4.72 or higher for browser output.

Getting

Started with FrontPage 2000

Objectives

- ► **Understand Web servers and sites**
- ► **Start FrontPage 2000**
- ► **Plan a new Web site**
- ⌐MOUS⌐ ► **Create a new Web with a FrontPage 2000 Wizard**
- ⌐MOUS⌐ ► **Work with the Tasks list**
- ⌐MOUS⌐ ► **View the FrontPage window**
- ► **Create Web folders**
- ► **Get Help**
- ⌐MOUS⌐ ► **Close the Web and exit FrontPage 2000**

FrontPage 2000 is a powerful program designed to help you develop dynamic, interactive World Wide Web sites. A **Web site** is a collection of documents that can be published via the **Internet**, a worldwide communications network. FrontPage 2000 management features make it easy to organize and maintain the numerous files and folders that make up an ever-expanding Web site, while FrontPage 2000 makes it easy to create and edit Web pages or Web documents. ✐ Connie Lee is the marketing director for Computer Corner. Connie maintains that it is important for Computer Corner to develop an Internet presence, and will develop a Web site for her company. In this first unit, she plans and creates the initial Computer Corner Web site.

Understanding Web Servers and Sites

A computer **network** consists of two or more computers linked together to share information. The Internet connects computer networks from all over the world. Millions of computers are currently connected to the Internet through telephone lines, cables, satellites, and other telecommunications media. The Internet allows users to share information in many different forms, including text, graphics, sound, and video, through the World Wide Web. The two main components of the World Wide Web are Web clients and Web servers. **Web clients** host computer programs called browsers. A **browser**, such as Netscape Communicator or Microsoft's Internet Explorer, can request a Web page from a **Web server**, which is typically a remote computer running Web server software, as depicted in Figure A-1. The Web client and the Web server software use agreed-upon mutual languages, known as **protocols**, to communicate. For example, clients and servers use a protocol called **HTTP (Hypertext Transfer Protocol)** to send and receive documents. To reach Web pages that are located on Web servers, you can enter the server's network address or its **URL (Uniform Resource Locator)**. FrontPage 2000 provides a rich set of tools that help maintain Web sites and servers. Connie can use FrontPage 2000 to complete the following tasks:

Details

Create a Web

A large Web site may encompass several independent business or personal sites. FrontPage uses the term **Web** to describe these component sites. A Web usually consists of multiple folders containing Web pages, image files, sound files, and video files.

Create Web pages

FrontPage 2000 provides a **WYSIWYG (What You See Is What You Get)** editor that helps you create Web pages without any prior knowledge of the **HTML (Hypertext Markup Language)** programming language. All Web pages must be written in HTML, but FrontPage makes the task easier by generating the HTML code for you.

Manage a Web

FrontPage provides many powerful tools to help you manage a Web. You can create and move folders, as well as import and export files. A **Tasks** list helps you keep track of the tasks that need to be completed.

Publish a Web

FrontPage Webs can be published to any remote computer running Web server software and FrontPage Server Extensions. The **FrontPage Server Extensions** are software components that enable the FrontPage management tools to work with many different kinds of Web server software. The **Publish Web** feature automates the task of transferring your Web files from your local computer to the remote computer.

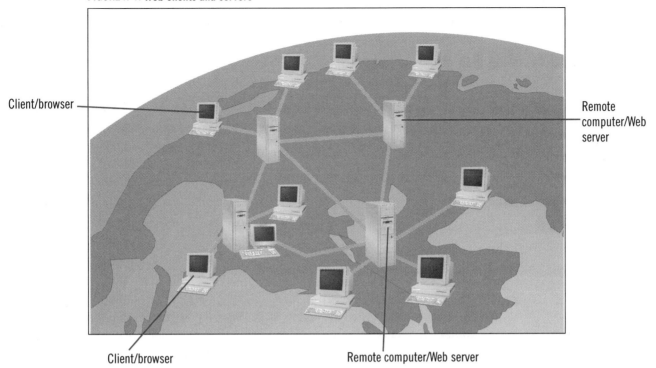

Client/browser

Remote computer/Web server

Client/browser

Remote computer/Web server

Using HTML (Hypertext Markup Language)

Web documents are created using a programming language called HTML. In HTML, commands are entered within lesser than (<) and greater than (>) tags. For instance, the following command is used to bold text: . HTML is a paired-tag language, because it requires a tag to "turn off" this bold command. Thus, the following code will bold the word "Hello": Hello. Web browsers interpret the HTML code and display the results in the browser window. Because HTML files are always saved in standard ASCII code, or text format, Web pages are platform-independent. That means that a UNIX or Macintosh machine can read the files just as easily as a PC.

Starting FrontPage 2000

To start FrontPage, you click the Start button on the **taskbar**. (A different procedure may be necessary if you are working on a network.) Ask your instructor or technical support person if you need help locating FrontPage. ⟍ Connie has decided to use FrontPage 2000 to develop the Computer Corner Web. She begins by starting the FrontPage program.

Steps

1. Click the **Start button** 🏁Start on the taskbar, as shown in Figure A-2
To start FrontPage, Windows must be running.

2. Point to **Programs** on the Start menu
The Programs menu, located at the top of the Start menu, lists all programs installed on your computer. Microsoft FrontPage is in this list along with all other available Microsoft programs, as shown in Figure A-2.

Trouble?
If Microsoft FrontPage is not on the Programs menu, ask your instructor or technical support person for help.

3. Click **Microsoft FrontPage** on the Programs menu
The FrontPage 2000 window appears, as shown in Figure A-3.

FIGURE A-2: Programs menu

Start menu

Programs menu

Start button

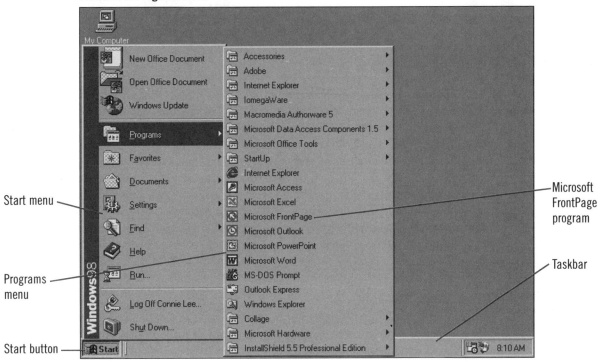

Microsoft FrontPage program

Taskbar

FIGURE A-3: FrontPage 2000 window

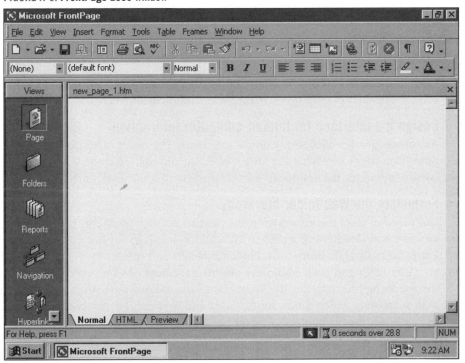

Planning a New Web Site

Whether you are developing a Web site for commercial, educational, or personal use, you are never really "done." The dynamic environment of the World Wide Web allows Web sites to take on a life of their own, growing and maturing along with the vision of their creators. Web development tools like FrontPage 2000 have made it easier to manage sites and author pages, leading to a rapid increase in the number of Web sites. However, the amount of time you earmark for planning will be directly proportional to your overall satisfaction during the rest of the development process. Remember that planning a Web site involves both *content* and *structure*. The planning phase typically includes setting goals, evaluating your audience, brainstorming for content, interviewing interested parties, designing the interface, and formulating the Web folder hierarchy. Connie uses the following guidelines to plan the Computer Corner Web site:

Details

Write a mission statement

Connie begins the planning process by writing a short, concise statement of the major goals she wants to accomplish with the Web site: "The Computer Corner Web site is intended as a storefront for all of its products and services."

Evaluate the intended audience

Connie asks, "Who is going to use the site?" She describes the demographics and the characteristics of her intended audience. Are they young? Are they old? Do they intend to use her products for professional or personal purposes? What is their average income? She is as precise as possible because her audience will largely determine the methods used to achieve her goals.

Brainstorm for content

Connie gathers together everyone involved with the project and brainstorms ideas for the actual content of the site. During this process, she keeps in mind that all ideas may be possible with some refinement.

Interview interested parties

Connie interviews all people interested in the Web site, not just those directly involved in the project. She talks to employees, management, and customers.

Design the interface for human-computer interaction

As she designs her Web site, Connie anticipates the needs of visitors to her site. She reviews other Web sites to see what she feels is effective and well designed. She thinks about the overall layout, the colors, the graphics—what features of the site work particularly well?

Formulate the Web folder hierarchy

Connie takes all of the information she gleaned through goal setting, brainstorming, and interviewing, and sketches out an initial Web folder hierarchy for her site. She plans for expansion. Using the natural divisions found in her business and subject matter, she subdivides Web folders. After talking to both employees and management of Computer Corner, Connie envisions the following hierarchy for the Web: Hardware and Software must each be a major category, with subfolders under Hardware for Sales and Service. Her complete plan for the Web folder hierarchy for the Computer Corner site is shown in Figure A-4.

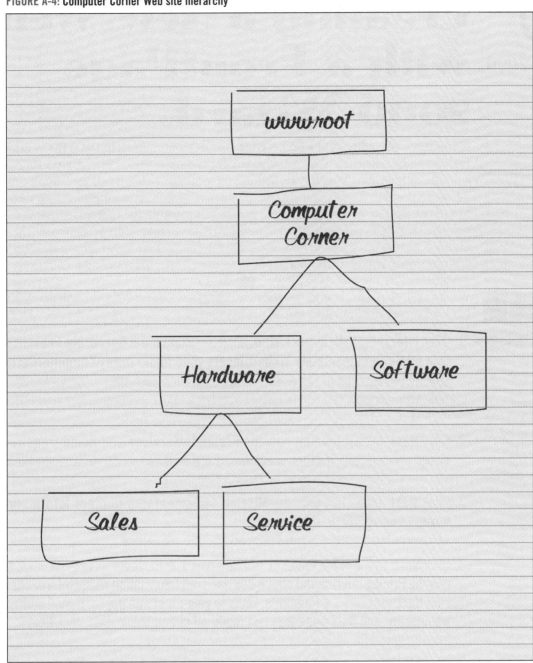

Defining a Web folder hierarchy

Web server software acts like an electronic filing cabinet that can be accessed from anywhere on the Internet. Every folder in a Web server's folder hierarchy stems from the main folder or root folder. Microsoft Web servers for Windows 95, 98, and NT use "wwwroot" as the name for the default root folder. Each individual Web within the main folder has its *own* root folder, designated by its name. For instance, ComputerCorner is the root folder for the Computer Corner Web. When a browser sends a folder's URL, or Internet address, the server automatically retrieves the default file from the folder named in the URL. The default file is usually designated as index.htm or default.htm, depending on the Web server being used. When the URL at http://*your.server.name*/ComputerCorner is accessed, the server automatically retrieves the index.htm file from the ComputerCorner folder and sends it to the browser. All HTML files will have either an .htm or .html extension.

FrontPage 2000

Creating a New Web with a FrontPage 2000 Wizard

A FrontPage Web consists of a **home page** (the index.htm or default.htm file in the Web's root folder) and its associated files, including images and other digital files. A FrontPage wizard will automatically create a Web for you. To use a FrontPage Web wizard, you simply answer a few questions posed in a series of dialog boxes. The Web wizard customizes the new Web according to your answers to the questions. Webs usually reside within the root folder that the Web server software creates; if you are using a Microsoft Web server, that folder is wwwroot. If you have not installed Web server software, however, FrontPage 2000 provides options to develop Webs elsewhere on your hard drive or on a floppy disk. In this case, the root folder will be the folder you designate when the Web is created. Connie wants to use the Corporate Presence Wizard as the basic framework for the new Computer Corner Web. She will develop the site on her hard drive before publishing it to the Internet.

Steps

QuickTip

The Computer Corner Web can be saved to several alternate locations, such as a hard drive, a network drive, or external media. Due to the size of the completed Web, it is not recommended that it be saved to floppy disk. If you have saved the Computer Corner Web in a different location, enter the path to the alternate location.

1. Click **File**, point to **New**, click **Web,** click the icon for the **Corporate Presence Wizard,** type **C:\My Documents\My Webs\\[insert your name here]\ComputerCorner** in the Specify the location of the new web text box, then click **OK**
   You can insert your first and last name to create a folder that is uniquely your own. Your dialog box should be consistent with that shown in Figure A-5.

2. Click **Next**, then verify that only the **Products/Services** and **Home (required) check boxes** are selected, if other check boxes are selected, click to deselect them
   You can always deselect a checkbox by clicking it.

3. Click **Next**, then click only the **Mission Statement** and **Contact Information check boxes** to select them, if necessary
   The Corporate Presence Wizard presents the next dialog box.

4. Click **Next**, type **2** in the Products text box, type **1** in the Services text box, click **Next**, click only the **Pricing information check box** and both **Information request form check boxes**, click **Next**, click only the **Page title**, **Links to your main web pages**, **E-mail address of your webmaster**, and **Date page was last modified check boxes**, then click **Next**
   The Corporate Presence Wizard presents the next dialog box.

5. Click the **Yes option button** (if necessary), click **Next**, type the company information shown in Figure A-6, click **Next**, type **888-555-1111** in the What is your company's telephone number? text box, type **888-555-2222** in the What is your company's FAX number? text box, type **samantha@computercorner.com** in the What is the e-mail address of your webmaster? text box, type **joel@computercorner.com** in the What is the e-mail address for general info? text box, then click **Next**
   The Corporate Presence Wizard presents the next dialog box.

6. Click **Choose Web Theme**
   The Choose Theme dialog box appears. You can preview a theme in the Theme Preview section.

Trouble?

Depending on the speed of your computer, the wizard may take a few minutes to create the Web.

7. Scroll to and click **Expedition**, click **Vivid colors**, click **Active graphics**, click **Background picture**, click **OK**, click **Next**, then click **Finish**
   The Corporate Presence Web Wizard creates the Computer Corner Web. The Web opens in Tasks View, as shown in Figure A-7. FrontPage has assigned tasks to help you customize the new Web.

FIGURE A-5: New dialog box

Corporate Presence Wizard

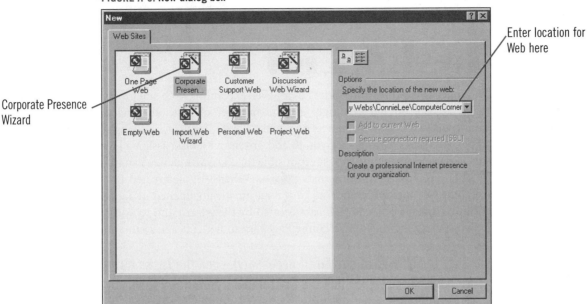

Enter location for Web here

FIGURE A-6: Company information for Corporate Presence Web Wizard

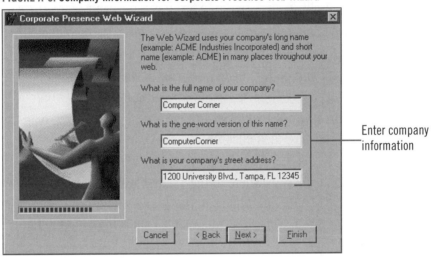

Enter company information

FIGURE A-7: Tasks View of Computer Corner Web

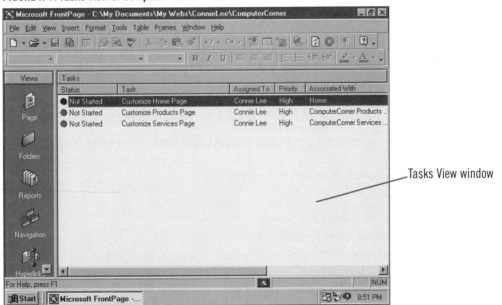

Tasks View window

Working with the Tasks List

The collection of files and folders in an ever-expanding Web site grows quickly, making it hard to keep track of the seemingly endless number of tasks that need to be completed. The FrontPage Tasks feature offers a convenient way to keep track of what needs to be done within a Web site. **Tasks View** allows you to add or remove a task, assign a level of priority to the task, sort tasks, and designate who is responsible for a task. Later, you can mark the task as completed or simply remove it from the list. When Connie created the Computer Corner Web using the Corporate Presence Wizard, it automatically opened in Tasks View. Connie will work with the Tasks List to edit the tasks created by the wizard and to add new tasks. She will begin by reassigning the Customize Home Page task to her colleague Samantha.

Steps

1. Click the **Maximize button** (if necessary), click the **Tasks button** 📋 in the Views bar (if necessary), right-click the **Customize Home Page task** at the top of the list, then click **Edit Task**

   The Task Details dialog box appears, as shown in Figure A-8. The name that appears automatically in the Assigned to text box is the name of the current user.

2. Type **Samantha** in the Assigned to text box, then click **OK**

   The Customize Home Page task is now assigned to Samantha.

3. Click **Edit** on the menu bar, point to **Task**, then click **Add Task**

   The New Task dialog box appears, as shown in Figure A-9.

4. Type **Rework Tasks List** in the Task name text box, type **Connie Lee** in the Assigned to text box, then click **OK**

   FrontPage adds the Rework Tasks List task to the list for the Computer Corner Web.

5. Right-click anywhere in the **Tasks View window** (but not on a task), click **New Task**, type **Create Subfolders** in the Task name text box, type **S** in the Assigned to text box (the name Samantha will appear), click **High** in the Priority options list, then click **OK**

   The Create Subfolders task is added to the list.

6. Double-click on the **Create Subfolders task**, type **Add the planned subfolders to the Web site** in the Description text box, then click **OK**

   The description is added to the Create Subfolders task. To view the task description, use the horizontal scroll bar or double-click on the task itself to bring up the dialog box.

7. Click the **Priority button** at the top of the Tasks View window

   The list of tasks is automatically sorted according to level of priority. If you click the priority button a second time, the sort order will reverse. You can sort tasks by other factors, such as Status, Assigned To, or Task, by clicking the corresponding button at the top of the Tasks View window.

8. Right-click the **Rework Tasks List task**, then click **Mark as Completed**

   FrontPage changes the task status from red to green, indicating that the task has been completed, as shown in Figure A-10.

Viewing Task History

To view the list of all tasks added to the Tasks list since the Web was created, right-click in the Tasks View window, then click Show Task History. When Show Task History is selected, all completed and uncompleted tasks appear in the Tasks View window. If Show Task History is not selected, tasks you have marked as completed will not appear on the Tasks list once you have switched to another FrontPage view, such as Folders View.

FIGURE A-8: **Task Details dialog box**

Task name text box

Assigned to text box

Description text box

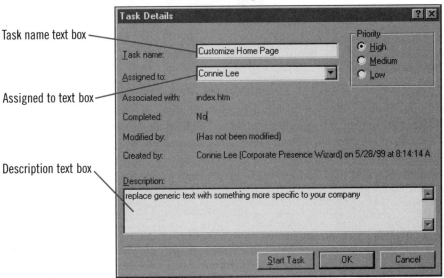

FIGURE A-9: **New Task dialog box**

Enter name of
task here

Set priority here

Enter description
here

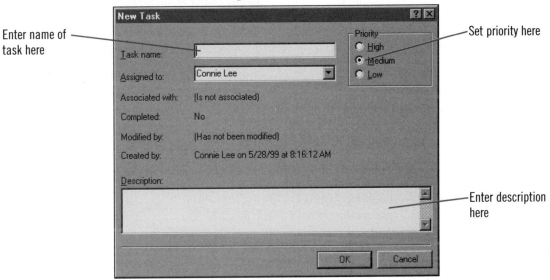

FIGURE A-10: **Tasks View with Rework Tasks List task marked as completed**

Task marked as
completed

Priority button

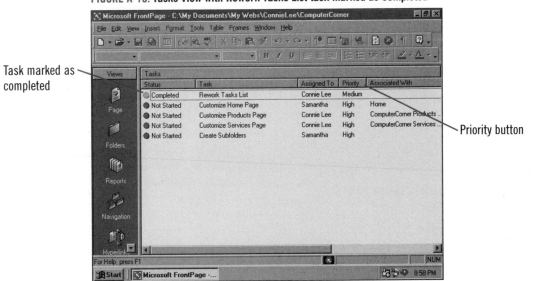

FrontPage 2000

Viewing the FrontPage Window

In addition to Tasks View, FrontPage provides several alternate views to help you manage the files, folders, and hyperlinks that make up a Web. **Hyperlinks** are highlighted words, phrases, and graphics that open other Web pages when you click them. **Hyperlinks View** displays an overview of the site and the *existing* hyperlinks between Web pages. **Navigation View** shows the navigation structure of the Web. **Folders View** illustrates the folder hierarchy of the entire Web site. **Reports View** creates reports to help you analyze your Web and manage its contents. **Page View** provides the interface to FrontPage, enabling you to create and edit Web pages. Some elements of FrontPage that provide access to additional features are identified in Figure A-11. ✏️ Connie decides to familiarize herself with the FrontPage window before creating the folders for the Computer Corner Web site.

Steps

1. Click the **Hyperlinks button** 🖼️ in the Views bar of the FrontPage window
   FrontPage displays the Hyperlinks View of the Computer Corner Web, showing the hyperlinks to the products and services pages created by the Corporate Presence Wizard.

2. Click the **Navigation button** 🖼️ in the Views bar of the FrontPage window
   FrontPage presents the navigational structure of the Computer Corner Web.

3. Click the **Reports button** 🖼️ in the Views bar of the FrontPage window
   FrontPage lists a summary report of files, hyperlinks, and other elements of your Web. The window provides more detailed reports for each element listed, as shown in Figure A-12.

4. Click the **Page button** 🖼️ in the Views bar of the FrontPage window
   FrontPage presents a Web page template incorporating the theme you selected with the Corporate Presence Wizard. FrontPage templates can be edited and incorporated into the Web.

5. Click the **Folders button** 🖼️ in the Views bar of the FrontPage window
   FrontPage presents your Web site in Folders View, showing the folders and files that were added automatically when you created the new Computer Corner Web, as shown in Figure A-13.

Using ScreenTips

You will find ScreenTips on the FrontPage 2000 toolbar. If you are unfamiliar with a toolbar button, you can view its ScreenTip by placing your mouse pointer over the button. A ScreenTip appears, providing information about the function of the button. The Status bar simultaneously displays an expanded version of the ScreenTip information.

FIGURE A-11: Navigation View of Computer Corner Web

Title bar
Standard toolbar
Views bar
Page button
Folders button
Reports button
Navigation button
Hyperlinks button
Task bar

Menu bar
Status bar

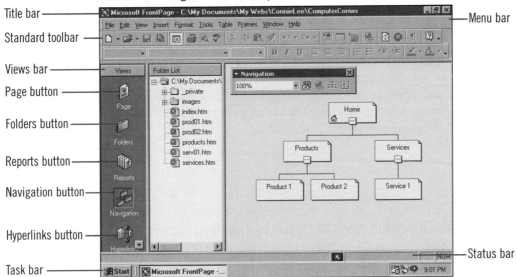

FIGURE A-12: Reports View of Computer Corner Web

Select report type here

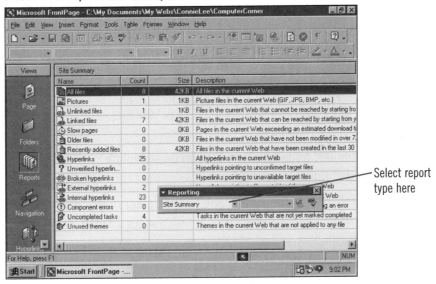

FIGURE A-13: Folders View of Computer Corner Web

All folders in Web

Contents of current folder

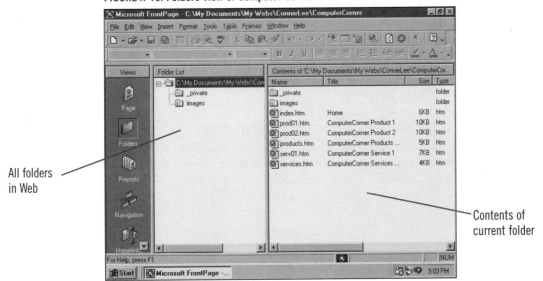

Creating Web Folders

Folders View in FrontPage provides an easy way to manage files and folders. The Folders View window is divided into two panes. The left pane displays the entire Web folder hierarchy, and the right pane lists the contents of the selected folder. You can use Folders View to copy, delete, rename, and move the files and folders contained in your Web site. Connie will use the Folders View window to re-create the hierarchy of folders for the Computer Corner Web site, as planned in preceding lessons.

Steps

1. Click **File** on the menu bar, point to **New**, then click **Folder**

FrontPage creates a new folder in the right pane of the Folders View window, as shown in Figure A-14.

2. Type **Hardware**, then press **[Enter]**

A Rename dialog box may briefly open while FrontPage creates the new folder. Once the folder is renamed, the Hardware folder will appear in both the Web hierarchy area of the left pane and the contents area of the right pane.

3. Right-click in the **right pane** of the Folders View window, then click **New Folder**

FrontPage creates another new folder in the right pane of the Folders View window.

4. Type **Software**, then press **[Enter]**

The Software folder appears in both the Web hierarchy area of the left pane and the contents area of the right pane.

5. In the left pane, click on the **Hardware** folder

The right pane displays the contents of the empty Hardware folder.

6. Right-click in the **right pane** of the Folders View window, then click **New Folder**

FrontPage creates a new folder within the Hardware folder in the right pane of the Folders View window.

7. Type **Sales**, then press **[Enter]**

FrontPage creates the Sales folder within the Hardware folder and displays it in the right pane of the Folders View window.

8. Right-click in the **right pane** of the Folders View window, then click **New Folder**

FrontPage creates another new folder within the Hardware folder in the right pane of the Folders View window.

9. Type **Service**, then press **[Enter]**

FrontPage creates the Service folder within the Hardware folder and displays it in the right pane of the Folders View window.

10. Click the **plus sign** next to the Hardware folder

The Hardware folder is expanded, and the complete, updated version of the Computer Corner hierarchy appears in the left pane of the Folders View window. Compare your Folders View window with the window shown in Figure A-15.

FIGURE A-14: Add a new folder in Folders view

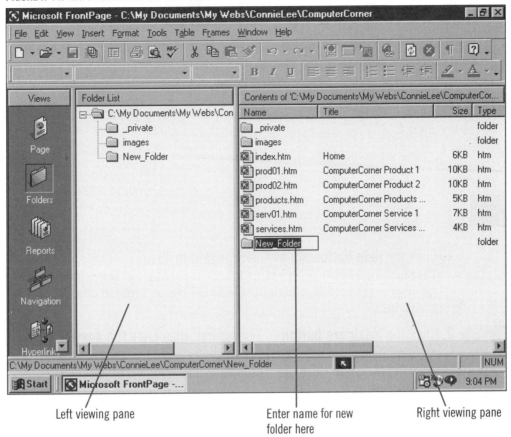

Left viewing pane

Enter name for new folder here

Right viewing pane

FIGURE A-15: Computer Corner Web folder hierarchy

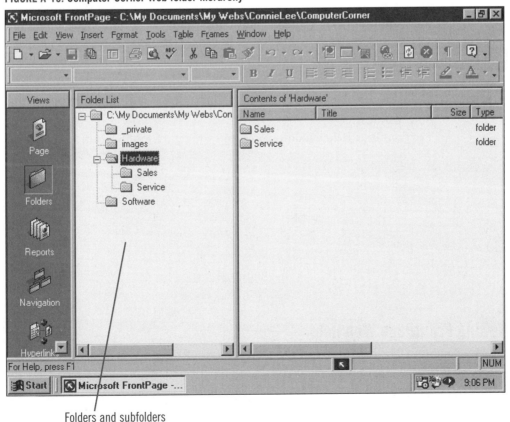

Folders and subfolders

Getting Help

FrontPage 2000 includes an extensive Help system with information and instructions about its features and commands. The Help system provides lists of related topics, definitions of terms, step-by-step procedures, and search capabilities that allow you to get immediate help with the task at hand. As Connie works, she realizes that there may be some information about working with Webs that could make her job easier. She consults the FrontPage Help system to learn more.

Steps 1 2 3 4

1. Click the **Help button** on the Standard toolbar

The Microsoft FrontPage 2000 Help dialog box opens. Don't worry if the foremost tab appearing on your screen differs from the one in the figure. Each tab offers a different method for getting help.

> **QuickTip**
>
> If you are using FrontPage Help for the first time, a Find Setup Wizard dialog box opens. Choose the database size option that fits your needs, click Next, then click Finish. If you are unsure which option to choose, accept the default value.

2. Click the **Maximize button** (if necessary), then click the **Answer Wizard** tab, if it is not already the foremost tab

The Answer Wizard tab opens, as shown in Figure A-16. The Answer Wizard tab allows you to search the Help system by entering a question, making it easy to find a specific topic quickly.

3. Type **How do you open a Web?** in the What would you like to do? text box, then click **Search**

The Help system displays a list of relevant topics, as shown in Figure A-17, and automatically displays the first topic on the list.

4. Click **Open the last web automatically when ...** in the Select topic to display area

The topic displayed in the right pane of the dialog box changes and presents step-by-step instructions on how to automatically open the Web you were working on when you last exited FrontPage 2000, as shown in Figure A-18.

5. Read the text in the dialog box, then click the **Close button** in the FrontPage Help window

The FrontPage Help window closes, and you return to the FrontPage window.

Getting FrontPage Web Help

FrontPage provides additional help if you are working while connected to the Internet. Click Help on the menu bar, then click Office on the Web. FrontPage automatically opens your Web browser and connects to Microsoft's FrontPage World Wide Web site. You can then search Microsoft's site for more information on FrontPage.

FIGURE A-16: FrontPage 2000 Help dialog box

Answer Wizard tab

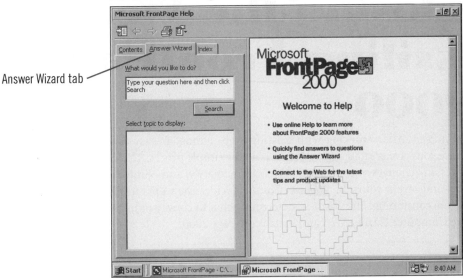

FIGURE A-17: Answer Wizard tab dialog box

Type question here

Search button

List of relevant topics

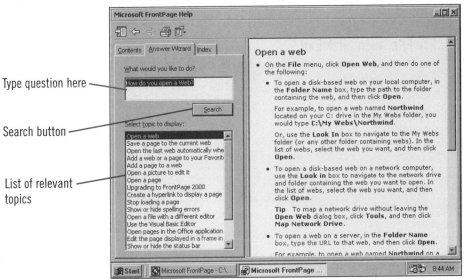

FIGURE A-18: Help dialog box with the Open the last web automatically when you start FrontPage topic displayed

Select topic for display here

Topic displayed here

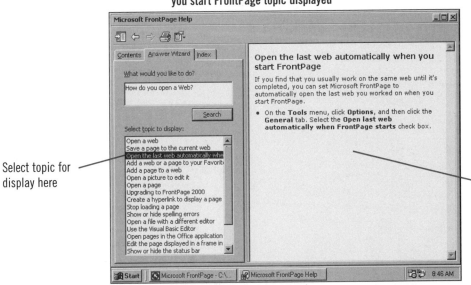

Closing the Web and Exiting FrontPage 2000

FrontPage makes working with existing Webs almost as easy as working with individual files. Once you have created a new Web, it is a very simple process to close it. FrontPage automatically saves any changes you make to a Web immediately, and eliminates the need to take that extra step and save it yourself. ✐▬▬ Connie decides she wants to give her Web site more thought before continuing. She wants to determine what to convey in her Web pages. For now, she closes the Computer Corner Web and exits FrontPage 2000.

1. **Click File on the menu bar**

   The File menu appears, as shown in Figure A-19.

2. **Click Close Web**

   FrontPage saves any changes you made to the Web, and then closes the Web.

3. **Click File, then click Exit**

   FrontPage 2000 closes, and returns you to the desktop.

FIGURE A-19: Expanded File menu options

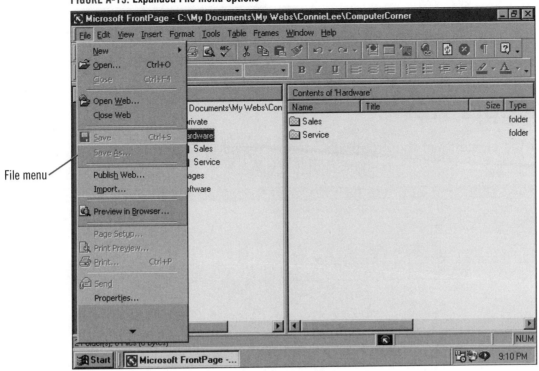

File menu

Opening an existing Web

You can open an existing Web in several ways. For example, FrontPage will automatically open the last Web that was worked on, if you like. You can set this preference by clicking Tools, clicking Options, and then clicking in the check box next to Open last Web automatically when FrontPage starts. You can also open existing Webs by clicking File and then clicking Open Web. The Open Web dialog box appears, as shown in Figure A-20. Navigate to the Web of your choice, and click Open. To open a Web published on the Internet, simply enter the URL and Web name in the Folder name text box.

FIGURE A-20: Open Web dialog box

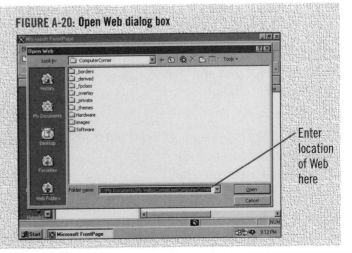

Enter location of Web here

Practice

▶ Concepts Review

Label each of the elements of the FrontPage window shown in Figure A-21.

FIGURE A-21

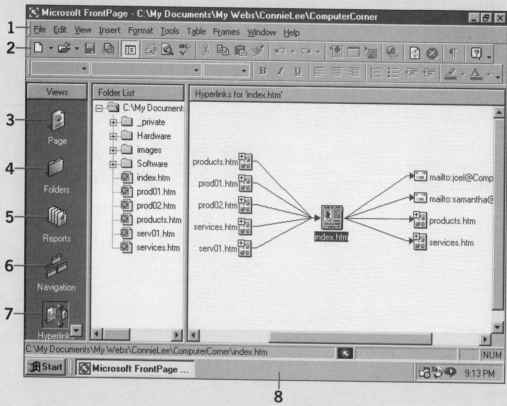

Match each term with the statement that describes it.

9. Web browser
10. Internet
11. HTML
12. Hyperlink
13. Web site

a. A collection of Web documents
b. Opens another Web page when clicked
c. The language used to encode Web pages
d. A global network connecting computers from around the world
e. Web client software that reads HTML

Select the best answer from the list of choices.

14. Which is NOT part of a Web server?

a. Web server software
b. Browser

c. Folders
d. Image files

15. Which of the following is NOT part of the planning phase of developing a Web site?

a. Brainstorming for content
b. Interviewing interested parties

c. Installing a Web server
d. Evaluating your intended audience

16. FrontPage Folders View provides

a. All the current hyperlinks of the Web.
b. The structure and files of the Web.

c. The URL addresses for the Web.
d. Site Visit statistics for the Web.

17. The Start button is located on the
a. Taskbar.
b. Menu bar.
c. Status bar.
d. Toolbar.

18. When you point the mouse at a button in FrontPage, additional information about that button is displayed
a. In a toolbar.
b. On the menu bar.
c. In a ScreenTip.
d. In the title bar.

19. A Tasks list allows you to indicate all of the following, except the
a. Priority level of the task.
b. Name of the task.
c. Person responsible for the task.
d. Deadline date for completion of the task.

20. To perform a search by asking a question in FrontPage 2000 Help, you would choose the
a. Contents tab.
b. Answer Wizard tab.
c. Index tab.
d. Properties tab.

▶ Skills Review

1. Start FrontPage 2000.
a. Make sure your computer is on and Windows is running.
b. Click the Start button, point to Programs, then click Microsoft FrontPage.

2. Create a new Web with a FrontPage 2000 Wizard.
a. Click File, point to New, then click Web.
b. Click the Personal Web icon.
c. Specify the location and name for the Web.
d. Click OK.

3. Work with a Tasks list.
a. Click the Tasks button.
b. Click File, click New, then click Task.
c. Type "Learn about Tasks lists" in the Task name text box.
d. Type your name in the Assigned to text box.
e. Assign a high priority to the task, then click OK.
f. Right-click the Learn about Tasks lists task, click Edit Task, type a description of the task, then click OK.
g. Right-click the task again, then click Mark as Completed.
h. Add a new task called "Write a mission statement", assign a medium priority to the task, then type your name in the Assigned to text box.
i. Add a new task called "Brainstorm for content", assign a high priority to the task, then type your name in the Assigned to text box.
j. Sort the tasks by priority.

4. View the FrontPage window.
a. Click the Hyperlinks button.
b. Click the Folders button.
c. Click the Reports button.
d. Place the mouse pointer on each of the buttons on the Standard toolbar to view each ScreenTip.
e. Click the Navigation button.
f. Click the Page button.

5. **Create Web folders.**
   a. Click the Folders button.
   b. Click File, point to New, then click Folder.
   c. Type **Resume**, then press [Enter].
   d. Create another folder.
   e. Name the new folder *Interests*, then press [Enter].
   f. Click the Resume folder in the left window pane.

6. **Get Help.**
   a. Click the Help button on the Standard toolbar.
   b. Click the Answer Wizard tab.
   c. Type in a question concerning FrontPage.
   d. Click a topic of your choice.
   e. Click the Index tab.
   f. Type in a keyword.
   g. Click on a topic of your choice.
   h. Close the FrontPage Help window.

7. **Close and exit.**
   a. Close the FrontPage Web.
   b. Click File, then click Open Web.
   c. Select a Web, then click OK.
   d. Close the Web.
   e. Exit FrontPage.

▶ Independent Challenges

1. You are the president of MultiMedia Magic, and you want to develop a Web site. You have just purchased FrontPage. You have created one Web with several folders, but you are not sure what to do next. In trying to envision your home page, you realize you do not know much about laying out a Web page. You decide to consult the FrontPage Help menu.

To complete this independent challenge:

a. Start Microsoft FrontPage.
b. Open an existing Web.
c. Explore the FrontPage Help facilities by clicking Help on the menu bar, then clicking Microsoft FrontPage Help.
d. Select the Answer Wizard tab if it is not the foremost tab, and type "What are frames?" in the appropriate text box, as shown in Figure A-22. Find out about frames by exploring the topics that are presented in the topics area.
e. Click the Index tab and learn more about what is included in FrontPage 2000.
f. Cancel Help and close the Web.

FIGURE A-22: **Answer Wizard tab in Help dialog box**

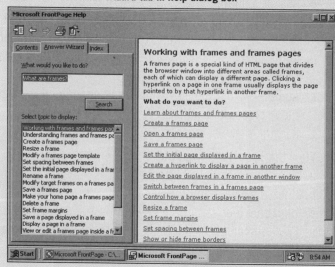

2. You have been appointed Webmaster for HomeTown Cycles, Inc. Your responsibilities include planning and developing the new HomeTown Web site. Your first task is to create a plan for the structure of the Web. Using the following guidelines, sketch on a piece of paper a possible Web folder hierarchy for the HomeTown Web.

To complete this independent challenge:

a. Write a mission statement.

b. Evaluate your intended audience.

c. Brainstorm for content.

d. Formulate the Web folder hierarchy.

3. As manager of Max's Fruit and Vegetable Shop, you decide that your shop needs a Web site where you can advertise your fresh produce. Sketch a plan for the Web site. The finished sketch should include the proposed Web structure.

To complete this independent challenge, review your sketch of the folder hierarchy and perform the following tasks:

a. Create a new One Page Web named *Max*.

b. Using Folders View, create a Web folder hierarchy based on your sketch. Include at least two subfolders—one for *Fruits* and one for *Vegetables*.

c. Look at your Web using Navigation View.

d. View your subfolders.

e. Close your Web.

An Internet connection is required to complete the following Independent Challenge.

4. You are considering starting your own pet-sitting business. To find out whether you have any competitors who are using the Web to advertise their services, spend some time online visiting other Web sites devoted to pet services. See what you like and don't like about their Web pages. Look at their layout and design. Read their text. See if they have hyperlinks to other sites and, if so, which ones.

To complete this independent challenge:

a. Log on to the Internet and use your favorite browser.

b. Perform an Internet search using "pets" as the keyword.

c. Analyze your two most favorite and two least favorite sites.

d. Keep track of the most interesting sites you find by listing their URLs for future reference.

e. Start FrontPage and create a One Page Web called *Pets*.

f. Click the Tasks button and add a new task.

g. Type **Analyze competing Web sites** in the Task name text box and assign the responsibility to yourself.

h. Describe what you found in the Description text box and assign it a high priority.

i. Click the Folders button.

j. Create a folder called *Analysis of Competing Web Sites*.

k. Create two subfolders—one called *Favorite Sites* and one called *Least Favorite Sites*.

l. Close the Web. Disconnect from the Internet and exit FrontPage.

▶ Visual Workshop

Create a One Page Web called *Workshop*. In Tasks view, add tasks to the Tasks list so it contains the same tasks as those shown in Figure A-23.

FIGURE A-23: Workshop Tasks list

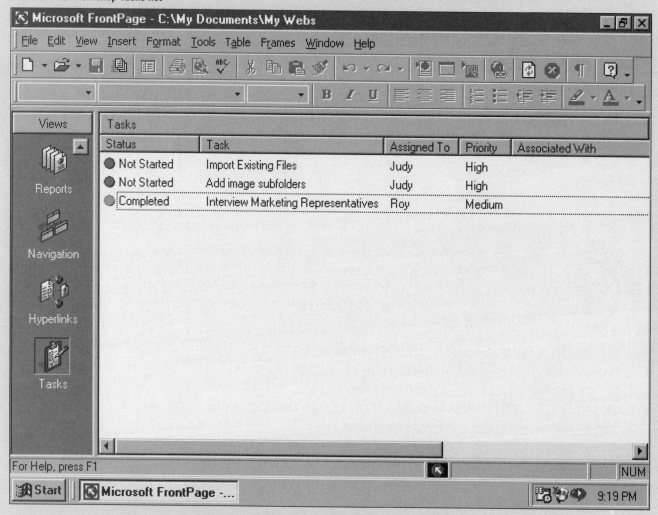

Unit
B

FrontPage 2000

Working
with Web Page Templates

Objectives

▶ **Understand FrontPage**
▶ **Open a Web page**
⌐MOUS⌐ ▶ **Edit a Web page**
⌐MOUS⌐ ▶ **Preview, save, and close a Web page**
⌐MOUS⌐ ▶ **Create a new Web page from a template**
⌐MOUS⌐ ▶ **Add a banner and navigation bars**
⌐MOUS⌐ ▶ **Create a new page in Navigation View**
⌐MOUS⌐ ▶ **Use shared borders**

The World Wide Web consists of Web sites (referred to as Webs) that contain documents (known as **Web pages**) with text, graphics, audio, video, and hyperlinks. Hyperlinks are "hot spots" in a document that link one Web page to another. And, hyperlinks can link to local pages (within the same Web) or to Web pages located on remote sites. FrontPage 2000 provides many shortcuts that automate the tasks required to create Webs and Web pages. FrontPage wizards create Webs, inserting a series of Web page **templates** based on your responses. Templates are pre-designed Web pages that can contain page and format settings, and text elements. Any template added to a Web can be edited or deleted at a later time. ⌐ Connie Lee wants to take full advantage of these exciting FrontPage features. She will edit the home page template created by the Corporate Presence Wizard.

Understanding FrontPage

Documents on the Web are created using a computer language known as HTML (Hypertext Markup Language). After HTML documents are created, they must be saved with a file extension of .html or .htm (traditionally, the .html extension is used in the UNIX and Macintosh world, and the .htm extension is used in the PC world). HTML commands can be entered in a text editor such as Notepad. Numerous HTML command tags can be used to apply styles to text, to add colors to text or to backgrounds, and to create hyperlinks to other Web pages. Typing the HTML commands to designate type styles and other document features can be tedious and time-consuming. FrontPage eliminates the need to manually type HTML commands by providing a visual interface for creating Web pages. Because the HTML commands are automatically generated, you do not need to type, edit, or even view them. Figure B-1 shows an example of a Web page created using FrontPage, while Figure B-2 shows the HTML code that was generated when the page was created. Using FrontPage you may never need to enter HTML code manually, however you can edit the code at any time, if desired. As Connie Lee begins using FrontPage to edit Computer Corner's Web pages for their Web site, she starts to appreciate the many advantages that FrontPage offers, including:

Details

Visual interface

Connie likes using the visual interface of FrontPage to create and edit her Web documents. Instead of typing HTML command tags, she merely clicks various toolbar buttons and menu bar options to add styles and formatting to her Web pages.

Integration with other FrontPage features

Connie uses FrontPage through Page View to create and edit her Web pages, and she uses the other FrontPage 2000 views to organize the pages on her Web site. It is very easy for Connie to switch back and forth between Page View and other views through the buttons located on the Views Bar.

Quick preview of Web pages

After entering information into FrontPage, Connie can view her Web pages with the Preview tab or with a Web browser (such as Netscape Communicator or Internet Explorer) to see how her pages will look to the rest of the world.

FIGURE B-1: A Web page created with FrontPage

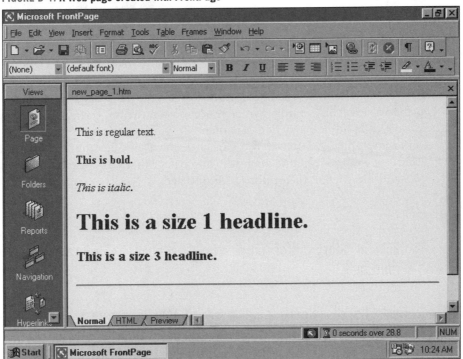

FIGURE B-2: The HTML code generated for the same Web page

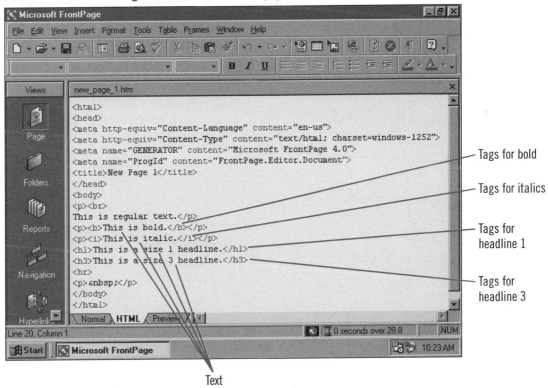

Tags for bold

Tags for italics

Tags for headline 1

Tags for headline 3

Text

Planning a Web page

Before creating Web pages, you should develop a master plan of the structure of the page, often called a storyboard. Relying on the mission statement, audience evaluation, and usability analysis done earlier, decide on the elements (such as text and graphics) that the page will include, then sketch an outline of its content and layout. You should also create or locate the graphics you want to use in your Web page and record the URLs for any Web pages that you might want to include as destination pages for your hyperlinks.

Opening a Web Page

The initial Web page at a Web site is often called the home page. It usually provides a welcome statement and an overview of the contents provided at the Web site. When you created a new Web with the Corporate Presence Wizard, the wizard inserted a home page into the Web. The elements included on the home page are based on the answers you provided to the wizard. For example, when you choose a theme, certain colors and text styles are added to the home page. You can then edit this home page in FrontPage, exactly as you would any other Web page. You can click the Page View button for quick access to the FrontPage. ◆ Connie opens the home page that was created for the Computer Corner Web and investigates the options in FrontPage.

Steps 1 2 3 4

1. **Click the Start button on the taskbar, point to Programs, then click Microsoft FrontPage**
   FrontPage 2000 starts.

2. **Click File, click Open Web, browse to C:\My Documents\My Webs\[insert your name here]\ComputerCorner, then click Open**
   The Computer Corner Web opens in the FrontPage window.

3. **Click the Page button 🗐 (if necessary)**
   Page View of the Computer Corner Web appears, displaying a blank Web page, as shown in Figure B-3. Numerous toolbars and menu options are available with FrontPage active.

4. **Click File on the menu bar, click Open, then double-click index**
   FrontPage opens the home page in the document window in Page View.

FIGURE B-3: Page View open to blank Web page

Standard toolbar
Formatting toolbar
Page button
Views bar

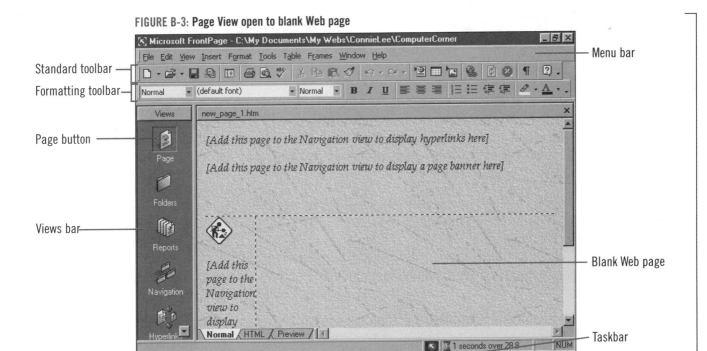

Menu bar
Blank Web page
Taskbar

FIGURE B-4: Page View open to Computer Corner home page

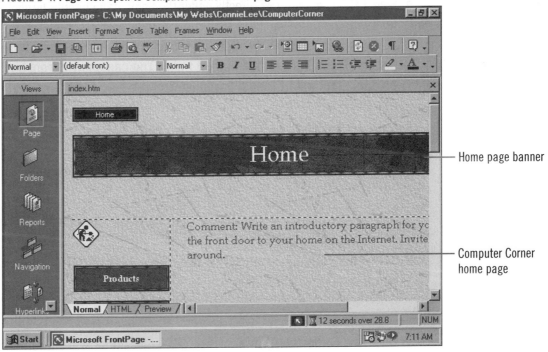

Home page banner
Computer Corner home page

Opening the existing home page

Opening a page through File menu bar options (as outlined above) can be accomplished in any view. FrontPage will automatically switch to Page View and display the document. You can also open a Web document, such as the home page, from alternate views by double-clicking the document. From Navigation View, double-click the Home icon. From Folders View, double-click the name of the file (index.htm). From Hyperlinks View, double-click the Home icon.

Editing a Web Page

FrontPage 2000 includes a variety of Web and Web page templates. A template is a ready-made Web page that you can customize to suit your particular needs. When you use a wizard, multiple pages are included that will enhance your Web. For example, in addition to the home page, the Corporate Presence Web Wizard also created several Products/Services pages when creating the Computer Corner Web. The Products/Services pages are actually a series of Web pages that are linked together to provide product and service information for visitors to your Web site. Hyperlinks are automatically provided to the Products/Services pages from the home page. Any page added to a Web by a wizard can be customized at any time. ➤ For now, Connie uses FrontPage to customize the home page that was included, using the Corporate Presence Web Wizard.

Steps

1. **Double-click the Home page banner** located at the top of the home page
   The Page Banner Properties dialog box appears, as shown in Figure B-5.

2. Select the text **Home** in the Page banner text box, type **Computer Corner**, then click **OK**
   The text on the Home page banner is changed to read Computer Corner.

3. Click on the text **[Edit the properties for this Navigation Bar to display hyperlinks here]** directly below the banner to highlight it, then press **[Delete]**
   The comment is deleted.

4. Select the comment text directly under the home page banner by clicking the text beginning with the word Comment, type the following text exactly (include the spelling error of *periphrals*) **Computer Corner provides the highest quality in computers and periphrals available on the market today. You can choose from a wide assortment of products that will fit almost any budget.**
   This paragraph replaces the template's text.

5. Click the **Save button** 💾 on the Standard toolbar, then click the **Spelling button** ✔ on the Standard toolbar
   The Spelling dialog box opens, as shown in Figure B-6. FrontPage's spell checker identifies any misspelled words and suggests options for correction. You can click the Ignore button if a word is spelled correctly. You can also make a correction by replacing the selected misspelled word with the new spelling in the Change to text box in the Spelling dialog box, and then clicking the Change button.

6. Click **Change** in the Spelling dialog box to accept the suggested spelling change for peripherals, then click **OK**
   A dialog box appears with information that the spelling check is complete, and the spelling tool closes. FrontPage 2000 also provides for global spell checking of the entire Web site.

7. Click the **Folders button** 📁, click ✔, click the option button next to **Entire web**, then click **Start**
   The FrontPage spelling tool checks every page in the site and presents a list of files with spelling errors. To correct the errors, you double-click the file and respond to the dialog boxes.

8. Click the **Close button** on the dialog box
   The spelling tool is closed. The Computer Corner home page template should look like Figure B-7.

FIGURE B-5: Page Banner Properties dialog box

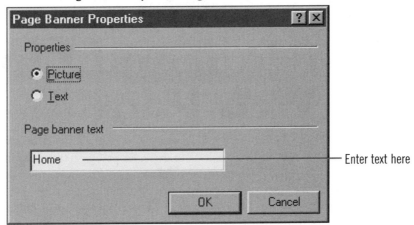

Enter text here

FIGURE B-6: Spelling dialog box

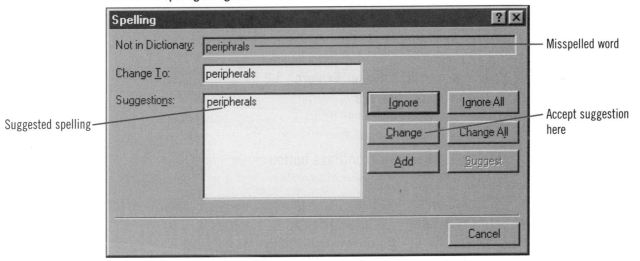

Misspelled word

Accept suggestion here

Suggested spelling

FIGURE B-7: Customized Computer Corner home page

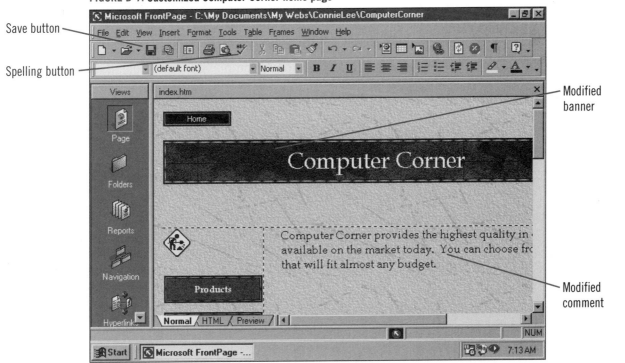

Save button

Spelling button

Modified banner

Modified comment

Previewing, Saving, and Closing a Web Page

As you create Web pages, it is important to periodically **preview** (test) the pages with a Web browser to see how they will look to users. FrontPage 2000 makes it easy to switch back and forth between the editor and a browser. ◄◄◄ Connie knows that the Web page she is working on may not have exactly the same appearance when viewed with a Web browser. She decides to preview her page using Internet Explorer, to see how it would appear to visitors to the Computer Corner Web site, before saving, printing, and closing the home page.

Steps 1 2 3 4

1. Click **File** on the menu bar, then click **Preview in Browser**

   The Preview in Browser dialog box opens, as shown in Figure B-8. The Web browsers available on the system appear in the Preview in Browser window.

> **Trouble?**
>
> If your Preview in Browser window does not list a Web browser, click Add and then Browse to locate a browser on your computer.

2. Click **Microsoft Internet Explorer 5.0** in the Preview in Browser dialog box, click **Preview**, then click **Yes**

   Internet Explorer opens and displays the Computer Corner home page, as shown in Figure B-9.

3. Click the **Microsoft FrontPage button** on the taskbar

   The document now appears in Page View for editing.

4. Scroll down if necessary, click the comment text under Contact Information, then press **[Delete]**

   The Contact Information comment is deleted.

5. Click the **Save button** 🖫 on the Standard toolbar

   The file is saved.

6. Click the **Print button** 🖨 on the Standard toolbar

   The modified Home page is printed.

> **Trouble?**
>
> If the comment area has not been deleted from the home page, click the Refresh button.

7. Click the **Preview in Browser button** 🔲 on the Standard toolbar, then scroll to verify that the comment is deleted

   The document appears in Microsoft Internet Explorer.

8. Click **File**, then click **Close**

   Internet Explorer closes.

9. Click **Microsoft FrontPage** on the taskbar if necessary, click **File**, then click **Close**

   The Computer Corner home page is closed.

FIGURE B-8: Preview in Browser dialog box

Save button

Print button

Preview in Browser button

Select browser

Find alternate browswers

Preview Web page

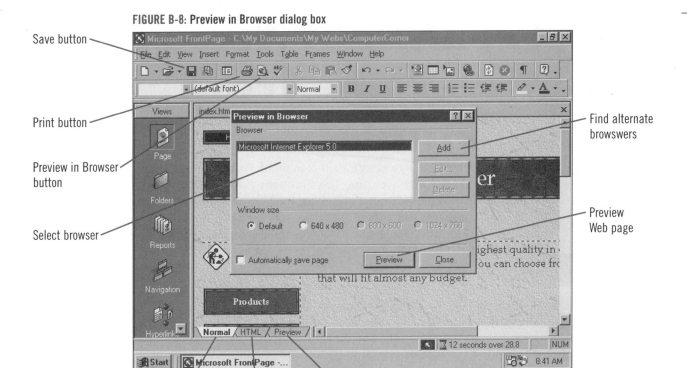

Normal tab   HTML tab   Preview tab

FIGURE B-9: Computer Corner home page opened in Internet Explorer Web browser

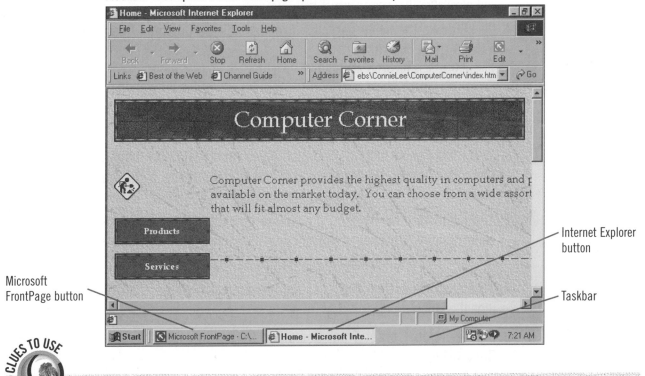

Internet Explorer button

Taskbar

Microsoft FrontPage button

CLUES TO USE

Using the Normal, Preview, and HTML tabs

You can obtain a quick preview of your Web page in Page View by clicking the Preview tab at the bottom of the screen. Although this method does not open a Web browser, it does provide a quick way to test your page. After viewing the page, click the Normal tab to

return to the Normal view. Click the HTML tab to review your Web page's HTML codes. Altering anything in this view will change your Web page. (Do not type anything into the HTML code for the lessons in this book.)

FrontPage 2000

Creating a New Web Page from a Template

Effective Web sites are designed with visitors in mind. FrontPage templates provide a quick and easy way to enhance your Web site. The **Frequently Asked Questions** (FAQ) template is designed to answer common questions about your business or service. Connie wants to add a Web page that will answer typical questions about Computer Corner. She creates the page using the FrontPage Frequently Asked Questions template, changes the title, and then edits the first question.

Steps 1234

1. **Click File on the menu bar, point to New, then click Page**
   The New Page dialog box opens.

2. **Click the Frequently Asked Questions page template on the General tab**
   A description and preview of the template appear in the New Page dialog box. You can click other templates to preview them and read their descriptions, as shown in Figure B-10.

3. **Click OK**
   A Frequently Asked Questions page appears in the document window. It includes banner and navigation bar comments.

4. **Click File on the menu bar, click Properties, type Common Questions in the Title text box, then click OK**
   The new title is incorporated into the page based on the template. Keep in mind that editing the title of a Web page changes the title in the title bar, but not on the page itself.

5. **Click the Save button, then click Save**
   The Common Questions page is saved as common_questions.

6. **Select the Comment text, then type Many new customers have questions about Computer Corner. Here are some of the questions you might have.**
   The comment is replaced by your text.

7. **Replace the text for Question 1 with How do I order from Computer Corner? in the same manner in both the table of contents and the list of questions below the table of contents, then replace the answer text as shown in Figure B-11**

8. **Click the Save button, then click the Preview tab, located at the bottom of the document window**

9. **Click How do I order from Computer Corner? to test the hyperlink, then click Back to Top**
   The Back to Top hyperlink returns you to the top of the list of questions.

10. **Click the Normal tab, located at the bottom of the document window**
    The page is returned to editing mode.

FIGURE B-10: **New Page dialog box**

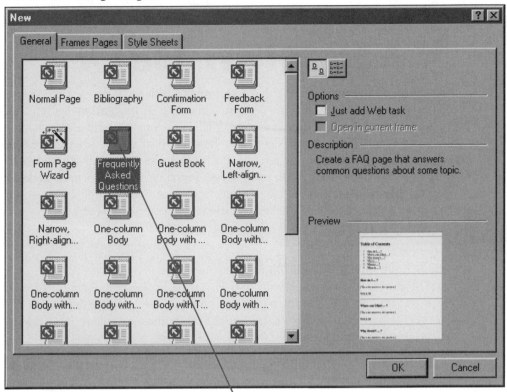

Frequently Asked
Questions template

FIGURE B-11: **Frequently Asked Question 1 displayed with answer**

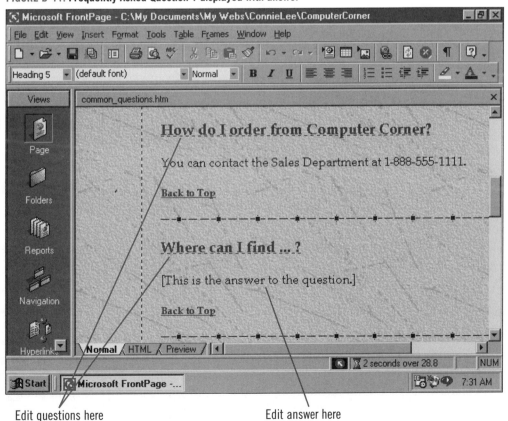

Edit questions here

Edit answer here

FrontPage 2000

Adding a Banner and Navigation Bars

Providing effective navigation tools for visitors to a Web site is a necessity. Without an intuitive and consistent means of moving around a site, such as **navigation buttons** and **navigation bars**, users can easily become disoriented. Visitors seldom return to a Web site that is confusing and frustrating. When you use **Navigation View** in FrontPage 2000, navigation buttons and bars are automatically placed at the top and at the left-hand side, or the **shared borders**, of every page in the Web site. They list the other pages in the Web site and can be clicked for easy navigation. ▨▨ Connie uses Navigation View to add navigation buttons and bars to the Computer Corner Frequently Asked Questions Web page she just created.

Steps 1234

1. **Click the Navigation button** ▨
   The files are listed alphabetically in the left pane, as shown in Figure B-12. Notice that there is one **orphan file** (common_questions.htm) in the left pane, which is not linked to any other pages in the right pane. The index.htm (home page) file is not considered an orphan because it is at the top of the Navigation hierarchy.

2. **Click and drag common_questions.htm from the left pane to a location directly below the Computer Corner home page in the right pane of Navigation View**
   FrontPage adds the Frequently Asked Questions page to the navigational hierarchy for the Computer Corner Web site. It also adds a banner and navigational bars to the FAQ template.

3. **Click the Page button** ▨
   The Frequently Asked Questions page appears in the document window.

4. **Click the Preview tab at bottom of the document window**
   A banner, displaying the page title, and a navigation bar have been added to the page, as shown in Figure B-13.

5. **Click the Normal tab at the bottom of the document window**
   The page is returned to editing mode.

6. **Double-click the text [Edit the properties for this Navigation Bar to display hyperlinks here], located at the far left side of the page**
   The Navigation Bar Properties dialog box appears.

7. **Click the check box for Home Page under Additional pages, then click OK**
   A button that links back to the home page is added to the left navigation bar, as shown in Figure B-14.

8. **Click the Save button, click File, click Close, then click Yes**
   The Frequently Asked Questions page is saved and closed.

Setting navigation bar properties

To change a navigation bar's properties in FrontPage, double-click on a button in the navigation bar. You can choose to have the navigation bar display buttons for **parent** pages (above the page in the hierarchy), **child** pages (below the page in the hierarchy), or pages on the same level. You can also display Back and Next buttons. You can display the bar as buttons or text, and choose its orientation (horizontal or vertical). You can also choose to display additional pages on the navigation bar, including the home page and the parent page.

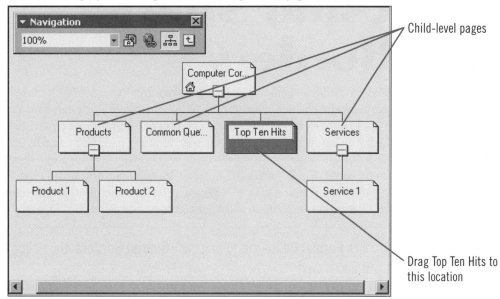

Child-level pages

Drag Top Ten Hits to this location

FIGURE B-16: Top Ten Hits in Page View

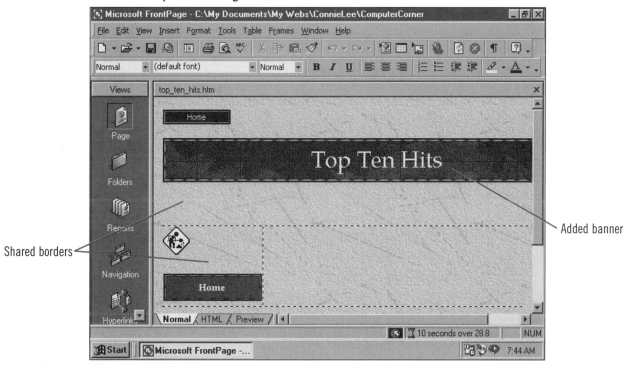

Added banner

Shared borders

Changing a Web theme

You can change a Web theme at any point during the development of your Web site. You can also select different themes for different pages of the Web. To change a Web theme for the entire Web from any view, click Format, click Theme, and then choose All Pages. To change a Web theme for individual pages, click the Folders, Hyperlinks, or Navigation button on the Views bar, select the page or pages that you want to format, click Format, click Theme, and then choose Selected pages. You can preview themes on the right and select new themes from the list on the left. You can also modify individual elements of theme, such as text color, by clicking Modify. When you have selected a new theme for the Web, click OK.

Using Shared Borders

When you add navigation bars using Navigation View, the FrontPage **shared borders** feature is automatically enabled. Shared borders include navigation bars and buttons, but they can also include other elements, such as text comments, graphics, or hyperlinks. Shared borders can be placed at the top, bottom, left, or right areas of the page. You can edit the information in a shared border on any page, and your edits will be reflected on other pages throughout the Web site that use the same shared borders. However, the shared borders feature can be turned off at any time on individual pages, if desired. 🖎 Connie uses the shared borders feature to add a copyright notation for Computer Corner to the bottom of each Web page.

Steps

1. Click **Format** on the menu bar, click **Shared Borders**, then click the **Bottom check box** (if necessary)

   The Shared Borders dialog box appears. Shared borders will appear on the top, left, and bottom of the page. The selected check boxes should reflect Figure B-17.

2. Click **OK**

   The top, left, and bottom borders are a part of every page in the Web site with shared borders enabled.

3. Scroll down to the bottom of the page, then click immediately after the date last modified

   All shared borders on the page are highlighted, as shown in Figure B-18. Note also that the Rice Paper theme has been applied to the Top Ten Hits page.

4. Press [Enter], type **Copyright 2000 Computer Corner**, click the **Center button** 🔲 on the Formatting toolbar, click outside the shared border to deselect it, then click the **Save button**

   The copyright notation for Computer Corner is added automatically to all pages in the Web site that use shared borders. This process may take a few minutes.

5. Click **File**, click **Open**, then double-click **index**

   The home page becomes the current page in Page View. Note the navigational links that have been created for the Common Questions and Top Ten Hits pages, as shown in Figure B-19. Also notice that the Expedition theme has not been changed on the home page.

6. Click the **down scroll arrow** to scroll to the bottom of the page, note that the copyright notation has been added, click **File**, then click **Close**

   The home page closes.

7. Click **File**, then click **Close**

   The Top Ten Hits page closes. FrontPage 2000 also provides a method to turn off the shared borders feature on individual pages.

8. Click the **Folders button** 📁, double-click **common_questions**, click **Format**, click **Shared Borders**, click **Current Page**, click **Bottom** (to deselect it), then click **OK**

   Note that the Computer Corner 2000 copyright notation in the bottom shared border that you added is removed from the Common Questions page. The bottom shared border remains on all other pages in the Web.

9. Click **File**, then click **Close**, click **Yes** (if necessary), click **File**, then click **Close Web**, click **Yes** (if necessary)

   The Common Questions page is closed. The Computer Corner Web is closed.

FIGURE B-17: Shared Borders dialog box

Select shared borders to include

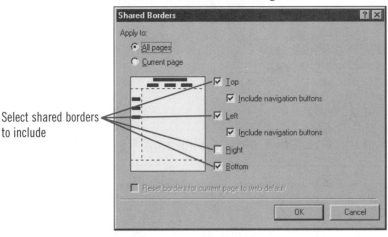

FIGURE B-18: Shared borders highlighted on Top Ten Hits page

Shared borders

Click here to enter text

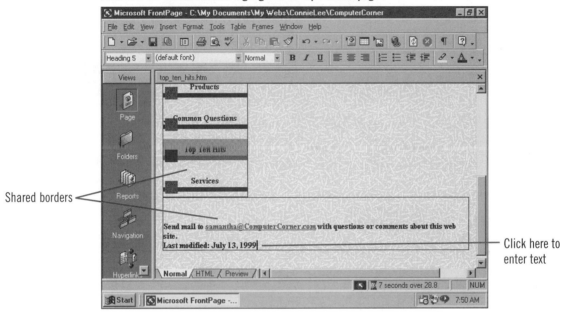

FIGURE B-19: Computer Corner home page

Added navigational links

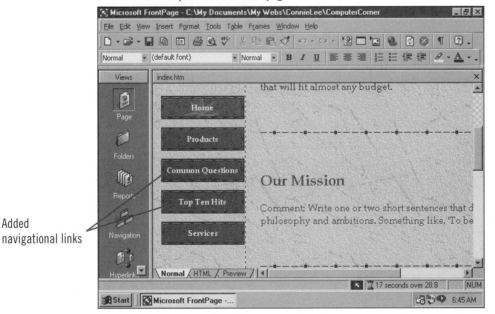

FrontPage 2000

Practice

► Concepts Review

Label each of the elements of the FrontPage window shown in Figure B-20.

FIGURE B-20

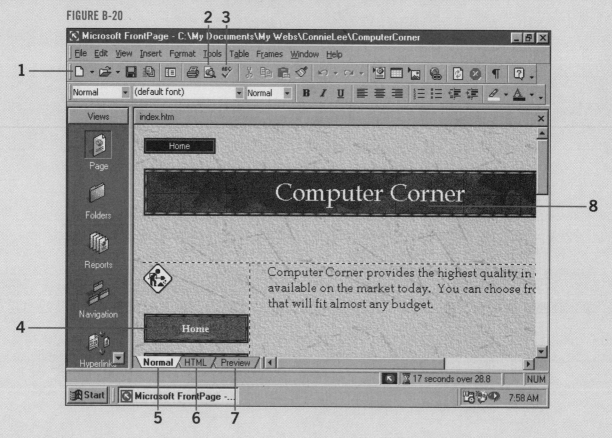

Match each term with the statement that describes it.

9. **Page Properties**
10. **HTML tab**
11. **Preview tab**
12. **Web page template**
13. **Page View**

a. Opens FrontPage in preview mode
b. Ready-made framework that can be customized
c. Opens FrontPage
d. Opens FrontPage in code-editing mode
e. Where the page title can be entered

Select the best answer from the list of choices.

14. **A navigation bar lets you include buttons on your Web page to**
    a. Link to parent pages.
    b. Link to child pages.
    c. Link to pages at the same level.
    d. Include Back and Next buttons.
    e. All of the above

15. **Which view lets you automatically create navigation bars and shared borders on every page?**
    a. Shared Border View
    b. Navigation View
    c. Hyperlinks View
    d. Reports View

16. **Which of the following statements is NOT true?**
    a. Shared borders appear on every page unless you select an individual page and turn off the shared border feature.
    b. Shared borders can be placed only on the top or left side of a page.
    c. Shared borders can include navigation bars, text, graphics, and buttons.
    d. Shared borders can be included in a Web theme.

17. **To edit a shared border for an individual page,**
    a. From Page View, click View on the menu bar, then click Shared Borders.
    b. Click the Shared Borders View button on the Views bar in FrontPage.
    c. From Page View, click Format on the menu bar, then click Shared Borders.
    d. Click Insert on the menu bar in Navigation View, then click Shared Borders.

18. **The view that lets you work with a Web's hierarchy is called**
    a. Report View.
    b. Navigation View.
    c. Folders View.
    d. Hyperlinks View.

19. **Using FrontPage, you can spell check**
    a. An individual Web page.
    b. An entire Web site.
    c. Filenames.
    d. Both a and b

20. **In FrontPage, you can create a new Web page using a template by**
    a. Clicking the Navigation button.
    b. Clicking File, then clicking Open.
    c. Clicking File, pointing to New, then clicking Page.
    d. Clicking File, then clicking Wizard.

▶ Skills Review

1. Open a Web page template.
   a. Click the Start button on the taskbar.
   b. Point to Programs and open Microsoft FrontPage.
   c. Click File, point to New, then click Web.
   d. Select Personal Web, name the new FrontPage Web [insert your last name here], then save it to the location where you store all the files for this book.
   e. Click OK.
   f. Click the Navigation View button.
   g. Double-click the Home Page icon.

2. Edit a Web page.
   a. Replace the opening paragraph with a statement about the purpose of your home page.
   b. Click the Save button, click File, then click Close.
   c. Click Navigation, then double-click interest.htm.
   d. Edit the three interest areas by adding your own interests.
   e. Check the spelling, then click the Save button.
   f. Click File, then click Close.

3. Preview, save, and close a Web Page.
   a. Click File, click Open, then double-click photo.
   b. Create a list of photos to display in your Web.
   c. Rewrite the text of the opening paragraph to reflect your own personal introduction.
   d. Click the Preview in Browser button.
   e. Note how your page looks in a Web browser.
   f. Click File, then click Close to close the Web browser.
   g. Save the page.
   h. Close the page.

4. Create a new Web page from a template.
   a. Make sure that you are in Page View.
   b. Click File, point to New, then click Page.
   c. Select Guest Book in the New dialog box, then click OK.
   d. Save the page as *guests*.
   e. Right-click on the page, click Page Properties, make the title of the page **Guest Book**, then click OK.
   f. Replace the Comment with the text: **I want to know about you. What do you like about my home page? What would you like to see in the future?**, then save the page.
   g. Preview and close the page.

5. Add a banner and navigation bars.
   a. Switch to Navigation View.
   b. Drag guests.htm to the right pane, directly beneath the home page.
   c. View the Guest Book page in Page View, then preview it in your Web browser.
   d. Change the page banner to read **My Guest Book**.
   e. Save the page, preview it in your Web browser, and then close the browser.
   f. Switch back to FrontPage and close the My Guest Book page, saving any changes.

6. **Create a new page in Navigation View.**
   a. Switch to Navigation View.
   b. Right-click the Home Page icon, then click New Page.
   c. Rename the new page **My Resume**.
   d. Open the page in Page View.
   e. Click below the banner and enter an introductory paragraph.
   f. Save and preview the page in your Web browser.
   g. Close the page.

7. **Use shared borders.**
   a. Open the home page.
   b. Change the page banner title to reflect your name.
   c. Double-click the text comment directly below the page banner, click the check box for Child pages under Home, under Hyperlink to add to page in the Navigation Bar Properties dialog box, then click OK.
   d. Click Format, then click Shared Borders.
   e. Click the Bottom check box, then click OK.
   f. Add your own personal quote or message to the bottom shared border.
   g. Save the page and preview it in your Web browser.
   h. Check the links to the pages to verify that the new bottom border is added to each page.
   i. Close both the page and the browser.
   j. In FrontPage open the photo page, click Format, then click Shared Borders.
   k. Click the Current page option button, click the Bottom check box to deselect it, then click OK.
   l. Preview the page in the browser to verify the absence of the bottom border.
   m. Close the browser, return to FrontPage, then save and close the Web.

▶ Independent Challenges

1. You are the Webmaster for a new online newspaper called XtraXtra. The only way your venture can make any money is by selling advertising to companies that want to reach your readers. Your first challenge is to make the site more user-friendly by adding Frequently Asked Questions and Bibliography pages.
  To complete this independent challenge:

  a. Create a new Web named *Xtra* with the One-Page Web template.
  b. Click Format, and then click Theme and select a theme for your Web.
  c. Change the name of the home page to **Xtra**, then switch to Page View.
  d. Add a Frequently Asked Questions page as a child of the home page.
  e. Insert four questions that you think visitors to the site would ask.
  f. Add a Bibliography page as a child of the home page.
  g. Save the page, then preview it.
  h. Print the page.
  i. Close FrontPage.

2. You are the Webmaster for a bookstore chain called Best Books, Incorporated. You have been charged with designing a Web site for the chain. You plan to develop a Web site with the following navigational structure:

- Best Books home page
  - Youth Literature
    - Picture
    - Early Reader
    - Young Adult
- Adult Literature
  - Mystery
  - Contemporary
  - Classics
  - Poetry
- Recent Awards

You also want to include shared borders on the top and left of every page. The top border will have a navigation bar with buttons linking to the home page and second-level pages. Before you worry about content, you decide to complete the navigational structure.

To complete this independent challenge:

a. Use the One-Page Web template and create a new one-page Web named *BestBooks*.

b. Click Format, then click Theme and assign any theme to the Web.

c. Name the home page **Best Books**.

d. Switch to Navigation View, if necessary, and add three second-level pages: **Youth Literature**, **Adult Literature**, and **Recent Awards**.

e. Include navigation bars in all new pages.

f. Rename the pages in Navigation View as you create them.

g. Select the Youth Literature page and add three pages below it called **Picture**, **Early Reader**, and **Young Adult**.

h. Select the Adult Literature page and add four pages to the next level: **Mystery**, **Contemporary**, **Classics**, and **Poetry**.

i. Open the Recent Awards page and delete the navigation bar in its left shared border, save and preview in a browser, then print the page.

j. Close FrontPage.

3. Your maternal grandmother has recently taken to surfing the Web. She's fascinated with the idea of creating a family home page, but doesn't know anything about programming. She has asked for your help. Together, the two of you will use FrontPage to create a Web called Family.

To complete this independent challenge:

a. Draw a family tree, starting with your maternal grandparents. (You can use your own family or a fictional family.)

b. Create a one-page Web called *Family*, using the One Page Web template.

c. Preview a number of themes and choose one that reminds you of your family.

d. Switch to Navigation View.

e. Title the home page with your grandparents' names.

f. Create child pages in Navigation View—one for each child and spouse pair in your mother's generation.

g. Create a third level for your generation.

h. Create a fourth level if you or your siblings have children.

i. Switch to Page View, open the home page, and add a right shared border to all pages.

j. Save, preview, and print the page.

k. Return to Normal view.

l. Close FrontPage.

4. Many sites on the World Wide Web use the features found in FrontPage 2000. For example, you'll see shared borders, page banners, and navigation bars at many sites. As Webmaster for Treats, a mail-order pet-supply company, you are interested in updating your site with the newest features that FrontPage offers. You decide to see how other online mail-order companies use these features.

To complete this independent challenge:

a. Connect to the Internet and use your favorite browser.

b. Use a search engine to find the Amazon online bookstore and print its home page. (You can also visit a different mail-order company, if you want.)

c. Mark the different features, such as shared borders and navigation bars, on your printout.

d. Hand in the printout with your comments.

▶ Visual Workshop

Create a single Web page in FrontPage that looks exactly like the Bibliography page depicted in Figure B-21. (*Hint*: This page uses the Bibliography template and the Citrus Punch theme.) Preview the page in your browser, then print a hard copy of it.

FIGURE B-21

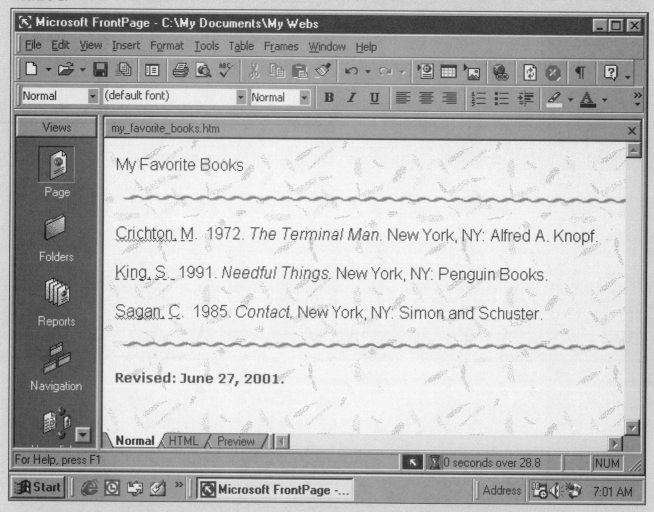

Working
with Web Pages

<MOUS> ▶ **Remove shared borders and themes**

<MOUS> ▶ **Set page properties**

<MOUS> ▶ **Enter text into a Web page**

<MOUS> ▶ **Format text**

<MOUS> ▶ **Format paragraph styles**

▶ **Print a Web page**

<MOUS> ▶ **Import a Web page**

▶ **Delete and export Web pages**

Although FrontPage templates and wizards are very efficient for creating a consistent "look and feel" for a Web site, you may want to create a unique look for a specific Web page or for an entire site. Microsoft FrontPage provides many options to customize a page and to incorporate unique colors, styles, and sizes for text and paragraphs on a Web page. It is also easy to print, import, export, and delete Web pages.
   The president of Computer Corner has asked Connie Lee to create a Web page that provides a personal welcome message. Although he likes the template Connie is using for the rest of the site, he wants his page to be unique.

Removing Shared Borders and Themes

To attract attention or address a specific issue, you may want one or more pages on a Web site to be unique or different. In this case, you can create a new Web page and then remove any shared borders and themes. To create a new Web page, you can use the File option on the menu bar or the New button on the Standard toolbar. ◀━━ Connie creates a new Web page in the Computer Corner site for the president of the company. This page provides a welcome to the Web site message from the president.

Steps 1234

QuickTip

The Computer Corner Web can be saved to several alternate locations, such as a hard drive, a network drive, or external media. Due to the size of the completed Web, it is not recommended that it be saved to floppy disk. If you have saved the Computer Corner Web in a different location, enter the path or browse to locate the Web.

QuickTip

If the filename is not highlighted, you can right-click the new file, click Rename, and type the new name (President.htm).

1. Start **Microsoft FrontPage**, click **File**, and then click **Open Web**
   The Open Web dialog box appears.

2. Click the **Computer Corner Web**, then click **Open**
   The Computer Corner Web opens in the FrontPage window.

3. Click the **Folders button** ⬚, then click the **New Page button** ⬚ on the Standard toolbar
   A new file (new_page_1.htm) appears in the file listing.

4. Type **President.htm** to rename the file and press **[Enter]**
   The new page has been renamed, and President.htm appears in the listing.

5. Double-click **President.htm** to open it in Page View
   The page opens, as shown in Figure C-1. The new page has the same theme and shared borders as the other pages in the Computer Corner Web.

6. Right-click anywhere on the page and select **Page Properties**
   The Page Properties dialog box opens.

7. Click the **General tab** to make it foremost (if necessary), type **President Buckwood's Welcome Page** in the Title box, then click the **Custom tab**
   The Custom area of Page Properties appears, as shown in Figure C-2.

8. Click **Microsoft Border**, then click **Remove**
   The shared borders will be removed from this Web page.

9. Click **Microsoft Theme**, click **Remove**, then click **OK**
   The president's page appears, as shown in Figure C-3. The template and the shared border have been deleted from this page.

10. Click the **Save** button ⬚ on the Standard toolbar
    The page is saved.

FIGURE C-1: President.htm in Page view

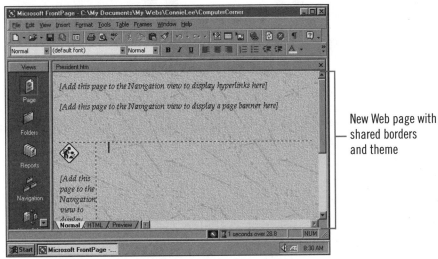

New Web page with shared borders and theme

FIGURE C-2: Page Properties dialog box (Custom tab)

Custom tab

Indicates borders and theme associated with current page

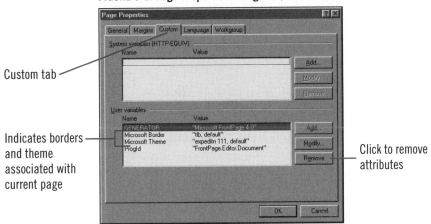

Click to remove attributes

FIGURE C-3: President.htm in Page view, showing deletions

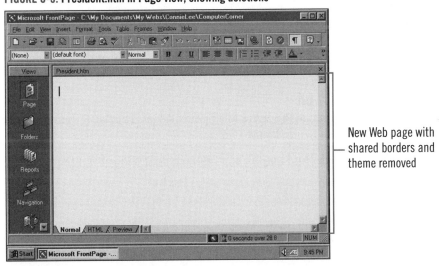

New Web page with shared borders and theme removed

Using descriptive titles for Web pages

It is important to specify a descriptive title for each Web page. Titles serve to help the developers identify and locate Web pages. In addition, if a user sets a bookmark to a particular Web page or adds the page to the Favorites list, it is the title that becomes the reference. Titles can also assist others in locating your Web page through an Internet search engine.

Setting Page Properties

The overall appearance of a Web page can be set in the Page Properties dialog box. Through the options in Page Properties, you can specify the title of the page, select the colors of the background and text, set the margins, and define other features. ➤ Connie wants to set the background and text colors for the president's page.

Steps 1234

1. **Right-click anywhere in the document window, select Page Properties, and click the Background tab**
   The Background section appears with options for setting the background, text, and hyperlink colors.

2. **Click the Background list arrow, then click Navy**
   Navy becomes the active background color.

3. **Click the Text list arrow, then click White**
   White becomes the active color in the text list, as shown in Figure C-4.

4. **Click the Margins tab and click Specify left margin**
   A check mark appears in the Specify left margin box.

5. **Select the 0 in the Specify left margin number box, then type 30**
   The left margin is set to 30 pixels, as shown in Figure C-5.

6. **Click the Workgroup tab**
   The Workgroup section appears with options for selecting a category, assigning files, and specifying the review status.

7. **Scroll down the Available categories list and click the VIP check box**
   The VIP option is selected. Specifying a category for a file allows you to sort and group by category in the Reports view.

8. **Click OK**
   The Page Properties dialog box closes. The background of the president's page is now navy, as shown in Figure C-6.

9. **Click the Save button 🔲 on the Standard toolbar**

FIGURE C-4: **Page Properties dialog box (Background tab)**

Background tab

Background color

Text color

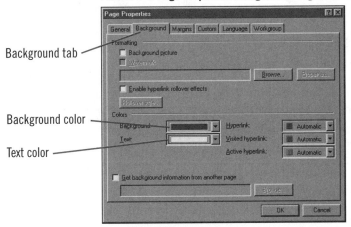

FIGURE C-5: **Page Properties dialog box (Margins tab)**

Margins tab

Number of pixels in
left margin

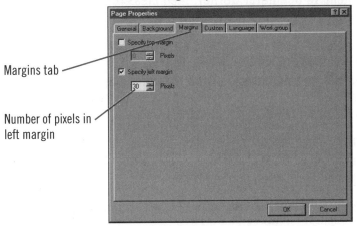

FIGURE C-6: **President's page with navy background**

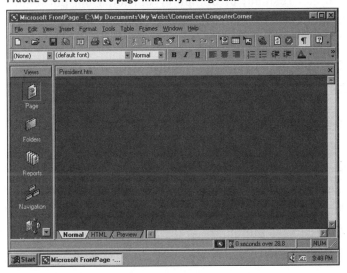

Contrasting text and background colors

A well-designed page should have a definite contrast between the text color and the background color. Most pages use a white or light-colored background with black or dark-colored text. You can also use a dark background with light text. Always test your pages to ensure that they are easy to read before determining the final colors.

Entering Text into a Web Page

Text is often a big part of Web pages, primarily because text files are generally smaller and can transfer over the Internet faster than large graphics files. With Microsoft FrontPage, entering text for a Web page is as easy as entering text in a word-processing program. The president wants his page to begin with a personal welcome. To create this introduction, Connie begins by entering the text on the president's page.

Steps

1. Type **Welcome to Computer Corner**, then press **[Enter]**
The text appears on the left of the screen, and the insertion point moves down to the beginning of the second line.

2. Type **Our company is dedicated to providing the very best prices in computer equipment for your home and office. We offer the following advantages:**
The text appears on the screen. Note that the text automatically wraps to the next line when you reach the right margin.

3. Press **[Enter]** and type the following phrases:
Low prices, then press **[Enter]**
Free technical support, then press **[Enter]**
Fast, friendly service, then press **[Enter]**
The phrases appear on three separate lines.

4. Type **As President of Computer Corner, I am personally committed to ensuring that the customers are happy.**, then press **[Enter]**
The Web page appears as shown in Figure C-7.

5. Select the word **happy**, click **Tools**, then click **Thesaurus**
The Thesaurus dialog box opens, as shown in Figure C-8. "Contented" and other words are listed as possible synonyms.

6. Click **Look Up**, then click **Replace**
The word "happy" is replaced by the word "satisfied," as shown in Figure C-9.

7. Deselect the text, click the **Spelling button** on the Standard toolbar, then click **OK**
If the typing was correct, a dialog box appears confirming that the spelling check is complete. If there is an error, the Spelling dialog box appears with recommended corrections.

8. Click the **Save button** on the Standard toolbar
The page is saved.

FIGURE C-7: President's page with text

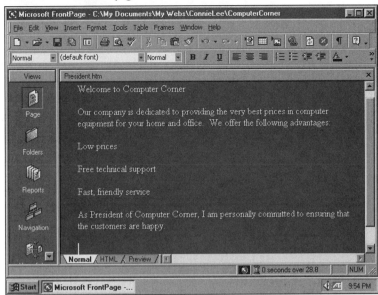

FIGURE C-8: Thesaurus dialog box

Synonyms associated with highlighted meaning

Alternate meanings

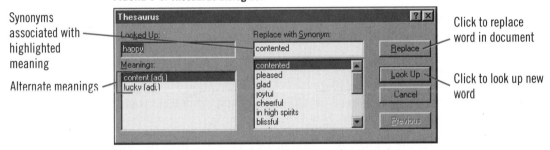

Click to replace word in document

Click to look up new word

FIGURE C-9: President's page with replacement from Thesaurus

Replaced word

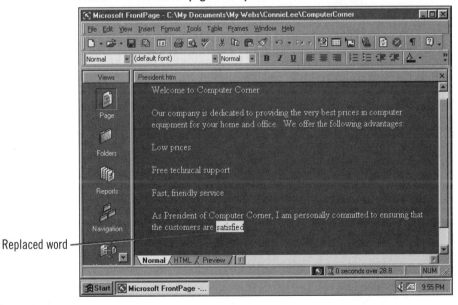

Using the Thesaurus

Prior to selecting a synonym in the Thesaurus, it is important to make sure that the correct meaning is selected. For example, many words can be used as adjectives, nouns, or verbs. When using the Thesaurus, first click the correct meaning for the word, then select a synonym to Look Up or Replace.

Formatting Text

To emphasize various parts of a text page, you can apply different font sizes, colors, and formatting styles. For example, you can increase or decrease the size of your text, you can change the color and style of your text, or you can alter the background color of your page. Figure C-10 shows the **Formatting toolbar**, whose buttons provide quick access to formatting changes; additional options are available through menu selections. ◄▬▬ Connie wants the president's page to attract attention. She uses the Formatting toolbar and dialog boxes to enhance its appearance.

Steps

1. Double-click the word **Computer** in the top line to select it

QuickTip

Use text colors sparingly. Never include more than five or six colors on a page.

2. Click the **Font Color list arrow** on the Formatting toolbar
   The drop-down color box appears, as shown in Figure C-11. The options allow you to select Standard Colors or access More Colors.

3. Click **Yellow**, then click anywhere to deselect the text
   The font color box closes, and the word "Computer" changes to yellow.

4. Select the word **Corner**, click the **Font Color button** 🅰 on the Formatting toolbar, then deselect the text
   The word "Corner" changes to yellow. Since Yellow was the previously selected color, it is not necessary to open the Font Color list.

5. Select the phrase **very best prices**, click the **Bold button** 🅱 on the Formatting toolbar, then click anywhere to deselect the text
   The text appears in bold, causing it to seem larger and slightly darker than the surrounding words.

6. Select the phrases **Low prices**, **Free technical support**, and **Fast, friendly service**
   To select large quantities of text, you can drag the mouse pointer over the text or click at the beginning of the text, hold the [SHIFT] key, and click at the end of the text. It is also possible to select an entire line of text by clicking to the left of the first letter.

7. Click the **Increase Indent button** 📧 on the Formatting toolbar, then click the **Save** icon 💾 on the Standard toolbar
   The three phrases move slightly to the right, as shown in Figure C-12.

FIGURE C-10: Formatting toolbar

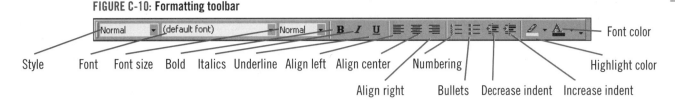

Style
Font
Font size
Bold
Italics
Underline
Align left
Align center
Align right
Numbering
Bullets
Decrease indent
Increase indent
Highlight color
Font color

FIGURE C-11: Color dialog box

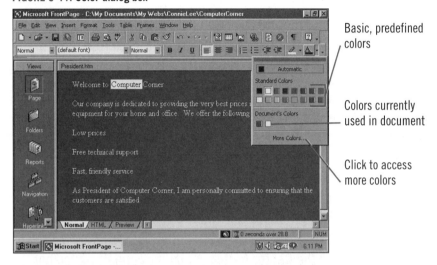

Basic, predefined colors

Colors currently used in document

Click to access more colors

FIGURE C-12: President's page

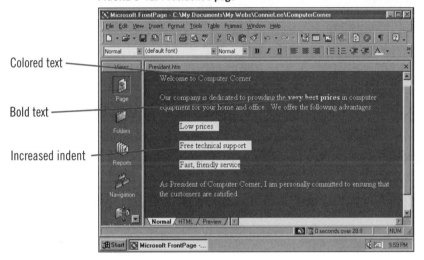

Colored text

Bold text

Increased indent

Accessing the Font dialog box

Another way to select the colors, sizes, and styles of text is through the Font dialog box, shown in Figure C-13. To access the Font dialog box, select the text and then click the right mouse button to display the pop-up menu. Click Font to open the Font dialog box.

FIGURE C-13: Font dialog box

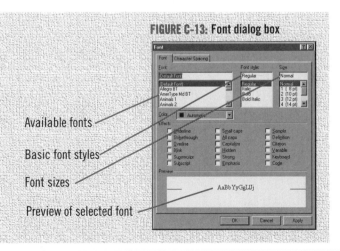

Available fonts

Basic font styles

Font sizes

Preview of selected font

FrontPage 2000

Formatting Paragraph Styles

Styles can be applied to text or paragraphs to add variety to your Web pages. A **style** is a combination of settings. For example, one style might set the text to a 12-point font that is bold and centered. Applying a predefined style to text is generally a one-step process, and is much faster than applying individual formats. The Formatting toolbar in Microsoft FrontPage contains several paragraph styles that can help clarify the organization of your text by creating lists and various styles of headings. The **Style** list includes six levels of headings, ranging from Heading 1 to Heading 6. Heading 1 generally is set to a large, bold font and is used for major headings. Heading 6, on the other hand, is generally the smallest font and is used for minor headings. Connie wants to increase the size of the welcoming message for the president's page. She also wants to add bullets to highlight the important points about Computer Corner.

1. Select the phrase **Welcome to Computer Corner**

2. Click the **Style list arrow**, then select **Heading 1**
   The Heading 1 level is applied to the phrase, causing it to appear in large, bold type, as shown in Figure C-14.

3. Click the **Center button** 🖿 on the Formatting toolbar
   The phrase centers on the page.

4. Select the phrases **Low prices**, **Free technical support**, and **Fast, friendly service**

   QuickTip

   If you want bullets to appear instead of numbers, click the Bullets button 🖿.

5. Click the **Numbering button** 🖿 on the Formatting toolbar
   The text automatically indents, and numbers appear in front of the words, as shown in Figure C-15.

6. Right-click anywhere on the numbered list and select **List Properties**
   The List Properties dialog box opens, as shown in Figure C-16.

7. Click the **A. B. C.** option, then click **OK**
   The numbers change to A. B. and C.

8. Click the **Decrease Indent button** 🖿 on the Formatting toolbar, then click anywhere to deselect
   The lettered list moves slightly to the left, as shown in Figure C-17.

9. Click the **Save button** 🖿 on the Standard toolbar

FIGURE C-14: Heading 1 style

Style list arrow

Heading 1 in style list

Heading 1 applied to first line

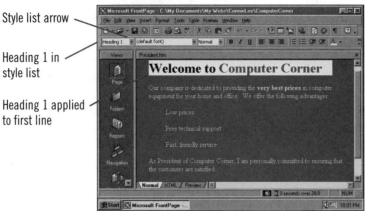

FIGURE C-15: Centered text and numbered list

Centered text

Numbered list

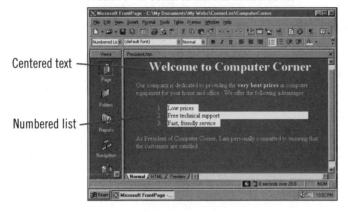

FIGURE C-16: List Properties dialog box

Numbers tab

First number in list

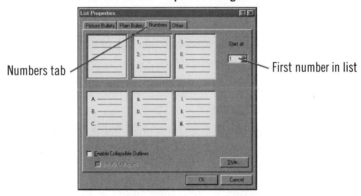

FIGURE C-17: President's page with lettered list

Numbers changed to letters

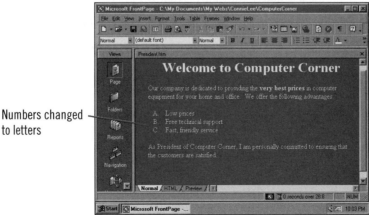

FrontPage 2000

Printing a Web Page

It is easy to print Web pages with FrontPage. To save paper, make sure that your Web page is ready to be printed, by previewing it using the **Print Preview** option. Buttons at the top of the Print Preview window provide options to **Zoom In**, **Zoom Out**, **Close**, and **Print**. Before printing a page, it is advisable to check the Page Setup. The Print Page Setup dialog box allows you to set the margins for printing and specify whether or not you want to print the file path and page numbers. Connie wants a printout of the Web page to show to the president. She begins by previewing the page and checking the Page Setup to make sure the format and layout are as she intended them to be; then she prints a hard copy.

Steps

1. Click File on the menu bar, then click Print Preview

A small image of the page appears in the Print Preview window, as shown in Figure C-18.

2. Click Zoom In

The Zoom In option increases the size of the page on the screen. You can then examine the text as well as the layout of the page.

3. Click Zoom Out

The Zoom Out option decreases the size of the page on the screen.

4. Click Close

The Print Preview window closes.

5. Click anywhere in the document window, click File on the menu bar, then click Page Setup

The Print Page Setup dialog box appears, as shown in Figure C-19. The &T in the Header box indicates that the filename and path will be printed at the top of the page. The Page &P in the Footer box indicates that the word "Page," followed by the page number, will be printed at the bottom of the page.

6. Double-click in the top margin box and type .75, then click OK

The Top margin is changed to ¾-inch.

7. Click File on the menu bar, then click Print

The Print dialog box enables you to select the printer, the range of pages to print, and the number of copies.

> **Trouble?**
> The options for your printer may be different.

8. Click the Properties button, then select 2 up in the Layout section

The Properties dialog box opens, and the layout is set to print two pages, side by side, or a single page on the left side of the paper, as shown in Figure C-20.

9. Click OK twice, then click the Save button 🖫 on the Standard toolbar

The Print dialog box closes, and the current Web page prints on the selected printer.

FIGURE C-18: Print Preview window

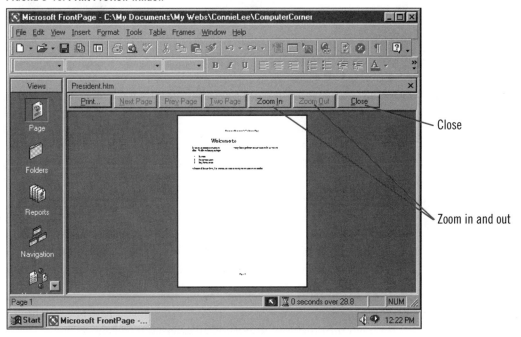

Close

Zoom in and out

FIGURE C-19: Print Page Setup dialog box

Indicates that file-name and path will print at top of page

Indicates that the word "Page" and the page number will print at bottom of page

Set margins for printout

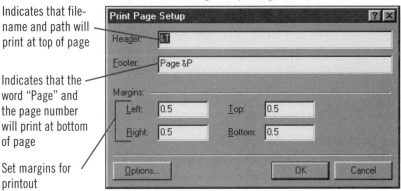

FIGURE C-20: Print Properties dialog box

Paper tab

Indicates paper size

Will print two pages on one sheet of paper

Prints vertical page

Prints horizontal page

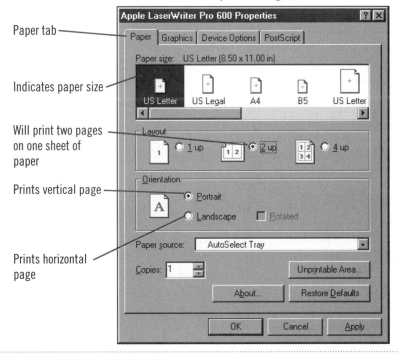

FrontPage 2000

Importing a Web Page

FrontPage provides a rich set of tools that simplify file management. The Import command lets you quickly copy external files or folders into your Web from a local file system, corporate intranet, or the World Wide Web. For example, there may be Web pages in a different Web (either on your computer or at a remote location) that you would like to be able to access, organize, and manage from within your current Web. In addition to Web pages, you can import graphics and any other type of file that your operating system supports (such as Microsoft Word documents and Microsoft Excel spreadsheets). Connie wants to import a Web page from a remote site that focuses on copyright issues.

Steps

1. Click Folders, click File on the menu bar, then click Import

The Import to FrontPage Web dialog box is displayed, as shown in Figure C-21.

2. Click From Web

The Import Web Wizard – Choose Source dialog box opens. The Wizard will guide you through the process of importing an external Web page.

QuickTip

Before downloading Web pages, graphics, or other elements from the Web, always check to make sure there are no copyright restrictions.

3. Click From a World Wide Web site (if necessary), and type www.loc.gov/copyright/cpypub/circ1a.html in the Location box

The location for the United States Copyright Office: A Brief History and Overview is entered as the source for the import, as shown in Figure C-22. Make sure you type a numeral one in the file name circ1a.html.

4. Click Next

The Import Web Wizard – Choose Download Amount dialog box appears.

5. Click the Down Arrow to change the levels below to 0

The download amount will be limited to 500 KB and 0 levels (beyond the current page), as indicated in Figure C-23. When the levels below is set to 0, FrontPage will import only the starting page, plus any images or other files on that page. If the levels below is set to 1, the starting page and its contents will be imported, as well as all of the files and pages that are connected to the hyperlinks.

Trouble?

If you cannot access the copyright page, enter a different URL or import a local file.

6. Click Next, then click Finish

7. Right-click circ1a.html, select Rename, type copyright.htm, press [Enter], then click Yes

The file, circ1a.htm, is renamed to copyright.htm.

8. Double-click copyright.htm

The International Copyright page appears in Page View, as shown in Figure C-24.

9. Click the Save button 🖫 on the Standard toolbar

Setting the download limit

Because most Web pages have multiple links that lead to subdirectories (folders), you must be very careful about limiting the numbers of levels that you import from another location. Setting the download levels to more than one or two could result in hundreds of files, if each Web page links to multiple pages. For example, if you download a Web page that has four images and six hyperlinks (each of which links to a page that has four images and six hyperlinks), and you set the number of levels to 1, you will import 35 files. (Each page has one .htm file and four image files.) If each of those pages then linked to pages with four images and six hyperlinks, and you set the levels to 2, you would import 245 files!

FIGURE C-21: Import dialog box

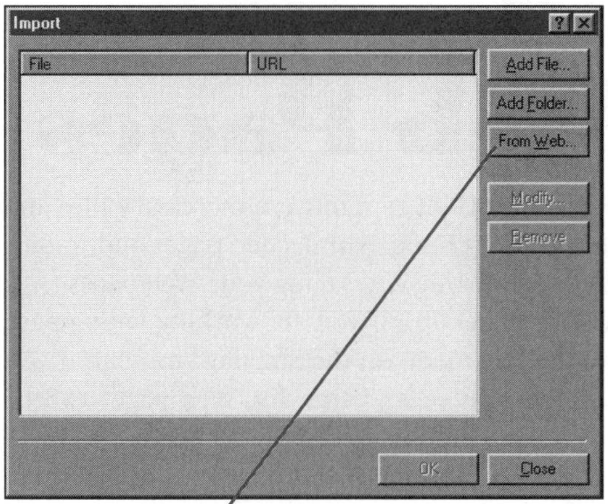

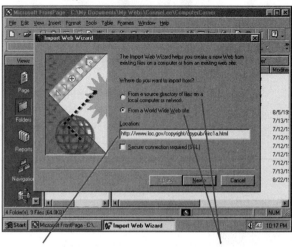

Imports documents from
World Wide Web

FIGURE C-22: Import Web Wizard – Choose Source

URL of file to be imported   Import source options

FIGURE C-23: Import Web Wizard – Choose Download Amount

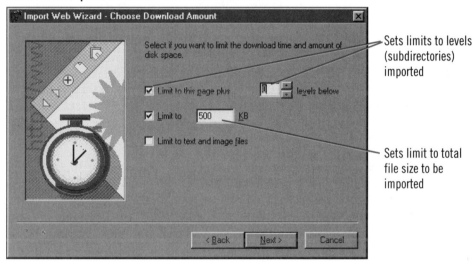

Sets limits to levels
(subdirectories)
imported

Sets limit to total
file size to be
imported

FIGURE C-24: Copyright page

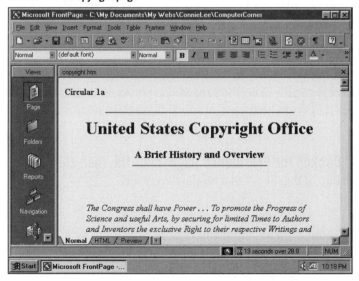

Deleting and Exporting Web Pages

As your Web site grows, you will find that it is very important to remove unnecessary files and folders. Using the **Delete** command, you can permanently remove unneeded pages and folders from your Web. Several options are also available for exporting and saving your Web pages (you should always save your file in a separate location, as a backup). If you are working with a page you have previously saved, you can select Save on the File menu on the Standard toolbar. If you want to change the name or location of a page, you can select **Save As**. Web pages can be exported and saved on a hard drive, a floppy disk, or a remote Web server. Connie decides to delete the copyright page she imported. She realizes that the information will be more accurate and current if she links to the Library of Congress Web site. She also wants to save a backup of the president's page.

Steps

QuickTip
You also can delete files from the Navigation and Hyperlinks Views.

1. Click the **Folders button** 📁
   The folders and files in the Computer Corner Web appear.

QuickTip
Multiple files can be selected by using the Shift key.

2. Select the **copyright.htm**, click **Edit** on the menu bar, then click **Delete**
   The Confirm Delete dialog box appears, as shown in Figure C-25.

3. Click **Yes**
   The dialog box closes, and the file is permanently removed from the Web.

4. Double-click **President.htm**
   The president's page appears in Page View.

5. Click **File** on the menu bar, then click **Save As**
   The Save As dialog box opens, as shown in Figure C-26.

6. Navigate to your floppy disk drive for the Save in box
   The Save in box displays 3½ Floppy (A:).

7. Click **Change**
   The Set Page Title dialog box appears, as shown in Figure C-27. Changing the title of the file makes it easier to keep track of which files are originals and which are backups.

Trouble?
If you cannot save the file on a floppy disk, select another location on the hard drive or network.

8. Type **Backup for President's page**, click **OK**, then click **Save**
   A backup of the file is saved on the floppy disk.

9. Close your browser, close the Web, then exit FrontPage

FIGURE C-25: Confirm Delete dialog box

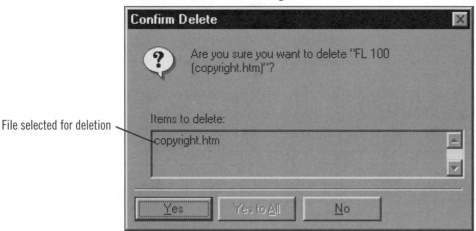

File selected for deletion

FIGURE C-26: Save As dialog box

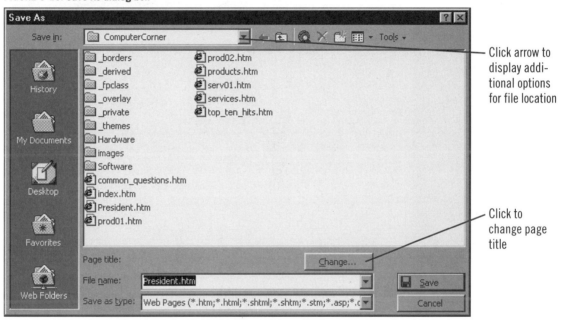

Click arrow to display additional options for file location

Click to change page title

FIGURE C-27: Set Page Title dialog box

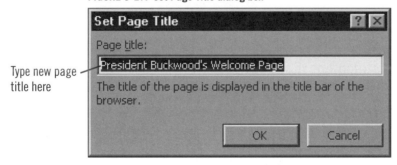

Type new page title here

Maintaining backups for Web pages

It is important to maintain backups of your Web pages. In most cases, you should save each file in a couple of different places, such as on a floppy disk or a hard drive, so that you will be able to recover the information if a file is lost or becomes corrupted. As you back up the files and save them, be sure to keep track of dates and times so that you can use the most recent versions.

Practice

► Concepts Review

Label each of the elements of the FrontPage window shown in Figure C-28.

FIGURE C-28

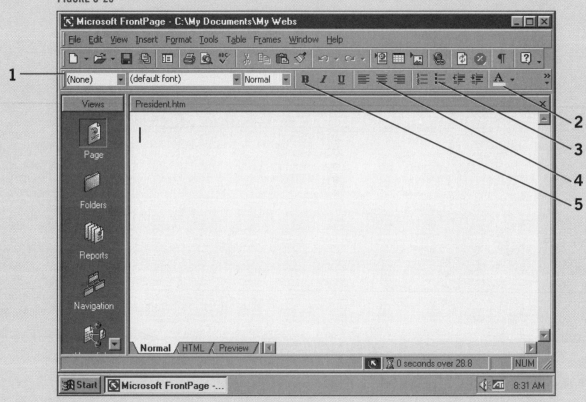

Match each term with the statement that describes it.

6. Heading 6
7. File
8. Page Properties
9. Font dialog box
10. Edit

a. Menu on which Delete command is located
b. Where font size can be specified
c. Where the background color can be specified
d. The smallest level of style on a Web page
e. Menu on which Save As command is located

Select the best answer from the list of choices.

11. **To change the color of the text, which tab should you click in the Page Properties dialog box?**
    a. General
    b. Background
    c. Margins
    d. Custom

12. **Which heading level formats the text in the largest font for the most global title?**
    a. Level 1
    b. Level 6
    c. Level A
    d. Level B

13. **Why are descriptive titles important for Web pages?**
    a. Because the title cannot be changed
    b. Because search engines often index by the titles
    c. Because each title must be unique
    d. Because the title is the first line of text that appears on a page

14. **Which button will provide access to Help in FrontPage?**
    a.
    b.
    c.
    d.

15. **Which button will increase the indent in FrontPage?**
    a.
    b.
    c.
    d.

16. **If you want to create a backup and change the location of a page, which command should you use?**
    a. Save As
    b. Save
    c. Export
    d. Import

17. **In the Print Page Setup box, which of the following indicates that the filename and path will be printed?**
    a. &F
    b. &P
    c. &R
    d. &T

▶ Skills Review

1. **Remove shared borders and templates.**
    a. Start Microsoft FrontPage.
    b. Create a new Web (select the Project Web template) named *New*.
    c Click the Folders button.
    d. Click the New Page button.
    e. Double-click the new page.
    f. Right-click anywhere on the page and select Page Properties.
    g. Select the Custom tab.
    h. Click Microsoft Border, then click Remove.
    i. Click Microsoft Theme, click Remove, then click OK.

2. Set text and background color.

a. Right-click the page.

b. Click Page Properties.

c. Type a descriptive title in the Title text box.

d. Click the Background tab.

e. Select a color for the background.

f. Select a color for the text.

g. Click OK.

3. Enter text and apply text styles.

a. Type the following text: **Microsoft FrontPage is a great way to create Web pages. It is easy to use and very efficient.**

b. Drag the mouse pointer over the word "great" to select it.

c. Click the Bold button on the Formatting toolbar.

d. Drag the mouse pointer over the words "Microsoft FrontPage" to select them.

e. Click the Italics button on the Formatting toolbar.

f. Drag the mouse pointer over both sentences to select them.

g. Click the Cut button to delete all of the text.

4. Format paragraph styles.

a. Type the following text:

Delicious Chocolate Chip Cookies

To bake delicious cookies, follow this recipe:

Go to the supermarket

Buy frozen cookie mix

Place the cookies on a cookie sheet

Bake at 350 degrees

Eat the cookies

b. Highlight the first line and apply the Heading 1 style.

c. Highlight the second line and center it on the page.

d. Apply the Heading 2 style to the second line.

e. Highlight the rest of the lines and format them as a bulleted list.

f. Change the formatting of the recipe to a numbered list.

g. Add a note at the bottom of the page (using the Address style) to call 1-800-COOKIES, if the visitor has questions.

h. Save the changes to your document.

5. Print a Web page.

a. Select Print Preview on the File menu.

b. Preview the page by zooming in.

c. Zoom back out to the miniature view of the page.

d. Close the Print Preview window.

e. Click the Print button on the Standard toolbar.

f. Indicate that you want one copy of the printout.

g. Click OK.

6. **Import a Web page.**
   a. From Folders View, click File and Import.
   b. Click Add File.
   c. Navigate to the Computer Corner Web site and select President.htm.
   d. Click OK.
   e. View the page in Page View.

7. **Delete a Web Page.**
   a. Change to Folders View.
   b. Highlight the President.htm file.
   c. Click Edit, click Delete, then click Yes.

8. **Export a Web page.**
   a. Click anywhere on the page, click File on the menu bar, then click Save As.
   b. Change the name of the Web page to *mypage.htm*.
   c. Save the Web page on a floppy disk.
   d. Exit FrontPage.
   e. Close your browser.

▶ Independent Challenges

1. You have just moved to a new neighborhood and want to meet people. You have been trying to meet your neighbors, but they are busy and it has been hard to find people with whom you have things in common. One of your friends has suggested that you create a Web page where you could list your interests and hobbies. That way, you might locate others, near or far, who share your interests. You like the idea and decide to use Microsoft FrontPage to create a Web site and Web page.

To complete this independent challenge:

a. Start FrontPage and create a new Web (One-Page Web) called *Moving*.
b. Open the home page. Using the Page Properties dialog box, title the Web page [*your name*]'s **Home Page**.
c. Make the background color red and the text color white.
d. Enter your name in the Web with an introductory sentence about your interests, then include a list of four hobbies. End with the sentence, **I have located some great Web sites about these hobbies.**
e. Add a line of text at the top of the page (in Heading 1 style) that contains **All About** [*your name*].
f. Format the hobbies as a bulleted list.
g. Italicize the last sentence.
h. Save the page, preview it, print the page, then close FrontPage.

2. You plan to graduate from college within the next two months and have noticed that several of your friends were able to line up job interviews and employment opportunities through their Web pages. Create a Web site and Web page about your education, experience, and career goals.

To complete this independent challenge:

a. Create an outline of the page that includes a rough draft of the layout you plan to use. Include the following items: your name, address, education, experience, and career goals.

b. Start FrontPage and create a new Web (One-Page Web) called *Job*.

c. Open the home page.

d. In the Page Properties dialog box, title the page with your name.

e. Select a text color and a background color.

f. Type the text on the page. List your career goals in the order in which they would logically occur, and describe the skills that you can offer prospective employers.

g. Format your page in a way that calls attention to your most notable accomplishments. Use at least two different heading levels and two different text colors on your page. Save your page.

h. View the page in a Web browser; if any changes are necessary, make them.

i. Print and save the page, then close the Web browser and FrontPage.

3. The mayor of the town you lived in as a child has heard that you are learning how to create effective Web pages. She has contacted you through a mutual acquaintance to ask for your assistance in creating a Web site for the town (or city). Because many of the citizens have older computer systems, which have fairly slow modems, you decide to design the home page with text only (no graphics).

To complete this independent challenge:

a. Start FrontPage and create a new Web (One Page Web) called *HomeTown*.

b. Open the home page.

c. Title the page with the name of the town where you lived as a child.

d. Design the content of the page so key points about the town are emphasized.

e. Sketch the layout of the page on a piece of paper, then enter it into FrontPage. Include at least three paragraphs, one bulleted list, and one numbered list.

f. Add a sentence at the bottom of the page that includes your name as the Webmaster.

g. Save the page.

h. Preview, save, and print the page. Then close FrontPage.

4. Your boss has assigned you the task of designing the layout for the new company Web page. Because of the high visibility this page will have, both internally and externally, you decide to research alternate layouts for Web pages. A friend has advised that the best way to learn about the possibilities for the layout of Web pages is to explore the Web and investigate several different sites, noting good and not-so-good features of each site. She also mentioned that many Web style guides are available (on the Web) to provide guidance for the layout of your Web pages.

To complete this independent challenge:

a. Log on to the Internet.

b. Use your browser to find at least six different Web sites. Use the Web page evaluation form in Table C-1 to assess at least six different Web pages on the different Web sites. Write down the address and title of each site.

c. If you have trouble locating Web pages with varied designs, use your browser to go to http://www.course.com. Go to the Student Online Companion for this book, then click the link for Unit C.

d. Using the six pages that you investigated, print the Web page you liked the best and the one you liked the least.

e. Many style guides are available on the Web. Use your browser to go to http://www.course.com. Go to the Student Online Companion for this book, then click the link for Unit C. Click Web Style Guides.

f. Review at least two of the available style guides.

TABLE C-1: **Web Page Evaluation**

Evaluation Question		
Is there a heading and introduction at the top of the page?	Yes	No
Are the spelling and grammar correct on the page?	Yes	No
Is the contrast between the text color and background color sufficient?	Yes	No
Is the layout appealing and easy to read?	Yes	No
Is there a date on the page that tells when it was last updated?	Yes	No
Are the hyperlinks easy to find and follow?	Yes	No
Does the page take more than 20 seconds to load?	Yes	No
Are the pictures on the page relevant to the information provided?	Yes	No

▶ Visual Workshop

One of your college professors has asked for your assistance in placing some of the content for a course on the Web. Use the skills you learned in this lesson to create a Web page similar to the one in Figure C-29. Save the file as *multi.htm*.

FIGURE C-29

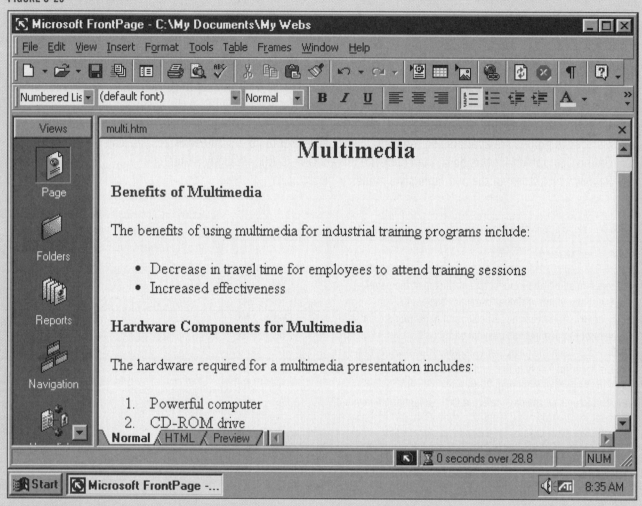

Enhancing
Web Pages

Objectives

- MOUS ► **Insert a picture**
- MOUS ► **Edit a picture**
- ► **Insert a horizontal line**
- MOUS ► **Insert a hyperlink to a local Web page**
- ► **Test a hyperlink**
- MOUS ► **Create hyperlinks to remote Web pages**
- ► **Link to an e-mail address**
- ► **Insert a hyperlink to a bookmark**
- MOUS ► **Use a picture for a hyperlink**

Web pages can contain pictures, lines, and hyperlinks, which allow you to enhance the appearance and value of the pages. Images such as title banners at the top of the page, colorful bullets for items in a list, or pictures that add to the content of the page can help communicate your message effectively if you use them wisely. Other elements, such as horizontal lines, can be used to divide major sections of a page so that the information is presented in easily digestible chunks. In addition, hyperlinks can be added to Web pages to provide easy access to other Web pages that are either local (located in your site) or remote (located on another site). ✎ Connie Lee is ready to add and edit a picture on the president's page. She also wants to incorporate hyperlinks that will link to local or remote sites when someone clicks on underlined text or on the picture.

Inserting a Picture

The old adage "a picture is worth a thousand words" is certainly true for a Web page. Pictures, in the form of illustrations or photographs, can make a Web page more interesting and exciting. Web pages can display images that are stored in two different formats—JPG and GIF. The JPG (or JPEG) format is typically used for photographic images. The GIF format is commonly used for line drawings, such as bar charts. Pictures for Web pages are generally inserted from clip art, scanned into a computer, or created with a software program such as Adobe PhotoShop. With FrontPage, you can insert an image into your Web page easily and effectively. ✎ Connie wants to insert a picture of a computer on the president's page.

Steps 1234

1. Start **Microsoft FrontPage**, click **File**, then click **Open Web**
The Open Web dialog box appears.

2. Click the **[insert your name here]** folder, if necessary, click the **ComputerCorner** Web, click **Open**, click the **Folders button** 🗁, then double-click **President.htm**
The President.htm page appears in Page View.

3. Click at the bottom of the page, press **[Enter]**, then click the **Insert Picture From File button** 🖼 on the Standard toolbar
The Picture dialog box appears, as shown in Figure D-1.

4. Click **Clip Art**, click in the **Search for clips text box**, type **computer**, then press **[Enter]**
Several pictures of computers appear in the window, as shown in Figure D-2.

5. Click the picture titled **computers** or a similar picture that has a white background
A menu appears, as shown in Figure D-3. To view a picture's description, keywords, file type, filename, file size and other details in the Clip Art Gallery, right-click the picture, then select Clip Properties.

6. Click **Insert clip** 🖼 on the menu
The computer picture appears on the president's page.

7. Click the **Save button** 🖫, click **Rename**, then type **computer.gif**
The Save Embedded Files dialog box opens. You can use a descriptive name for each image.

8. Click **Change Folder**, click **images**, then click **OK** twice
The picture is saved in the images folder of the Computer Corner Web. The president's page now has a picture at the bottom of the page, as shown in Figure D-4. Don't worry if the size of your picture is different. You will resize the picture in the next lesson.

FIGURE D-1: **Picture dialog box**

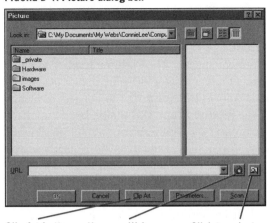

Clip Art button   Use your Web browser to select a page or file   Click to select a file on your computer

FIGURE D-2: **Clip Art Gallery with computer pictures**

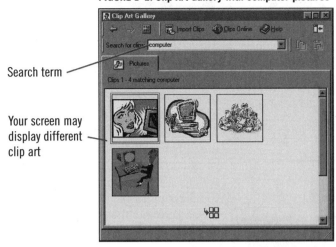

Search term

Your screen may display different clip art

FIGURE D-3: **Pop-up menu**

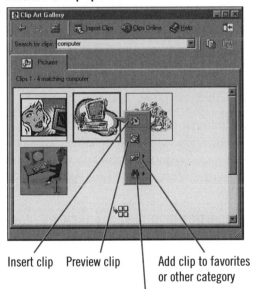

Insert clip   Preview clip   Add clip to favorites or other category

Find similar clips

FIGURE D-4: **President's page with computer picture at bottom**

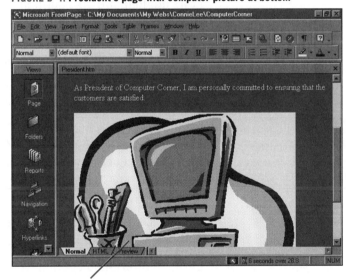

Picture appears at bottom of page

CLUES TO USE

Inserting a picture, text, or a hyperlink from a Web browser

If you find a picture, text, or a hyperlink on the Web that you would like to include on your Web page, you can simply drag and drop it from Internet Explorer into your Web page in FrontPage. To do this, open both FrontPage and Internet Explorer. Then click on the picture (or other element) in the browser that you want to copy, and drag it over to the FrontPage window. (Be aware that there are copyright restrictions on many of the pictures on the Web.) The same procedure works for text and hyperlinks; click slightly in front of the hyperlink and drag over it without clicking *on* the hyperlink.

Editing a Picture

Although pictures are not generally created in FrontPage, they can be edited in Page view of FrontPage. When you select a picture, the Pictures toolbar appears. The **Pictures toolbar** contains editing tools that can be used with tools on the Format toolbar to alter the color, size, or placement of a picture or to select a transparent color. When a color is **transparent**, it disappears or blends into the background of the page. You can also use the **Picture Properties dialog box** to interlace a picture. An **interlaced** picture initially appears on a Web page with very poor resolution (it looks fuzzy). Slowly, as the picture is downloaded, its resolution improves and the picture quality sharpens. Many pictures on the Web are interlaced because interlaced images seem to appear faster; therefore, visitors are more likely to wait for them to appear fully. ✎ Connie notes that the computer in her picture appears against a white rectangle. If the rectangle were the same color as the background, the computer would blend into the page and the rectangle would appear to be transparent. She also wants to interlace the picture.

1. **Click the computer picture on the president's page**
   Small squares, called **sizing handles**, surround the picture to indicate that it is selected. In addition, the Pictures toolbar appears below the document window.

2. **Click and drag the sizing handle at the lower-right corner of the picture to decrease (or increase if you selected another smaller image) the size of the picture to about ¼ of its original size, as shown in Figure D-5**
   As you click and drag the sizing handle, the insertion point turns into a double-headed arrow.

3. **Click the Set Transparent Color button** ✎ **on the Pictures toolbar**
   A warning dialog box may appear informing you that the picture will be converted to the GIF format and that the number of colors in the picture may be reduced.

4. **Click OK, then click the white rectangle in the picture**
   The warning dialog box closes. As the mouse pointer moves over the picture, its shape changes to that of a pencil eraser. When you click the picture, the white color disappears and becomes the same color as the background. The picture now appears to blend into the background, and it no longer retains its rectangular shape.

5. **Right-click the picture, then select Picture Properties from the pop-up menu**
   The Picture Properties dialog box opens. Note that the Transparent box is checked.

6. **Click the Interlaced box and type Computer Picture in the Text box under Alternative representations**
   A checkmark appears for the Interlaced option, as shown in Figure D-6. The Transparent and Interlaced options are available only if the graphic is a GIF image. If the picture is in JPEG format, you have the option to set the Quality of the image. Quality settings range from 1 to 100. Selecting a higher quality improves the appearance of the image but results in a larger file.

7. **Click OK to close the Picture Properties dialog box, then click the Center button** 🖼 **on the Formatting toolbar**
   The picture is centered on the Web page, as shown in Figure D-7.

8. **Click outside the picture to deselect it, click the Save button** 💾 **on the Standard toolbar, then click OK**
   The file and picture are saved.

FIGURE D-5: **Computer picture and Picture toolbar**

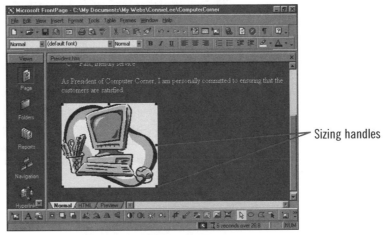

Sizing handles

FIGURE D-6: **Picture Properties dialog box (General tab)**

Name and location of picture

Options for GIF image

Alternative text for image

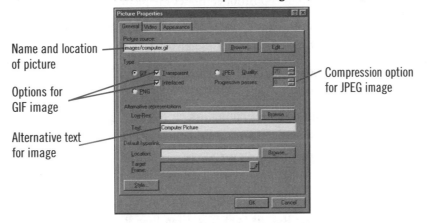

Compression option for JPEG image

FIGURE D-7: **President's page with transparent picture**

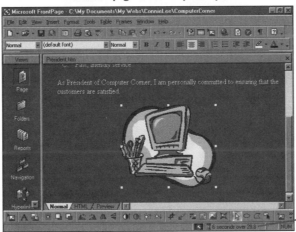

Estimated time to download at 28.8 Kbps

Downloading pictures

Pictures can enhance a Web page, but they also can frustrate users if the files are too large and require too much time to transfer and display. In the lower corner of the document window, you can see the estimated time to download a page at 28.8 Kbps. A modem operating at 28.8 Kbps is a common speed for Internet connections from homes and small offices. If the estimated time to download exceeds 15 seconds, you should use a smaller picture, limit the number of pictures, or shorten the page length.

Inserting a Horizontal Line

As you browse the Web, you are likely to see a variety of horizontal lines on Web pages. These lines are easy to insert and can help divide Web pages into topical areas. Through the Horizontal Line Properties dialog box, which can be accessed by right-clicking on a horizontal line, you can specify the color of the line and set its width, height, and alignment. ✎ Connie wants to add a line under her picture. She thinks a thick, gray line will help separate the picture from the text she plans to add below.

Steps

QuickTip
To delete the line, simply click the horizontal line and press [Delete] or [Backspace].

1. **Click to the right of the picture and press [Enter]**
   The insertion point is positioned under the picture.

2. **Click Insert on the menu bar and select Horizontal Line**
   A horizontal line appears under the picture.

3. **Place the mouse pointer over the line, then right-click**
   The pop-up menu appears, as shown in Figure D-8.

4. **Select Horizontal Line Properties on the pop-up menu**
   The Horizontal Line Properties dialog box opens.

5. **Double-click the Width text box, then type 75**
   The width of the line can be set as either a percentage of the window (75% in this case) or a specific number of pixels.

6. **Double-click the Height text box, then type 8**
   This action determines the thickness of the line. The higher the number, the thicker the line.

7. **Click the Color list arrow, click Gray, then click the Solid line (no shading) check box if necessary**
   Compare your screen to Figure D-9.

8. **Click OK, then click outside the selection**
   The Horizontal Line Properties dialog box closes, and a thick, gray line appears, as shown in Figure D-10.

9. **Click the Save button 🖫 on the Standard toolbar**

FIGURE D-8: Pop-up menu

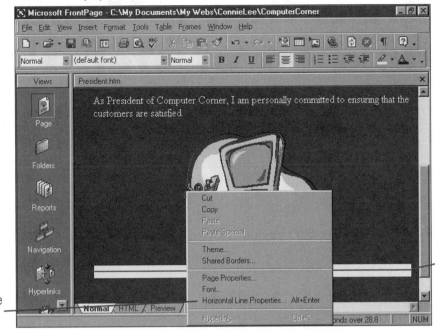

Horizontal Line
Properties

Highlighted
horizontal line

FIGURE D-9: Horizontal Line Properties dialog box

Sets width of line

Sets thickness
of line

Sets alignment

Specifies color

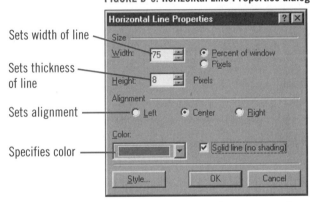

FIGURE D-10: Web page with thick, gray line

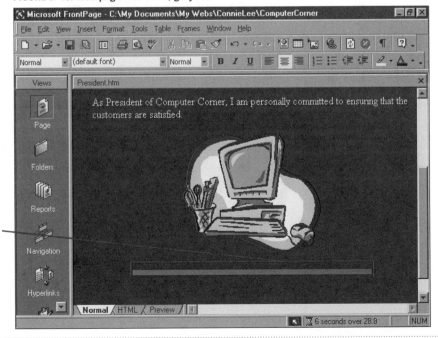

Line length equals
75% of screen

FrontPage 2000

Inserting a Hyperlink to a Local Web Page

Hyperlinks are used to connect one Web page to another. For example, if you have several related Web pages, you can create hyperlinks that will link each of your Web pages to a home page or to the other Web pages. You also can create hyperlinks that connect your Web pages to other Web sites throughout the World Wide Web to provide quick, easy access to related information. To create a hyperlink, simply highlight the text or graphic image that you want to trigger the link, then specify the destination Web page in the **Create Hyperlink dialog box**. The hyperlink can connect to another Web page in the current Web (local link) or to a remote Web page on the Internet. ◄━━ Connie wants to link the president's page she is currently developing to the home page for the Computer Corner Web.

Steps

1. Click at the bottom of the president's page and type **Visit the Computer Corner Home Page**

   The text appears on a new line centered at the bottom of the page.

2. Select **Computer Corner Home Page**, then click the **Hyperlink button** 🖫 on the Standard toolbar

   The Create Hyperlink dialog box opens.

Trouble?

If the file index.htm does not appear in your window, ask your instructor or technical support person for assistance.

3. Click **index.htm**

   The file index.htm appears in the URL text box, as shown in Figure D-11.

4. Click **OK**, then click anywhere outside the selection

   The Create Hyperlink dialog box closes, and the text "Computer Corner Home Page" appears in blue text with an underline. This is the default style for hyperlinks.

5. Right-click anywhere in the document window and select **Page Properties**

   The Page Properties dialog box appears.

6. Click the **Background tab**, click the **Hyperlink list arrow**, then click **White**

   White becomes the active color for hyperlinks, as shown in Figure D-12.

7. Click **OK**, then click the **Save button** 🖫 on the Standard toolbar

   The Page Properties dialog box closes, and the Web page is saved. The hyperlink is white text with an underline, as shown in Figure D-13.

FIGURE D-11: Create Hyperlink dialog box

Home page for
Computer Corner Web

Name of selected file

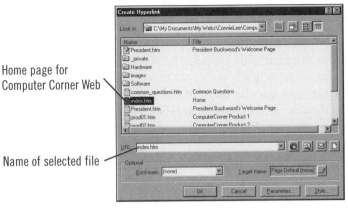

FIGURE D-12: Page Properties dialog box (Background tab)

Background tab

Color for text
of hyperlink

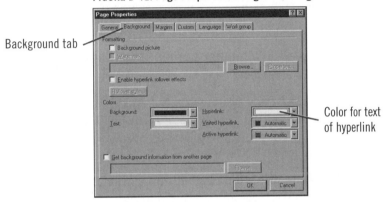

FIGURE D-13: President's page with white hyperlink

Hyperlink

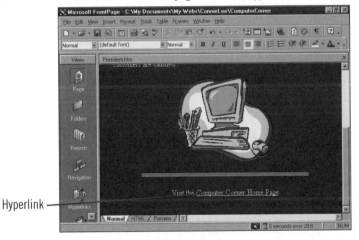

Creating hyperlinks

The following guidelines will help make the hyperlinks on your Web pages more user-friendly to your visitors:

- Create descriptive hyperlinks. For example, say, "Click to visit the White House" instead of "Click here to go to the White House." A descriptive hyperlink specifies the location of the destination for the link.

- Connect every page on your Web site to your home page; otherwise, your pages can become dead ends for your users.
- Make the hyperlinked word or phrase large enough that users can easily click on it. Never use a small word or just one letter for a hyperlink.

FrontPage 2000

Testing a Hyperlink

The best way to test your hyperlink is to view the Web page in a Web browser and click the hyperlink. If the link does not work properly, it is easy to modify the settings in FrontPage. You should make a habit of periodically testing all links on your pages. The Internet changes constantly, and links that work one day may not function the next. ➤ Connie wants to make sure her first hyperlink works correctly before she creates additional links on the page.

Steps

Trouble?

If you do not have a browser loaded on your computer, or if you receive an error message when trying to open the browser, contact your instructor or technical support person.

QuickTip

If you are using Microsoft Internet Explorer and the settings are correct, you can also click the Edit button on the browser toolbar (see Figure D-14) to return to FrontPage.

1. Click the **Preview in Browser button** 🔍 on the Standard toolbar
   Microsoft Internet Explorer opens the president's Web page.

2. Scroll to and click **Computer Corner Home Page**
   As the mouse pointer moves over hyperlinks, it changes to a 👆. When you click the hyperlink, the Computer Corner home page appears in the browser window, as shown in Figure D-14.

3. Click the **Back button** ⬅ on the browser toolbar
   The link on the president's Web page may now be a purple color. Hyperlinks that have been clicked are called **visited links**.

4. Click the **Microsoft FrontPage button** on the taskbar
   The president's Web page appears in FrontPage.

5. Right-click anywhere in the document window, then click **Page Properties**
   The Page Properties dialog box appears.

6. Click the **Background tab**, click the **Visited Hyperlink list arrow**, click **Gray**, then click **OK**
   Gray becomes the active color for visited hyperlinks.

7. Click the **Save button** 💾 on the Standard toolbar
   The Web page is saved.

8. Click the **Preview in Browser button** 🔍 on the Standard toolbar, then scroll to and click **Computer Corner Home Page**

9. Click ⬅ on the browser toolbar, then click away from the hyperlink
   The visited hyperlink should now appear in gray, as shown in Figure D-15.

10. Click the **Microsoft FrontPage button** on the taskbar
    The president's Web page appears in FrontPage.

FIGURE D-14: **Computer Corner home page viewed in Microsoft Internet Explorer**

Back button

Address (URL) of page

Edit button

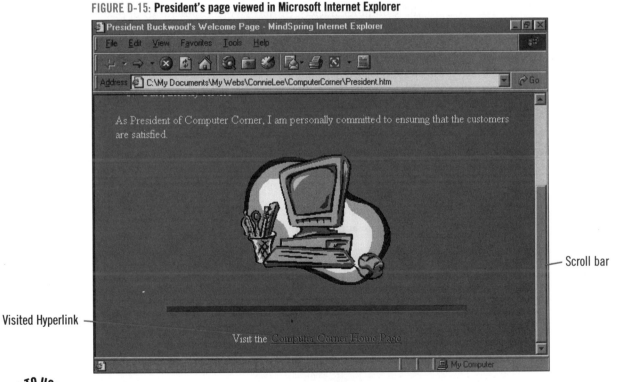

FIGURE D-15: **President's page viewed in Microsoft Internet Explorer**

Scroll bar

Visited Hyperlink

Correcting your hyperlinks

If your link does not work correctly in the browser preview, there is an easy way to examine possible problems. Return to FrontPage, right-click the hyperlink to activate the pop-up menu, and then select Hyperlink Properties. In the Edit Hyperlink dialog box, locate the correct destination for the hyperlink and click on it. You then can return to the browser and test the link.

Creating Hyperlinks to Remote Web Pages

In addition to creating hyperlinks to other pages on your Web, you can link your Web pages to **remote Web pages** (pages that are located on other sites) throughout the world. If you know the Web address, or **URL** (Uniform Resource Locator), of a particular site, you can type it in the destination box (the URL text box) for the hyperlink. If you do not know the URL and you are connected to the Internet, you can use the Browse feature and navigate to the remote site to determine the URL. ✏️ Connie provides a hyperlink on the president's page to the Web site of the Computer Society.

Steps

1. Click the end of the Computer Corner Home Page hyperlink, press **[Enter]**, then type **The Computer Corner is a proud member of the Computer Society.**

2. Select **Computer Society** and click the **Hyperlink button** 🔲 on the Standard toolbar
   The Create Hyperlink dialog box opens, with http:// appearing in the URL text box. The "http" stands for Hypertext Transfer Protocol, the hyperlink type used to access Web pages located on remote servers. Other hyperlink types, described in Table D-1, can be used in Microsoft FrontPage as well.

3. In the URL text box, type **www.computer.org**
   The URL for the Computer Society (http://www.computer.org) appears in the URL text box, as shown in Figure D-16.

4. Click **OK**, then click outside the selection
   The new link is added to the president's Web page, as shown in Figure D-17.

5. Click the **Save button** 🔲 on the Standard toolbar
   The revised page is saved in the Computer Corner Web.

6. Click the **Preview tab** at the bottom of the document window, click <u>Computer Society</u>, then connect to the Internet
   The Computer Society Web site appears, as shown in Figure D-18.

7. Click the **Normal tab** at the bottom of the document window.
   The president's Web page appears in FrontPage.

CLUES TO USE

Creating a hyperlink to a new Web page

If you want to create a hyperlink to a Web page that has not yet been created, you can create the page when you add the hyperlink. To do this, create the text that you want to act as the hyperlink, highlight the text, and select the Hyperlink button. In the Create Hyperlink dialog box, click the New Page button 🔲. A new page will be created for the hyperlink.

FIGURE D-16: **Create Hyperlink dialog box**

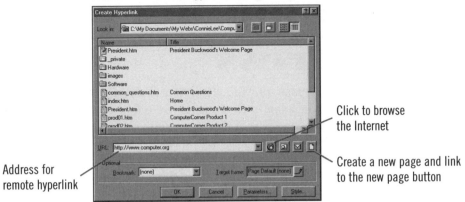

Address for
remote hyperlink

Click to browse
the Internet

Create a new page and link
to the new page button

FIGURE D-17: **President's Web page**

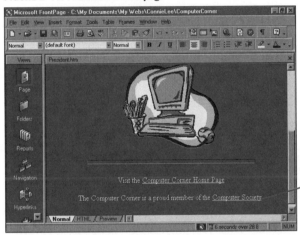

Hyperlink to
Computer Society

FIGURE D-18: **Computer Society Web site**

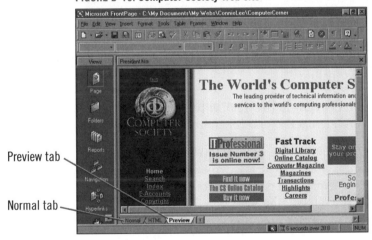

Preview tab

Normal tab

TABLE D-1: **Hyperlink types**

hyperlink type	description
ftp	File Transfer Protocol: used for transferring files
http	Links to Web pages
file	Links to a file on a local drive
news	Links to Internet newsgroups and discussion forums
telnet	Links to remote computer systems

Linking to an E-mail Address

E-mail (electronic mail) provides a way to send messages from one computer to another, and it is rapidly becoming a preferred means of communication for many people. With e-mail, messages can be sent at any time of the day or night, and you do not need to buy a postage stamp! **E-mail hyperlinks** on Web pages can be created to automatically enable users to send e-mail messages. In this manner, companies can use their Web pages to solicit information, answer questions, and respond quickly to issues. To provide visitors with an easy way to send comments to the company president, Connie adds an e-mail link to the bottom of his Web page.

Steps 123 4

1. Click at the end of the Computer Society hyperlink, press **[Enter]**, then type **Please send comments or questions to John Buckwood, President.**
   The sentence appears at the bottom of the Web page.

2. Select the entire sentence, click the **Center button** if necessary, then click the **Style list arrow** and select **Address**
   The sentence is centered and appears in italics.

3. Select **John Buckwood, President**, then click the **Hyperlink button** on the Standard toolbar
   The Create Hyperlink dialog box opens.

4. Click the **Make a hyperlink that sends E-mail button**
   The Create E-mail Hyperlink dialog box opens, as shown in Figure D-19.

5. Type **president@computercorner.com**, then click **OK**
   The Create E-mail Hyperlink dialog box closes, and the president's e-mail address appears in the URL text box.

6. Click **OK**, click anywhere to deselect the text, then click the **Save button** on the Standard toolbar

7. Click the **Preview in Browser button** on the Standard toolbar
   Microsoft Internet Explorer (or another Web browser) opens the president's Web page.

8. Click the hyperlink for **John Buckwood, President**
   The Untitled (or New) Message composition box opens, as shown in Figure D-20, with the president's e-mail address automatically entered into the To area. If you know a valid e-mail address, you can type the address in this To area and click the Send button to send the message.

9. Click the **Close button** on the title bar, click **No**, then click **Microsoft FrontPage** on the taskbar
   The Untitled Message composition box closes, and the president's page appears in FrontPage, as shown in Figure D-21.

Trouble?

The Configure Mail Wizard may appear if your Internet mail is not properly configured. If you receive an error message, contact your instructor or technical support person.

FIGURE D-19: Create E-mail Hyperlink dialog box

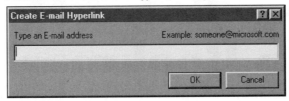

FIGURE D-20: New Message dialog box

Send button ———

Close button

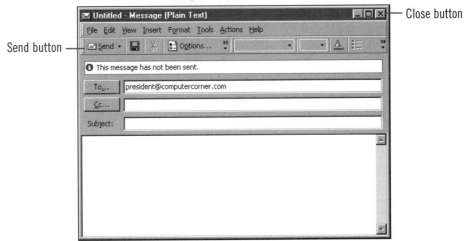

FIGURE D-21: President's page with e-mail hyperlink

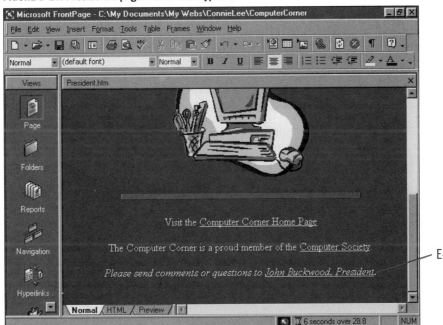

E-mail hyperlink

Addressing E-mail

E-mail addresses begin with a name or identifier (such as Suzanne, Jones, or MSmith), followed by an @ sign. The end of the e-mail address contains the server name and the domain name of the computer that stores the e-mail account. For example, Connie's e-mail address contains computercorner.com, meaning that her e-mail account is on the computercorner server in the commercial (com) domain. Other common e-mail domains in the United States include: gov (government), edu (education), org (nonprofit organizations), mil (military), and net (network organizations).

Inserting a Hyperlink to a Bookmark

A **bookmark** in Microsoft FrontPage is a specific location or text on a page that has been tagged or marked. Bookmarks can be used as destinations for hyperlinks, to allow the user to access a relevant part of a page, rather than the top of the page. Many of the FrontPage templates contain pages with preassigned bookmarks. ◄▬▬ Connie decides to add information about the president on the Common Questions page. She will create a hyperlink to the pertinent bookmark on that page.

Steps 1234

1. From Folders View, open the **Common Questions** page
   The Common Questions page appears.

2. Select question #4 in the Table of Contents, then type **Who is the president of Computer Corner?**
   The text for the fourth option changes to focus on the president of Computer Corner.

3. Scroll down the page and change the **Who is...?** question and answer area to match the text in Figure D-22, then click the **Save button** 🖫 on the Standard toolbar
   The text is changed to match.

4. Click the **Folders** button 📁, then double-click **President.htm**

5. Click after the sentence that ends with **satisfied**, press [Spacebar], then type: **For more information about my background, visit the Common Questions page.**
   The text is added to the president's page.

6. Select the words **Common Questions**, then click the **Hyperlink button** 🔗
   The Create Hyperlink dialog box opens.

7. Click **common_questions.htm**, click the **Bookmark list** arrow, then click **who**
   The common_questions.htm file appears in the URL box, and the Bookmark list appears with who, as shown in figure D-23.

8. Click **OK**, click the **Preview in Browser button** 🔍 on the Standard toolbar, click **Yes**, then click **Common Questions**
   The Common Questions page appears, with "Who is the president of Computer Corner?" at the top of the page, as shown in Figure D-24.

9. Click **Microsoft FrontPage** on the taskbar
   The president's page appears in FrontPage, as shown in Figure D-25.

Inserting bookmarks

If you have a relatively long Web page, you may want to insert bookmarks to easily navigate the page. To insert the bookmark, open the page in Page view, then position the insertion point where you want the bookmark. Click Insert on the menu bar, click Bookmark, then enter a name for the bookmark.

FIGURE D-22: Text for Common Questions page

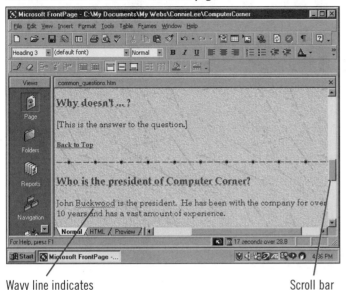

Wavy line indicates
spell-checker does
not recognize word

Scroll bar

FIGURE D-23: Create Hyperlink dialog box

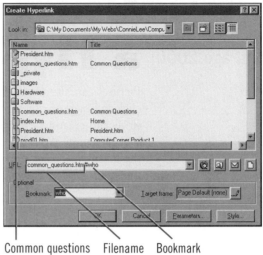

Common questions   Filename   Bookmark
file

FIGURE D-24: Common Questions page

Page opens to
bookmarked location

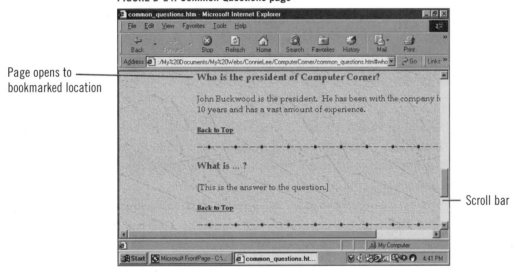

Scroll bar

FIGURE D-25: President's page

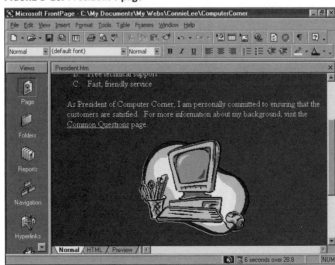

Using a Picture for a Hyperlink

Pictures can also be used for hyperlinks. Instead of clicking a word or phrase, the user might click an image or a picture to link to another Web page. Creating a hyperlink for a picture is very similar to creating a hyperlink for text. The destination for the link can be a page on the local Web, a remote Web site, or an e-mail address. ✎ Connie decides to resize the picture on the President's page, move it to the top of the page, and make it a hyperlink. If a user clicks on the picture, he or she will be linked to the Computer Corner Home Page.

Steps

1. **Click the picture of the computer**
   Sizing handles appear on the edges of the picture to indicate that it is selected.

2. **Click in the center of the computer picture, drag the ⬚ to the top left of the page, then release the mouse when the insertion point appears at the top of the page**
   The picture appears at the top of the page, as shown in Figure D-26.

3. **Click to the right of the picture, press [Enter], then click the picture and click the Hyperlink button 🔗 on the Standard toolbar**
   The Create Hyperlink dialog box opens.

4. **Click index.htm, then click OK**
   The Create Hyperlink dialog box closes.

5. **Click the Save button 💾 on the Standard toolbar, click OK if necessary, click the Preview tab, then click the picture of the computer**
   The Computer Corner home page appears in the Preview window.

6. **Click the Normal tab**
   The president's page appears in FrontPage, as shown in Figure D-27.

7. **Click the Close button on the title bar of FrontPage, click Yes if necessary, then click the Close button on the title bar of the browser**

FIGURE D-26: Computer picture moved to the top of the page

FIGURE D-27: President's page

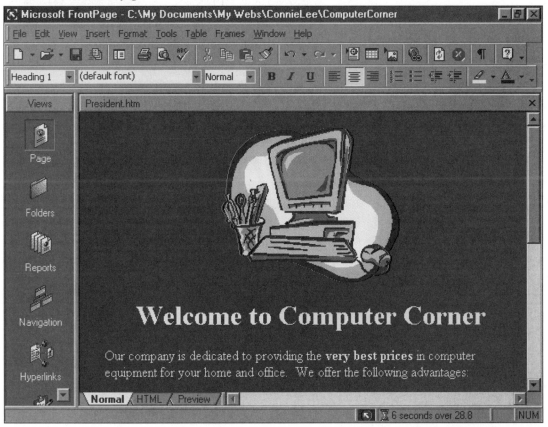

Practice

▶ Concepts Review

Label each of the elements of the Microsoft FrontPage window shown in Figure D-28.

FIGURE D-28

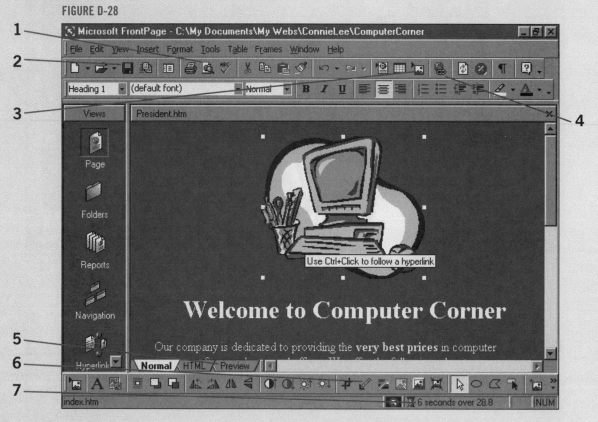

Match each of the terms with the statement that describes it.

8. http   **a.** Image format used for line drawings

9. URL   **b.** Image format used for photographic images

10. GIF   **c.** The address for a Web page

11. Transparent   **d.** A color that disappears to match the background color

12. JPEG   **e.** The hyperlink type for Web pages on a server

13. Interlaced   **f.** The domain for the e-mail address for the U.S. president

14. gov   **g.** A picture that appears gradually on a page

Select the best answer from the list of choices.

15. One of the graphics formats used for images on the Web is

    a. GIF.   **c.** TIFF.

    b. BMP.   **d.** MPEG.

16. If you have a photograph that you want to use on a Web page, what is the best format?

    a. MPEG   **c.** TIFF

    b. GIF   **d.** JPEG

17. Which of the following might be a valid e-mail address?
- **a.** barron@mail@usf.edu
- **b.** barron@mail.usf
- **c.** mail.usf.edu@barron
- **d.** barron@mail.usf.edu

18. How can you determine if a text hyperlink has been previously clicked?
- **a.** The color of the text changes.
- **b.** A check appears.
- **c.** The underline disappears.
- **d.** The text becomes bold.

19. Pictures that appear gradually on a Web page are
- **a.** Transparent.
- **b.** Hotspots.
- **c.** Hyperlinks.
- **d.** Interlaced.

▶ Skills Review

1. Insert and edit a picture.
- **a.** Start Microsoft FrontPage.
- **b.** Create a New Web (select One Page Web) named *NASA*.
- **c.** Select a blue color for the background (click the Background tab in the Page Properties dialog box).
- **d.** Click the Insert Picture From File button to insert a picture of an airplane from Clip Art (type airplane in the Search for clips text box).
- **e.** Click the Set Transparent Color button on the Pictures toolbar to change one of the colors in the picture to a transparent color.
- **f.** Right-click the picture and click the Interlaced check box in the Picture Properties dialog box to interlace the picture.
- **g.** Save the Web page as *airplane*.htm.
- **h.** Click the Preview in Browser button to view the page with your Web browser.

2. Insert a horizontal line.
- **a.** Make sure that the airplane.htm file is open in Page View.
- **b.** Click Insert on the menu bar to insert a horizontal line below the airplane picture.
- **c.** Right-click the line and open the Horizontal Line Properties dialog box.
- **d.** Change the width of the line to 50% of the window.
- **e.** Change the height of the line to 5 pixels.
- **f.** Center the line.
- **g.** Change the line color to yellow.
- **h.** Close the Horizontal Line Properties dialog box.

3. Insert a hyperlink to a local Web page.
- **a.** Create a new Web page.
- **b.** Save the page as linking.htm and enter **Linking** as the title of the page.
- **c.** At the top of the page, type **This is a hyperlink to My Airplane Page.**
- **d.** Select the text "My Airplane Page."
- **e.** Click the Hyperlink button to insert a hyperlink that connects the Linking page to the Web page saved as airplane.htm.
- **f.** Save the changes to the linking.htm Web page.

4. Test a hyperlink.
- **a.** Make sure that the linking.htm file is open in Page View.
- **b.** Click the Preview in Browser button to view the Linking Web page with a Web browser.
- **c.** Click the hyperlink for My Airplane Page.
- **d.** Click the Back button to return to the Linking page.
- **e.** Click the Microsoft FrontPage button on the taskbar to return to FrontPage.

5. Add hyperlinks to remote Web pages.
- **a.** Make sure that the linking.htm file is open in Page View.

b. At the bottom of the page, type **Yahoo is a great search engine!**

c. Click the Hyperlink button to insert a hyperlink that links the word "Yahoo" to the Web page at http://www.yahoo.com.

d. Click the Preview in Browser button to view the linking.htm Web page with a Web browser.

e. Test the hyperlink to Yahoo.

f. Print the Yahoo home page.

g. Return to the Linking page.

h. Return to FrontPage.

6. Add hyperlinks to e-mail addresses.

a. Make sure that the linking.htm file is open in Page View.

b. Type **Click to send a message to** [*insert your name*]. in the document window.

c. Highlight your name, then click the Hyperlink button to insert a hyperlink that allows users to click your name to send a message to your e-mail address.

d. Click the Preview tab to test your hyperlink.

e. Click the new hyperlink.

f. In the New Message window, type **Sending e-mail is fun and easy.**

g. Send the message. (If you have not set up the e-mail facility in your Web browser, you will get an error message when you select the e-mail hyperlink. Ignore this error.)

h. Return to the Normal window.

7. Insert a hyperlink to a bookmark.

a. Click File on the menu bar to create a new Web page (select Frequently Asked Questions), and save the file as *FAQ.htm*.

b. Open the Linking page, and type **This is a link to a bookmark.**

c. Highlight "bookmark," then click the Hyperlink button to insert a hyperlink to FAQ.htm.

d. Click the Bookmark list arrow to link to the "what" bookmark in the FAQ.htm file.

e. Click the Preview tab to test the new hyperlink.

f. Click the Normal tab.

8. Use a picture for a hyperlink.

a. Open the airplane.htm file in Page View.

b. Click the picture, then click the Hyperlink button to create a hyperlink to the NASA Space Center at http://www.nasa.gov.

c. Save the airplane.htm Web page.

d. Click the Preview tab to test the hyperlink.

e. Print the NASA home page.

f. Return to the Airplane page (airplane.htm).

g. Print the Airplane page.

h. Close the Web and exit FrontPage.

▶ Independent Challenges

1. Your friend John just opened a surf and scuba shop that caters to college students. He has asked you to create a Web page. He also wants you to add a hyperlink to a Weather site at http://www.weather.com so that his clients can obtain daily weather reports.

To complete this independent challenge:

a. Create a new One Page Web.

b. Title the Web *John* and save it.

c. At the very top of the home page, insert a picture from the Clip Art Gallery that relates to the page.

d. Center the picture.

e. Enter the text **Visit the Weather site for daily weather reports.**

f. Create a hyperlink that will link the words "Weather site" to http://www.weather.com.

g. Save the file.

h. Test the file to verify the link.

i. Return to the index.htm file.

j. Print the Web page.

k. Close the Web and the browser.

2. A small retail company that sells computer software has hired you to enhance its Web page. It wants you to add links to the major computer companies so that its customers can check out the latest prices in hardware.

To complete this independent challenge:

a. Create a new One Page Web named *Computer*.

b. Create hyperlinks that will link the name of the computer company to the URL listed here:

Apple Computer, Inc.	http://www.apple.com
Dell Computer Company	http://www.dell.com
IBM Corporation	http://www.ibm.com
Microsoft Corporation	http://www.microsoft.com

c. Save the Web page.

d. Preview the Web page with a Web browser and test the hyperlinks.

e. Make a printout of the Web page and a printout of the home pages of each of the computer companies.

f. Return to FrontPage.

g. Close the Web and the browser.

3. You have been hired by a ribbon company, Color Ribbons International, to help create a Web page that is unique and colorful. The company has asked that you make a Web page with an aqua background and white text that contains at least three different colorful lines.

To complete this independent challenge:

a. Create a new One Page Web titled *Ribbons*.

b. Create a new Web page titled *Color*.

c. Make the background color aqua and the text color white.

d. Add three different colorful lines from the clip art collection provided with Microsoft FrontPage. (*Hint*: Use the Web Dividers category.)

e. Add a large, bold title at the top of the page with the name of the company.

f. Save the page and preview it with a Web browser.

g. Print the Web page.

h. Close the Web and the browser.

WEB WORK

4. As the person in charge of creating Web pages for your school, you are always looking for good, copyright-free clip art. A friend told you that there are many clip art resources on the Web that you should investigate. You decide to start your search with one of the powerful search engines available (Yahoo).

To complete this independent challenge:

a. Connect to the Internet.

b. Access the Yahoo search engine at http://www.yahoo.com.

c. Enter "clip art" for the search word.

d. Investigate at least five clip art resources.

e. If you have trouble locating Web pages with clip art, go to http://www.course.com. Go to the Student Online Companion for this book, then click the link for Unit D.

f. Print the home page from at least three different clip art resources.

g. Create a new One Page Web titled *ClipArt*. On the home page, include hyperlinks to your favorite clip art sites for future use.

h. Print the home page.

i. Close the Web and the browser.

▶ Visual Workshop

Harvest Acres has hired you to create a Web page for their company. Use the skills you learned in this unit to create a Web page similar to the one in Figure D-29. The picture of the tree is located in the Clip Art section of FrontPage. If this clip art is not available, select other appropriate pictures. Save the file with the filename *harvest.htm*.

FIGURE D-29

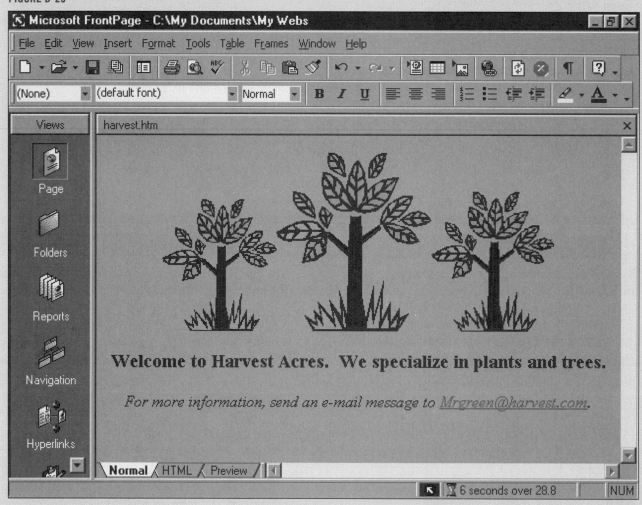

Unit
E

Adding
Graphic Features to Web Pages

Objectives

- ▶ Set custom colors
- ▶ Use an image for a background
- ▶ Download clip art from the Web
- ▶ Use the Pictures toolbar to modify images
- ▶ Align text to an image
- ▶ Create and edit hotspots
- ▶ Add a scrolling marquee
- ▶ Add page transitions and animations

Microsoft FrontPage offers many advanced graphics features for Web pages. For example, you can easily create custom colors for backgrounds, pictures, and text. You can also add a background image and add text or hotspots on top of pictures. You can even add a scrolling **marquee** (words that move across the Web page) or animate the text or pictures. The president of Computer Corner wants Connie to create a Web page for a special employee travel program. Connie decides to include a graphic in the background, hotspots on a picture, and a scrolling marquee.

Setting Custom Colors

Microsoft FrontPage provides a selection of colors that can be applied to backgrounds, text, hyperlinks, and other objects. You can also define a **custom color** by selecting values on a color **gradient**, or scale. Once you have created a custom color, you can use it on any Web pages in the current Web. ━━━━ Connie decides to create a custom color (light pink) for the background color of the Travel page.

Steps 1 2 3 4

QuickTip

The Computer Corner Web can be saved to several alternate locations, such as a hard drive, a network drive, or external media. Due to the size of the completed Web, it is not recommended that it be saved to a floppy disk. If you have saved the Computer Corner Web in a different location, enter the path or browse to locate the Web.

1. Start **Microsoft FrontPage**, click **File** on the menu bar, click **Open Web**, click the [*insert your name here*] **folder**, if necessary, select the **ComputerCorner Web**, then click **Open**
   The Computer Corner Web opens.

2. From Folders View, click the **New Page button** 🗋, then type **travel.htm** and press **[Enter]**
   A new page is created and named travel.htm.

3. Double-click **travel.htm**, right-click anywhere, select **Page Properties**, type **Employee Travel Program** in the Title box, then click the **Custom tab**
   The Page Properties dialog box opens to the Custom tab.

4. Click **Microsoft Border**, click **Remove**, click **Microsoft Theme**, click **Remove**, then click **OK**
   The dialog box for the Custom tab closes and the shared borders and theme are removed from the Web page.

5. Click **Format** on the menu bar, then click **Background**
   The Background tab of the Page Properties dialog box appears.

QuickTip

Your screen may look slightly different if your computer is set to display fewer colors.

6. Click the **Background color list arrow**, click **More Colors**, click **Select**, move 🖊 over a pink color and click
   As the Select tool moves over the colors, the color changes in the New box. In addition the hexidecimal equivalent for the color changes in the Value area, as shown in Figure E-1. FrontPage stores the hexidecimal value of the color in the HTML code.

7. Click **Custom** and drag the **arrow** on the color bar up to a lighter pink color
   The color indicator is located on the pink area of the color matrix, as illustrated in Figure E-2. You can click anywhere in this matrix to define a custom color. As you drag the arrow up, the color in the Color Solid section changes to a lighter pink. Note that the numerical values for Green, Blue, and Red change as well.

QuickTip

You can use the same procedure to create a custom color for text or hyperlinks.

8. Click **Add to Custom Colors**, then click **OK** three times
   The Color dialog box closes, and the Custom color is displayed in the Background section of the Page Properties dialog box. When the Page Properties dialog box closes, the background color for the page is light pink, as shown in Figure E-3.

9. Click the **Save** button 🖫 on the Standard toolbar

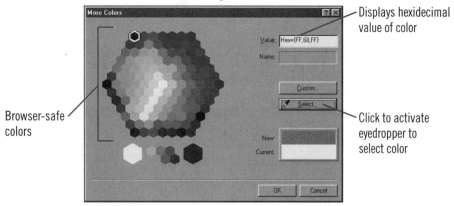

FIGURE E-1: More Colors dialog box

Displays hexidecimal value of color

Browser-safe colors

Click to activate eyedropper to select color

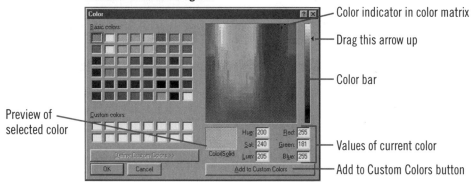

FIGURE E-2: Color dialog box

Color indicator in color matrix

Drag this arrow up

Color bar

Preview of selected color

Values of current color

Add to Custom Colors button

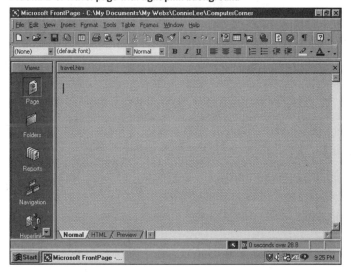

FIGURE E-3: Travel page with light pink background

CLUES TO USE

Understanding color values

All of the colors on a computer screen are composed of combinations of red, green, and blue. The values of each of these three colors can range from 0 to 255. If red is 255 and green and blue are both 0, then the color you see is bright red. Additional color values include hue, saturation, and luminosity (see Figure E-2). The **hue** of a color represents its place on the color matrix: red is 0, green is 80, and blue is 160. **Saturation** is the amount of color used: 240 is deep, and 120 is less deep. **Luminosity** is the amount of white added to the color: a higher number corresponds to a brighter color. In most cases, it is best to simply select your color by dragging the arrow on the color bar; the values are generated automatically.

Using an Image for a Background

A background image is a graphic that is **tiled**, or repeated over and over again, until it completely fills the background of a page. Background images are often used to add texture to a Web page. Sometimes they include a company's logo or other trademark. Connie is not completely satisfied with the custom color she created for the background. Instead of using the solid pink color, she decides to insert a background image that includes a subtle texture.

Steps

1. Click **Format** on the menu bar, then click **Background**
   The Background tab of the Page Properties dialog box opens.

2. Click the **Background picture check box**, click **Browse**, then click **Cancel** in the Select File dialog box
   A check mark appears in the Background Picture check box, and the Watermark check box becomes available. A **watermark** is a background image that does not scroll as the user scrolls the Web page. The Select Background Picture dialog box opens, as illustrated in Figure E-4.

3. Click **Clip Art** in the Select Background Picture dialog box, then click the **Backgrounds** category
   Several options for background images appear, as shown in Figure E-5.

4. Click a light textured background, click the **Insert clip button** , then click **OK**
   The textured background appears.

5. Press **[Enter]**, then type the text shown in Figure E-6, using the styles indicated in the callouts
   The new text appears on the background.

6. Click the **Save** button on the Standard toolbar, click **Rename**, then type **pinkbkgd.gif**
   The background image is renamed to pinkbkgd.gif.

7. Click **Change Folder** (if necessary), then click **images**
   The background file is saved in the images folder, as shown in Figure E-7.

8. Click **OK**

FIGURE E-4: Select Background Picture dialog box

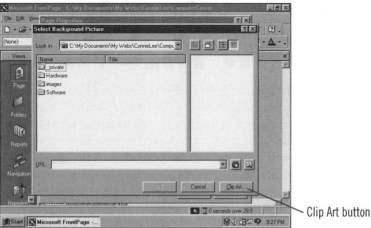

Clip Art button

FIGURE E-5: Images in Background category

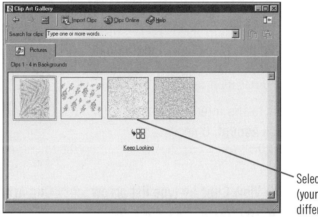

Select light background
(your screen may display
different graphics)

FIGURE E-6: Web page with tiled background image and new text

Heading 1
style

Normal size

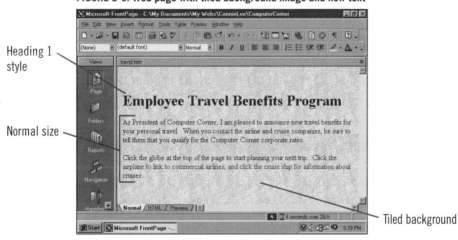

Tiled background

FIGURE E-7: Embedded files to save dialog box

New name for
background
picture

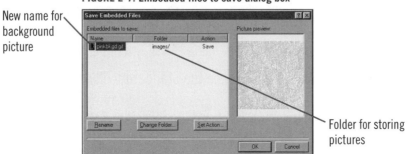

Folder for storing
pictures

Downloading Clip Art from the Web

Although Microsoft FrontPage supplies numerous clip art images, there are times when you will want a wider selection. In the Clip Art section of FrontPage there is a link to an online gallery that is maintained by Microsoft. This resource provides an extensive list of clip media in the form of clip art, photos, sounds, and motion. It is possible to search by media type or keyword and to browse through numerous categories. Connie decides to access the online gallery to locate a small picture of an airplane for the travel page.

Steps

Trouble?

The Select File dialog box may appear when you click the Insert Picture From File button. If it does, simply click Cancel.

1. Click at the bottom of the travel page, press **[Enter]**, then click the **Insert Picture From File button** 🖼 on the Standard toolbar
   The Picture dialog box appears.

2. Click **Clip Art**, then click **Clips Online**
   The Connect to Web for More Clip Art, Photos, Sounds dialog box may appear, depending on your installation, as shown in Figure E-8.

3. Connect to the Internet, if necessary, click **OK**, then read the Microsoft Agreement and click **Accept**, if necessary
   The first time you access the online gallery, the Microsoft agreement will appear. After you click Accept, the Microsoft Clip Gallery Live site will open.

4. Click the **View Clips by type list arrow**, click **Clip Art**, type **cruise ship** in the **Search by keyword** text box, then click **go**
   Search results appear in the document window, as shown in Figure E-9.

5. Click a picture of a ship to see a preview
   A preview of the picture appears on the left side of the screen.

6. Click the preview picture to download the picture
   The picture is automatically downloaded into the Microsoft Clip Art Gallery on your computer, as shown in Figure E-10.

QuickTip

If the Microsoft Clip Gallery 5.0 window is open after you add the clip to the Favorites category, close the window, then return to the Clip Art Gallery window.

7. Click the picture in the Microsoft Clip Art Gallery dialog box, then click **Add clip to Favorites or other category button**, then click **Add**
   The picture is stored in the Favorites category of the Clip Art Gallery. Saving pictures in this category can make them easier to locate in the future.

8. Click the **All Categories button** 🔲, click **Favorites**, click the picture of the ship, click the **Insert clip button** 🔲, then return to FrontPage if necessary
   The picture appears at the bottom of the Travel page.

9. Click the picture, click the **Bevel button** 🔲 on the Pictures toolbar, then deselect the picture
   A bevel is added around the picture, as shown in Figure E-11.

10. Click the **Save** button 🔲 on the Standard toolbar, click **Rename**, type **ship.gif**, then click **OK**
    The background image is renamed to ship.gif and saved in the images folder.

FIGURE E-8: Connect to Web for More Clip Art, Photos, Sounds dialog box

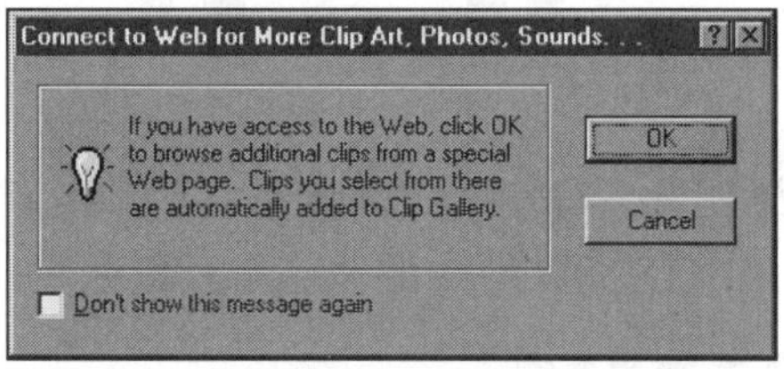

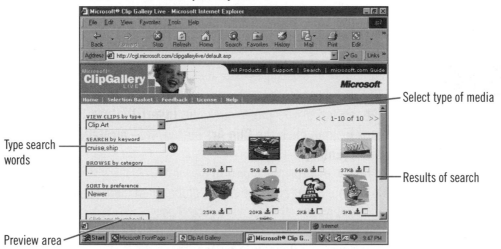

FIGURE E-9: Microsoft Clip Gallery Live site

Select type of media

Type search words

Results of search

Preview area

FIGURE E-10: Microsoft Clip Gallery

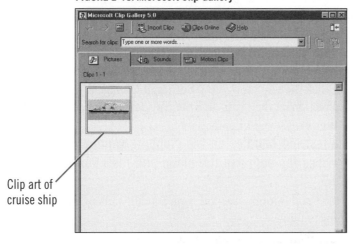

Clip art of cruise ship

FIGURE E-11: Travel page with beveled picture of cruise ship

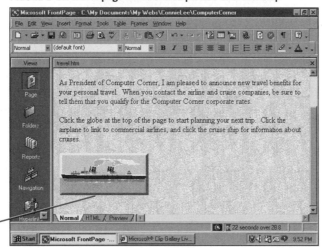

Beveled clip art

Using the Pictures Toolbar to Modify Images

The Pictures toolbar in FrontPage offers a wide variety of features. For example, when a picture is selected, you can click options that will crop, rotate, or flip the image. You can also alter the picture's contrast or brightness. Connie needs to add a picture of an airplane and globe at the top of the Travel page. After she inserts the picture, she plans to increase the contrast of the picture. She also wants to change its size and to experiment with flipping and cropping the image.

Steps

1. **Click at the top of the page, click the Insert Picture From File button 🖾 on the Standard toolbar, click the Clip Art button, type airplane in the Search for clips box, then press [Enter]**
   Several images of airplanes appear in the Clip Art Gallery window.

2. **Click a picture of an airplane and a globe, then click the Insert clip button 🖾**
   The picture appears at the top of the Travel page.

QuickTip

After you resize an image, it is wise to resample it. Resampling changes the file size of the image to match its current display size.

3. **Click the picture and drag one of the corner resizing handles to reduce the size by about 50%, then click the Resample button 🖾 on the Pictures toolbar**
   Be sure to select a corner resizing handle to maintain the aspect ratio and correct proportions. If you select a resizing handle on the side, the picture will become distorted. The picture should appear as shown in Figure E-12.

4. **Click the Flip Horizontal button 🔼 on the Pictures toolbar, then click the Crop button 🖾 on the Pictures toolbar**
   When you click the Flip Horizontal button, the image is reversed (and the airplane faces the opposite direction). When you click the cropping button, a cropping window appears on top of the picture, as shown in Figure E-13.

5. **Using the resizing handles on the cropping window, resize the cropping window so that it touches the edges of the plane and the globe, then click 🖾 on the Pictures toolbar**
   Clicking the Crop button a second time actually cuts or crops the image to the area within the cropping window.

6. **Click the Set Transparent Color button 🖾 on the Pictures toolbar, click OK if necessary, then select the white portion of the airplane picture**
   The white portion becomes transparent.

7. **Click the Less Brightness button 🖾 on the Pictures toolbar repeatedly until the image becomes darker**
   As you click the Less Brightness button, the image becomes darker, as shown in Figure E-14. The Pictures toolbar contains buttons to add more contrast, less contrast, more brightness, and less brightness. You must click repeatedly before the picture changes dramatically.

QuickTip

If you do not like the edits you have made on a picture (such as cropping or resizing), you can click the Restore button on the Pictures toolbar and undo all the changes you have made to the picture since you last saved it or added it to the page.

8. **Click the Save button 🖾 on the Standard toolbar, then click Rename, type airplane.gif, then click OK**
   The picture is saved as airplane.gif in the images folder of the current Web.

FIGURE E-12: Travel page with airplane picture

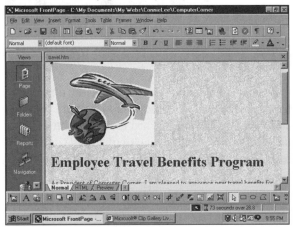

FIGURE E-13: Cropping window on picture

Cropping window

Resizing handles

Less Brightness

Crop

Set Transparent Color

Flip Horizontal

Resample

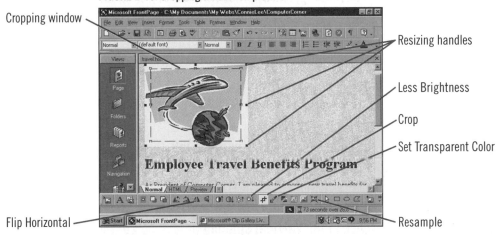

FIGURE E-14: Travel page with airplane picture, reduced brightness

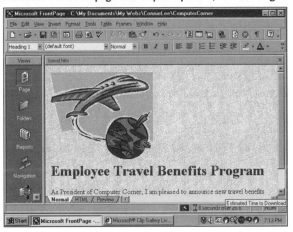

Sizing an image

Sometimes it is difficult to determine the exact size of an image by clicking and dragging it. If you need precise measurements for an image, you can click Specify Size in the Appearance section of the Picture Properties dialog box. The picture's width and height can be specified either in pixels or in percentages. If the Keep Aspect Ratio check box is selected, the image will retain the current width and height proportions.

Aligning Text to an Image

When you insert an image, the text automatically **aligns** with the bottom of the image. This default text placement is known as **bottom alignment**. To add more variety to the layout of your Web pages, you can align one line of text to the **middle** or **top** of the image. You can also align the image to the **left** (with the text flowing on the right) or to the **right** (with the text flowing on the left). Connie decides to align the text on her Web page to the left of the airplane picture.

Steps 1 2 3 4

1. Click the **airplane picture**, press **[Alt][Enter]**, then click the **Appearance tab**
   The Appearance tab of the Picture Properties dialog box appears.

2. Click the **Alignment list arrow**
   The alignment options appear, as shown in Figure E-15.

3. Click **Right**, then click **OK**
   The Picture Properties dialog box closes, and the text wraps to the left side of the airplane picture.

4. Press **[Alt][Enter]**, click the **Appearance tab**, then double-click in the **Horizontal spacing** area and type **20**
   The Horizontal spacing setting determines how many pixels will separate the side of the picture from the text.

5. Double-click in the **Vertical spacing** area, type **20**, then click **OK**
   The picture appears on the Travel page, with increased separation from the text, as shown in Figure E-16. The Vertical spacing setting determines how many pixels will separate the bottom or top of the picture from the text.

6. Click the picture of the cruise ship and then click the **Hyperlink button** 🖼 on the Standard toolbar
   The Create Hyperlink dialog box appears.

7. Type **www.cruise.com** in the URL text box, then click **OK**

8. Click the **Save button** 🖫 on the Standard toolbar

9. Click the **Preview tab** to test the page
   The page appears as shown in Figure E-17. The cruise ship links to a remote page.

10. Click the **Normal tab**

FIGURE E-15: Alignment options for pictures

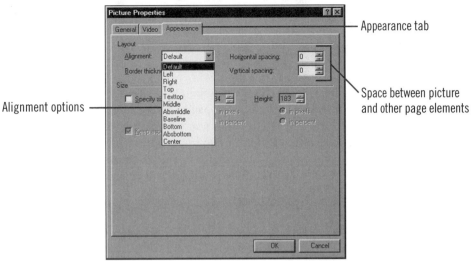

Appearance tab

Alignment options

Space between picture
and other page elements

FIGURE E-16: Travel page with airplane picture

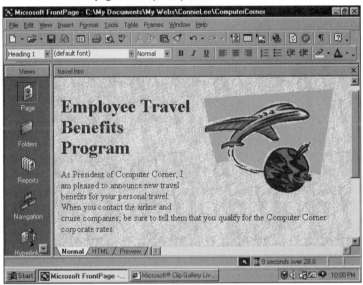

FIGURE E-17: Travel page with Preview tab

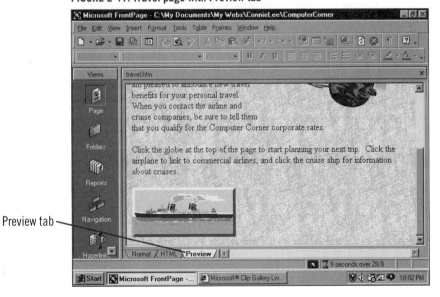

Preview tab

Creating and Editing Hotspots

Hotspots are areas on images that contain hyperlinks. For example, many Web pages include an image at the top or bottom of the page offering several options, such as Menu, Next, Back, Glossary, and Search. With hotspots, you can include multiple hyperlinks on a single image, each linking to a different URL. The hotspots are invisible to the user of your Web site, although you can see them when you create them. ➤ Connie wants to create hotspots on the picture at the top of the Travel page. She will create one hotspot on top of the globe and another on the airplane.

Steps

1. Select the airplane picture at the top of the page, then click the **Circular Hotspot button** ⊙ on the Pictures toolbar

The Circular Hotspot tool becomes the active tool.

Trouble?

If you are dissatisfied with the placement or size of the circle, click Cancel, click the circular Hotspot button to start again.

2. Move the insertion point to the center of the globe, then click and drag to create a circle that encompasses the globe

As the mouse moves over the image, it turns into a pencil. When you drag the mouse pointer, a circle appears, as shown in Figure E-18. After you draw the circle and release the mouse button, the Create Hyperlink dialog box opens.

3. Type **www.mapquest.com** in the URL text box, then click **OK**

The Select File dialog box closes.

4. Click the **Polygonal Hotspot button** ◁ on the Pictures toolbar, and click the nose of the airplane

The Polygonal Hotspot button is used to create hotspots that are not circular or rectangular.

QuickTip

If the Create Hyperlink dialog box does not open, press [Esc].

5. Move the mouse pointer and click on the edges of the plane until you return to the nose of the plane, as shown in Figure E-19

When you return to the original point (and complete a polygon), the Create Hyperlink dialog box opens.

6. Type **air-online.com/AIRwelcome.shtml** in the URL text box, and click **OK**

When a visitor clicks anywhere on the airplane, it will link to the air-online.com site on the Web.

7. Click the **Save button** 🖫 on the Standard toolbar

8. Click the **Preview in Browser button** 🔍 on the Standard toolbar, click the **globe**, click the **Back button**, then click the **airplane**

First the MapQuest page appears in the document window, and then the Airline page appears.

9. Click the **Microsoft FrontPage button** on the taskbar

The Travel page appears in the document window, as shown in Figure E-20.

FIGURE E-18: Circular hotspot on globe

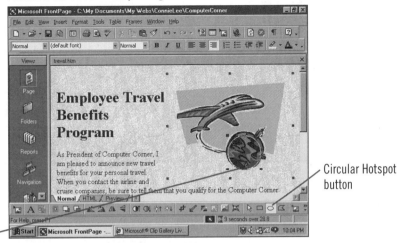

Circular hotspot

Circular Hotspot button

FIGURE E-19: Creating a polygonal hotspot on the airplane

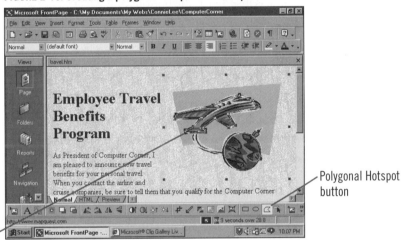

Polygonal hotspot

Polygonal Hotspot button

FIGURE E-20: Travel page

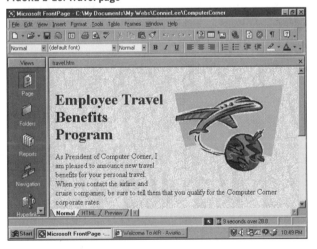

Editing hotspots

To change the size of a hotspot, simply click the hotspot and drag one or more of the resizing handles. If you cannot find the hotspots on a page, click the Highlight Hotspots button on the Pictures toolbar. You can also change the destination of the hyperlink by double-clicking the hotspot.

FrontPage 2000

Adding a Scrolling Marquee

You can add action and interest to a Web page by including a moving text area, called a **marquee**. When you create a marquee, you can control the size of the window, the speed with which the words cross the screen, and the marquee's colors. The options for marquee properties are described in Table E-1. To call attention to the release of the Travel awards, Connie decides to add a marquee to the bottom of her Web page.

Steps 1 2 3 4

1. Scroll to and click the bottom of the Web page, then press **[Enter]** twice
   A blank line is inserted at the bottom of the page.

2. Click **Insert** on the menu bar, point to **Component**, then click **Marquee**
   The Marquee Properties dialog box opens.

3. Type **Announcing the Employee Travel Program** in the text box
   The text appears in the text box, as shown in Figure E-21.

4. Click the **Background color list arrow**, then click **Red**
   The background color for the marquee changes to red.

5. Click **Style**, click **Format**, then select **Font**
   The Font dialog box opens, as illustrated in Figure E-22.

6. Set the Font Size to **24pt**, then click **OK** three times
   A red rectangle with text appears on the bottom of the page. To view the marquee in action, you must preview the page.

7. Click the **Save button** 🖫, then click the **Preview tab** to see the marquee
   The marquee moves across the page, as shown in Figure E-23.

8. Click the **Normal tab**

FIGURE E-21: Marquee Properties dialog box

Enter text here ——

Style button ——

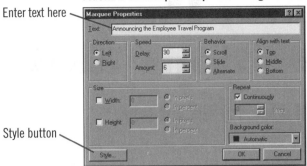

FIGURE E-22: Font dialog box

—— Set font size

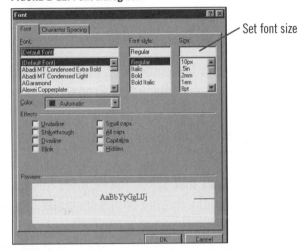

FIGURE E-23: Travel page with marquee

Scrolling marquee ——

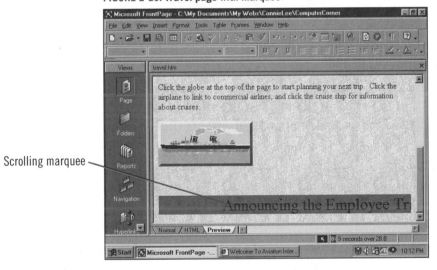

TABLE E-1: Marquee properties

property	description
Scroll	Text continuously scrolls across the page
Slide	Text scrolls across the page and stops
Alternate	Text moves back and forth from one side of the screen to the other
Movement Speed: Delay	Measured in milliseconds; the larger the delay, the slower the marquee will move
Movement Speed: Amount	Measured in pixels; the larger the amount, the faster the marquee will move

Adding Page Transitions and Animations

FrontPage makes it easy to add exciting features, such as page transitions and text animations, to Web pages. **Animations** affect the way that an element (such as text or an image) appears on the page. They include movement, such as zooming or flying in from the left or right of the page. A **page transition** is a special effect, such as vertical blinds or checkerboards, that appears as the page is displayed. Connie decides to experiment with the page transitions and animation features of FrontPage for the Travel page.

Steps

1. From Folders View, double-click **President.htm**, then right-click the picture at the top of the page, click **Hyperlink Properties**, type **travel.htm**, and click **OK**
   The hyperlink for the picture is changed to the Travel page.

2. Click the **Text button** [A] on the Pictures toolbar and type **Travel**, press **[ENTER]**, and type **Program**

3. Click the **Select tool** on the Pictures toolbar, then click and drag inside the text box to position the text box on the computer monitor screen
   The text appears as shown in Figure E-24.

4. Click **Format** on the menu bar, then click **Page Transition**
   The Page Transitions dialog box opens, as shown in Figure E-25. You can set transitions for events, such as entering or exiting a page.

5. Click the **Event list arrow**, click **Page Exit**, click **Vertical blinds** for the Transition effect, then click **OK**
   The Page Transitions dialog box closes.

6. Select the phrase **Welcome to Computer Corner**, click **Format** on the Standard menu bar and select **Dynamic HTML Effects** (if it is already checked, do not select it)
   The DHTML Effects toolbar appears. The toolbar may be **docked**, which means that it is located under the Formatting toolbar, or it may float on the screen. You can dock the toolbar by clicking and dragging it under the Formatting toolbar.

7. Click the **On list arrow** and select **Page Load**
   The On option changes to Page Load and the Apply area becomes active.

8. Click the **Apply list arrow**, select **Fly in**, then select **From right** for the Effect
   The DHTML Effects toolbar selections are shown in Figure E-26. To view the animation, you must preview the page.

9. Click the **Close box** on the DHTML Effects toolbar, click the **Save button** , click the **Preview tab** to see the animation, then click the **computer picture** to link to the Travel page (and see the transition)
   The transition and the animation appear on the page.

10. Click the **Normal tab**

11. Click the **Close button** on the title bar of FrontPage and click the **Close button** on the title bar on the browser

Trouble?

If the text is too large (or small), right-click on the text box and select Font from the pop-up menu. Select an appropriate size for the font, then click OK.

Trouble?

Page transitions and animations will appear only in new browsers, such as Internet Explorer 4.0.

FIGURE E-24: Text box on computer monitor

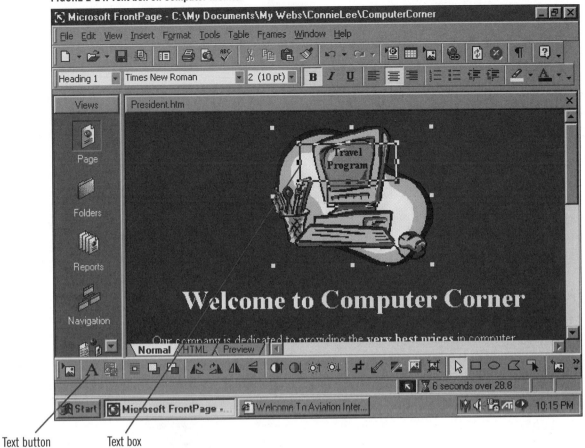

Text button   Text box

FIGURE E-25: Page Transitions dialog box

Options for page transitions

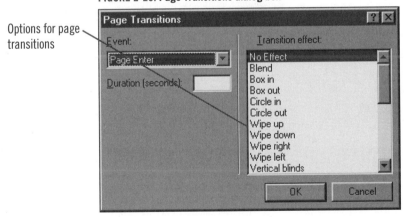

FIGURE E-26: DHTML Effects dialog box

You can dock your toolbar by clicking and dragging it under the Formatting toolbar

Practice

► Concepts Review

Label each of the elements of the FrontPage window shown in Figure E-27.

FIGURE E-27

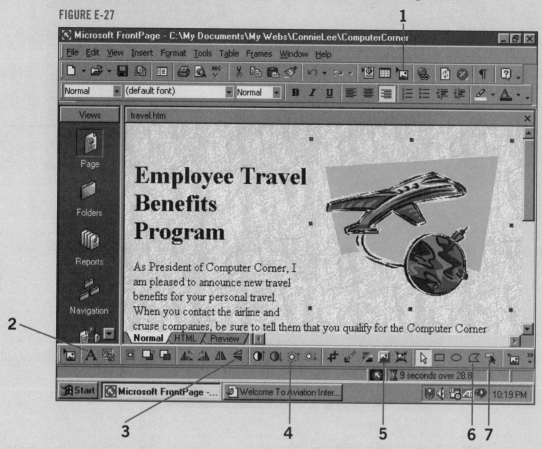

Match each term with the statement that describes it.

8. Hotspot
9. Marquee
10. Alignment
11. Scroll (movement)
12. Slide (movement)
13. Page transition
14. Tiled

a. A portion of an image that has a hyperlink
b. A special effect that appears when a Web page opens or closes
c. An image that is repeated both horizontally and vertically
d. Text that continuously moves in one direction across a page
e. The way text lines up with a picture
f. An active element on a page that includes moving text
g. Text that scrolls across the page and then stops

Select the best answer from the list of choices.

15. A color that you define for a background or text is a
a. Custom color.
b. Defined color.
c. Gradient color.
d. Tailored color.

16. All colors on a computer screen consist of combinations of which colors?
a. Red, green, and yellow
b. Red, white, and yellow
c. Red, black, and white
d. Red, green, and blue

17. Which button will highlight all of the hotspots on a page?
a.
b.
c.
d.

18. If you want the text to wrap to the left of an image, which alignment should you select?
a. Top
b. Middle
c. Right
d. Left

19. If you want to change both the height and width of a picture, what should you click and drag?
a. One of the corner resizing handles
b. The center of the image
c. A resizing handle on the side
d. The outside of the image

20. If you want to move an image without changing the size, where should you click?
a. One of the corner resizing handles
b. The center of the image
c. A resizing handle on the side
d. The outside of the image

21. How can you convert a GIF image to a JPEG image?
a. Click the image, access Picture Properties, and click JPEG.
b. Click Save and change the name in the Save Embedded Files dialog box.
c. Change the name in Folders View.
d. GIF images cannot be converted to JPEG format.

22. If you want to draw a polygonal hotspot, how do you define the area?
    a. Click the mouse on the screen and drag until you have the desired shape.
    b. First draw a rectangular hotspot, then add a circular hotspot.
    c. Click a series of points, then click the selection arrow button.
    d. Click a series of points, then click the first point again.

23. If you want a marquee that will scroll onto the screen and then stop, which movement should you select?
    a. Scroll
    b. Slide
    c. Alternate
    d. Wipe

24. What image formats must be used on a Web page?
    a. BMP and TIF
    b. GIF and TIF
    c. BMP and JPG
    d. GIF and JPG

 # Skills Review

1. Set custom colors.
    a. Start Microsoft FrontPage and create a new One Page Web named *Computerweb*.
    b. Type **Computers are an integral part of business today.** on the Web page.
    c. Select the text, click Format on the menu bar, and select Font.
    d. Select More Colors in the Font color list, then click Custom.
    e. Click a hot pink color, then click Add to Custom Colors.
    f. Click OK three times, then deselect the text.
    g. Save the Web page as *Business.htm*.

2. Use images as backgrounds for Web pages.
    a. Make sure the Business.htm file is open in Page View.
    b. Click Format on the menu bar, then select Background.
    c. Click the Background picture check box.
    d. Click Browse and Clip Art to access the Clip Art Gallery.
    e. Scroll down to the Web Background category.
    f. Select a background picture and click Insert clip.
    g. Click OK, then save the Web page and save the background as *back.gif* in the images folder.
    h. Preview the page with your Web browser.

3. Download clip art from the Web.
    a. Make sure the Business.htm file is open in FrontPage.
    b. Click the Insert Picture From File button.
    c. Click Clip Art, then click Clips Online.
    d. Search for clip art related to satellites, then click the picture to preview it.
    e. Click the preview to download the clip and insert it into the Clip Art Gallery.
    f. Click the picture, then click Insert clip, resize if necessary.
    g. Save the Web page and rename the picture to *satellite.gif*.

4. **Use the Pictures toolbar to modify the images.**
   a. Click New Page to open a new Web page.
   b. Click the Insert Picture From File button and access the Clip Art Gallery.
   c. Search for clips that are related to computers.
   d. Insert two computer pictures on your page, each on a separate line. (Click Insert clip after you select the pictures you want.)
   e. Click More Contrast to increase the contrast of the first image.
   f. Use the resizing handles to change the size of the second image (make it twice as big).
   g. Click Flip Vertical to flip the second picture vertically.
   h. Save the Web page as *computer.htm* (rename the pictures as *comp1.gif* and *comp2.gif*).

5. **Align text to images.**
   a. Add a sentence of text beside each computer image. Type the following:
      Computers are very important business tools. (by the first image)
      Computers are also important personal tools. (by the second image)
   b. Click each picture, then press [Alt][Enter] to access the Picture Properties dialog box.
   c. Click the Appearance tab and select Top alignment for the first picture and Right alignment for the second picture.
   d. Preview the Web page with the Preview tab.
   e. Return to Normal view.
   f. Save the Web page.

6. **Create image hotspots.**
   a. Click New Page to open a new Web page.
   b. Insert a picture of a person on a bicycle from the Clip Art Gallery.
   c. Click and drag the resizing handles to make the bicycle twice as large.
   d. Create a circular hotspot on the front wheel, then link it to http://www.bicycle.com.
   e. Create a circular hotspot on the back wheel, then link it to http://www.bikes.com.
   f. Save your page as *bike.htm* and the picture as *bike.gif* in the images folder.

7. **Add a marquee.**
   a. Make sure that the bike.htm file is open, and press [Enter].
   b. Click Insert on the menu bar, then select Component.
   c. Select Marquee.
   d. Type **Welcome to my Bicycle Page!** in the text box.
   e. Select Slide for Behavior and Right for Direction, click OK.
   f. Save the Web page.
   g. Click the Preview in Browser button to view the marquee.
   h. Return to FrontPage, then save and print the page.

8. **Add animations and page transitions.**
   a. Make sure that bike.htm is open in FrontPage.
   b. Click Format and click Page Transition.
   c. Select Page Enter for the Event and Vertical blinds for the effect.
   d. Add a line after the marquee and enter the following text: **Riding a bicycle is very good exercise.**
   e. Select the text and make sure the Dynamic HTML Effects toolbar is visible. If it is not, click Format and Dynamic HTML Effects.

    f. Use the following setting: On: Page Load; Apply: Spiral.

    g. Save the Web page.

    h. Preview the Web page in your Web browser.

▶ Independent Challenges

1. Your boss has asked you to design a series of Web pages containing information about your company. The first page will introduce the company with the following text: "Terry's Travel Company can schedule your trips, provide up-to-date weather reports, and deliver the tickets to your front door. Click the Next button to view the latest airline prices." The second page provides a table with airfares to the following cities: "Chicago—$400; New York—$800; San Diego—$1200; Paris—$2000. Click the Back button to return to the Introduction." Your boss would like you to create the two pages and add a "Next" button and a "Back" button to link them together.

    To complete this independent challenge:

a. Create a new One Page Web called *Terry*.

b. Create two new Web pages in the Web. The first page should be named **Introduction** (*intro.htm*) and the second page **Prices** (*price.htm*).

c. On Page One, insert a right arrow image from the Clip Art Gallery.

d. On Page Two, insert a left arrow image from the Clip Art Gallery.

e. Make each arrow button a hyperlink, with the right arrow on Page One linking to Page Two, and the left arrow on Page Two linking to Page One.

f. Save the Web pages.

g. Test the files with the Preview tab.

h. Print the Web pages, then close the Web and FrontPage.

2. Your ABC Arts and Crafts Company is designing a new Web page and needs a unique look. Your supervisor likes one of the banners provided in the Microsoft Clip Art Gallery, but would like to create a custom background color to match the banner.

    To complete this independent challenge:

a. Create a new one-page Web named *Arts*.

b. On the home page, insert the Web Banner with the autumn leaves on it from the Clip Art Gallery. If you do not have this file, select another one.

c. Stretch the banner until it covers your screen width.

d. Create a custom background color that complements the light tan color.

e. Create a custom text color that matches the dark brown color in the banner.

f. Enter a few lines of text about arts and crafts, such as "ABC Arts and Crafts can meet all of your creative needs."

g. Save the page.

h. Print the page, then close the Web and FrontPage.

3. Your college, International University, wants to announce the Homecoming game on its Web page. The provost has asked that you experiment with a marquee to see if you can create one that matches the school colors (dark green and yellow).

    To complete this independent challenge:

a. Create a new One Page Web named *IU*. Name the Web IU.

b. On the home page, add a background image from the Web Backgrounds section of the Clip Art Gallery.

c. Insert a marquee with the following settings:
   Text: Homecoming Game October 27!
   Direction: Right
   Behavior: Alternate
   Delay: 100
   Amount: 10
   Align with Text: Middle
   Font Style: 24 pt
   Width: 80%
   Height: 50 pixels
   Background Color: Dark green
   Text Color: Yellow
d. Save the page.
e. Preview the page.
f. Print the page, then close the Web and FrontPage.

4. As the Webmaster for your company (JobsRUs), you are in charge of designing and developing Web pages. You would like to add some textured backgrounds to the pages, but you do not have a graphic artist to create the images. Your friend suggested that you look on the Internet for copyright-free backgrounds.
To complete this independent challenge:

a. Connect to the Internet.
b. Access the Excite search engine at http://www.excite.com.
c. Enter **+graphics +background** for the search words.
d. Investigate at least three sites that offer background graphics.
e. Make sure that the graphics can legally be used on a commercial Web site.
f. If you have trouble locating Web sites with graphics, go to http://www.course.com. Go to the Student Online Companion for this book, then click the link for Unit E.
g. Select a graphic and incorporate it into a Web page. Name the Web and Web page *JobsRUs*.
h. Print your Web page.

► Visual Workshop

The SoundWorld Warehouse has hired you to help market their products on the Web. Use the skills you learned in this lesson to create a Web page similar to the one in Figure E-28. The images are available in the Microsoft Clip Art Gallery. Save the file with the filename *stereosales.htm*. (*Hint:* The banner is a marquee.)

FIGURE E-28

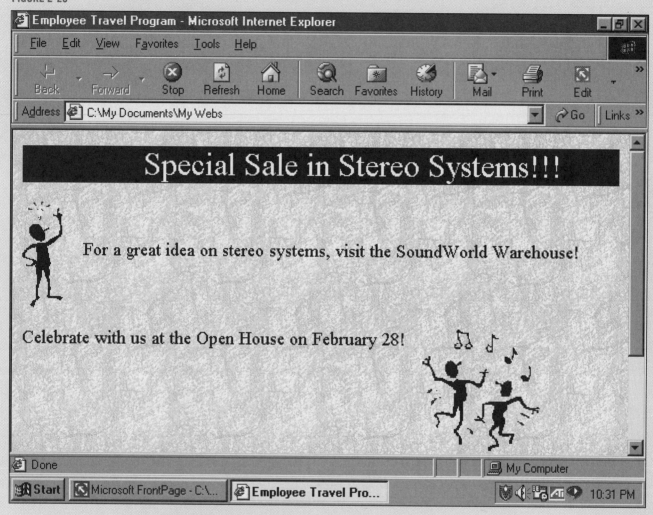

FrontPage 2000

Unit **F**

Creating
Tables and Frames

Objectives

- ▶ **Insert a table**
- ▶ **Modify table properties**
- ▶ **Add rows, columns, and captions to a table**
- ▶ **Modify cell properties**
- ▶ **Create a Web page with frames**
- ▶ **Set frame targets**
- ▶ **Modify frame properties**
- ▶ **Exit a frame page**

Tables and frames are two features in Microsoft FrontPage that can help organize the information on your Web pages. **Tables** allow you to organize text, hyperlinks, and graphics into columns and rows to improve the design of your Web pages. **Frames** enable you to display several Web pages at the same time. ✎ Connie Lee wants to add definitions and details about the hardware products to the Computer Corner site. To organize and display this information, she decides to add some tables and frames to her pages.

Inserting a Table

Like many word-processing programs, FrontPage provides a feature that inserts tables into your documents. Tables are a great way to organize a lot of information on a Web page so that it is logical and easy to read. The basic component of a table is a **cell**, the intersection of a vertical column and a horizontal row. If you have ever used a spreadsheet program, such as Microsoft Excel or Lotus 1-2-3, you have worked with cells. ◄──── Connie wants to provide a list of computer peripherals on the company's Web site. To accomplish this goal, she creates a Web page in the Hardware folder and inserts a table to draw attention to the technology products.

Steps

1. Start **Microsoft FrontPage**, click **File**, then click **Open Web**
   The Open Web dialog box appears.

2. Click the [*insert your name here*] **folder**, if necessary, click the **ComputerCorner** Web, click **Open**, click the **Folders button** ▣, then double-click the **Hardware** folder
   The Hardware directory opens.

3. Click the **New Page button** ▯ on the Standard toolbar, type **peripheral.htm**, and press **[Enter]**
   A new page is created and named peripheral.htm.

4. Click the **Navigation button** ▱ and drag the new file under **Product 1** on the flowchart
   A new file is added to the Navigation flowchart of the site, as shown in Figure F-1. The hyperlinks and the page banner are automatically added to the new page.

5. Double-click **Hardware/peripheral.htm**, then right-click anywhere on the page banner (the large graphic at the top of the page), and select **Page Banner Properties**
   The Page Banner Properties dialog box opens.

6. Select the contents of the Page banner text box, type **Computer Peripherals**, then click **OK**
   The Page Banner Properties dialog box closes and Computer Peripherals appears in the page banner.

7. Click in the middle of the page, click **Table** on the menu bar, click **Insert**, then click **Table**
   The Insert Table dialog box appears, as shown in Figure F-2.

8. In the Size section, increase the number of Rows to **4**, deselect **Specify width**, if necessary, then click **OK**
   The table appears at the far-left margin of the center section, as shown in Figure F-3. Notice that the insertion point is automatically placed in the first table cell. Because you did not specify a table width, the table will adjust to fit the text as you enter it.

9. Click the top-left table cell, if necessary, and type **Peripheral**, then press **[Tab]** to move to the next cell, and type **Types**
   The text appears just as you typed it.

10. Use the **[Tab]** key to navigate through the table and enter text until the table resembles the table in Figure F-4

11. Click the **Save button** ▣ on the Standard toolbar
   FrontPage saves the Computer Peripherals page.

FIGURE F-1: Navigation View

Hardware folder ——
New file ——

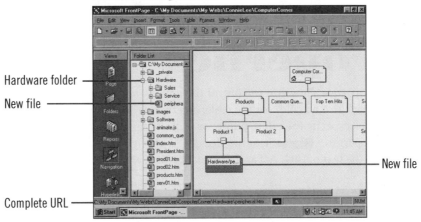

New file

Complete URL ——

FIGURE F-2: Insert Table dialog box

Specify layout ——

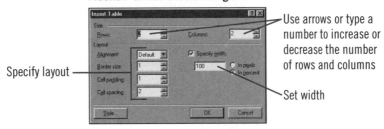

Use arrows or type a number to increase or decrease the number of rows and columns

Set width

FIGURE F-3: Empty Computer Peripherals table

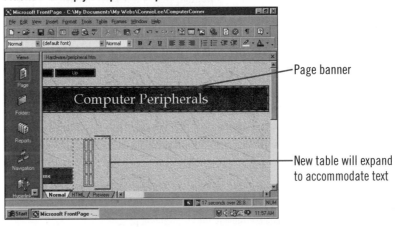

Page banner

New table will expand to accommodate text

FIGURE F-4: Completed Computer Peripherals table

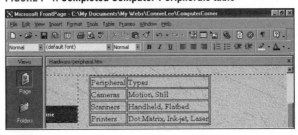

CLUES TO USE

Setting the table width

You can use the Table Properties dialog box to specify the width of a table, either as a percentage of the available window width or as a number of pixels. If you specify a percentage (such as 50%), the table will adjust to the window size available on the user's screen. Therefore, the table may have a slightly different appearance when viewed by different users. If you specify the number of pixels (dots on the screen) as 400, the table will remain at 400 pixels, regardless of the user's window size.

Modifying Table Properties

Table properties allow you to control the appearance of the entire table. For example, you can select a background color for the table, determine the width of the border, change the alignment of the table, specify the cell padding, or indicate the cell spacing. Table F-1 defines the available table properties. Connie decides to change the color of her table and alter the space between the text of each cell and the cell border.

Steps

1. **Right-click anywhere in the table, then select Table Properties from the pop-up menu**
   The Table Properties dialog box appears.

QuickTip

You can also select a background image for the entire table or for an individual cell in the table.

2. **Double-click in the Border Size text box and type 6, double-click in the Cell spacing text box and type 8, click the Background Color list arrow, then click White**
   The settings for the Table Properties are shown in Figure F-5.

3. **Click Style, click Format, then click Font**
   The Font dialog box opens.

4. **Select Times New Roman (or a similar font) for the Font, then click OK three times**
   The Peripherals page appears with the settings applied to the entire table.

5. **Right-click anywhere on the table and select Table Properties**
   The Table Properties dialog box opens.

6. **Double-click in the Cell padding box, type 8, double-click in the Cell spacing box and type 2, then click OK**
   The space between the text and the borders of each cell increases, and the space between cells decreases.

7. **Click the Save button 🖫 on the Standard toolbar**
   The table appears as shown in Figure F-6.

TABLE F-1: Table properties

table property	description
Alignment	Aligns the table to the left, right, or center of the window
Float	Determines whether text outside the table flows around the table (Left or Right) or not at all (Default)
Border size	Specifies the thickness of the lines on the outside edge of the table
Cell padding	Specifies the distance between the cell's contents and its border
Cell spacing	Specifies the thickness of the borders between cells
Minimum size Width/height	Determines the width and height of the table as either a percentage of the window width or a number of pixels
Custom background image	Determines the background image for the table
Custom background color	Determines the background color of the entire table
Custom border color	Determines the color of the table's border
Custom light border color	Determines the color of the table's top and left borders
Custom dark border color	Determines the color of the table's bottom and right borders

FIGURE F-5: Table Properties dialog box

Specify layout —

Size options —

Table border options —

Set background color —

Style button —

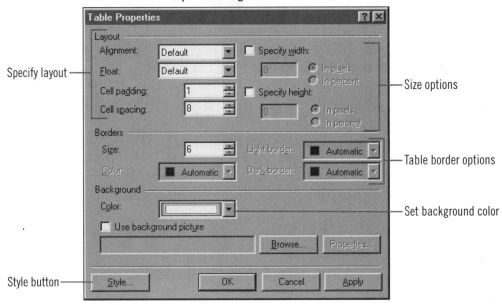

FIGURE F-6: White table with narrow border and increased cell padding.

Border set to 6 —

Cell padding set to 8 —

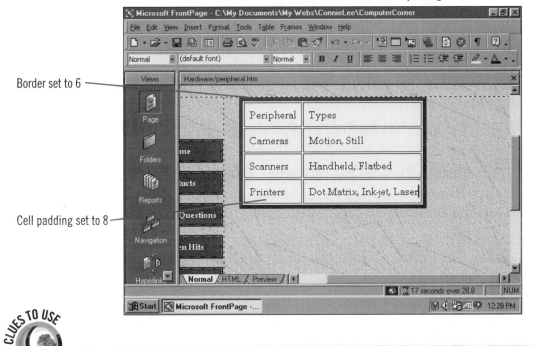

Peripheral	Types
Cameras	Motion, Still
Scanners	Handheld, Flatbed
Printers	Dot Matrix, Ink-jet, Laser

CLUES TO USE

Understanding cell spacing and cell padding

The differences between cell spacing and cell padding are illustrated in Figure F-7. When the cell spacing is set to 10 and the cell padding is 0, the text is next to the borders, but the borders are wide. In contrast, when the cell padding is 10 and the cell spacing is 0, substantial space separates the text and the borders.

FIGURE F-7: Cell spacing and cell padding

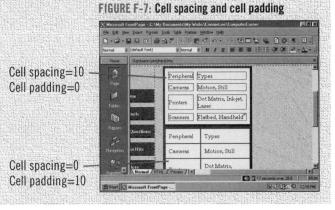

Cell spacing=10
Cell padding=0

Cell spacing=0
Cell padding=10

Adding Rows, Columns, and Captions to Tables

After you have created a table, you may decide to add another row or column to the table. You may also want to add a caption above or below the table. FrontPage makes it very easy to insert or delete table rows, columns, and captions. ◆━━ Connie decides that she needs one more row at the bottom of her table.

Steps

1. **Click anywhere in the bottom row of the table, click Table on the menu bar, click Insert, then click Rows or Columns**
   The Insert Rows or Columns dialog box opens.

2. **Select Rows, if necessary, click the Below selection option button** (the dialog box is shown in Figure F-8), **then click OK**
   A new row appears in the table, as shown in Figure F-9.

3. **Click the first cell of the new row, then type DVD drives can play CD-ROM discs.**
   The column expands to fit the new text, as shown in Figure F-10.

4. **Click Table on the menu bar, click Insert, then click Rows or Columns**
   The Insert Rows or Columns dialog box opens.

5. **Click Columns, click the Right of selection option button, if necessary, then click OK**
   A new column appears in the center of the table.

6. **Click Table on the menu bar, click Insert, then click Caption**
   The insertion point moves above the table.

7. **Type Now Available at Computer Corner**
   The caption appears centered above the table.

8. **Right-click the caption, select Caption Properties from the pop-up menu, then click Bottom of Table**
   The Caption Properties dialog box appears.

9. **Click OK, then click the Save button 🖫 on the Standard toolbar**
   The table appears with three columns and the caption below the table, as shown in Figure F-11.

FIGURE F-8: **Insert Rows or Columns dialog box**

Specify number of rows —

Specify placement — of rows

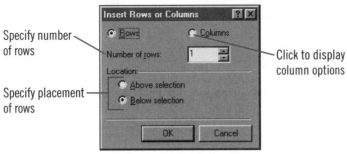

— Click to display column options

FIGURE F-9: **New blank row inserted into table**

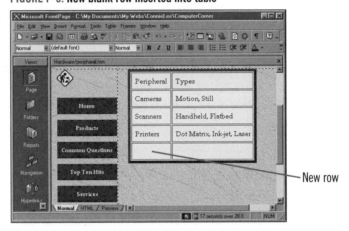

— New row

FIGURE F-10: **Table with text in new row**

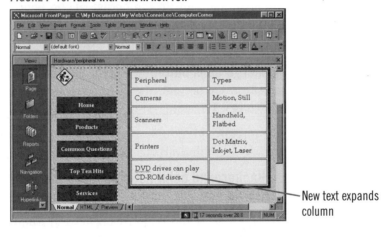

— New text expands column

FIGURE F-11: **Table with three columns**

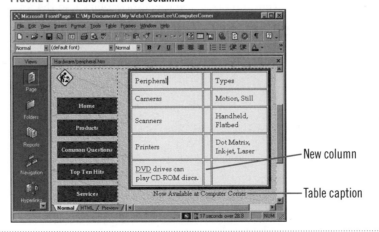

— New column

— Table caption

Modifying Cell Properties

In some cases, you may not want to change the settings of the entire table. Instead, there may be only a few cells (or a single cell) that you would like to modify. The **Cell Properties** dialog box provides many options for changing cells, including the alignment of the text in the cells, the width of the cells, the color, and the **cell span** (the number of rows or columns covered by the cell). Table F-2 lists several Cell Properties options. Connie decides to delete the center column of her table. She also wants to make the text in the bottom row span two columns.

Steps

1. Move the insertion point to the border on top of the center column until it turns into a downward-pointing arrow, then click
   The center column turns black, indicating that it is selected.

2. Click **View** on the menu bar, click **Toolbars**, then click **Tables** if necessary
   The Table toolbar is displayed, as shown in Figure F-12.

3. Drag the **Tables toolbar** up to just under the Formatting toolbar, if necessary
   The toolbar docks (or attaches) to the other toolbars.

QuickTip

You cannot delete a single cell unless the row or column consists of only one cell.

4. Click the **Delete Cells button** on the Tables toolbar
   The highlighted cells in the center column are deleted.

5. Move the insertion point to the border at the beginning of the bottom row until it turns into a black right-pointing arrow, then click
   The bottom row turns black, indicating that it is selected.

6. Click the **Merge Cells button** on the Table toolbar
   The two cells in the bottom row merge into one large cell that spans both columns, as shown in Figure F-13.

7. Select the top row of the table, right-click, and select **Cell Properties**
   Be sure to select only the cells that you want to change.

8. Click the **Background color list arrow**, select **Black**, click **OK**, then deselect the row
   The background changes to black.

9. Select the top row of the table (if necessary), right-click, select **Font**, change the font color to **White**, click **OK**, then deselect the table
   The background of the top row is now black and the text is white, as shown in Figure F-14.

10. Click the **Save button** on the Standard toolbar

FIGURE F-12: Tables toolbar

Draw table

Eraser | Insert rows | Insert columns | Delete cells | Merge cells | Split Cells | Align Top | Center vertically | Align bottom | Distribute rows evenly | Distribute columns evenly | Fill color

AutoFit

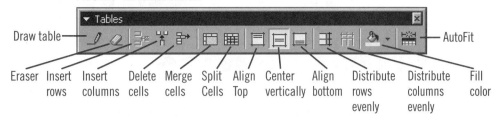

FIGURE F-13: Table with cells in bottom row merged

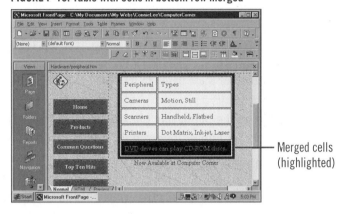

Merged cells (highlighted)

FIGURE F-14: Peripherals table

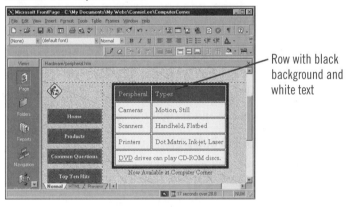

Row with black background and white text

TABLE F-2: Cell properties

cell property	description
Horizontal alignment	Aligns the text to the left, right, or center of the cell
Vertical alignment	Aligns the text to the top, bottom, or center of the cell
Header cell	Displays the cell contents in bold
No wrap	Restricts the cell contents from wrapping to the next line
Specify width	Determines the width of the cell, measured either as a percentage of the table width or as a number of pixels
Specify height	Determines the height of the cell, measured either as a percentage of the table height or as a number of pixels
Custom background color	Determines the background color of the cell, which overrides the table color
Custom background image	Determines the background image, for example, a bitmap; this setting overrides the table's background image
Custom border color	Determines the color of the cell border
Number of rows spanned	Lets one cell cover multiple rows
Number of columns spanned	Lets one cell cover multiple columns

Creating a Web Page with Frames

Frames allow you to display more than one Web page on a single screen. With this feature, each Web page uses only a portion of the screen, and the user can interact with the pages independently. For example, a Web page might consist of two frames; the frame on the left side of the screen might display a Web page with a table of contents, while the frame on the right side displays a Web page with the content corresponding to a selection from the table of contents. Connie decides to create two Web pages, a list of computer terms (terms.htm) and an introduction (intro.htm). She uses a Frame template to create a Web page that will simultaneously display both of these pages in frames.

1. **Click File on the menu bar, click New, click Page, then click the Frames Pages tab**
   The options for frames appear in the New dialog box, as shown in Figure F-15.

2. **Click Contents, then click OK**
   A new page opens with two frames—a narrow column on the left and a wide column on the right, as shown in Figure F-16. Additional tabs for No Frames and Frames Page HTML appear at the bottom of the screen.

3. **Click New Page in the left frame**
   A new background appears on the left side of the page.

4. **Type Cameras, press [Enter], type Scanners, and press [Enter]**
   The words appear on separate lines in the left frame.

5. **Click New Page in the right frame and enter the text shown in Figure F-17**
   The text appears in the right frame.

6. **Click the Save button** 💾
   The Save As dialog box appears. Note that the left frame is darker, indicating that it is the page that will be saved.

7. **Double-click the Hardware folder, select the contents of the File name box, type terms.htm, then click Save**
   The left frame is saved as terms.htm in the Hardware folder. The right frame is now highlighted, as shown in Figure F-18.

8. **Select the contents of the File name box, type intro.htm, then click Save**
   The right frame is saved as intro.htm. The highlight now surrounds the entire page.

9. **Select the contents in the File name box and type frames.htm, click the Change button, type Master Frames page in the Page title box, click OK, then click Save**
   The new frames page is saved in the Hardware folder of the Computer Corner Web. This page is the **master** page—each time it is displayed, it will pull terms.htm into the left frame and intro.htm into the right frame.

FIGURE F-15: New dialog box

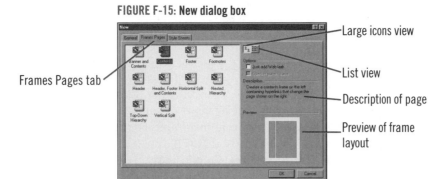

Frames Pages tab

Large icons view

List view

Description of page

Preview of frame layout

FIGURE F-16: New page with two frames

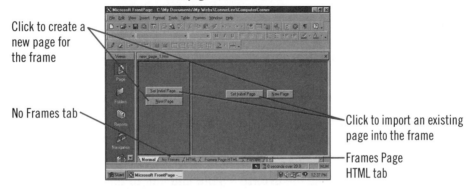

Click to create a new page for the frame

No Frames tab

Click to import an existing page into the frame

Frames Page HTML tab

FIGURE F-17: Frames with initial pages displayed

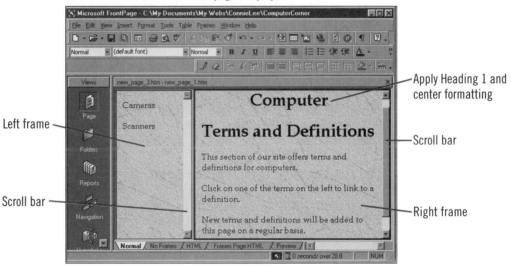

Apply Heading 1 and center formatting

Left frame

Scroll bar

Scroll bar

Right frame

FIGURE F-18: Save As dialog box

Current file

FrontPage 2000

Setting Frame Targets

Frame pages are often used to display tables of contents, with the list of contents appearing in one frame and the selected topic in another frame. For the frames to operate in this manner, you must create hyperlinks in one frame that will display the corresponding Web pages (the frame **targets**) in the other frame. ✐ Connie wants to create hyperlinks in the left column of her frame page so that when a user clicks a term, the appropriate definition appears in the right frame.

Steps 1 2 3 4

1. Select **Cameras** in the left frame, then click the **Hyperlink button** 🔗 on the Standard toolbar

   The Create Hyperlink dialog box opens.

2. Click the **Change Target Frame button** 🔲, then click the **right frame**

   The Target Frame dialog box opens and the right frame is selected, as shown in Figure F-19. This indicates that the link will display a new page in the right-hand frame.

3. Click **OK**, click the **Create a page and link to the new page button** 🔲, click **Normal Page**, then click **OK**

   A new page appears in Page view. Even though the page now appears in full view, it will be displayed only in the right-hand frame.

4. Click in the center of the page and type **There are many new, digital cameras available. These cameras do not use film; they can save the photos directly to a computer.**

   The text appears on the page, as shown in Figure F-20.

5. Click the **Save button** 💾 on the Standard toolbar, type **cameras.htm** in the File name box, then click **Save**

   The page is saved in the Hardware folder.

6. Click **Folders**, double-click **frames.htm**, select **Scanners**, and click 🔗 on the Standard toolbar

   The Create Hyperlink dialog box appears.

7. Click 🔲, then click the **right frame**

   This ensures that the link will display a new page in the right-hand frame.

8. Click **OK**, click 🔲, then click **Normal Page** and click **OK**

9. Type **Scanners can be used to digitize photographs. Most scanners offer many different color options.**

   The text appears on the page.

10. Click 💾 on the Standard toolbar, type **scanners.htm** in the File name box, then click **Save**

    The page is saved in the Hardware folder.

11. Click **Folders**, double-click **frames.htm**, and click the **Preview tab**

    The frames page appears, as shown in Figure F-21.

12. Test both of the links, then click the **Normal tab**

FIGURE F-19: Target Frame dialog box

Current target for frame

Change Target Frame button

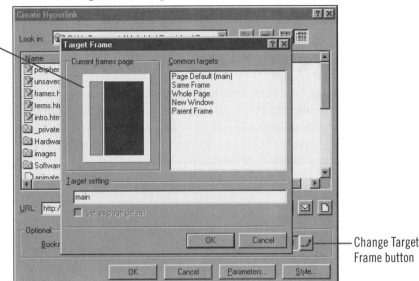

FIGURE F-20: Cameras page with text

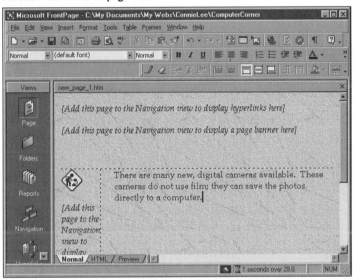

FIGURE F-21: Frame Page displayed in Preview view

Hyperlinks

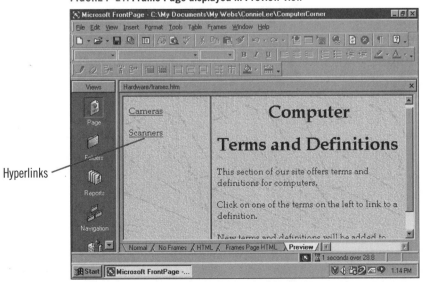

Modifying Frame Properties

Each frame on a page is an individual Web page; consequently, each frame can have a unique color and other attributes. In addition, you can modify **Frame Properties**, such as whether the user can resize the frames or whether a scroll bar will appear on the frames. Connie wants to make the left frame a little wider. She also wants to ensure that users cannot inadvertently change the size of the frames.

Steps 1234

1. Move the pointer over the border between the two frames until it changes into a ↔, then click and drag the border slightly to the left
   As the border is moved to the left, the right frame becomes slightly wider.

2. Right-click anywhere in the right frame, then click **Frame Properties** on the pop-up menu
   The Frame Properties dialog box opens.

3. Deselect **Resizable in Browser**, if necessary
   When this option is not checked, users cannot move the border or make the frames larger or smaller.

QuickTip

If the Show Scrollbars option is set to If Needed, the scroll bar will appear only when the frame cannot display its entire contents on one screen.

4. Click the **Show Scrollbars** list arrow, then click **Always**
   The changes are reflected in the Frame Properties dialog box, as shown in Figure F-22.

5. Click **OK**
   The Frame Properties dialog box closes.

6. Click the **Preview tab** on the View bar to test the page, then click **Cameras**
   The border between the frames remains locked in place and the scroll bar appears, as shown in Figure F-23.

7. Click the **Normal tab** on the View bar, then click the **Save button** 🖫
   The changes are saved.

FIGURE F-22: Frame Properties dialog box

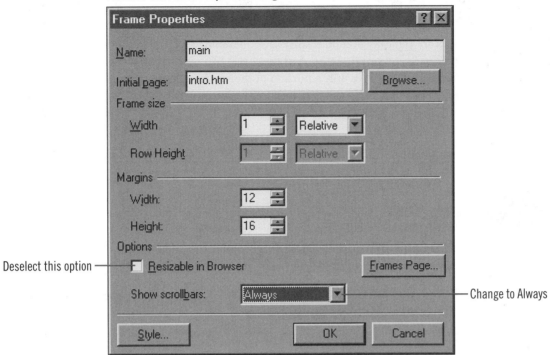

Deselect this option ——

Change to Always

FIGURE F-23: Frame page for Cameras in Preview view

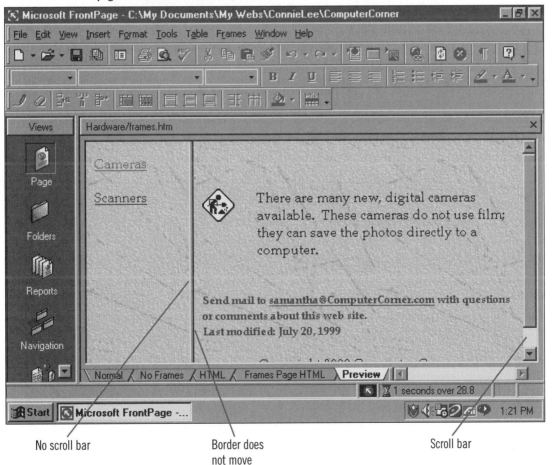

No scroll bar

Border does
not move

Scroll bar

Exiting a Frame Page

Frames are typically used to display several Web pages on the same screen. When you exit from a frame page, it is important to reset the screen to a whole page—otherwise, Web pages may continue to be displayed in only a portion of the screen. ➤ Connie decides to add a hyperlink on her framed page that takes the user to the Computer Corner home page.

Steps 1 2 3 4

1. Type **Computer Corner Home Page** under the second option in the left frame
   The new text appears, as shown in Figure F-24.

2. Select **Computer Corner Home Page**, then click the **Hyperlink button** on the Standard toolbar
   The Create Hyperlink dialog box opens.

3. Click the **Change Target Frame button**
   The Target Frame dialog box appears, as shown in Figure F-25. It lists the **common targets**, which are frame settings recognized by all Web browsers.

4. Click **Whole Page**, then click **OK**
   When this link is activated, the linked page will fill the entire screen, rather than just the default target (the right frame).

5. Scroll to and click **index.htm**, then click **OK**
   The Create Hyperlink dialog box closes.

6. Click the **Save button** on the Standard toolbar
   The file is saved with the new hyperlink.

7. Click the **Preview tab** on the View bar, then click **Computer Corner Home Page**
   The Computer Corner home page fills the entire screen.

8. Click the **Normal tab** and deselect the text
   The frames appear as shown in Figure F-26.

9. Click the **Close button** on the title bar of FrontPage

FIGURE F-24: New text in left frame

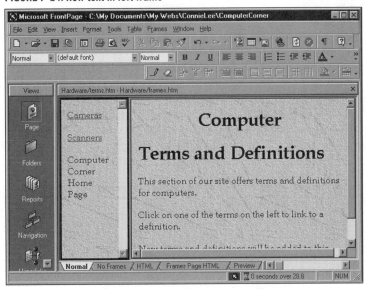

FIGURE F-25: Target Frame dialog box

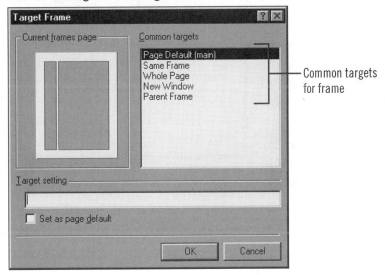

Common targets for frame

FIGURE F-26: Frames page

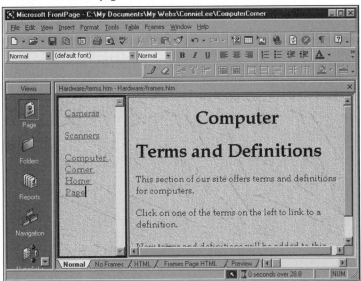

Practice

► Concepts Review

Label each of the elements of the FrontPage window shown in Figure F-27.

FIGURE F-27:

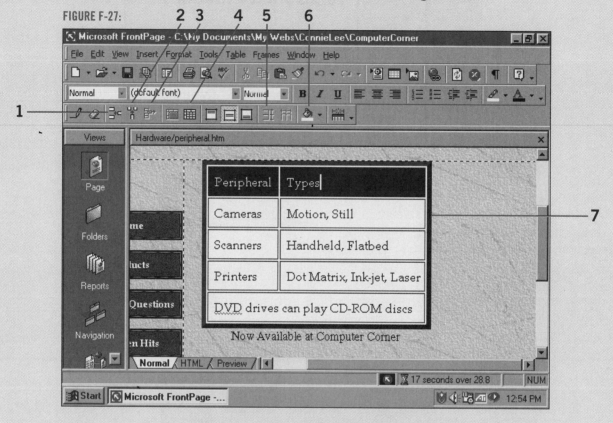

Match each of the descriptions with the correct term.

8. The distance between the cell's content and the border
9. When a cell covers more than one row or column
10. A horizontal group of cells
11. A vertical group of cells
12. The thickness of the cells' border
13. The frame in which a Web page is displayed
14. A title for a table

a. Cell padding
b. Cell spacing
c. Spanning
d. Caption
e. Target
f. Row
g. Column

Select the best answer from the list of choices.

15. The individual parts of a table are called
    a. Cells.
    b. Frames.
    c. Rows.
    d. Partitions.

16. If you want to change the background color of one row in a table, which dialog box should you open?
    a. Table Properties
    b. Cell Properties
    c. Page Properties
    d. Row Properties

17. If you want to change the background color of an entire table, including the caption, which dialog box should you open?
    a. Table Properties
    b. Cell Properties
    c. Page Properties
    d. Row Properties

18. How can you edit the message that viewers will see if they access your frame page, but their browsers do not support frames?
    a. Access Page Properties.
    b. Access Frame Properties.
    c. Create a new page and write a new message.
    d. Click the No Frames tab on the View bar.

19. How do you add another frame to a page?
    a. You cannot add another frame to a page that already has one frame.
    b. Click Frame Properties and select Add Frame.
    c. Delete the frame you are in and then create a new page.
    d. Select an existing frame, click Frame on the menu bar, then click Split Frame.

20. If you have two frames on a page and you want to make one larger and one smaller, what procedure would you follow?
    a. Select Page Properties and enter the new dimensions.
    b. Click and drag the border between the frames.
    c. Delete the page and create a new page with different dimensions.
    d. Create a new page for each frame.

▶ Skills Review

1. **Create a table.**
    a. Start Microsoft FrontPage. Create a new One Page Web and save it as *Finance*.
    b. Create a new Web page.
    c. Click Table on the File menu, click Insert, then click Table.
    d. Set the number of rows to 3 and the number of columns to 4.
    e. Set the Cell padding to 12.
    f. Enter the following text into each cell:

Month	January	February	March
Income	$4320	$3670	$5500
Expenses	$1280	$3200	$4000

    g. Save the Web page with **Profit** as the title and *profit.htm* as the filename.

2. **Modify table settings.**
   a. Make sure the profit.htm file is open in FrontPage.
   b. Right-click the table to open the Table Properties dialog box.
   c. Set the Border Size to 10 and the Cell spacing to 20. Leave the dialog box open.
   d. Set the Background color to Aqua, the Light border color to Silver, and the Dark border color to Black. Leave the dialog box open.
   e. Center the table in the window, then close the dialog box.
   f. Save the Web page.
   g. Preview the page.

3. **Add a row and a column to a table.**
   a. Make sure the profit.htm file is open in FrontPage.
   b. Click in the last column of the table and select Insert Rows or Columns.
   c. Add a column to the right of the current position.
   d. Type **April** into the first cell of the new column.
   e. Save the Web page.

4. **Modify cell properties.**
   a. Select all of the cells in the middle row of the table.
   b. Right-click to open the Cell Properties dialog box and set the horizontal alignment to right.
   c. Select the Income and Expenses cells, then click the Merge Cells button to merge them.
   d. Save and print the Web page.

5. **Create a Web page with frames.**
   a. Click File on the menu bar, point to New, then click Page.
   b. Click the Frames Pages tab.
   c. Select the Contents template.
   d. Save the page as *frame1.htm*.
   e. Click New Page in the small frame, type **Florida**, press [Enter], then type **Illinois**.
   f. Save the left frame page as *menu.htm*.
   g. Click New Page in the large frame, and type **Click Florida or Illinois to learn about the state**. Save this page as *intro.htm*.

6. **Set frame targets.**
   a. Make sure that the frame1.htm file is open.
   b. Select Florida and click the Hyperlink button, then click the Create a page and link to the new page button.
   c. On the new page, type **Florida is often referred to as the "Silicon Valley" of the East**.
   d. Save the frames page as *florida.htm*. Return to frame1.htm.
   e. Select Illinois and click the Hyperlink button, then click the Create a page and link to the new page button.
   f. On the new page, type **Illinois is known as the "Land of Lincoln"**.
   g. Save the target page as *illinois.htm*.
   h. From Folders View, open the frame1.htm file.
   i. Click the Preview tab on the View bar and test your hyperlinks.

7. **Modify frame properties.**
   a. Return to Normal View.
   b. Right-click the left frame and select Frame Properties.

c. Deselect the option for Resizable in Browser, if necessary.

d. Preview the page and try to move the border between the two frames (it should not move).

e. Return to Normal View and save the page.

8. Exit a frame page.

a. In the left frame, add the word **EXIT** under the link to the Illinois frame.

b. Select EXIT and click the Hyperlink button.

c. Click the Change Target Frame button and select Whole Page.

d. Select profit.htm as the target page.

e. Save the Web page.

f. Preview the Web page and test the EXIT hyperlink.

g. Close the Web, then close FrontPage.

▶ Independent Challenges

1. Your friend, Jerry, wants you to help him create a short newsletter for his school. Jerry decides to use a table so that the text will line up correctly; he plans to set the Border Size to 0 so that lines will not appear on the page.

You need to create a table with the following text:

Centennial College	
Student receives award Molly Flap received an award yesterday as the oldest student to ever graduate from Centennial College. Molly will turn 89 next month.	**Football team loses** The football team extended its record number of losses with a 57-3 defeat at the hands (and feet) of WauWau State.
Professor wins lottery Dr. Luck bought one lottery ticket last week and was lucky enough to hold the winning ticket for $1.2 million. Visit his Web page to see how he plans to spend the money.	**Classes canceled on Friday** All classes have been canceled next Friday to celebrate Homecoming.

To complete this independent challenge:

a. Create a new One Page Web named *News*.

b. Insert a table into the home page and enter the text. The table should have three rows and two columns. The cells in the top row should be merged.

c. Set the Border Size to 0 and the Cell padding to 8.

d. Make the first column Aqua and the second column Fuchsia.

e. Save the home page.

f. Test the page with the Preview tab.

g. Print the Web page, then close the Web.

2. Your mother, a fourth-grade teacher, has asked you to help create a Web page about North and South America. You decide to develop a frame page so that the students can click on either North America or South America and see information about that continent.

To complete this independent challenge:

a. Create a new empty Web named *Geography*, and create three Web pages as follows:
  1. A page with the names for two continents (North America and South America) aligned at the left margin. Save this page as *cont.htm*.
  2. A Web page with several sentences about North America. Save this page as *NA.htm*.
  3. A Web page with several sentences about South America. Save this page as *SA.htm*.
b. Create a new frames page with a template (Contents page).
c. Place the cont.htm page on the left side.
d. Place the NA.htm page on the right side.
e. Create a hyperlink so that, when a student clicks North America, the NA.htm page is displayed on the right.
f. Create a hyperlink so that, when a student clicks South America, the SA.htm page is displayed on the right.
g. Save the page as *Geo.htm*, then print it.
h. Test the hyperlinks, then close the Web.

3. You have been hired by a multimedia company, Multimedia Magic, to create a unique and attractive Web page. The company has asked that you develop a three-frame design for its page. The content and the hyperlinks will be added after Multimedia Magic approves the general look of the page. The company would like to have a banner at the top of the page with its name appearing in large, bold print. The left frame will contain the table of contents, and the right frame will display information related to the company.

To complete this independent challenge:

a. Create a new empty Web named *Multimedia*, and create a new frames page in FrontPage.
b. Select the Banner and Contents template.
c. Click New Page in each of the frames and design a page for each frame.
d. Add a large, bold title in the frame at the top of the page with the name of the company.
e. Add the words **Resources**, **Services**, and **Products** in the left frame.
f. In the right frame, type **Welcome to the Home Page of Multimedia Magic!**
g. Preview the page with the Preview tab.
h. Drag and move the borders to enlarge the banner area at the top.
i. Save the pages, then close the Web.

4. As the Webmaster for your company, you are charged with creating a reference area for the employees. Because they travel a great deal, you decide to create a table that provides information on airlines and their Web pages. Conduct a search on the Web and find the URLs for the following airlines: United, American, Delta, Southwest, and US Airways. Then create a table that provides a concise arrangement of the airline name, URL, and telephone number.

To complete this independent challenge:

a. Connect to the Internet.

b. Access the Yahoo! search engine at http://www.yahoo.com.

c. Enter the name of the airline for the search word (in most cases, it is best to use the full name in quotation marks, such as "Delta Airlines").

d. Obtain the URL for each airline, access the Web page, and locate the telephone number (if possible).

e. If you have trouble locating Web sites for the airlines, go to http://www.course.com. Go to the Student Online Companion for this book, then click the link for Unit F.

f. Create a new Web named *Airlines* with a page that contains a table with three columns and six rows (one is for the column heading).

g. Add a caption to the table.

h. Save and print the Web page that you created, then close the Web.

► Visual Workshop

A large computer company has hired you to create tables that present information about computer cables. Use the skills you learned in this lesson to create a Web page similar to the one in Figure F-28. Save the file with the filename *cable.htm*.

FIGURE F-28

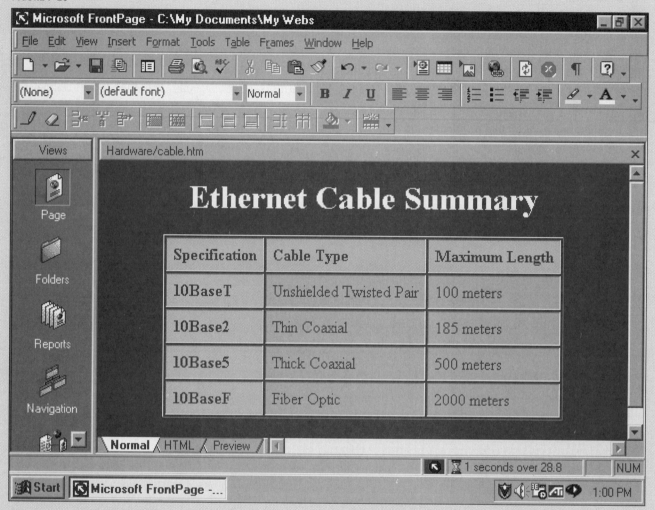

Unit **G**

Working

with HTML Forms

Objectives

- ► **Understand HTML Forms**
- `MOUS` ► **Create an HTML form with a wizard**
- `MOUS` ► **Set form properties**
- `MOUS` ► **Add text boxes**
- `MOUS` ► **Set form field properties**
- `MOUS` ► **Insert radio buttons**
- `MOUS` ► **Add check boxes**
- `MOUS` ► **Insert a drop-down menu**

When visiting most basic Web sites, users can move locally from page to page within the site and jump remotely from site to site, but cannot interact with the site. Using forms, you can create a dynamic Web site that facilitates two-way communication by inviting input from the user. Users can respond to the forms you design, to accomplish all kinds of tasks, from registering for free software to ordering a pizza. The most common method of collecting input from a visitor is the HTML form. ◢ Connie Lee decides to create an HTML form that lets visitors to the Computer Corner site order a free catalog. She will include the standard HTML form fields, such as text boxes, radio buttons, drop-down menus, and check boxes.

Understanding HTML Forms

HTML forms are used to collect data from a user. You can include these forms on any Web page. After a user completes a form, the Web browser sends the data to other software for processing. The processing software usually resides on a Web server, which in turn sends a confirmation to the user that the transaction is complete. The confirmation typically consists of a "thank you" message or a set of results. A good example of this type of transaction is a Web search. A Web search site provides an HTML form that accepts a search topic. The browser sends the topic to the search site's Web server for processing, and then the search site's server returns a list of hits to the user as confirmation. FrontPage 2000 provides many tools and templates that help you create forms that enable visitors to interact with your Web pages.  Connie Lee can use FrontPage 2000 to create the following types of forms:

 Guest Book

A guest book form provides visitors to your site a place to sign in and submit a brief comment about your site's services.

 Feedback

You can tailor a feedback form to accept user responses to specific questions about your site or any relevant topics.

 User Registration

A user registration form allows a visitor to supply a name, a place of business, an e-mail address, and other types of personal information while registering for a service provided by the Web site. Figure G-1 is an example of a registration form.

 Search

A search form provides a text box in which to enter search topics. It submits the topic input to the server for further processing, then returns a list of hits related to the keyword(s) entered.

 Confirmation

A confirmation form acknowledges receipt of a Web page that was submitted to and received by the server. It usually includes a short message and a hyperlink to return to the Web site's home page.

 Custom

You can create a custom HTML form for almost any personal, business, or academic need that requires input from visitors to your site.

FIGURE G-1: Registration form with form fields

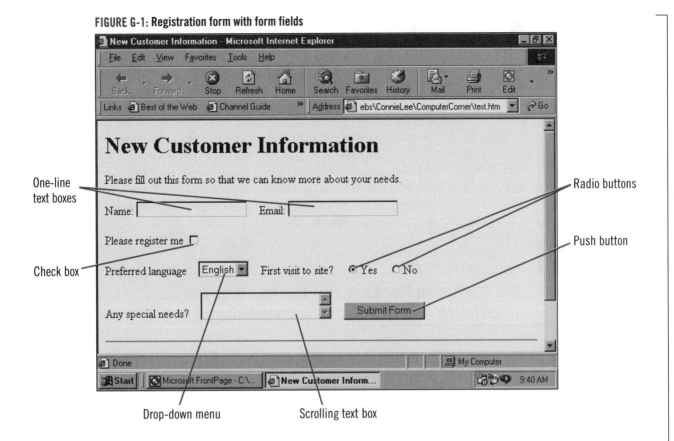

One-line
text boxes

Check box

Radio buttons

Push button

Drop-down menu

Scrolling text box

Creating an HTML Form with a Wizard

FrontPage 2000 provides a variety of ways to include forms on your Web site. You can create forms by using the FrontPage 2000 **Form Page Wizard**, or you can create your own customized HTML form on any Web page in your site. Forms include any **form fields** necessary for the collection of data. Table G-1 describes the types of form fields that are available. A Guest Book, for example, might provide a scrolling text box field in which visitors can enter comments. When you use a wizard, the form also automatically includes the necessary **push buttons** that allow the user to submit the data for processing. ◄━━ Connie Lee decides to allow visitors to the Computer Corner Web to order a catalog online. She uses the Form Page Wizard to create the form and then customizes it to suit Computer Corner's needs.

Steps 1 2 3 4

1. Start **Microsoft FrontPage**, click **File**, click **Open Web**, click the [*insert your name here*] **folder**, if necessary, click the **ComputerCorner Web**, then click **Open**
   The Computer Corner Web opens in the FrontPage window.

2. Click the **Page button** 📄 on the Views bar, click **File**, point to **New**, click **Page**, click **Form Page Wizard**, then click **OK**
   The Form Page Wizard dialog box opens.

3. Click **Next**
   This dialog box lets you revise an existing form, as shown in Figure G-2. You can add new questions or edit existing questions. Since you have not yet entered any questions in the form, the list is empty.

4. Click **Next**, click the **as normal paragraphs option button**, click the **no option button**, then click the **use tables to align form fields check box**
   This dialog box lets you choose presentation options. Questions can appear in paragraph form or as a numbered or bulleted list. Compare your dialog box to Figure G-3.

5. Click **Next**, click the **save results to a web page option button**, select the contents of the **Enter the base name of the results file text box**, type **catalog_form_results**, click **Next**, then click **Finish**
   The Form Page Wizard creates and opens a new form for customization. The results file is where FrontPage will store the information entered into the form by visitors.

6. Select **New Page 1**, type **Order a Computer Corner Catalog**, click the **Center button** 🖷 on the Formatting toolbar
   The place holder page title is replaced and centered.

7. Select **This is an explanation...**, type **This form provides Computer Corner with information about you, our valued customer, and gives you the opportunity to receive a FREE catalog.**, press [Enter], select **Author information goes here**, then type **Webmaster Computer Corner**
   Compare your Computer Corner Catalog form to Figure G-4.

8. Click **File**, click **Save As**, type **catalog_form.htm** in the File name text box, then click **Save**
   The Computer Corner catalog order form is saved as catalog_form.htm.

FIGURE G-2: Form revision options

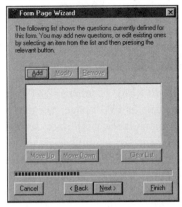

FIGURE G-3: Form presentation options

Choose presentation option here

Adds Table of Contents to page

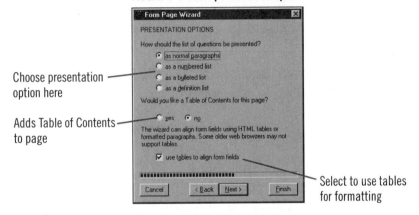

Select to use tables for formatting

FIGURE G-4: Computer Corner catalog order form

Replaced header text

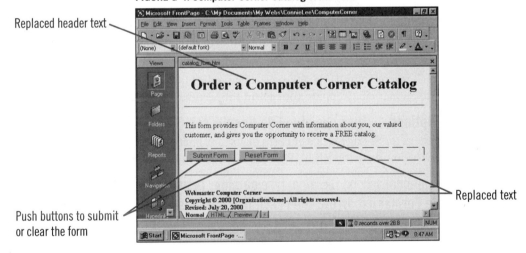

Replaced text

Push buttons to submit or clear the form

TABLE G-1: Form fields

form field	description
One-line text box	Provides space for one line of data entry
Scrolling text box	Provides space for multiple lines of data entry using a scroll bar
Check box	Creates check box entries that enable visitors to make multiple choices
Radio button	Allows visitors to make a single choice from multiple entries
Push button	Provides a button for submitting the data or resetting the form
Drop-down menu	Allows visitors to make either single or multiple selections from a menu containing multiple choices

Setting Form Properties

Once you create an HTML form, FrontPage 2000 offers several options for processing the data it collects. You can save the data to a Web page, save it to a text file, send it to an e-mail address, or send it to a custom CGI (Common Gateway Interface) script for processing. The best method of processing data varies from form to form. For a simple feedback form, an e-mail message to the Webmaster may be the most appropriate approach. For a form that creates a mailing list, a text file that can later be imported into a database may work better. FrontPage 2000 includes a number of formatting options for saving the data to a file, as shown in Table G-2. ➤➤➤ Connie Lee continues to customize the form. She chose to save the Computer Corner results in a Web page (catalog_form_results.htm) during the Form Page Wizard process but decides that it would also be a good idea to save the data collected from the catalog order form in a text file that can later be imported into a spreadsheet or database program. She will also have an e-mail notification sent to her Webmaster, Samantha.

Steps 1 2 3 4

1. **Right-click anywhere on the page, click Page Properties, type Catalog Order Form, then click OK**
   The title of the page is changed to Catalog Order Form. Adding a title to every Web page is important, but remember that the title appears in the title bar of the browser and not on the page itself.

2. **Right-click inside the form area (the form is defined by dashed lines), then click Form Properties**
   The Form Properties dialog box opens. Note that the filename catalog_form_results.htm you entered in the Form Page Wizard appears as the place to store the results collected from the form.

3. **In the Where to store results area, type samantha@computercorner.com in the E-mail address text box, then in the Form properties area, type Catalog Order Form in the Form name text box**
   After each visitor submits the form by clicking the Submit button, the results will be sent via e-mail to Samantha. Compare your Form Properties dialog box to Figure G-5.

4. **Click Options…, then click the File Results tab (if necessary)**
   The Options for Saving Results of Form dialog box opens. Note that the results file is once again listed as catalog_form_results.htm and formatted as an HTML definition list (see Table G-2).

5. **In the Optional second file area, type catalog_results.txt in the File name text box, click the File Format list arrow, then click Text database using comma as a separator**
   After each visitor submits the form by clicking the Submit button, the results will also be appended to a comma-delimited text file that can be imported into another software program, such as Access or Excel. Compare your Options for Saving Results of Form dialog box with that shown in Figure G-6.

6. **Click the E-mail Results tab, in the Email message header area type Catalog Order in the Subject line text box, click OK, click OK, click No, then click the Save button 🖫 on the Standard toolbar**
   The text Catalog Order will be added as a subject line on each message sent to Samantha. The e-mail response can be configured as you develop the Web on a hard or floppy disk, but for the e-mail feature to work properly, the Web must be published on the Internet.

FIGURE G-5: Form Properties dialog box

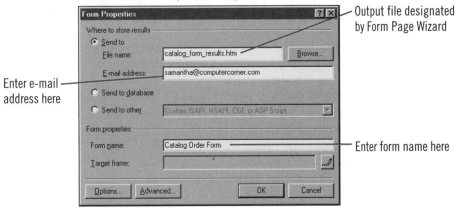

Enter e-mail address here

Output file designated by Form Page Wizard

Enter form name here

FIGURE G-6: Options for Saving Results of Form dialog box

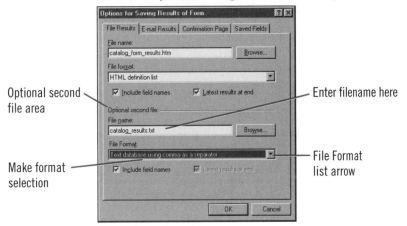

Optional second file area

Enter filename here

File Format list arrow

Make format selection

TABLE G-2: File formatting options

file format	description
HTML	Creates a standard Web page
HTML definition list	Creates a Web page formatted like a dictionary, including a name and definition
HTML bulleted list	Creates a Web page formatted as a bulleted list
Formatted text with HTML	Formats the text for easy reading in a Web browser
Formatted text	Formats the text for easy reading in a text editor
Text database using comma, tab, or space as a separator	Enters the form results into a text format that can be used in spreadsheet or database applications

CLUES TO USE

Comparing Common Gateway Interface (CGI) to FrontPage Server Extensions

The Common Gateway Interface provides one method by which Web clients and servers can communicate. CGI scripts are computer programs that reside on the Web server and process the information sent to the server from HTML forms on the Web browser. They can be written in many computer programming languages, such C, C++, and Perl. The Web browser sends and receives data to and from the Web server through the CGI protocol. As an alternative, you use FrontPage Server Extensions when you use forms in FrontPage 2000. The extensions enable FrontPage components to process the information from HTML forms, mitigating the need for CGI scripts. They also provide an additional means of communication between the browser and any Web server on which the server extensions are installed.

Adding Text Boxes

A standard HTML form field lets you collect data. Form fields include text boxes, radio buttons, check boxes, and drop-down lists. A text box lets a visitor to the Web site enter text, such as a name or address, into the form. Two basic types of text fields are available: **one-line text boxes** and **scrolling text boxes**. A one-line text box provides space for one line of data entry. In contrast, you can customize a scrolling text box to provide space for multiple lines using a scroll bar.
Connie Lee inserts three one-line text boxes into the Computer Corner catalog form to hold the visitor's name, street address, and city and state. She also adds a scrolling text box to accept visitor comments.

Steps

1. **Click immediately before the Submit Form push button, press [Enter], then click the top-left corner of the form**
   The push buttons move down one line, providing space for the insertion of text and form fields, as shown in Figure G-7.

2. **Type Customer Name:, press [Tab], click Insert on the menu bar, point to Form, then click One-Line Text Box**
   The text "Customer Name:" and a one-line text box field are added to the form, as shown in Figure G-8.

3. **Press [Enter], type Street Address:, press [Tab], click Insert on the menu bar, point to Form, then click One-Line Text Box**
   The text "Street Address:" and a one-line text box field are added to the form.

4. **Press [Enter], type City and State:, press [Tab], click Insert on the menu bar, point to Form, then click One-Line Text Box**
   The text "City and State:" and a one-line text box field are added to the form.

5. **Press [Enter], type Comments:, press [Enter], click Insert on the menu bar, point to Form, then click Scrolling Text Box**
   The text "Comments:" and a scrolling text box field are added to the form. Compare your form with Figure G-9.

6. **Click the Save button on the Standard toolbar**
   The form fields are saved on the form.

FIGURE G-7: Computer Corner catalog order form

Insertion point

Form area

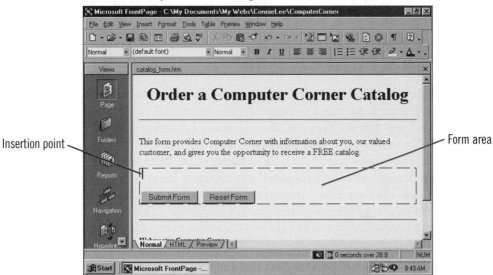

FIGURE G-8: Computer Corner catalog order form with Customer Name text box

One-line text box

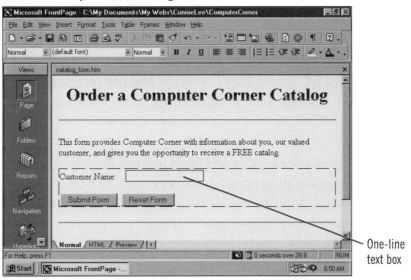

FIGURE G-9: Computer Corner catalog order form with all text boxes included

One-line text boxes

Scrolling text box

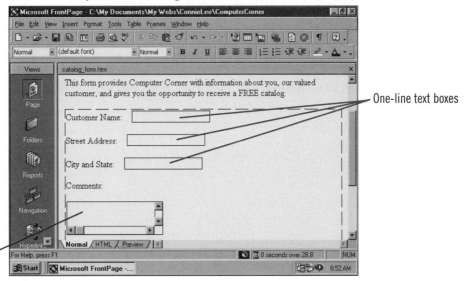

Setting Form Field Properties

Each form field has a set of properties that defines its name, appearance on the page, and initial value, among other characteristics. You can manipulate a form field's properties to customize the field for different types of forms. Initially FrontPage assigns a meaningless name to each field. You can create a more meaningful field name so that it describes the data that will be collected. The browser sends the data in **name/value pairs** for processing. For instance, the field named Street Address will contain the value entered into the form by the user. When the form is processed, the data values are paired with the names of the form fields. ➤ Connie Lee decides to change the properties for each of the text fields she created before she previews the form. As she adjusts the size of the text boxes, she names each text box field.

Steps

1. Right-click the **one-line text box field** to the right of the text Customer Name:, then click **Form Field Properties**
   The Text Box Properties dialog box opens. By default, FrontPage gives the first text box form field the name T1. You will change the name so that it is more meaningful.

2. Type **Name** in the Name text box, then type **30** in the Width in characters text box
   Compare your Text Box Properties dialog box with Figure G-10.

3. Click **OK**, double-click the **Street Address text box field**, type **Address** in the Name text box, type **40** in the Width in characters text box, then click **OK**
   The Name text box is now 30 characters wide, and the Street Address text box is now 40 characters wide.

4. Double-click the **City and State text box field**, type **City** in the Name text box, type **40** in the Width in characters text box, then click **OK**
   The City and State text box is now 40 characters wide.

5. Double-click the **Scrolling Text Box field** below the text Comments:
   The Scrolling Text Box Properties dialog box opens.

6. Type **Comments** in the Name text box, type **50** in the Width in characters text box, type **4** in the Number of lines text box, then click **OK**
   The size of the scrolling text box is changed.

7. Click the **Preview tab** on the View bar
   The Web page appears in Preview mode, as shown in Figure G-11. Use the scroll bar to see what the form will look like in a Web browser.

8. Click the **Normal tab**, then click the **Save button** 🖫 on the Standard toolbar

FIGURE G-10: Text Box Properties dialog box

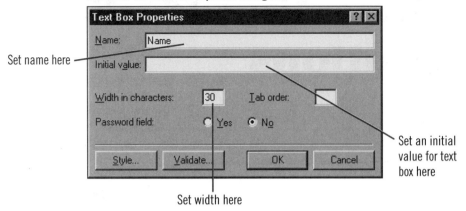

Set name here ——
Set width here
Set an initial value for text box here

FIGURE G-11: Preview of Computer Corner catalog order form

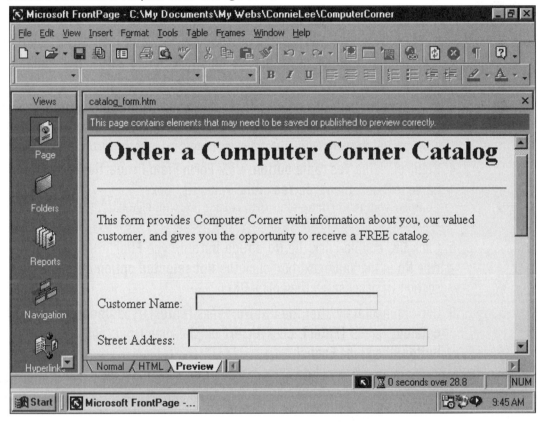

Setting other field properties

You can specify other properties in the Text Box and Scrolling Text Box dialog boxes, including Initial value, which is the text displayed in the text box when the form first appears, and Tab order, which is the order in which the field is activated on the form when the user presses the Tab key. You can also password-protect a field so that only users who know the field's password can alter its value.

Inserting Radio Buttons

Text box fields give visitors to your Web site a great deal of freedom in submitting data. Sometimes, however, it is useful to limit them to a range of choices. Radio Button, Check Box, and Drop-Down Menu fields let you control the content of the data submitted by users. For example, radio buttons are grouped together by group name. A user can select only one radio button at a time in any one group. You assign a value to each radio button (for example, Yes or No), thereby limiting the user's choice of acceptable responses. When the user submits the form, the selected radio button is processed as the value for the named group. ▬▬ Connie Lee decides to allow users of the Computer Corner catalog order form to choose whether they will be placed on a mailing list for sales fliers. She creates a radio button group named Fliers that contains two radio buttons, one for "Yes" and one for "No." She also sets the initial selection value to the "Yes" radio button. Multiple radio button groups can be used on each form. Connie Lee will add a second group of radio buttons that gives the visitor three language choices.

Steps 1 2 3 4

1. Click immediately after the **City and State text box field**, then press **[Enter]**

2. Type **Would you like to be placed on the monthly sales flier mailing list?**, then press **[Enter]**

3. Click **Insert** on the menu bar, point to **Form**, click **Radio Button**, type **Yes**, press **[Tab]**, click **Insert** on the menu bar, point to **Form**, click **Radio Button**, then type **No**
   The text and the two radio button fields are entered into the form, as shown in Figure G-12.

4. Right-click the **Yes radio button**, click **Form Field Properties**, type **Flier** in the Group name text box, then type **Yes** in the Value text box
   Compare your Radio Button Properties dialog box with Figure G-13. Because Computer Corner would like to send out more catalogs, setting the initial value to "Yes" is the desired choice.

5. Click **OK**, double-click the **No option button**, type **Flier** in the Group name text box, type **No** in the Value text box, click the **Not selected option button** in the Initial State section (if necessary), then click **OK**

6. Click immediately after the text **No**, Press **[Enter]**, type **Choose a language for your catalog.**, press **[Enter]**, click **Insert** on the menu bar, point to **Form**, click **Radio Button**, then type **English**

7. Press **[Tab]**, click **Insert** on the menu bar, point to **Form**, click **Radio Button**, type **French**, press **[Tab]**, click **Insert** on the menu bar, point to **Form**, click **Radio Button**, then type **Spanish**

8. Double-click the **English radio button**, type **Language** in the Group name text box, type **English** in the Value text box, click the **Selected radio button** in the Initial State area, click **OK**

9. Double-click the **French radio button**, type **Language** in the Group name text box, type **French** in the Value text box, click **OK**, double-click the **Spanish radio button**, type **Language** in the Group Name text box, type **Spanish** in the Value text box, click **OK**, then click the **Save button** 🖫 on the Standard toolbar
   The French and Spanish radio buttons are added to the Language radio button group. The changes to the catalog order form are saved. Compare your catalog order form with Figure G-14.

FIGURE G-12: Catalog order form with Yes and No radio buttons

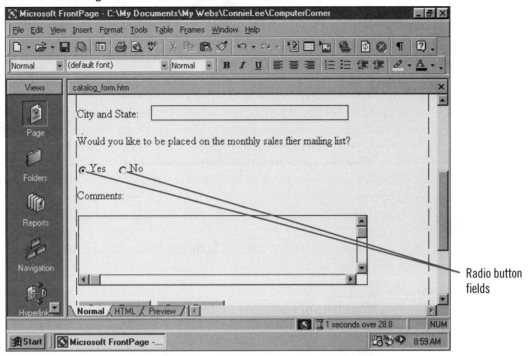

Radio button fields

FIGURE G-13: Radio Button Properties dialog box

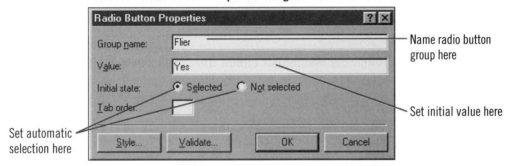

Name radio button group here

Set initial value here

Set automatic selection here

FIGURE G-14: Catalog order form with language radio buttons

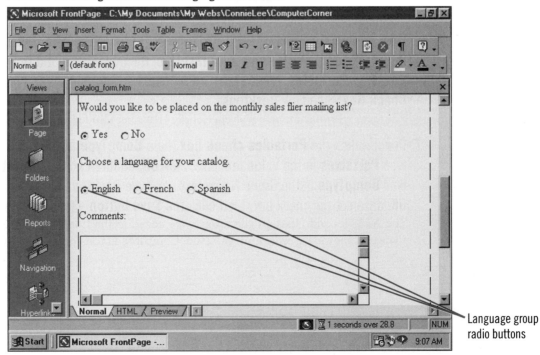

Language group radio buttons

FrontPage 2000

Adding Check Boxes

Like radio button fields, check box fields let you control the value of the data submitted by visitors to your Web site. Check boxes are also organized in groups, and multiple check box groups can be included in each form. However, unlike radio buttons, check boxes do not limit the user to a single choice. Users can select multiple check boxes within a single group. As the designer, you assign a value to each check box. When the user submits the form, the server processes all values assigned to the selected check boxes and associates those values with the group name. ◥ Connie Lee decides to elicit some information from users that better defines their product preferences. She creates a check box group named OS that contains three check boxes: Macintosh, Windows, and UNIX, and a second check box group named CompType that contains two check boxes: Portables and Desktops.

Steps

1. Click immediately after the text **Spanish**, then press **[Enter]**

   A blank line is inserted between the language radio button group and the Comments scrolling text box.

2. Type **What type of operating system(s) do you use?**, then press **[Enter]**

   The text is inserted into the form.

3. Click **Insert** on the menu bar, point to **Form**, click **Check Box**, type **Macintosh**, press **[Tab]**, click **Insert** on the menu bar, point to **Form**, click **Check Box**, type **Windows**, press **[Tab]**, click **Insert** on the menu bar, point to **Form**, click **Check Box**, then type **UNIX**

   The text and the three check box fields are entered into the form, as shown in Figure G-15.

4. Right-click the **Macintosh check box**, click **Form Field Properties**, type **OS** in the Group Name text box, then type **Macintosh** in the Value text box

   Compare your Check Box Properties dialog box with Figure G-16.

5. Click **OK**, double-click the **Windows check box**, type **OS** in the Group Name text box, type **Windows** in the Value text box, click **OK**, double-click the **UNIX check box**, type **OS** in the Group Name text box, type **UNIX** in the Value text box, then click **OK**

   The Macintosh, Windows, and UNIX check boxes have been assigned to the check box group named OS.

6. Click immediately after the text **UNIX**, press **[Enter]**, type **What type(s) of computers interest you?**, press **[Enter]**, click **Insert** on the menu bar, point to **Form**, click **Check Box**, type **Portables**, press **[Tab]**, click **Insert** on the menu bar, point to **Form**, click **Check Box**, then type **Desktops**

   The text and two computer type check boxes have been added to the form.

7. Double-click the **Portables check box**, type **CompType** in the Group Name text box, type **Portables** in the Value text box, click **OK**, double-click the **Desktops check box**, type **CompType** in the Group Name text box, type **Desktops** in the Value text box, click **OK**, deselect the check box, then click the **Save button** 🖫 on the Standard toolbar

   The Portables and Desktops check boxes are added to the CompType check box group. The changes to the catalog order form are saved. Compare your catalog order form with Figure G-17.

FIGURE G-15: Catalog order form with Macintosh, Windows, and UNIX check boxes

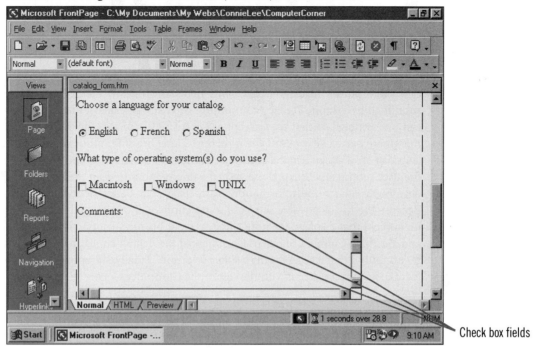

Check box fields

FIGURE G-16: Check Box Properties dialog box

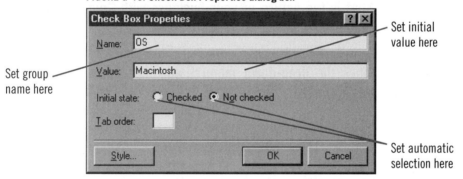

Set group
name here

Set initial
value here

Set automatic
selection here

FIGURE G-17: Catalog order form with CompType check boxes

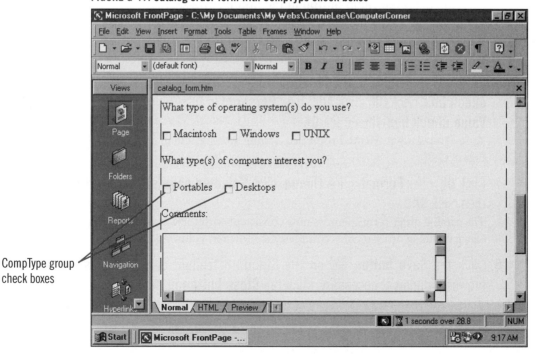

CompType group
check boxes

Unit G

FrontPage 2000

Inserting a Drop-Down Menu

Like radio button fields and check box fields, drop-down menu fields let you control the data submitted by visitors. Unlike radio button or check box fields, however, drop-down menu fields can be restricted so that they accept either a single selection or multiple selections. Drop-down menus are particularly useful when there is a long list of items, or when a list is to be updated at a later date. You assign a name and value to each choice added to the drop-down menu field. When the user submits the form, the assigned value is submitted for each choice. ➤ Connie Lee decides to elicit some information from users that better defines their business transactions. Because the list of possible business transactions will be updated later, she creates a drop-down menu field that displays, for now, three types of business transactions: Commercial, Educational, and Personal. Connie Lee makes Commercial the default choice, and she restricts the drop-down menu field so that it accepts only a single selection. Finally, she applies the Expedition theme to the form to keep it consistent with the rest of the Computer Corner Web.

Steps

1. **Click immediately after the text Desktops, then press [Enter]**
   A blank line is inserted between the CompType check box group and the Comments scrolling text box.

2. **Type What is the nature of your business with Computer Corner?, press [Enter], click Insert on the menu bar, point to Form, then click Drop-Down Menu**
   A drop-down menu field is inserted into the form.

3. **Right-click the drop-down menu field, click Form Field Properties, then type Business in the Name text box**
   Compare your Drop-Down Menu Properties dialog box with Figure G-18.

4. **Click Add**
   The Add Choice dialog box opens.

5. **Type Commercial in the Choice text box, click the Specify Value check box, then click the Selected radio button in the Initial state section**
   Compare your Add Choice dialog box with Figure G-19. The commercial choice is set to Selected so that the drop-down menu will automatically display the first choice in the list of possible business transaction types.

QuickTip

Click Move Up and Move Down to change the position of the highlighted choice in the dialog box.

6. **Click OK, click Add, type Educational in the Choice text box, click the Specify Value check box, click OK, click Add, type Personal in the Choice text box, click the Specify Value check box, then click OK**
   Your Drop-Down Menu Properties dialog box should match the dialog box shown in Figure G-20.

7. **Click OK, click Format, click Theme, click Selected page(s), click (Default) Expedition, then click OK**
   The catalog order form theme is now consistent with the rest of the Web site. The Computer Corner catalog order form is complete, as shown in Figure G-21.

8. **Click the Save button 🖫 on the Standard toolbar, click the Close button in the browser window if necessary, click the Close button in the FrontPage 2000 window**

FIGURE G-18: Drop-Down Menu Properties dialog box

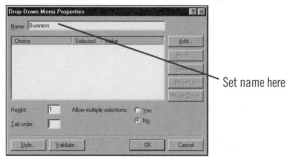

Set name here

FIGURE G-19: Add Choice dialog box

Set menu list
item name here

Commercial

Specifies list
name as value

Set automatic
selection here

FIGURE G-20: Completed Drop-Down Menu Properties dialog box

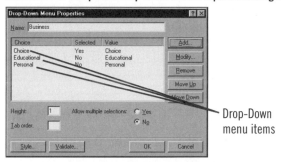

Drop-Down
menu items

FIGURE G-21: Completed Computer Corner catalog order form

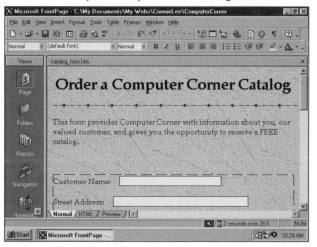

Viewing the results file

If you are working from a Web server, the results of all submissions from the Computer Corner catalog order form will be saved in two files in the root folder of the Web: catalog_form_results.htm and catalog_results.txt. The text file is formatted as a text database, with the fields separated by commas. The catalog_form_results.htm file can be viewed in any Web browser. The catalog_results.txt file can be read in any program that can read a text file, such as Notepad or Word, or can be imported into a spreadsheet or database program, such as Excel or Access.

Practice

► Concepts Review

Name each type of form field shown in Figure G-22.

FIGURE G-22

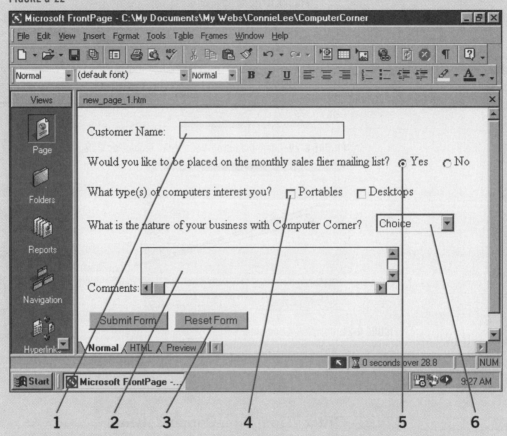

Match each of the terms with the correct description.

7. Form Field Properties dialog box   a. Allows users to submit data

8. Scrolling text box   b. General name for a method to collect data from an HTML form

9. Push button   c. Actual data sent to the Web server when the form is submitted

10. HTML form field   d. Place for form field settings, such as group name and initial value

11. Form field value   e. Lets form users enter multiple lines of text

Select the best answer from the list of choices.

12. **Which grouped HTML form field limits users to a single choice?**
    a. Check box
    b. Drop-down menu
    c. One-line text box
    d. Radio button

13. **FrontPage 2000 provides methods to record the results of a form in a(n)**
    a. E-mail message.
    b. Text file.
    c. HTML file.
    d. All of the above

14. **You can create an HTML form by answering the questions presented in dialog boxes by the FrontPage**
    a. Template.
    b. Form field.
    c. Form Page Wizard.
    d. Radio button.

15. **Which HTML form field allows you to either limit users to a single selection or allow users to make multiple selections?**
    a. Check box
    b. Drop-down menu
    c. One-line text box
    d. Radio button

16. **To work properly, a FrontPage HTML form must interact with**
    a. A radio button.
    b. A Web server.
    c. A text file.
    d. A dialog box.

17. **Which grouped HTML form field allows for only multiple selections?**
    a. Check box
    b. Drop-down menu
    c. One-line text box
    d. Radio button

18. **Which HTML form field allows users to enter unlimited amounts of information?**
    a. Scrolling text box
    b. Drop-down menu
    c. One-line text box
    d. Radio button

19. **A comma-delimited text file can be imported into which of the following types of application(s)?**
    a. Spreadsheet
    b. Database
    c. Both a and b
    d. None of the above

20. **Which dialog box allows you to associate a value with a user response?**
    a. Page Properties
    b. Form Properties
    c. Form Field Properties
    d. Form Validation

 # Skills Review

1. **Create a new HTML form.**
    a. Start FrontPage 2000 and create a new one-page Web named *Bookstore*.
    b. In Page View, click File, click New, then click Page.
    c. Click Form Page Wizard, then click OK.
    d. Click Next, then click Next.
    e. Present the questions in paragraph form, then click Next.
    f. Save the results to a file called *Books.txt*, then click Finish.

2. **Set form properties.**
    a. Highlight the placeholder title text, then type **Book Preferences**.
    b. Enter an explanation of the form's purpose: "This form will help us get to know you and your reading preferences so that we may better serve you."
    c. Right-click anywhere in the form area, then click Form Properties.
    d. Click Options, click the File Results tab (if necessary), then choose a file format for the results file from the drop-down list.
    e. Save the new Web page as *Books.htm*.

3. **Add text boxes.**
    a. Click before the Submit Form button and press [Enter], then type **Name:** on the top line of the form.
    b. Press [Tab], click Insert, point to Form, then click One-Line Text Box.
    c. Press [Enter], then type **E-mail address:**.
    d. Press [Tab], click Insert, point to Form, then click One-Line Text Box.
    e. Press [Enter], then type **About me:**.
    f. Press [Enter], click Insert, point to Form, then click Scrolling Text Box.
    g. Save the file.

4. **Set form field properties.**
    a. Right-click the "Name" one-line text box field, then click Form Field Properties.
    b. Type **Name** in the Name text box.
    c. Type **40** in the Width in characters text box.
    d. Select the E-mail text box and open the Form Field Properties dialog box. Use Email as the name and 25 as the width. (*Hint*: Do not use the hyphen in e-mail, as it is an invalid character.)

e. Double-click the Scrolling Text Box field.

f. Type **Feedback** in the Name text box.

g. Type **50** in the Width in characters text box.

h. Set the number of lines to 6.

i. Save your work.

5. Insert radio buttons.

a. Click before "About me:" and press [Enter].

b. Type **Do you enjoy reading?** at the beginning of the new line, then press [Enter].

c. Insert a Radio Button button.

d. Type **Yes**.

e. Press [Tab], then insert a Radio Button button.

f. Type **No**.

g. Double-click the Yes radio button and set the group name to **Enjoy** and the value to **Yes**.

h. Double-click the No radio button and set the group name to **Enjoy** and the value to **No**.

i. Save your work.

6. Add check boxes.

a. Click after the word "No" and press [Enter].

b. Type **Check the book genres you enjoy:**.

c. Press [Enter], insert a Check Box button, then type **Mystery**.

d. Add check boxes for Romance, Classics, and Contemporary.

e. Include all check boxes in the "Genre" group and set the value for each check box so that it coincides with the text label.

f. Save your work.

7. Insert a drop-down menu.

a. Click after "Contemporary" and press [Enter].

b. Type **Select your price range:**.

c. Press [Enter], then insert a Drop-Down Menu button.

d. Set the field name to **Price** in the Drop-Down Menu Properties dialog box.

e. Click the Add button, add the choice **Under $5**, then click Specify Value and set its initial state to Selected.

f. Click the Add button, add the choice **Under $10**, then click Specify Value.

g. Click the Add button, then add the choice **Under $15**, then click Specify Value.

h. Save your work.

i. Preview and print the form in your Web browser.

▶ Independent Challenges

1. You are the chief developer for LaraSoft Software Consultants. LaraSoft has just completed a beta version of a new WBT (Web-based Training) courseware management system. Beta versions of software programs are test versions. The beta version is the last version tested before the program is officially released to the public. The company is offering free downloads of the trial software. The only requirement for users is that they complete a registration form. Your task is to build an HTML registration form that includes the following items:

- Name
- City and State
- E-mail Address
- Operating System
- Type of Business

To complete this independent challenge:

a. Create a one-page Web named *BetaV*.
b. Create a form named *BetaV*, using the Form Page Wizard.
c. Type in text to describe the purpose of the form.
d. Create text box fields to hold the visitor's name and address data.
e. Create a drop-down menu field in which the user can select an operating system.
f. Create a radio button group to allow the user to indicate a type of business.
g. Save, preview, and print the form, then close the Web.

2. You are enrolled in an introductory computer course at your university. The instructor has assigned a brief research paper to be completed by the end of the term. As part of the project, you decide to conduct Web-based research to discover the types of computers and software your fellow students are using at home, and to determine what Internet service providers they use. Create a form for this research survey, which should seek answers to the following questions. Choose the most appropriate form field for each question.

- What type of computer do you own?
- What operating system do you use?
- Select the types of software programs you use most:
  - Database
  - Spreadsheet
  - Word processing
  - Enter software of choice
- What Internet service provider do you use?
- How long (in months) have you used the World Wide Web?
- How many hours per week do you spend surfing the Web?

To complete this independent challenge:

a. Create an empty Web named *Wresearch*.
b. Create a form using the Form Page Wizard and name it *Wresearch*.
c. Add introductory text to the form explaining its purpose.
d. Add the questions using the form fields you deem most appropriate.
e. Save, preview, and print the form, then close the Web.

3. You are the toys buyer for Kimto for Kids. Your job is to find the latest and greatest toys on the market, as well as to predict future customer buying trends. To gain insight into the current buying patterns of Kimto customers, you decide to create an HTML form that will indicate the types of products customers are buying.
To complete this independent challenge:

Create a one-page Web and an HTML form named Kimto that accomplishes the following tasks. Use your form-building skills to select the form field types best suited to the types of information to be collected by the form.

a. Gather the following demographic information for each customer:

- Name
- Address
- Phone Number

b. Ask how many toys the customer has purchased in the last year.
c. Provide a drop-down menu to determine what types of toys the customer bought in the last year.
d. Pose the following questions:

- What are the ages of your children?
- How much money did you spend on toys last year?
- How much money did you spend on Kimto toys?
- Will you have more money to spend on toys next year?
- Will you buy toys from Kimto again?

4. You are the Webmaster for the Brothers Group, a start-up software company. The president has asked you to survey visitors to its Web site to determine if they are satisfied with the home page and the information found there. You decide to see how a larger company, such as Microsoft, handles its home page and elicits visitor responses.
To complete this independent challenge:

a. Log on to the Internet and use your favorite browser.
b. Use a search engine to locate Microsoft's home page.
c. Explore the site and find the link that allows you to contact Microsoft.
d. Click Tell how www.microsoft.com can serve me better.
e. Fill out the form.
f. Print a hard copy of the form and identify form field types.
g. Click Cancel.
h. If you have trouble finding the home page, go to http://www.course.com. From there, click the Student Online Companion for this book, then click the link for Unit G.

▶ Visual Workshop

Create a Web page containing an HTML form similar to the Guest Notes page depicted in Figure G-23. Save the file as *guest.htm*, print the form, then close the Web and FrontPage.

FIGURE G-23

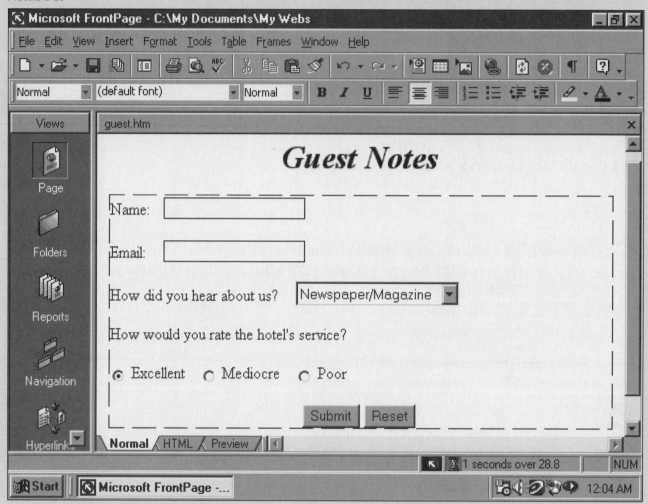

Unit
H

Enhancing
and Maintaining a Web Site

Objectives

MOUS ► **Insert a FrontPage component**

MOUS ► **Add a search form**

MOUS ► **Add content listings**

MOUS ► **Insert hover buttons**

► **Insert a banner ad manager**

MOUS ► **View and verify hyperlinks**

MOUS ► **Work with Reports View**

MOUS ► **Publish a Web site**

As a Web designer, you need to remember that Web sites are to be used by people. Great Web sites provide information quickly and easily in an aesthetically rich and pleasing environment. FrontPage 2000 provides many features that will help you to add richness to a Web site, such as search forms, hover buttons, banner ads, counters, and marquees, even if you have little or no programming knowledge. Browsing a site that is error-free also enriches the user experience, and FrontPage provides a host of additional features that make site maintenance easier by allowing you to produce reports to check the download speed of pages, and verify hyperlinks. ▰▬ In this unit, Connie Lee will add a variety of features that will make a visit to the Computer Corner Web site more enjoyable and friendlier for users. She will also review the site for errors and broken links before actually publishing the Computer Corner Web.

Inserting a FrontPage Component

Before tools like FrontPage 2000 were created, including exciting, interactive features in a Web site required extensive programming knowledge. For example, including a simple **hit counter**, to keep a tally of all visits to the Web page, required the Web designer to work in computer languages more complex than simple HTML. Today, FrontPage 2000 lets you add additional interactive elements through **FrontPage components**. FrontPage components are small software applications packaged for your convenience. Each component is programmed to perform a certain task and is an integral part of the FrontPage system. ✍ In order to keep track of the number of visitors to the Computer Corner Web site, Connie Lee decides to add a hit counter component to the Computer Corner home page. As a special effect, she also decides to add a welcome message for visitors, using the FrontPage **Marquee component**. Some components require interaction with a Web server to work properly. Consequently, Connie Lee will not be able to preview the hit counter until she actually publishes the Computer Corner Web.

Steps 1 2 3 4

1. Start **Microsoft FrontPage**, click **File**, then click **Open Web**
   The Open Web dialog box appears.

QuickTip

The Computer Corner Web can be saved to several alternate locations, such as a hard drive, a network drive, or an external media. Due to the size of the completed Web, it is not recommended that it be saved to floppy disk. If you have saved the Computer Corner Web in a different location, enter the path or browse to locate the Web.

2. Click the [*insert your name here*] folder, if necessary, click the **ComputerCorner Web**, then click **Open**
   The Computer Corner Web opens in the FrontPage window.

3. Click the **Folder List button** 📧 on the Standard toolbar to open the Folder List window, then double-click **index.htm**
   The Computer Corner home page opens in Page View.

4. Click 📧 to close the Folder List window, scroll to the bottom of the page, under Electronic Mail click immediately after the line **Webmaster: samantha@computercorner.com**, press **[Enter]**, press **[Enter]**, then type **You are visitor number:**
   The text is added to the bottom of the page area on the Computer Corner home page, as shown in Figure H-1.

5. Click **Insert** on the menu bar, point to **Component**, then click **Hit Counter**
   The Hit Counter Properties dialog box opens, as shown in Figure H-1.

6. Click the **third radio button**, click the **Fixed number of digits check box**, type **4** in the text box, then click **OK**
   FrontPage inserts a text place holder, [Hit Counter], where the actual customized hit counter component will be added to the Computer Corner home page upon Web site publication.

7. Scroll back to the top of the page, select the text **Computer Corner provides the highest quality**, click the **Font Color list arrow** ▲, select the color **White** under Standard Colors, click the **Insert Component button** 📧 on the Standard toolbar, then click **Marquee**
   The Marquee Properties dialog box opens, as shown in Figure H-2. The highlighted text has automatically been placed into the Text text box.

8. Click the **Width check box**, type **300** in the Width text box, click **In pixels**, click the **Background color list arrow**, select the color **Olive** (fifth color from left under Standard colors), click **OK**, then click the **Preview tab**
   The Marquee component has been added to the Computer Corner home page. Note that the text and background color have been changed, as shown in Figure H-3.

9. Click the **Save button** 📧 on the Standard toolbar, click **File** on the menu bar, then click **Close**
   The Computer Corner home page is closed.

FIGURE H-1: **Hit Counter text and properties dialog box**

Folder List button

Enter text here

Set style here

Insert Component button

Set number of digits here

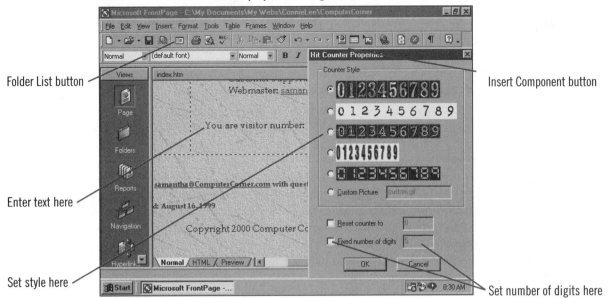

FIGURE H-2: **Marquee Properties dialog box**

Highlighted text
entered automatically

Set width here

Set background
color here

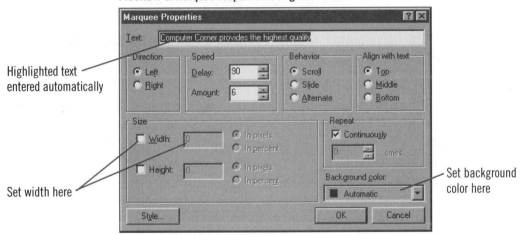

FIGURE H-3: **Marquee preview**

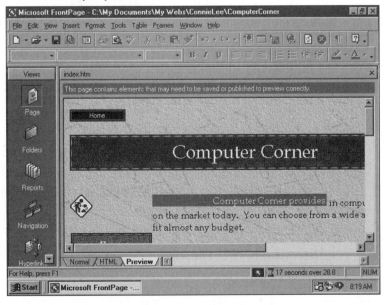

Adding a Search Form

FrontPage 2000 components not only let the Web designer add bells and whistles to a Web site, they also allow the designer to build in features that make the Web site ultimately more user-friendly. Including search forms is an excellent way to improve the usability for visitors. Visitors can use a search form to find information more quickly than by clicking through a series of Web pages. FrontPage search forms can be added in two ways. The New Page template provides for the inclusion of a separate **search page**, which can be linked to other pages within the Web and needs no further customization. The Insert Component feature provides for the inclusion of a **Search Form** on any page that is already a part of the Web. Both techniques allow visitors to perform a text search of every page in the Web by supplying a combination of keywords. Connie Lee decides to employ both search methods. She will create a separate search page that will be linked automatically to the other pages of the Computer Corner Web. She will also include a second search form on the Computer Corner products page that will allow visitors to search from that page without having to take time to click to access the separate search page.

Steps 1 2 3 4

1. Click **File** on the menu bar, point to **New**, click **Page**, click **Search Page**, click **OK**
   A search page appears in Page View.

2. Click the **Save button** 🖫 on the Standard toolbar, type **searchpage** in the Filename text box, then click **Save**
   The separate search page is saved as searchpage.htm in the Computer Corner Web.

3. Click the **Navigation button** 🖀 on the Views bar, drag the file **searchpage.htm** to a point directly below the home page in the navigation pane, right-click the page just added, click **Rename**, type **Search Page**, press **[Enter]**, click the **Page button** 📄, then scroll down the page
   A Search Page banner has been added to the page. Note that a button for the search page has been added to the left shared border and will be automatically added to the other pages containing a left shared border within the Computer Corner Web, as shown in Figure H-4.

4. Click 🖫, read the page, click **File** on the menu bar, then click **Close**
   The Computer Corner search page closes.

5. Click 🖽 to open the Folder List window, then double-click **products.htm**
   The Computer Corner products page opens in Page View.

6. Click the **Folder List button** 🖽 on the Standard toolbar to close the Folder List window, click **the comment**, press **[Delete]**, click the **Insert Component button** 🖾 on the Standard toolbar, then click **Search Form**
   The Search Form Properties dialog box opens, as shown in Figure H-5.

7. Click the **Search Form Properties tab** (if necessary), type **Search for Computer Corner Products** in the Label for Input text box, click the **Search Results tab**, click the **Display score (closeness of match) check box**, click the **Display file date check box**, click **OK**, then click the **Preview tab**
   A search form appears on the products page, as shown in Figure H-6.

8. Click the **Normal tab**, click **File**, click **Close**, then click **Yes**
   The customized products page closes.

FIGURE H-4: Computer Corner search page

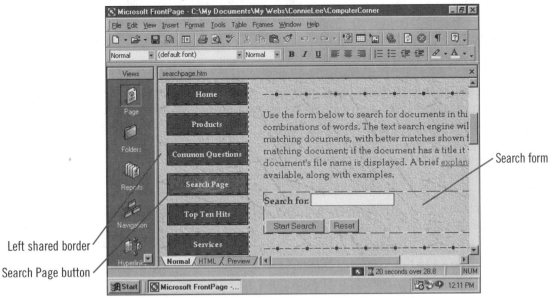

Left shared border

Search Page button

Search form

FIGURE H-5: Search Form Properties dialog box

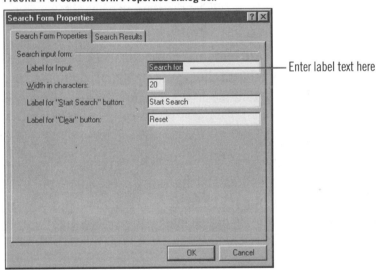

Enter label text here

FIGURE H-6: Computer Corner customized products page

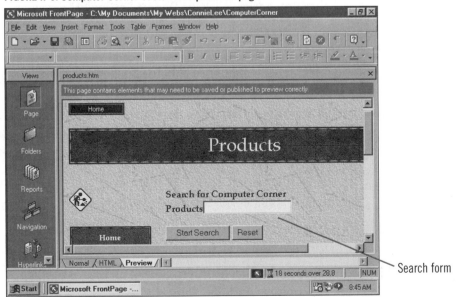

Search form

Adding Content Listings

FrontPage 2000

Adding table of content listings in the form of hyperlinks makes a Web site easier for visitors to use. FrontPage 2000 provides two methods that make it easy for the Web designer to create navigational hyperlinks. FrontPage allows the designer to create a separate global **Table of Contents** page, or to develop **Categories** and list pages independently of the global table of contents. The Table of Contents feature will automatically list the title of every page within the site as a hyperlink on a separate page. The Categories feature will list the title of every page within a defined category and the list of titles can be inserted on any individual page chosen by the designer. Connie Lee decides to add a global listing of content for the Computer Corner Web site, using the Table of Contents feature.

1. Click the **Page button** 🗋, click **File** on the menu bar, point to **New**, click **Page**, scroll to and click **Table of Contents**, then click **OK**

2. Scroll to and double-click <u>Table of Contents Heading Page</u>, type **index.htm** (if necessary) in the Page URL for the starting point of table area, click the **Heading font size list arrow**, click **2**, then click **OK**

3. Click the **Save button** 🖫, type **toc**, click **Save**, right-click in the document window, click **Page Properties**, type **Table of Contents**, click **OK**, click the **Preview in Browser button** 🔍 on the Standard toolbar, then click **Yes**
   Scroll down to see the table of contents page in Internet Explorer with the updated listings for all other pages within the Computer Corner Web, as shown in Figure H-7.

4. Click **Microsoft FrontPage** on the taskbar, click **File**, then click **Close**

5. Click the **Folder List button** 🗐 to open the Folder List window, double-click **products.htm** in the Folder List window, click 🗐 to close the Folder List window, then click immediately below the search form and before Name of product 1
   The Computer Corner Products page opens in Page View. The insertion point is immediately below the search form.

> **QuickTip**
> The Reporting toolbar may be docked under the Formatting toolbar.

6. Click the **Reports button** 🗐, click the **Report list arrow** on the Reporting toolbar, scroll to and click **Categories**, click the **Report Setting list arrow**, then click **(all categories)**
   All categories are listed for the Computer Corner Web, as shown in Figure H-8.

> **Trouble?**
> If the Reporting toolbar is not visible, click View, point to Toolbars, then click Reporting.

7. Click **prod01.htm**, hold down the **[Shift]** key, click **products.htm**, right-click on the three selected files (prod01.htm, prod02.htm, and products.htm), then click **Properties**
   The File Properties dialog box appears, as shown in Figure H-9.

8. Click the **Workgroup tab**, click **Categories**, type **Products** in the New category text box, click **Add**, click **OK**, scroll to and click the **Products check box** in the Available categories area, click **OK**, click the **Report Setting list arrow**, then click **Products**

9. Click 🗋, click the **Insert Component button** 🗐, click **Categories**, scroll to and click the **Products check box** in the Choose categories to list files by area, then click **OK**

10. Click 🔍 on the Standard toolbar, click **Yes**, then click **OK**
    The updated listing of pages within the Products category shown in Figure H-10.

11. Test the links, click **Microsoft FrontPage** on the taskbar, click **File**, then click **Close**

FIGURE H-7: Computer Corner Table of Contents page

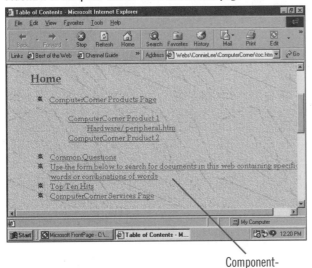

Component-
generated
Table of
Contents

FIGURE H-8: Categories report for Computer Corner Web

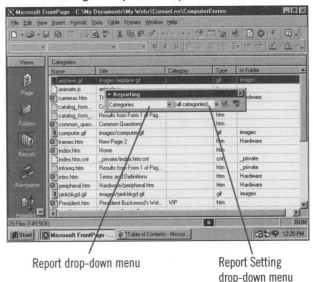

Report drop-down menu

Report Setting
drop-down menu

FIGURE H-9: File Properties dialog box

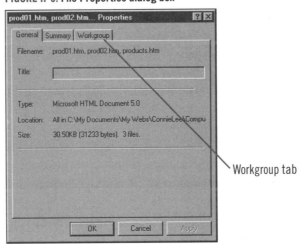

Workgroup tab

FIGURE H-10: Products page with Categories component

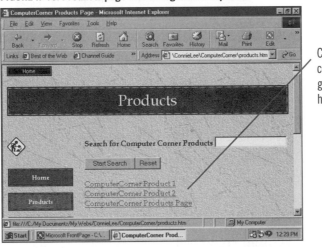

Categories
component-
generated
hyperlinks

Inserting Hover Buttons

A **hover button** is highlighted when a mouse moves over it, indicating to users that it will be the active button if it is clicked. **Hover buttons** are one of the more popular FrontPage components. FrontPage 2000 uses several methods to enable its active components: native FrontPage components, HTML forms, and **Java applets.** Hover buttons are actually Java applets that run through a Web browser. Java applets are self-contained software applications written in the Java programming language. Connie Lee will modify the Services page that was included when the wizard created the Computer Corner Web. She will remove the left border on only the Services page, and replace the built-in navigational buttons with customized hover buttons.

Steps

1. Click the **Folder List button** 🔲 on the Standard toolbar to open the Folder List window, double-click **services.htm** in the Folder List window, click 🔲 to close the Folder List window, right-click anywhere on the Services page, click **Shared Borders**, click the **Current page radio button**, click the **Left check box** to deselect it, click **OK**
The Services page appears without a left shared border.

2. Click on the comment, press **[Delete]**, click the **Insert Component button** 🔳 on the Standard toolbar, then click **Hover Button**
The Hover Button Properties dialog box appears, as shown in Figure H-11.

3. Type **Multimedia** in the Button text text box, click **Browse**, scroll to and click **serv01.htm**, click **OK**, click the **Button color list arrow**, click **Olive**, click the **Effect list arrow**, click **Bevel out**, click the **Effect color list arrow**, click **Yellow**, then click **OK**
The Multimedia hover button component is inserted into the Services page, as shown in Figure H-12.

QuickTip
You can insert the links at any time to the hover buttons.

4. Press **[Enter]**, click 🔳, click **Hover Button**, type **Repairs** in the Button text text box, click the **Button color list arrow**, click **Olive**, click the **Effect list arrow**, click **Bevel out**, click the **Effect color list arrow**, click **Yellow**, then click **OK**
The Repairs hover button is added to the Services page.

5. Press **[Enter]**, click 🔳, click **Hover Button**, type **Customers** in the Button text text box, click the **Button color list arrow** for Button color, click **Olive**, click the **Effect list arrow**, click **Bevel out**, click the **Effect color list arrow**, click **Yellow**, then click **OK**
The Customers hover button is added to the Services page.

6. Press **[Enter]**, click 🔳, click **Hover Button**, type **Home** in the Button text text box, click the **Browse button**, click **index.htm**, click **OK**, click the **Button color list arrow**, click **Olive**, click the **Effect list arrow**, click **Bevel out**, click the **Effect color list arrow**, click **Yellow**, then click **OK**

7. Click the **Save button** 🔲 on the Standard toolbar, click the **Preview in Browser button** 🔲 on the Standard toolbar, then move your mouse over the hover buttons
The Services page appears in Internet Explorer, as shown in Figure H-13.

8. Click the **Home hover button** on the Services page, then click the **Services button** on the home page
Navigational links are provided for both pages so that visitors can quickly and easily move among the pages.

9. Click **Microsoft FrontPage** on the taskbar, click **File** on the menu bar, then click **Close**
The Services page closes.

FIGURE H-11: Hover Button Properties dialog box

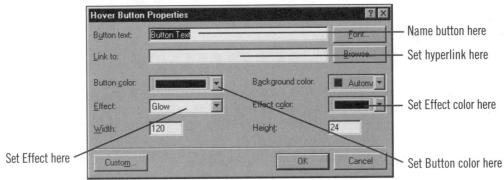

Set Effect here

Name button here
Set hyperlink here
Set Effect color here
Set Button color here

FIGURE H-12: Multimedia hover button

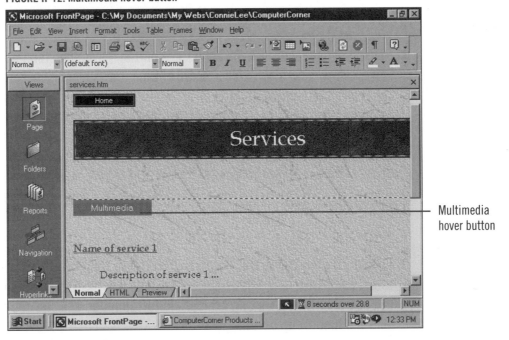

Multimedia
hover button

FIGURE H-13: Customized Services page

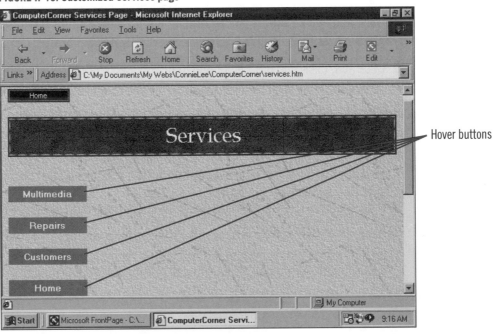

Hover buttons

FrontPage 2000

Inserting a Banner Ad Manager

Banner ad managers offer a convenient means of providing exposure for several advertisers on your site simultaneously. The advertisement switches from the banner of one company to the next automatically, eliminating the need to change the banner by hand on a daily or monthly basis. The banner ad manager can also be used to rotate images on a page, giving visitors a virtual slide show. ✒ Using a banner ad manager, Connie Lee decides to enhance the Services page by providing visitors with a slide show and link to the Multimedia page. She will use clip art from the Entertainment category for the slide show.

Steps 1234

1. Return to FrontPage, click the **Folder List button** 🔲 on the Standard toolbar to open the Folder List window, double-click **serv01.htm** in the Folder List window, click 🔲 to close the Folder List window, right-click anywhere on the page, click **Page Properties**, type **Multimedia** in the Title text box, click **OK**, double-click the **Page Banner**, type **Multimedia** in the Page banner text text box, click **OK**, select the text **This is a brief description of the service ...**, then press **[Delete]**
   The cursor is positioned at the top left of the text area, as shown in Figure H-14.

2. Press **[Enter]**, press **[Tab]**, click the **Insert Component button** 🔲 on the Standard toolbar, then click **Banner Ad Manager**
   The Banner Ad Manager Properties dialog box appears.

3. Type **200** in the Width text box, type **200** in the Height text box, click the **Transition effect list arrow**, click **Blinds Horizontal**, type **3** in the Show each picture for (seconds) text box, click **Add**, click **Clip Art**, click **Entertainment**, select a clip of your choice, then click the **Insert clip button** 🔲
   A reference to the clip art file is entered into the Pictures to display text box, as shown in Figure H-15.

4. Click **Add**, click **Clip Art**, click **Entertainment**, select a clip of your choice, then click 🔲
   A second reference is added to the Pictures to display text box.

5. Click **Add**, click **Clip Art**, click **Entertainment**, select a clip of your choice, then click 🔲
   A third reference is added to the Pictures to display text box.

6. Click **OK**, then click the **Save button** 🔲 on the Standard toolbar
   The Multimedia page is presented in normal mode with the first of the images displayed, and the Save Embedded Files dialog box opens.

7. Click **OK**, click the **Preview in Browser button** 🔲 on the Standard toolbar, then click **OK**
   The Multimedia page opens in Internet Explorer, as shown in Figure H-16. Note how the banner ad manager displays one image after another using the Horizontal Blinds transition.

8. Click the **Close button** in Internet Explorer, click **Microsoft FrontPage** (if necessary) on the taskbar, click **File** on the menu bar, then click **Close**
   Internet Explorer and the Multimedia page are closed.

FIGURE H-14: Insertion point for banner ad manager

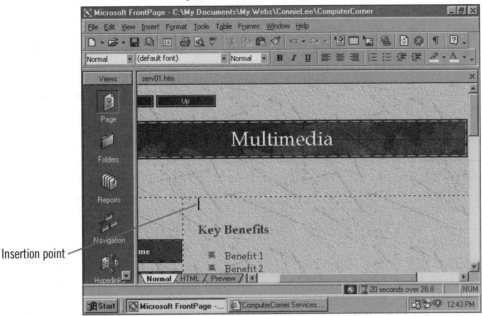

Insertion point

FIGURE H-15: Banner Ad Manager Properties dialog box with file reference

Set Width here

Set Height here

Set Transition effect here

Set time here

Click here to add image

File reference to first image

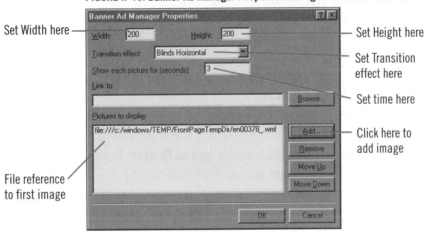

FIGURE H-16: Banner Ad Manager slide show

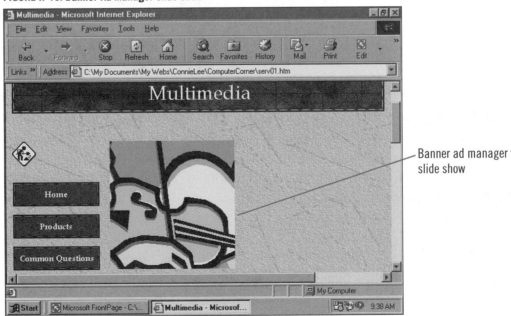

Banner ad manager slide show

Viewing and Verifying Hyperlinks

The World Wide Web is a dynamic environment. Web designers can add and modify the site frequently and easily, which makes the Web an exciting place to visit. Unfortunately, because Web developers modify sites often, sites are in constant flux. The Web sites you link to will change or move at a moment's notice, making the maintenance of your hyperlinks crucial to the usability of your Web site. Users will have a much more pleasant experience if everything in your Web works correctly. FrontPage 2000 provides several maintenance tools that help keep your sight error-free. Hyperlinks View and Report View combine to make the task of checking and maintaining your hyperlinks easier. ✐ Connie Lee will use Hyperlinks View to view the hyperlinks contained within the Computer Corner Web. She will then use the Recalculate Hyperlinks tool to fix any broken links that are local (*internal*) to the Web. Connie Lee will then check the status of any remote (*external*) hyperlinks through Report View.

Steps 1 2 3 4

1. Click the **Hyperlinks button** 📑 on the Standard toolbar, click on **index.htm**, then click the **Folder List button** 📼 on the Standard toolbar to close the Folder List window

Hyperlinks View presents a graphical representation of all the hyperlinks connected to the Computer Corner home page, as shown in Figure H-17. Note that all hyperlinks connected to the home page are local or internal links to another page within the Computer Corner site.

2. Right-click **President.htm**, then click Move to Center

The file that moves to center becomes the focal point for Hyperlinks View. All hyperlinks connected to the President's page are presented in the Hyperlinks View window. Note that of the hyperlinks linked to the President's page, one is a remote or external hyperlink.

3. Right-click **travel.htm**, click **Move to Center**

Note that the view graphically represents the travel page as a child of the President's page, containing three external hyperlinks, as shown in Figure H-18.

4. Click 📼, click **index.htm**, then click and drag the hyperlink in the Hyperlinks View window

The mouse cursor turns into a hand, allowing you to move the hyperlinks displayed in the window while still keeping the Folder List displayed.

5. Click **Tools** on the menu bar, click **Recalculate Hyperlinks**, then click **Yes**

The Recalculate Hyperlinks tool performs several functions that include: repairing all the internal hyperlinks in the Web, updating the shared borders and navigation bars, and synchronizing data and categories. The process may take a few minutes.

> **Trouble?**
> If the Reporting toolbar is not visible, click View, point to Toolbars, then click Reporting.

6. Click the **Reports button** 📑, click the **Report list arrow** on the Reporting toolbar, then click **Broken Hyperlinks**

A report is provided that lists all of the broken internal and external hyperlinks for the Computer Corner Web, as shown in Figure H-19.

> **Trouble?**
> If you are working without an Internet connection, all hyperlinks will be shown as broken. If you are working online, you may not have any broken hyperlinks.

7. Double-click a broken hyperlink

The Edit Hyperlink dialog box appears. Note that you can edit the hyperlink, and it will change on all the pages selected. The hyperlinks listed here will not be broken after publication, therefore, canceling out is the logical choice.

8. Click **Cancel**

Reports View once again presents the Broken Hyperlinks report.

FIGURE H-17: Hyperlinks View from Computer Corner home page

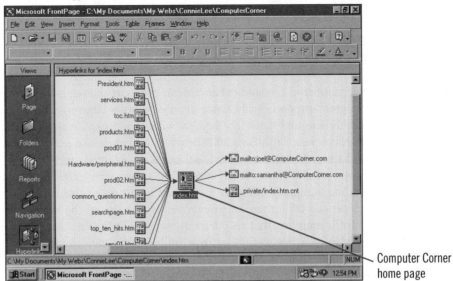

Computer Corner
home page

FIGURE H-18: Hyperlinks View from Travel page

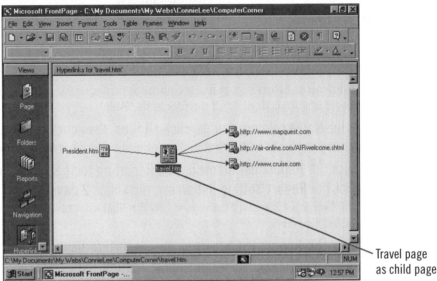

Travel page
as child page

FIGURE H-19: Broken Hyperlinks report

List of broken
hyperlinks

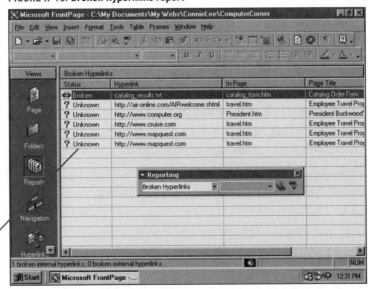

Working with Reports View

As the number of files and enhancements grows in an ever-expanding Web site, the possibility for errors grows proportionally. Once the site becomes large enough, checking to see that every page within the site, and that every element within each page, is working properly becomes a full-time and tedious task. FrontPage 2000 provides tools to make site maintenance easier. Reports View provides site information quickly and identifies potential problem areas. The Site Summary report gives an overview of the entire Web site and a quick view into individual reports. For example, listed in the Site Summary will be an individual report called Component Errors. At a glance, the Web developer can tell if there are any problems with any of the FrontPage components, such as a hit counter or marquee, that are currently included in the site. Additional individual reports provide detailed information about files, hyperlinks, assignments, etc. ◢━━━ Connie Lee will use Reports View as a precheck to publishing the Computer Corner Web. She will check the number of files contained in the site and check the download time for pages. She will see what has recently been added to the site and check the publish status for each new page. Connie Lee will also check to see which pages are assigned to the Products category.

1. **Click the Report list arrow on the Reporting toolbar, then click Site Summary**
   The Site Summary report appears in the Reports View window. Note that each individual report is listed in the left-hand column, as shown in Figure H-20. Note further that in the Component Errors report line a column is provided for a count of errors. The All files row provides a total count of all the files in the Web.

2. **In the Name column, double-click All files, then click the Title column**
   A complete list of all the files in the Computer Corner Web is shown alphabetically by title.

3. **Click the Report list arrow on the Reporting toolbar, click Recently Changed Files, click the Report Setting list arrow, then click 2 days**
   The Recently Changed Files report lists the filenames of all files that have been edited within the last two days.

4. **Click the Report list arrow on the Reporting toolbar, click Site Summary, double-click Slow Pages, click the Report Setting list arrow, click 30 seconds, click the Report Setting list arrow, click 10 seconds, click the Report Setting list arrow, then click 5 seconds**
   The Slow Pages report is presented three different times displaying the pages that take longer to download than the stipulated time. The number of files listed will increase as the amount of time is diminished. Figure H-21 shows a list of files for the Computer Corner Web that take more than 5 seconds to download to a user's browser.

5. **Click the Report list arrow on the Reporting toolbar, click Publish Status, select serv01.htm, click in the Publish column of the serv01.htm row, click the Publish list arrow, click Don't Publish, then click anywhere on the report to deselect the file**
   The publish status of the Multimedia page changes to Don't Publish.

6. **Click the Report list arrow on the Reporting toolbar, click Categories, click the Report Setting list arrow, then click Products**
   All the files assigned to the Products category are listed in the report.

7. **Click the Report list arrow on the Reporting toolbar, click Older Files, click the Report Setting list arrow, click 30 days**
   A list of the files contained in the Computer Corner Web that have not been modified in over 30 days appears, making the task of staying current easier.

FIGURE H-20: Reports View of Computer Corner Web

Count column

Names of individual reports

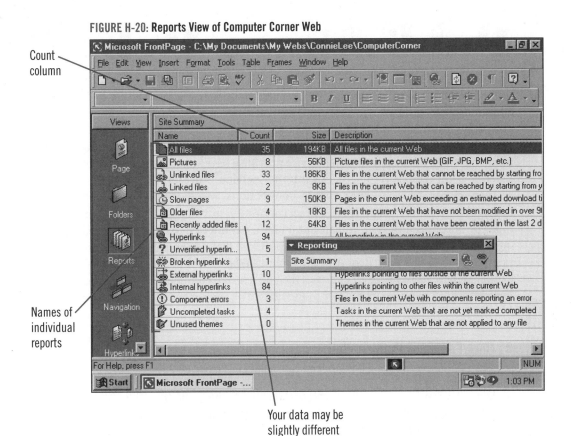

Your data may be slightly different

FIGURE H-21: Slow Pages report for 5 seconds

Download time

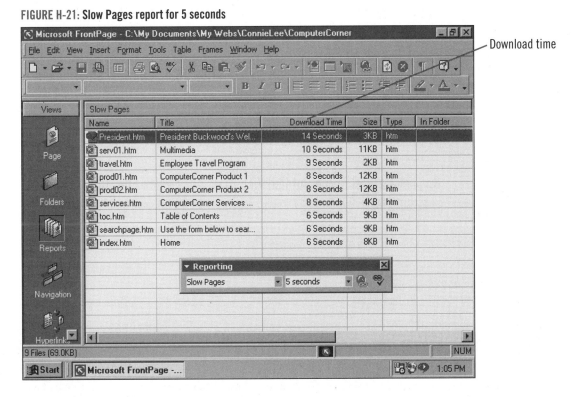

FrontPage 2000

Publishing a Web Site

FrontPage 2000 makes it easy to publish your Web pages to a remote server using Microsoft FrontPage Server Extensions. The **server extensions** must be installed on the remote server if all FrontPage features are to work properly. FrontPage allows you develop your Web pages on a local computer and then publish them to a remote server. You can use the publish feature whether you are connected to the remote server through a network connection or through a modem connection. Many Internet service providers have already installed the FrontPage Server Extensions for your convenience. An **Internet service provider (ISP)** supplies two basic types of Internet connection service: **direct connections** and **dial-up connections**. A school or business, for example, might lease a direct connection from an ISP. If your place of business has this type of connection, then you are automatically connected to the Internet each time you turn on your computer. For home use, you may purchase dial-up services from a variety of ISPs, such as Compuserve, AT&T, GTE, or America Online. ➤ Connie Lee will publish the Computer Corner Web to a remote server. She uses the Publish Web command to automatically transfer the Web pages from her local computer to the remote server.

Steps

1. **Click File, click Publish Web, then click Options**
   The Publish Web dialog box appears, as shown in Figure H-22.

2. **Click after http://, type *yourservername*/ComputerCorner, then click the Publish all pages, overwriting any already on the destination radio button**
   If you choose to publish, click Publish, and FrontPage 2000 will make the connection to the remote server. The remote server may ask for your username and password. When finished publishing, a Microsoft FrontPage dialog box appears.

3. **Click WPP's ...**
   Internet Explorer connects to the Microsoft Web Presence Providers Web site, as shown in Figure H-23.

4. **Scroll to and click Search by Location (U.S./Canada only), select your state, then click Go**
   A listing of Web Presence Providers located in your state is presented.

5. **Click the Close button in Internet Explorer**
   Internet Explorer closes.

6. **Click Cancel in the Publish Web dialog box, click File, then click Exit**
   FrontPage 2000 closes.

Setting server permissions

If you are creating your Web directly on a World Wide Web or Intranet server, you can set security properties so that only people to whom you give permission can browse, administer, or modify the Web. Browsing permission lets a user view the Web after it has been published. Authoring permission allows a user to create and edit the Web using Page View. Administering permission lets a user create new Webs and set permissions for others. To grant permissions, click Tools on the menu bar, click Permissions, then select the desired settings for groups and individual users.

FIGURE H-22: Publish Web dialog box

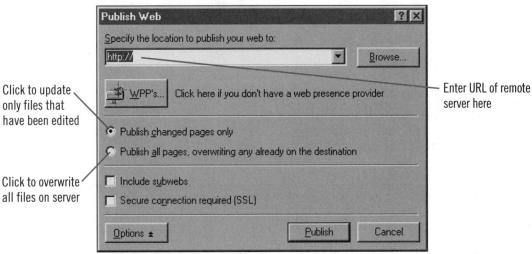

Click to update only files that have been edited

Click to overwrite all files on server

Enter URL of remote server here

FIGURE H-23: Microsoft Web Presence Providers for FrontPage Web site

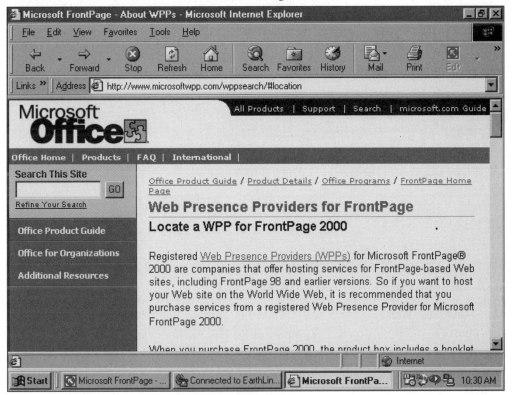

Practice

▶ Concepts Review

Describe each element of the component menu shown in Figure H-24.

FIGURE H-24

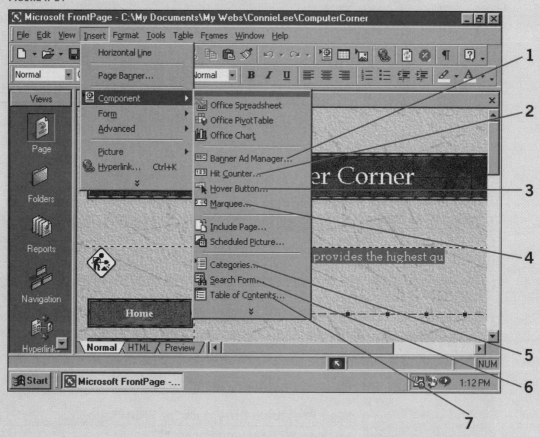

Match each of the terms with the correct description.

8. **Recently Changed Files report**   a. Provides file creation information.
9. **Slow Pages report**   b. Shows download information.
10. **All Files report**   c. Lists the titles of all pages in the Web site.
11. **Site Summary report**   d. Lists the names of all reports in the Web site.
12. **Old Files report**   e. Shows file update information.

Select the best answer from the list of choices.

13. **To use an ISP dial-up service, you need**
    a. A FrontPage component.
    b. A modem.
    c. A network adapter card.
    d. A Web server.

14. **The FrontPage component that tracks visitors to your site is called a**
    a. Search form.
    b. Substitution.
    c. Hit counter.
    d. Banner ad manager.

15. **If you want to let users find particular words or phrases on your Web pages, you can insert a**
    a. Find form.
    b. Search form.
    c. Hit counter.
    d. Replace form.

16. **Which statement about active elements is NOT true?**
    a. Active elements can be FrontPage components.
    b. Active elements can be Web pages.
    c. Active elements can be Java applets.
    d. Active elements can be HTML forms.

17. **Which active element displays alternate images when viewed in a Web browser?**
    a. Hover button.
    b. Ad banner manager.
    c. Marquee.
    d. Hit Counter.

18. **A hover button is a button that**
    a. Moves across the page in a browser.
    b. Appears to float on the page.
    c. Changes appearance when a mouse is positioned over it.
    d. Displays different images every few seconds.

19. **The FrontPage component that scrolls text across a Web page is called**
    a. A hit counter.
    b. A banner ad manager.
    c. A category.
    d. A marquee.

20. **For all FrontPage components to work properly when a site is published, the remote server must have installed**
   a. Search forms.
   b. An ISP.
   c. Substitution components.
   d. Server extensions.

 Skills Review

1. **Insert FrontPage components.**
   a. Start FrontPage 2000 and create a new one-page Web named *Acme*.
   b. Open the home page (index.htm) in Page View.
   c. Title the page Acme Computers, type Acme Computers at the top of the page, highlight the text, set the style to Heading 1, set the color to Navy blue, then center the text.
   d. Click after the text, press Enter twice, click Insert, point to Component, then click Marquee.
   e. Type an Acme welcome message of your own creation, set the background color to Yellow, set the marquee to repeat 5 times, click OK, then press Enter.
   f. Click Insert, point to Component, then click Hit Counter.
   g. Select a style of your choice, set the number of digits to 6, then click OK.
   h. Save the page, click the Preview tab, and close the page.

2. **Add a search form.**
   a. Click File, point to New, then click Page.
   b. Click Search Page, then click OK.
   c. Title the page **Acme Search Page**, save the page as *search.htm*, preview, and close the page.
   d. Click File, click Open, then double-click index.
   e. Click anywhere on the page under the marquee component, click the Insert Component button, then click Search Form.
   f. Click the Search Form Properties tab, type **Search Acme Computers**, click the Display score (closeness of match) check box on the Search Results tab, then click OK.
   g. Click the Preview tab, then save and close the page.

3. **Add content listings.**
   a. Click File, point to New, click Page, click Table of Contents, then click OK.
   b. Double-click the Table of Contents component.
   c. Type index.htm as the starting point of table if necessary, set the heading font size to 4, then click OK.
   d. Save the page as *toc.htm*.
   e. Click the Preview in Browser button and preview and print the page.
   f. Close the browser.
   g. Close the page.

4. Insert a hover button.
   a. Click the Folder List button, then double-click index.htm.
   b. Enter two blank lines below the marquee component, make sure the lines are left aligned, press Tab, click the Insert Component button, then click Hover Button.
   c. Name the button Sales, set the Button color to Navy, set the Effect color to Yellow, then set the Effect to Glow.
   d. Press Tab, click the Insert Component button, then click Hover Button.
   e. Name the button Service, set the Button color to Navy, set the Effect color to Yellow, then set the Effect to Bevel Out.
   f. Press Tab, click the Insert Component button, then click Hover Button.
   g. Name the button Search, click the Browse button, click search.htm, set the Button color to Navy, set the Effect color to Yellow, then set the Effect to Bevel Out.
   h. Click the Save button, click the Preview tab, move your mouse over the buttons, click the Normal tab, then close the page.

5. Insert a banner ad manager.
   a. Double-click index.htm, insert two blank lines below the hover buttons, click the Center button, click the Insert Component button, then click Banner Ad Manager.
   b. Type 300 in the Width text box, type 300 in the Height text box, then click Blinds Vertical in the Transition effect list arrow.
   c. Click Add, click Clip Art, click People, select a clip of your choice, then click the Insert Clip button.
   d. Click Add, click Clip Art, click People, select a second clip of your choice, then click the Insert Clip button.
   e. Click Add, click Clip Art, click People, select a third clip of your choice, then click the Insert Clip button.
   f. Click OK, then click the Save button and save the embedded files.
   g. Click the Preview in Browser button, then close the browser and the page.

6. View and verify hyperlinks.
   a. Click the Hyperlinks button, click the Folders List button, then click index.htm.
   b. Click search.htm, then click the Folders List button to close the Folders List window.
   c. Click Tools, click Recalculate Hyperlinks, then click Yes.
   d. Click the Reports button, then click the Broken Hyperlinks report.

7. Work with Reports View.
   a. Select Site Summary, click All files, then click the Name column to arrange the files alphabetically by Title.
   b. Select Recently Changed Files, then set the report setting to 4 days.
   c. Select Site Summary, double-click Slow Pages, then set the report setting to 30 seconds.
   d. Select Publish Status, then set the Publish status for search.htm to Don't Publish.
   e. Select Site Summary, double-click Older Files, then set the report setting to 365 days.

8. Publish a Web site.
   a. Click the Publish Web button.
   b. Type the URL for the remote server, click Publish all pages, overwriting any already on the destination.
   c. Click the WPP's button.
   d. View the Microsoft page, then close the browser.
   e. Click Cancel, then close FrontPage 2000.

▶ Independent Challenges

1. You are the Webmaster for Mercury Shoes, Inc. The president of the company wants you to create a company Web site using FrontPage. Your first step will be to create a new One-page Web that can be customized to suit Mercury's needs.

   To complete this independent challenge:

   a. Create a new Web named *Mercury* using the FrontPage One Page Web template.
   b. Select the Citrus theme and apply it to the Web.
   c. Change the page banner to read: **Mercury Shoes**.
   d. Delete the Shared Left border for the entire Web.
   e. Create a table of two columns and four rows.
   f. Place 4 blue hover buttons with green effects into the four rows of the left column of your table.

   - Sales
   - Domestic
   - Imported
   - Repairs

   g. Save and close the Web.

2. As Webmaster for Houston Tile, you have been charged with creating the company's first Web site. You have recommended using Microsoft FrontPage as the development software because it is easy to use and offers so many options.

   To complete this independent challenge, answer the dialog box questions in a manner that will ensure that the Houston Tile Web meets the following demands:

   a. Using the Corporate Presence Web Wizard, create a new *Houston Tile Web*.
   b. Include these main pages: What's New, and Products/Services.
   c. Include these topics on the home page: Introduction, Mission Statement, and Contact Information.
   d. Include these topics on the What's New Page: Web Changes and Press Releases.
   e. Set the number of products and services to 2.
   f. Choose a theme.
   g. Enter the name and address of the company as **Houston Tile, Inc., 1313 Main Street, MyTown, USA**. The one-word name should be **Houston**.
   h. Add a Search form to the home page that will search the entire Houston Web. Date the results from the search.
   i. Add a separate Table of Contents page to the Houston Tile Web that starts with the home page.
   j. Preview the completed Web in Page View, and a Web browser.
   k. Save and close the Web.

3. As a consultant for Auntie Jean's Homemade Cookies Company, you will review the Auntie Jean Web. You have decided to make a few changes to the Web to provide better service for Auntie Jean's customers. In particular, you will add a higher level of interactivity to the Web by inserting several FrontPage components.

To complete this independent challenge:

a. Create a Web called *Auntie* using the Customer Support Web template.

b. Add a hit counter component to the home page.

c. Using clip art, add a banner ad manager to the home page.

d. Delete the Frequently Asked Questions page.

e. Add a separate search page that will search the entire Auntie Jean Web.

f. Preview the search page in a browser.

g. Close the Web.

4. You are the Webmaster for the Chockles Nut Company. The president of the company has asked you to find an ISP for the Chockles Web site. The single greatest resource for any Web developer is the World Wide Web itself.

To complete this independent challenge:

a. Connect to the Internet and use your favorite browser to search using the keywords "Internet Service Provider."

b. Find three sites that provide information about ISPs.

c. Record the number of ISPs that use the FrontPage Server Extensions.

d. Make a note of the URLs that you find on a separate list, and print a copy of the home page for each site that you find.

► Visual Workshop

Open FrontPage 2000. Re-create a Web page similar to the page depicted in Figure H-25. You should create a one-page Web for this task named *Workshop*. Use the Rice Paper theme. Save the file as *CustomerRelations.htm* and print the page.

FIGURE H-25

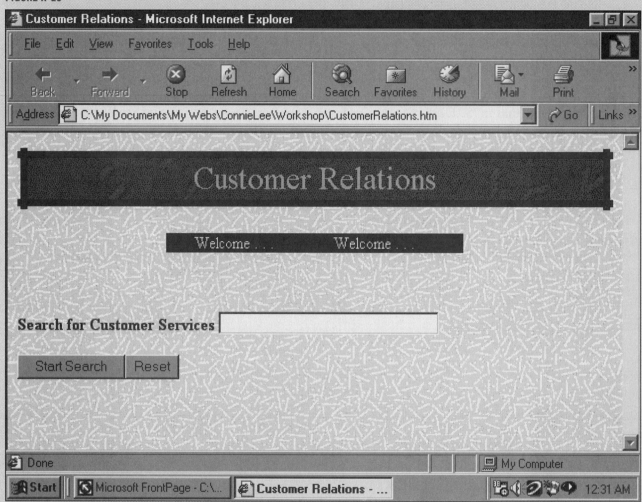

Working
with Tables and Frames in a Web Site

Objectives

- [MOUS] ► **Resize a table**
- [MOUS] ► **Resize a table cell**
- [MOUS] ► **Center a picture in a table cell**
- [MOUS] ► **Add a custom background color to a table**
- [MOUS] ► **Create a nested table**
- [MOUS] ► **Create a new frame in a frames page**
- [MOUS] ► **Delete a frame from a frames page**
- ► **Print a frames page in Internet Explorer**

Tables and frames are important ways to present information on Web pages. Tables help you organize information so it can be quickly and easily understood. Frames help you organize your Web site so its pages are readily available to visitors. FrontPage allows you to use both tables and frames on your Web pages. ✐ The Jenkins Publishing Company publishes books about Texas history, and as such, it has been very successful. Maureen Jenkins is the CEO of the company. Maureen wants to create a Web site that buyers can use to search for and learn about different authors and titles. For now, Maureen wants the Web site to list the in-stock titles for the company.

Resizing a Table

When data that you want to use on a Web page is stored as a table in another Office format, such as a Word document or an Excel workbook, you can copy and paste the table data on a Web page. The pasted table data appears on the Web page as a table that you can format, resize, and update. ◀━━━━ Maureen has a list of books stored in a Word table that she wants to use in the new Web site. She wants to copy this table data from the Word document, create a new one-page Web site, then copy the table data onto the new Web page.

Steps 123 4

1. Click the **Start button** 🔳Start on the taskbar, point to **Programs** on the Start menu, then click **Microsoft Word** on the Programs menu
   The Word window opens.

Trouble?

If you see the three-letter extension .doc on the file-name in the Open dialog box, Windows is set to show file extensions.

2. Click the **Open button** 🖾 on the Standard toolbar, click the **Look in list arrow**, open the **Unit I folder** on your Project Disk, then double-click **Books**
   The Books document opens in the Word window. This document contains a table with the author's name, title, subtitle, date, page count, ISBN, and price of each book.

3. Click anywhere in the table, click **Table** on the menu bar, point to **Select**, then click **Table**
   The entire table is selected.

4. Click the **Copy button** 🖹 on the Standard toolbar
   The table is copied to the Windows Clipboard.

QuickTip

The Jenkins Web can be saved to several locations, such as a hard drive, a net-work drive, or external media. Due to the size of the com-pleted Web, it is not recom-mended that it be saved to a floppy disk.

5. Click the **Close button** on the Word title bar to close Word, start **Microsoft FrontPage**, click **File** on the menu bar, point to **New**, click **Web**, click the **One Page Web icon**, type **C:\My Documents\My Webs\[insert your name here]\Jenkins** in the Specify the location of the new web text box, click **OK**, then click the **Folders button** 📁 on the Views bar
   You use your first and last names in the name of the Web site to create a folder that is unique to you. FrontPage creates the new Jenkins Web. The Jenkins Web opens in Folders View, as shown in Figure I-1.

6. Click the **New Page button** 🗋 on the Standard toolbar, type **Booklist.htm**, press **[Tab]**, type **Booklist**, press **[Enter]**, double-click **Booklist.htm** to open the page in Page View, then click the **Paste button** 🖺 on the Standard toolbar
   The table you copied from the Word document appears on the new Booklist Web page.

7. Click anywhere in the table to select it, click **Table** on the menu bar, point to **Properties**, then click **Table**
   The Table Properties dialog box opens, as shown in Figure I-2. You use the Table Properties dialog box to change attributes that relate to the entire table.

8. Click the **Specify width check box** to select it, press **[Tab]** and type **90**, click the **In percent option button**, click **OK**, then scroll to the top of the page
   The table changes to use 90% of the window width, as shown in Figure I-3. When you set a table to use a percentage of the window width, the table will always appear as a percentage of the browser window size, regardless of the browser screen size or monitor resolution.

9. Click the **Save button** 🖫 on the Standard toolbar
   FrontPage saves the Booklist Web page.

FIGURE I-1: Jenkins Web in Folders View

New Page button

Your name will appear here

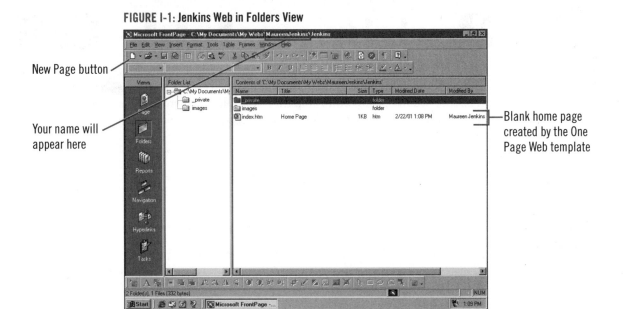

Blank home page created by the One Page Web template

FIGURE I-2: Table Properties dialog box

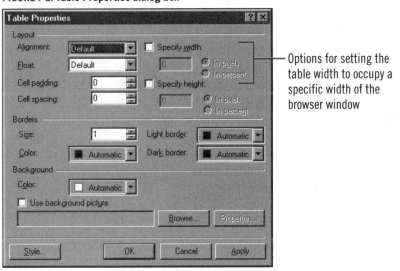

Options for setting the table width to occupy a specific width of the browser window

FIGURE I-3: Resized table

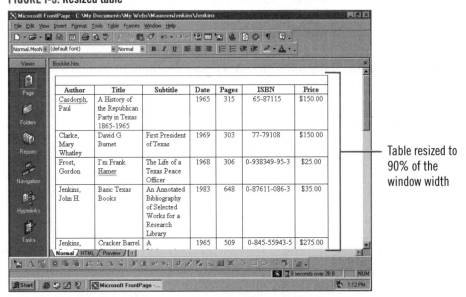

Table resized to 90% of the window width

Author	Title	Subtitle	Date	Pages	ISBN	Price
Casdorph, Paul	A History of the Republican Party in Texas 1865-1965		1965	315	65-87115	$150.00
Clarke, Mary Whatley	David G. Burnet	First President of Texas	1969	303	77-79108	$150.00
Frost, Gordon	I'm Frank Hamer	The Life of a Texas Peace Officer	1968	306	0-938349-95-3	$25.00
Jenkins, John H.	Basic Texas Books	An Annotated Bibliography of Selected Works for a Research Library	1983	648	0-87611-086-3	$35.00
Jenkins,	Cracker Barrel	A	1965	509	0-845-55943-5	$275.00

FrontPage 2000

Resizing a Table Cell

In the previous lesson, you learned how to resize a table to fit the width of the browser window. You can also resize the individual rows, columns, and cells in a table. Maureen wants to increase the width of the second column in the table so there is more room for the book titles. Then she wants to increase the height of the second row to make the labels easier to read.

Steps

1. Position the mouse pointer on the right border of the second column until it changes to ↔

2. Click and drag the border to the right (see Figure I-4)
When you drag the right border of a column to the right, you increase the width of the column. Dragging the right border to the left decreases the width of the column.

Trouble?

If your table looks different, use the pointer to resize the second column until it matches Figure I-4.

3. Release the mouse button
The width of the second column increases, as shown in Figure I-4.

4. Position the pointer on the bottom border of the second row until it changes to ↕

Trouble?

If your table looks different, use the pointer to resize the second row until it matches Figure I-5.

5. Click and drag the border down (see Figure I-5), then release the mouse button
The height of the second row increases, as shown in Figure I-5. When you drag the bottom border down, you increase the height of the row. Dragging the bottom border up decreases the height of the row.

6. Position the pointer on the left border of the second row until it changes to ➡, then right-click the second row
The second row is selected and a pop-up menu appears.

7. Click **Cell Properties** on the pop-up menu, click the **Vertical alignment list arrow**, click **Middle**, click **OK**, then click anywhere in the second row to deselect it
The labels in the second row of the table are still centered horizontally but vertically aligned in the middle of the cells, as shown in Figure I-6.

8. Click the **Save button** 🖫 on the Standard toolbar
FrontPage saves the Booklist Web page.

FIGURE I-4: Resized column

Right border of column 2 dragged to here

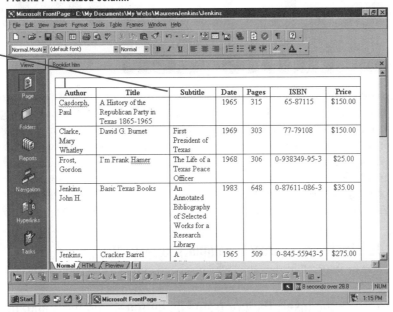

FIGURE I-5: Resized row

Left border of second row

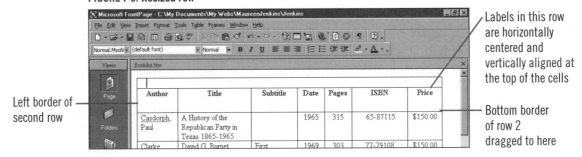

Labels in this row are horizontally centered and vertically aligned at the top of the cells

Bottom border of row 2 dragged to here

FIGURE I-6: New alignment of text in a row of cells

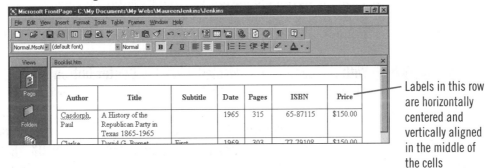

Labels in this row are horizontally centered and vertically aligned in the middle of the cells

CLUES TO USE

Using the pop-up menu to resize table rows and columns

In addition to setting a table's width and resizing individual rows and columns in a table, you can change the table so that all rows and columns have equal measurements. To set rows or columns to distribute evenly, select the rows or columns to resize, right-click them to open the pop-up menu, then click Distribute Rows Evenly or Distribute Columns Evenly. FrontPage resizes the table so that the selected rows or columns have equal measurements.

Centering a Picture in a Table Cell

When you insert a picture in a table cell, FrontPage automatically resizes the cell that contains the picture to accommodate the picture's size. If the picture is too large or too small for your needs, you can click it and use a sizing handle to make the picture smaller or larger. When you insert a picture in a table cell, you can change the picture using the same methods for changing other pictures that you use in a Web page. For example, you might add special effects to the picture, wash out the picture, or use the picture as a hyperlink that opens another Web page. Maureen wants to insert a picture in the first cell of the table to add visual interest to the book listing. She resizes and centers the picture in the cell.

Steps 123 4

1. **Click the cell in row 1, column 1 to select it**
   The first cell in the table, which is blank, now contains the insertion point.

2. **Click the Insert Picture from File button** ![icon] **on the Standard toolbar, click Clip Art, click in the Search for clips list box, type books, then press [Enter]**
   Several pictures of books appear in the Clip Art Gallery window.

   Trouble?
   If you can't find the picture shown in Figure I-7, select a similar picture in the Clip Art Gallery window.

3. **Locate and click the picture of three books (see Figure I-7), then click the Insert clip button** ![icon]
   The picture appears in the first cell of the table. The picture is too large, so you will resize it.

   Trouble?
   If necessary, continue to resize your picture so it is approximately the same size as the one shown in Figure I-7.

4. **Click the picture to select it, click and drag the sizing handle in the lower-right corner toward the middle of the picture to reduce the picture's size (see Figure I-7), then release the mouse button**
   The picture is smaller, as shown in Figure I-7. Notice that when you resize the picture, the height of the cell that contains it is also resized.

5. **Click the Resample button** ![icon] **on the Pictures toolbar**
   After resizing a picture, it is a good idea to resample it so the picture's file size matches the picture's actual size, optimizing the download time.

   QuickTip
   You can center, right-align, or left-align the contents of any cell by selecting the cell and then clicking the ![icon], ![icon], or ![icon] button, respectively, on the Formatting toolbar.

6. **With the picture still selected, click the Center button** ![icon] **on the Formatting toolbar**
   The picture is centered in the first cell of the table, as shown in Figure I-8.

7. **Click the Save button** ![icon] **on the Standard toolbar, click Rename, type Books.jpg, press [Enter], click Change Folder, click images, click OK, then click OK again**
   FrontPage saves the Books.jpg file in the Web site's images folder and saves the revised Booklist Web page in the Web site.

FIGURE I-7: Picture inserted in a cell

Resized cell accommodates the picture's size

Resized picture from the Clip Art Gallery

Resample button

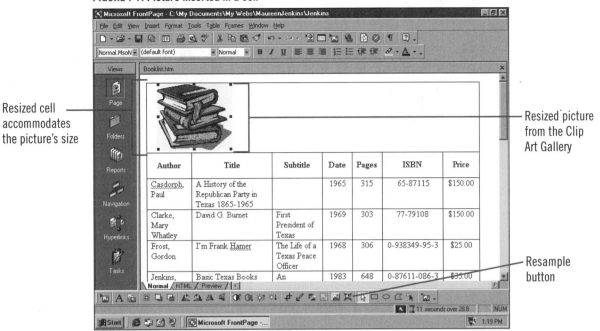

FIGURE I-8: Picture centered in a cell

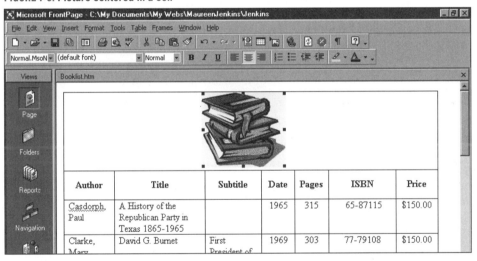

Centering a table on a Web page

Centering a table on a Web page is different from centering the contents of a cell within a cell. One uses table properties for the whole table, while the other uses cell properties for a portion of the table. To center a table on a Web page, click anywhere in the table, click Table on the menu bar, point to Properties, then click Table. Click the Alignment list arrow in the Layout section of the Table Properties dialog box, then click Center. You can also follow these same steps to change a table's alignment to left, right, or justified. The default alignment for a table is to left-align it. To change the alignment of the contents of cells within a table, select the cells, then click an alignment button on the Formatting toolbar.

Adding a Custom Background Color to a Table

You can add a background color to a table or to individual cells. Adding a background color to a table or to individual cells creates visual interest and calls attention to specific cell values. For example, if your table shows financial data, you might add a background color to the cell that identifies whether a project is under or over budget. FrontPage lets you apply standard colors, or you can create a custom color to get the exact shade that you want. When using background colors for tables and cells, make sure that the text is readable, that the color complements the Web page, and that the color is pleasing to the eye. ◣▬▬▬ Maureen likes the light blue color in the picture that you added to the table. She wants to match this color and apply it to the background of the table that appears in the Booklist Web page.

Steps 1234

1. Right-click anywhere in the table except the picture, click **Table Properties** on the pop-up menu, then drag the **Table Properties dialog box** to the right so you can see the picture in the first cell of the table

2. Click the **Color list arrow** in the Background section
   A color palette opens. You can select one of the standard colors, or you can choose a custom color. You will choose a custom color to match the blue in the books.

3. Click **More Colors**, then if necessary, drag the **More Colors dialog box** down so you can see the picture in the first cell of the table
   You can click any color in the color spectrum to use it, click Custom to create a custom color, or click Select to copy a color from any screen element.

4. Click **Select**
   The pointer changes to a dropper ✐. You select a color by clicking any color on the screen that you want to match.

Trouble?

If you inserted another picture in the first cell of the table, skip Step 5 and instead click the selected color, as shown in Figure I-9.

5. Move the pointer over the lower-left corner of the blue book until the color changes (see Figure I-9), then click the left mouse button
   The color you selected appears in the New section of the More Colors dialog box. If you are not able to select the correct color using the eyedropper, you can select the correct color in the More Colors palette.

6. If necessary, drag the **More Colors dialog box** so you can see **OK**, click **OK** to close the More Colors dialog box, then click **OK** to close the Table Properties dialog box
   The dialog boxes close and the custom background color is applied to the table background. The text in the table is easy to read and the new background color adds visual interest to the page.

QuickTip

If your picture is already in the GIF format, you won't need to convert it. In FrontPage, you can only make changes to pictures that are in the GIF format.

7. Click the **picture** in the first cell to select it, click the **Set Transparent Color button** 🖉 on the Pictures toolbar, click **OK** to convert the picture to GIF format (if necessary), click the **white background** of the picture, then click anywhere in the table to deselect the picture
   The picture now has a transparent background, as shown in Figure I-10.

8. Click the **Save button** 🖫 on the Standard toolbar, then click **OK**
   FrontPage saves the Booklist Web page and the Books.gif picture file.

FIGURE I-9: Custom color selected

Pointer on color to select

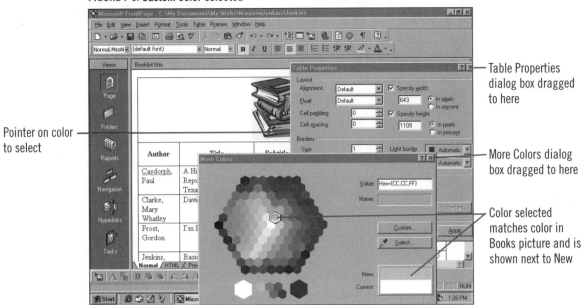

Table Properties dialog box dragged to here

More Colors dialog box dragged to here

Color selected matches color in Books picture and is shown next to New

FIGURE I-10: Custom background color applied to a table

Picture changed to use a transparent background

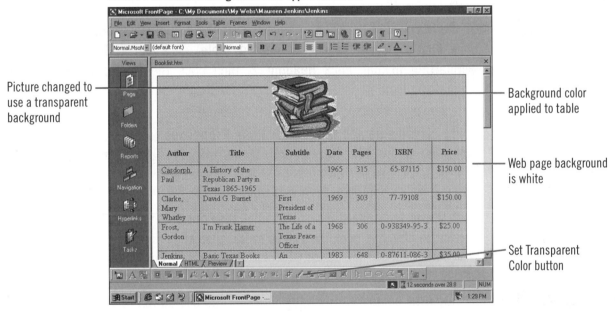

Background color applied to table

Web page background is white

Set Transparent Color button

Using the Format Painter to format table cells

When you apply complicated formats to one table cell and need to apply that same format to other table cells or to the rest of a table, you can use the Format Painter to copy and paste the formatting. The **Format Painter** lets you copy the format from existing formatted text and apply it to new text. To use the Format Painter, click the cell whose format you want to copy, click the Format Painter button on the Standard toolbar, then click the cell to which you want to apply the formatting. To paste the same formatting to more than one cell, double-click the Format Painter button on the Standard toolbar. You can paste the format as many times as needed, then click the Format Painter button on the Standard toolbar again to turn it off. You can use the Format Painter to copy and paste formats in any text, and not just in tables.

Creating a Nested Table

A **nested table** is a table that appears in one cell of another table. You might use a nested table to have more control over the format of your table's data. For example, a nested table can use a different background picture or color than the table that contains it. You might create a nested table to hold a logo, important data that uses a different background color for emphasis, or a grand total in a table that contains financial information. Maureen wants the first cell in the table to contain the company name, but with a different background color. She creates a nested table in the first cell, then applies a different background color.

Steps

Trouble?

If you click the picture in the first cell, press the right arrow key to move the insertion point to the right of the picture.

1. Click an empty area to the right of the picture in the cell in **row 1, column 1** to place the insertion point there

2. Click the **Insert Table button** on the Standard toolbar, then click the cell in **row 1, column 2** of the grid
   A new table with one row and two columns appears below the picture in the first cell, as shown in Figure I-11.

QuickTip

To select the nested table, click ➡ on its left border.

3. In the first cell of the nested table, type **Jenkins Publishing Company**, press [Tab], type **Austin, Texas**, select the **nested table**, click the **Style list arrow** on the Formatting toolbar, click **Heading 2**, then click the **Center button** on the Formatting toolbar
   The text that you typed is centered in the nested table.

QuickTip

To identify a color by name, position the pointer on it to view the ScreenTip.

4. Right-click the **nested table**, click **Table Properties** on the pop-up menu, click the **Color list arrow** in the Background section, click the **Teal color** in the Standard colors section, then click **OK**
   The teal color is applied to the nested table.

5. With the nested table still selected, click the **Font Color button list arrow** on the Formatting toolbar, click the **Yellow color**, then click anywhere in the table
   The background of the nested table is teal, which helps the yellow text stand out in the nested table.

Trouble?

Depending on your monitor resolution, the text in your nested table might appear on two lines. Don't worry, it should appear correctly in the browser.

6. Position the pointer on the right border of the nested table, drag the nested table's right border to the right (see Figure I-12), then release the mouse button
   The nested table is finished, as shown in Figure I-12.

7. Click the **Save button** on the Standard toolbar
   FrontPage saves the Booklist Web page.

FIGURE I-11: Nested table

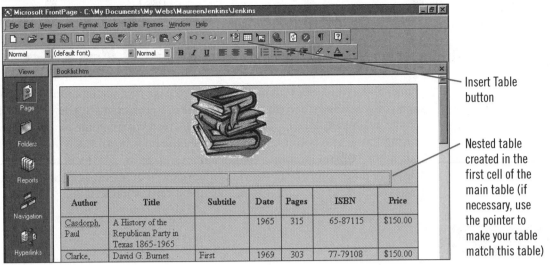

Insert Table button

Nested table created in the first cell of the main table (if necessary, use the pointer to make your table match this table)

FIGURE I-12: Completed nested table

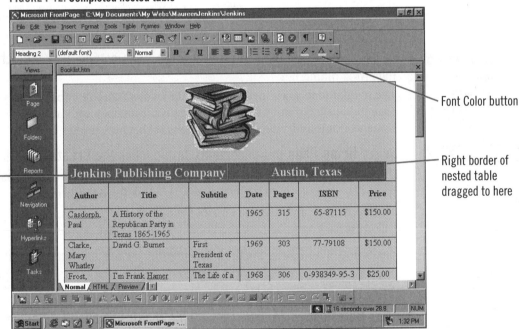

Nested table with a teal background and yellow text

Font Color button

Right border of nested table dragged to here

Applying border colors to tables and cells

In addition to applying a background color to a table, you can apply colors to its borders. To apply a border color, select and then right-click the table or cell(s) to which you want to apply the color, click Table Properties (to apply the border color to all cells in a table) or Cell Properties (to apply the border color to only the cell(s) you have selected) on the pop-up menu, click the Color list arrow in the Borders section, then choose a color or create a custom color.

You can create a three-dimensional effect for tables and cells by choosing complementary light and dark border colors. A **light border color** is applied to a cell's bottom and right borders; a **dark border color** is applied to a cell's top and left borders. You can only change the border colors for tables that you create in FrontPage; these steps do not work for tables that you import from other programs.

Creating a New Frame in a Frames Page

Frames allow you to show more than one Web page on a single screen. After you create a frames page, you might need to create another frame in it. For example, you might add a small frame to contain a company logo or name. When you create a new frame in a frames page, you **split** an existing frame into two frames. You can split frames horizontally or vertically, depending on your needs. ◤━━━━ Maureen creates a frames page using the Contents frames page template. The page in the contents frame will contain links that open pages in the main frame. Maureen creates a smaller frame corner to include the company name.

Steps 1 2 3 4

QuickTip

FrontPage includes several frames page templates that you can use to create new frames pages.

1. Click **File** on the menu bar, point to **New**, click **Page**, click the **Frames Pages tab**, then double-click the **Contents icon**
   The frames page contains a contents frame on the left and a main frame on the right.

2. In the contents frame, click **New Page**, type **Home Page**, press **[Enter]**, then type **Booklist**
   FrontPage creates a new Web page in the Web site that appears in the contents frame.

QuickTip

FrontPage created a blank home page named index.htm. when you used the One Page Web template to create the Jenkins Web.

3. In the main frame, click **Set Initial Page**, then double-click **index.htm** in the Create Hyperlink dialog box
   The blank home page opens in the main frame; you will create the content for the home page in Unit J. For now, the frames page is a container with a Web page that opens in the contents frame and a Web page that opens in the main frame.

QuickTip

When a dark blue border appears around a frame, it is selected.

4. Select **Home Page** in the contents frame, click the **Create Hyperlink button** 🖻 on the Standard toolbar, double-click **index.htm**, double-click **Booklist** in the contents frame to select it, click 🖻, then double-click **Booklist.htm**
   The Home Page and Booklist entries are now formatted as hyperlinks, which when clicked will open the home page and the Booklist page in the main frame.

5. Press and hold **[Ctrl]**, position the pointer on the top border of the contents frame until it changes to ↕, drag the top border down (see Figure I-13), then release **[Ctrl]**
   A new frame is created in the frames page, as shown in Figure I-13.

6. Click **New Page** in the new frame, type **Jenkins Publishing Company**, then click the **Center button** ☰ on the Formatting toolbar
   The text is centered in the new frame.

QuickTip

You already saved the home page in the main frame of the frames page as index.htm.

7. Click the **Save button** 🖫 on the Standard toolbar
   The Save As dialog box opens, as shown in Figure I-14. You will need to save the two new Web pages associated with the frames page in order to "save" the frames page. You will save the solid, dark blue frame shown in the dialog box first.

8. Type **Jenkins** in the File name text box, click **Save**, click **Change**, in the Page title text box type **Contents**, click **OK**, type **Contents** in the File name text box, click **Save**, click **Change**, in the Page title text box type **Frames Page**, click **OK**, type **Frames** in the File name text box, then click **Save**
   FrontPage saves the frames page and the two new pages that you created.

9. Click the **Preview tab**, then click **Booklist** in the contents frame
   The frames page appears, as shown in Figure I-15.

FIGURE I-13: New frame in a frames page

New frame created by splitting the contents frame

Contents frame

Hyperlinks to open the home page and the Booklist page in the main frame

Main frame

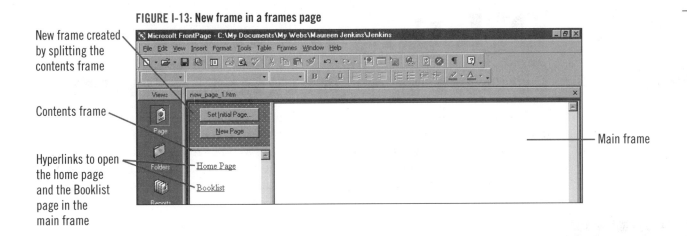

FIGURE I-14: Save As dialog box

Web pages currently saved in the Jenkins Web

Current title of the selected page

Page to save is selected

Click to change the selected page's title

Suggested filename of the selected page

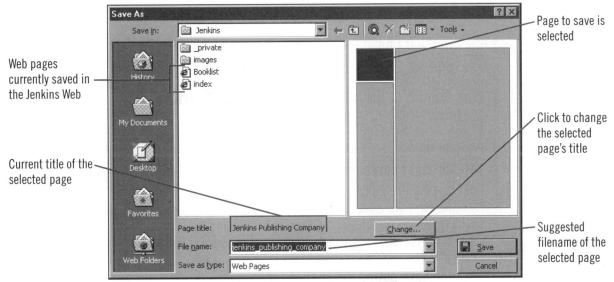

FIGURE I-15: Preview of the frames page

Jenkins.htm page

Contents.htm page

Preview tab

Booklist.htm page

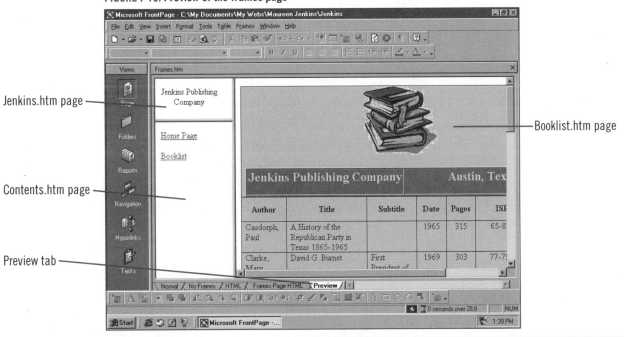

Deleting a Frame from a Frames Page

In some cases, you might need to delete a frame from a frames page. When you delete a frame from a frames page, you are only deleting the HTML code that *creates* the frame. You are not deleting the Web page that appears in the frame. ➤ Maureen decides to delete the frame that she created to hold the company name in order to be able to display more information in the contents frame. After deleting the frame, she resizes the contents frame to make it more narrow.

Steps

1. Click the **Normal tab**
   The frames page appears in Normal Page View.

2. Click in the **frame** in the upper-left corner to select it, if necessary
   The frame contains a dark blue border, indicating that it is selected.

3. Click **Frames** on the menu bar, then click **Delete Frame**
   The frame is deleted, as shown in Figure I-16.

4. Position the pointer on the right border of the contents frame until it changes to ↔, click the **right border** of the contents frame and drag it to the left (see Figure I-17), then release the mouse button
   As shown in Figure I-17, the size of the contents frame decreases and the size of the main frame increases. When you increase or decrease the size of a frame in a frames page, the relative sizes of the other frames in the frames page change as well.

5. Click the **Save button** 🖫 on the Standard toolbar
   FrontPage saves the Frames Web page.

6. Click the **Folders button** 🗁 on the Views bar
   Notice that the Jenkins.htm page still exists in the Jenkins Web, even though you deleted the frame that contained this page from the Frames page.

FIGURE I-16: Frames page after deleting a frame

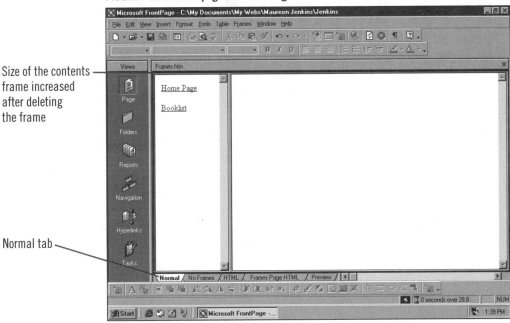

Size of the contents frame increased after deleting the frame

Normal tab

FIGURE I-17: Resized frames

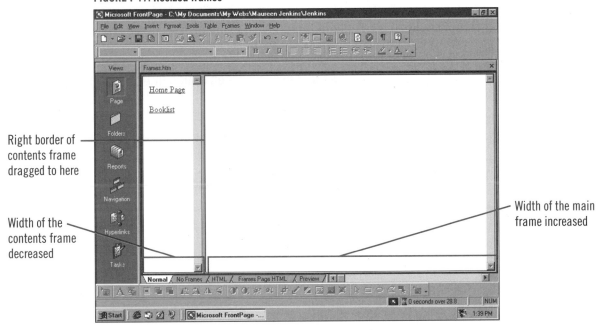

Right border of contents frame dragged to here

Width of the contents frame decreased

Width of the main frame increased

CLUES TO USE

Creating "no frames" pages for browsers that can't display frames

If visitors to your Web site use older browsers, they might not be able to see your frames pages. When a browser cannot display a frames page, it displays a message instead. When you create a frames page in FrontPage, FrontPage automatically creates a **No Frames page**, which provides a message that says "This page uses frames, but your browser doesn't support them." You can change the information in the No Frames page by clicking the No Frames tab in Page View, then editing the existing message or creating a new one. You can also create hyperlinks from the No Frames page to your Web's pages so people can still open them, even if they can't view the frames page.

Printing a Frames Page in Internet Explorer

As you browse the Web, you'll find many Web sites that use frames pages to organize the way that you view Web pages. Printing a frames page is different from printing a Web page that does not use frames. Each browser handles printing a frames page differently. In Internet Explorer, you have the option of printing the page as it appears in the browser, printing only the selected frame, or printing each frame on a separate sheet of paper. To print a frames page in these different ways, you need to use the Print command on the File menu. ✎ Maureen views her frames page in Internet Explorer, prints it as it appears on the screen, and then exits FrontPage.

Trouble?

If necessary, click the Maximize button on the Internet Explorer title bar to maximize the window.

1. With the Frames.htm page selected in Folders View, click the **Preview in Browser button** 🔍 on the Standard toolbar
   The Frames Web page opens in Internet Explorer.

2. Click **Booklist** in the contents frame
   The Booklist Web page opens in the main frame, as shown in Figure I-18.

3. Click **File** on the menu bar, then click **Print**
   The Print dialog box opens, as shown in Figure I-19.

4. If necessary, click the **As laid out on screen option button** in the Print frames section to select it

5. Click **OK**
   The Web page prints.

6. Click the **Close button** on the Internet Explorer title bar, then click the **Close button** on the FrontPage title bar
   Internet Explorer and FrontPage close.

FIGURE I-18: Completed frames page in Internet Explorer

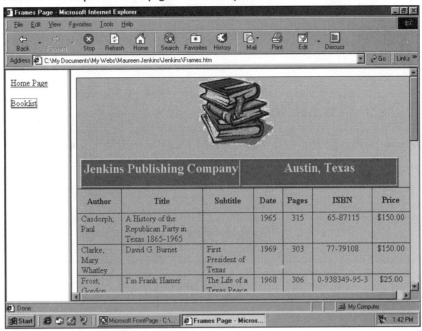

FIGURE I-19: Print dialog box in Internet Explorer

Your printer information will appear here

Options for printing frames page are enabled when a frames page is open in the browser

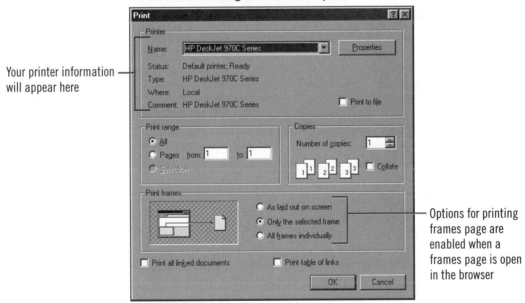

Other printing options in Internet Explorer

There are two other options in the Print dialog box that you might find useful when printing Web pages. If you select the Print all linked documents check box, you will print the page that appears in the browser window and all pages that are linked to that page. For example, you might print the home page and all pages that open using links on the home page. Use this option carefully, however, as some pages contain many links. If you select the Print table of links check box, you will print the page that appears in the browser window and a separate sheet that lists all of the documents that are linked to that page.

Practice

▶ Concepts Review

Label each of the elements of the Microsoft FrontPage window shown in Figure I-20.

FIGURE I-20

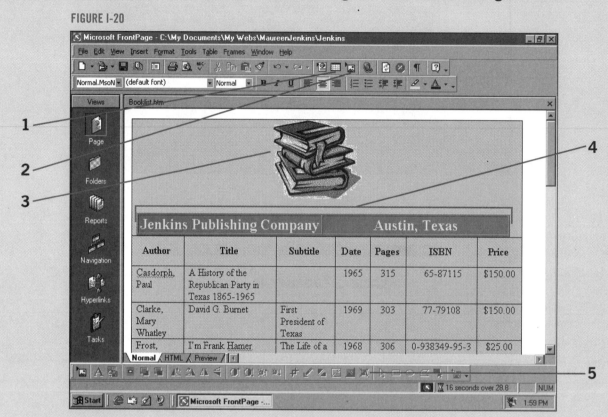

Match each of the terms with the statement that describes it.

6. Center button	a.	A table within another table
7. Format Painter	b.	Click to horizontally center a cell's contents within the cell
8. More Colors	c.	Click to select or create a custom color
9. Nested table	d.	Drag to change the size of a selected picture
10. Sizing handle	e.	Use to copy and paste cell formatting to other cells

Select the best answer from the list of choices.

11. Dragging a column's left border to the left will

a. Increase the column's width.

b. Decrease the column's width.

c. Delete the column.

d. Create a second column with the same width.

12. Dragging a row's top border up will

a. Increase the height of the row.

b. Decrease the height of the row.

c. Delete the row.

d. Create a second row with the same height.

13. Which of the following statements is NOT true?

a. You can apply a custom background color to a Web page.

b. You can apply a custom background color to a single table cell.

c. You can apply a custom background color to an entire table.

d. You can apply a custom background color to a table or a Web page, but not to both.

14. When you use a sizing handle to resize a picture that you added to a table cell,

a. FrontPage resizes the cell automatically to accommodate the picture's size.

b. You must also resize the cell that contains the picture to make it the appropriate size.

c. You must resample the picture before you can resize it.

d. None of the above.

15. How do you center a table on a Web page?

a. Select the entire table, then click the Center button on the Formatting toolbar.

b. Right-click anywhere in the table, then click Center Table on the pop-up menu.

c. Click anywhere in the table, click Table on the menu bar, point to Properties, click Table, click the Alignment list arrow, click Center, then click OK.

d. You cannot center a table on a Web page.

16. The Format Painter

a. Lets you copy and paste cell data from one location to another.

b. Lets you copy and paste cell formatting from one cell to another.

c. Lets you copy and paste non-table formatting from one location to another.

d. Both b and c are correct.

17. Applying complementary colors to light and dark borders will create a

a. Three-dimensional effect.

b. Solid cell border.

c. A border around the outside of the table.

d. None of the above.

18. To create a new frame in a frames page,

a. Press [Shift] while dragging a frame border.

b. Press [Ctrl] while dragging a frame border.

c. Click Frames on the menu bar, then click New Frame.

d. Click Frames on the menu bar, then click Frame Properties.

19. After deleting a frame from a frames page, you must

a. Resize the other frames to fill the void left by the deleted frame.

b. Re-create the Web page that appeared in the deleted frame.

c. Re-create the frames page.

d. Save the frames page if you want to save the change.

20. **To print a frames page exactly as displayed by Internet Explorer, click the**
   a. As laid out on screen option button in the Print dialog box.
   b. Only the selected frame option button in the Print dialog box.
   c. All frames individually option button in the Print dialog box.
   d. Print button on the toolbar.

▶ Skills Review

1. **Resize a table.**
   a. Start FrontPage and create a new Web using the Empty Web template and the name *CarLoan*.
   b. Create a new page in Folders View using the filename *CarLoan.htm* and the title **Car Loan**. Open the page in Page View.
   c. Start Word, open the *BMW* file from your Project Disk, select the table, copy it, then close Word.
   d. Paste the table into the Car Loan Web page.
   e. Change the table so it will occupy 85% of the width of the browser window.

2. **Resize a table cell.**
   a. Use the pointer to decrease the width of the first column in the table by approximately 25%.
   b. Use the pointer to make the second and third columns have approximately the same widths.
   c. Select all cells in the table, then use the Cell Properties dialog box to change the horizontal alignment to center and the vertical alignment to middle.
   d. Use the pop-up menu to change all of the columns and rows in the table to have equal measurements.

3. **Center a picture in a table cell.**
   a. Click after 6%, then create a new line in row 1, column 2 by pressing [Shift][Enter]. Use the Clip Art Gallery to insert a picture that represents money, such as a moneybag or a dollar sign, on the new line. (If you cannot locate an appropriate clip art image, use any clip art image that is available.) After you insert the picture, center it. If necessary, resize the picture to make it small enough so that the first row is not more than one inch high.
   b. Resample the picture, if necessary.
   c. Click after 7%, then create a new line in row 1, column 3 by pressing [Shift][Enter]. Copy and paste the picture you inserted in the cell in row 1, column 2 on the new line.
   d. Save the page. Save the picture that you inserted in the Web site's images folder using the filename *Money.gif*, even if the clip art you selected does not represent money.

4. **Add a custom background color to a table.**
   a. Apply any custom color that you choose to the table's background. Select a color that complements the text in the table.
   b. Change the background of the pictures you inserted in the first row to transparent so that the pictures blend with the background.
   c. Save the page. Overwrite the Money.gif file if prompted to do so.

5. **Create a nested table.**
   a. Create a nested table in the cell in row 2, column 1. The nested table should contain two rows and two columns.
   b. Add the following data to the nested table:

Amount Financed	$33,000
Term	48 months

   Note: Your word wrap may differ.

c. Create a second nested table in the cell in row 3, column 1. The second nested table should contain two rows and two columns and the following data:

Amount Financed	$39,000
Term	48 months

d. Save the page.

6. **Create a new frame in a frames page.**

a. Create a new Web page using the Horizontal Split frames page template.

b. Create a new page in the top frame, then type **Loan Data** in the new page.

c. Set the bottom frame to open with the CarLoan.htm page.

d. Decrease the size of the top frame so that it is approximately half its current height and so that the Car Loan table appears in the bottom frame.

e. Split the top frame vertically into two equally sized frames so that the Loan Data text appears in a frame on the left. Create a new page with the text **BMW** on the right.

f. Save the top-left frame using the filename *LoanData.htm* and the title **Loan Data**, save the top-right frame using the filename *BMW.htm* and the title **BMW**, and save the frames page using the filename *Frames.htm* and the title **Frames Page**.

7. **Delete a frame from a frames page.**

a. Delete the top-right frame from the frames page.

b. Save the frames page.

8. **Print a frames page in Internet Explorer.**

a. Preview the frames page in Internet Explorer.

b. Print the page as it appears in the browser.

c. Close Internet Explorer, close the Web, then close FrontPage.

► Independent Challenges

1. Your favorite snack is chips and salsa. Your favorite salsa just happens to be one you make yourself. In fact, you grow its ingredients from scratch. Your best friend, Sarita, also enjoys your homemade salsa recipe and she has been growing the ingredients from scratch as well. She is moving from northern South Carolina (climate zone 7) to northern Florida (climate zone 8) next spring. Sarita asks you for the different dates to plant tomatoes, peppers, and cilantro in her new location. You decide to create a Web page to provide her with the suggested planting dates in each location.

To complete this independent challenge:

a. Start FrontPage and create a new Web using the Empty Web template and the name *Zones*.

b. Create a new Web page in Folders View using the filename *Planting.htm* and the title **Planting Guide**.

c. Start Word, open the *Zones* file from your Project Disk, then copy and paste the table into the Planting Guide Web page. Close Word.

d. Add an appropriate clip art picture from the Clip Art Gallery in the cell in row 1, column 1. If necessary, resize the picture so it is approximately one inch high. Then center the picture, and resample it, if necessary. Save the Web page, and save the clip art picture as *Gardening.gif* in the Web site's images folder.

e. Add a background color of your choice to the table's background. If necessary, change the background of the picture in the first row to transparent.

f. Change the table's alignment to center.

g. Use the pointer to increase the height of rows 2 through 4 by approximately 100% (i.e., double the height of the rows). Then make sure that the rows have equal heights.

h. Change the alignment of the table cells to use the center horizontal and middle vertical alignments.

i. Save the page, preview it in a browser and print it, then close your browser, the Web, and FrontPage.

2. Ella Jacobsen is the director and owner of a childcare center. She wants to use the company's Web site to provide parents with information about state-mandated tests for three- and four-year-old children who attend the center. She asks you to help her create a frames page to make it easy for parents to get the information they need, depending on their children's ages.

To complete this independent challenge:

a. Start FrontPage and create a new Web using the Empty Web template and the name *Childcare*.
b. Create a new Web page in Page View using the Vertical Split frames page template.
c. Create a new Web page in the left frame. In this frame, type the following information on separate lines: **Required tests for three-year-old children** and **Required tests for four-year-old children**.
d. Create a new page in the right frame, then type **Hearing and vision tests are required by law.**
e. Save the frames page using the filename *Ages.htm* and the title **Ages** for the page in the left frame, the filename *Threes.htm* and the title **Three-Year-Olds** for the page in the right frame, and the filename *Frames.htm* and the title **Frames Page** for the frames page.
f. Create a new frame above the left frame. The frame should be approximately two inches high and contain a new page with the text **Ella's Childcare Center**.
g. Resize the frame on the right so it is approximately 25% larger.
h. Save the frames page, and save the page in the new frame using the filename *Ella.htm* and the title **Ella**.
i. Preview the frames page in a browser, then print only the frame that contains the childcare center's name.
j. Delete the frame that contains the name of the childcare center, then save your changes.
k. Close your browser, the Web, and FrontPage.

3. Jayne Van Meter runs the cafeteria at a large computer manufacturer. Each day, she posts the cafeteria's breakfast and lunch specials outside the cafeteria's main entrance. Many employees have asked her to post a Web page on the company's intranet, so they can see the breakfast and lunch specials using the browsers in their offices. Jayne asks you to help her create the menu for Friday.

To complete this independent challenge:

a. Start FrontPage and create a new Web using the Empty Web template and the name *Menu*.
b. Create a new Web page in Folders View using the filename *Friday.htm* and the title **Friday Menu**.
c. Open the Friday.htm page in Page View. Use the Insert Table button to create a new table with two rows and three columns, then enter the following data in the table. (*Note*: Your word wrap may differ.)

	Breakfast	Lunch
Friday, February 23	Breakfast tacos with egg, potato, bacon, and cheese Orange juice Coffee	Chicken fried steak Mashed potatoes with country gravy Green beans Roll Beverage

d. Add a picture from the Clip Art Gallery to the cell in row 1, column 1. If necessary, resize the picture so it is approximately one inch high, then resample the picture. Change the alignment of the picture to centered.
e. Resize the first column so it is slightly wider than the data it contains.
f. Use the Distribute Columns Evenly command to resize columns two and three so they have equal widths.
g. Set the table to occupy 85% of the browser window width and to use a centered alignment on the page.
h. Add a custom background color of your choice to the table. If necessary, change the picture that you added in the first cell to use a transparent background.

i. Save the page, and save the picture using the filename *Logo.gif* in the Web site's images folder.

j. Add a nested table with one row and two columns below the date. In the first cell of the nested table, type **Posted by**. In the second cell of the nested table, type your first and last names.

k. Preview the page in a browser and print the page. Then close your browser, the Web, and FrontPage.

4. A government class you are taking is studying population changes. Recently your focus has been on population changes in the United States. Your instructor has asked you to find the amount of population change in a county of your choice. You decide to use the Web to locate census information about the county where you live. Then you will create a Web page with the census information.

To complete this independent challenge:

a. Connect to the Internet.

b. Access the Yahoo! search engine at http://www.yahoo.com.

c. Enter **Census population and housing estimates** as your search keywords, click Search, then click the link to open the Web page that you locate. (*Hint*: The wording of this link will be similar to the following: Population and Housing Unit Estimates - from the U.S. Census Bureau.)

d. If you have trouble locating this Web page, go to http://www.course.com. Go to the Student Online Companion for this book, then click the link for Unit I.

e. Click the County link under the Population Estimates heading, click the first county population estimates link on the page, then click the link for your state. (If you do not live in the United States, click any state.) Scroll the list that opens and locate the line that contains data about the county in which you live. (If you do not know which county you live in, select any county in the list.)

f. Select the line of data for your county, then copy it to the Clipboard by pressing [Ctrl][C]. Close your browser.

g. Start FrontPage and create a new Web using the Empty Web template and the name *Population*.

h. Create a new Web page in Folders View using the filename *County.htm* and the title **County Population Estimates**. Paste the data that you copied into the new Web page. (You will enter this pasted data into a table.)

i. Use the Insert Table button to create a table with two rows and five columns, then enter the following data in the first row. Center these heading in the cells. *Note:* Your word wrap may differ.

FIPS State/County Code and Area Name	Estimate 1	Estimate 2	Numeric Population Change	Percent Population Change

j. In the second row, enter the data that you pasted from the Web, then select and delete the pasted data from the page.

k. Add a custom background color of your choice to the table, and resize any rows and columns as necessary to make the data easier to read.

l. Type **Researched by: [insert your name here]** below the table, save the page, preview the page in a browser, and then print the page.

m. Close your browser, the Web, and FrontPage.

Visual Workshop

Start FrontPage and create a new Web using the Empty Web template and the name *Pets*. Create the frames page shown in Figure I-21. Save the top frame using the filename *Contents.htm* and the title **Contents**, and save the bottom frame using the filename *Canine.htm* and the title **Canine Products**. Save the frames page using the filename *Frames.htm* and the title **Pet Corral**. Create the hyperlink in the top frame after saving the frames page. Print the page as displayed by the browser, then close your browser and FrontPage.

FIGURE I-21

Unit
J

Using

Shared Borders and Themes in a Web Site

Objectives

- MOUS ▶ **Create shared borders in a Web site**
- MOUS ▶ **Add pages to Navigation View**
- MOUS ▶ **Change the content of a shared border**
- MOUS ▶ **Turn off a shared border for a single Web page**
- MOUS ▶ **Add a page banner and navigation bar to a Web page**
- MOUS ▶ **Apply a Web theme to a Web site and change its attributes**
- MOUS ▶ **Customize a Web site's theme**
- MOUS ▶ **Customize a Web theme for a single Web page**

One of the easiest and most efficient ways of creating the hyperlinks that link the pages in your Web site is to create shared borders. A **shared border** is an area that appears on every page in a Web site. Shared borders often include navigation bars or page banners. After you create a shared border, you can change its properties or you can identify pages on which you don't want shared borders to appear. Another way to enhance your Web site's appearance is to apply a theme to it. A **theme** is a collection of coordinated graphics, colors, and fonts applied to individual pages or all pages in a Web site. FrontPage provides over 50 themes from which you can choose, or you can customize an existing theme to get the right look for your Web site. Maureen Jenkins wants to update the Jenkins Web to include shared borders and a theme. These changes will make the Jenkins Web easier to navigate and provide visual interest, while maintaining consistency across the entire site.

Creating Shared Borders in a Web Site

Some FrontPage Web templates and wizards automatically create shared borders. If your Web site does not contain shared borders, you can create them by using the Shared Borders dialog box. You use shared borders to display information that you want to appear on every page in a Web site, such as a company logo or a copyright message, and to display hyperlinks to other Web pages in your Web site. When you create shared borders in FrontPage, you identify which pages should be linked based on their relationships to one another. For example, you might create hyperlinks for the parent page and all its child pages. ⟨⟩ Maureen wants to create top and left shared borders for the Jenkins Web. The top shared border will include the page title and a link to the Jenkins home page. The left shared border will include links to the parent page and to child pages. First she creates a heading and an introductory paragraph in the home page, then she creates the shared borders.

Steps

1. Start **Microsoft FrontPage**, click **File** on the menu bar, click **Open Web**, click the **[insert your name here] folder**, select the **Jenkins Web** (if necessary), click **Open**, then click the **Folders button** 📁 on the Views bar
   The Jenkins Web opens in Folders View.

2. Double-click **index.htm** in the contents pane
   The blank home page opens in Page View. You want the heading for the Jenkins Web to appear on this page.

3. Click the **Style list arrow** on the Formatting toolbar, click **Heading 2**, type **Welcome to the Jenkins Publishing Company's Web Site!**, then click the **Center button** 🖿 on the Formatting toolbar
   This text is the heading for the home page.

4. Press **[Enter]**, click the **Align Left button** 🖿 on the Formatting toolbar, then type the introductory paragraph (see Figure J-1)

5. Click **Format** on the menu bar, then click **Shared Borders**
   The Shared Borders dialog box opens, similar to the one in Figure J-2. You can apply shared borders to all pages in the Web site or to only the current page. In addition, you can apply shared borders to one or more sides of the Web page: top, left, right, and bottom. The top and left shared borders can include navigation buttons that FrontPage creates and manages through Navigation View.

6. Click the **All pages option button**, click the **Top** and **Left check boxes** to select them, then click the **Include navigation buttons check boxes** under the Top and Left check boxes to select them
   As shown in Figure J-2, the sample page in the dialog box shows how each selected item will appear on a Web page.

7. Click **OK**
   The home page changes to include shared borders at the top and left of the page, as shown in Figure J-3. Notice FrontPage automatically adds a page banner to the top shared border that contains the page title. The page title "Home Page" was automatically generated by FrontPage because it is the page title associated with the file index.htm. After you create shared borders, you can return to the Shared Borders dialog box at any time to make changes, such as adding or removing navigation buttons. You will edit the properties of the navigation bars in the next lesson.

8. Click the **Save button** 🖫 on the Standard toolbar
   FrontPage saves the home page and the shared borders for the Web site.

FIGURE J-1: Home page for the Jenkins Web

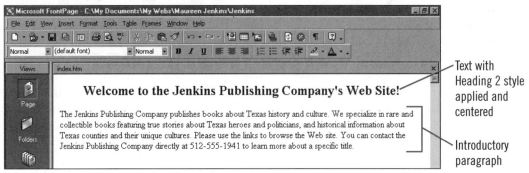

Text with Heading 2 style applied and centered

Introductory paragraph

FIGURE J-2: Completed Shared Borders dialog box

Applies shared border(s) to all pages in the site

Applies shared border(s) to the current page only

Sample page shows shared border selections

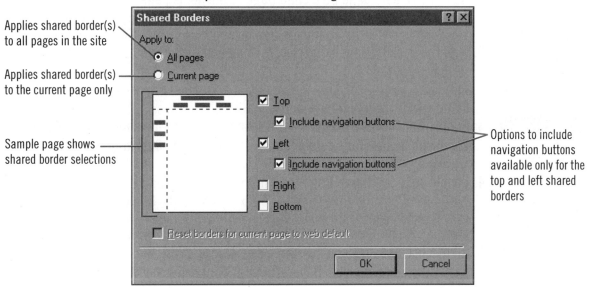

Options to include navigation buttons available only for the top and left shared borders

FIGURE J-3: Home page with shared borders

Page title (as seen in Navigation View) is added to the top shared border

Left shared border

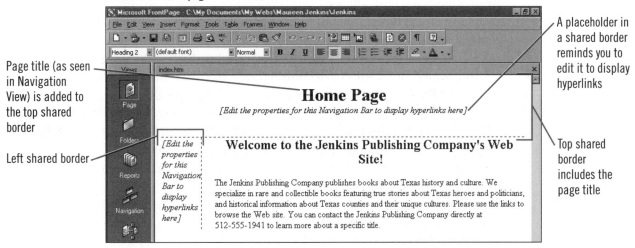

A placeholder in a shared border reminds you to edit it to display hyperlinks

Top shared border includes the page title

Adding Pages to Navigation View

After you create shared borders in a Web site, you must use Navigation View to tell FrontPage about the hierarchical relationships of your Web pages to each other. In most Web sites, the home page is the top-level page in the entire site. As you add new pages to the Web site below the home page, the home page becomes a parent page and the pages below it become child pages. As you continue adding pages to a Web site, you must return to Navigation View and add them to the Web site's navigation structure. ✏️ Maureen adds the Booklist page to the Web site as a child page of the home page. She also adds blank pages to the Web as placeholders for biographical information about some authors. After adding these new pages, she examines the navigation settings for each border.

Steps 123 4

Trouble?

If the Folder List does not appear, click the Folder List button 🔲 on the Standard toolbar. If the Navigation toolbar is blocking the Navigation pane, drag it out of the way.

QuickTip

Because this Web's frames page contains a Contents page with hyperlinks to open pages in the main frame, you usually won't include shared borders on the frames page or its related pages. Therefore, you will not add these pages to Navigation View.

1. Click the **Navigation button** 🔲 on the Views bar, then drag the **Booklist.htm page** from the Folder List to be a child page of the home page
   A line connects the Home Page and Booklist page icons indicating their relationship. FrontPage uses this information to create the correct hyperlinks in the Web site's shared borders.

2. With the Booklist page still selected, click the **New Page button** 🗋 on the Standard toolbar three times
   Three new pages—named New Page 1, New Page 2, and New Page 3—appear as child pages of the Booklist page, as shown in Figure J-4.

3. Right-click the **New Page 1 icon** to open the pop-up menu, click **Rename**, type **Casdorph**, press **[Tab]**, type **Frost**, press **[Tab]**, type **Sherman**, then press **[Enter]**
   You renamed the three new pages—one for each author.

4. Double-click the **Home Page icon** in the navigation pane
   The home page now displays a Booklist hyperlink in the left shared border—the Booklist page is a child page of the home page. The top shared border does not contain any hyperlinks because the home page is the top-level page in the Web site.

5. Right-click the placeholder text that begins **[Edit the properties...** in the top shared border, then click **Navigation Bar Properties** on the pop-up menu
   The Navigation Bar Properties dialog box opens, as shown in Figure J-5. When the top shared border was created, FrontPage used the default settings for creating button hyperlinks to same-level pages and to the home and parent pages in the top shared border.

6. Make changes as needed so that your Navigation Bar Properties dialog box looks like Figure J-5, click the **Parent page check box** to clear it, then click **OK**
   The Navigation Bar Properties dialog box closes. The top shared border looks the same, even though you made changes.

7. Right-click the **link** in the left shared border, then click **Navigation Bar Properties** on the pop-up menu
   The Navigation Bar Properties dialog box for the left shared border opens. Notice that the default setting for the left shared border creates vertical text links to child-level pages.

8. Click the **Parent page check box** to select it, then click **OK**
   The Navigation Bar Properties dialog box closes. The left shared border looks the same.

9. Click the **Save button** 🖫 on the Standard toolbar, click the **Preview in Browser button** 🔍 on the Standard toolbar, then click **Yes** if necessary
   FrontPage saves the home page and then opens it in a browser, as shown in Figure J-6.

10. Click the **Booklist link** in the left shared border
    The Booklist page opens in a browser, as shown in Figure J-7. FrontPage automatically created the hyperlinks on this page using the information you provided in Navigation View and in the Navigation Bar Properties dialog box.

FIGURE J-4: Navigation View of the Jenkins Web

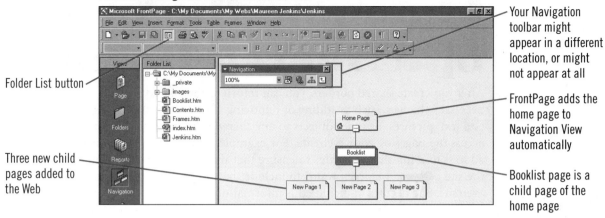

Folder List button

Three new child pages added to the Web

Your Navigation toolbar might appear in a different location, or might not appear at all

FrontPage adds the home page to Navigation View automatically

Booklist page is a child page of the home page

FIGURE J-5: Navigation Bar Properties dialog box for the top shared border

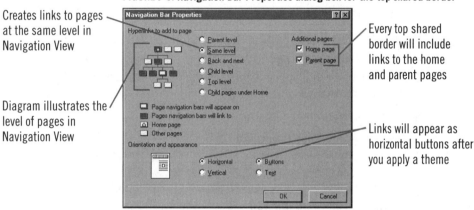

Creates links to pages at the same level in Navigation View

Diagram illustrates the level of pages in Navigation View

Every top shared border will include links to the home and parent pages

Links will appear as horizontal buttons after you apply a theme

FIGURE J-6: Home page in a browser

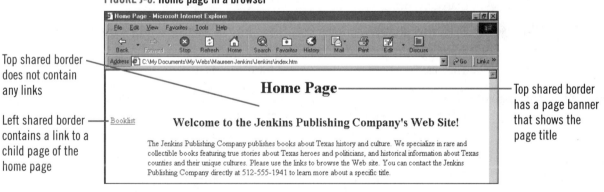

Top shared border does not contain any links

Left shared border contains a link to a child page of the home page

Top shared border has a page banner that shows the page title

FIGURE J-7: Booklist Web page in a browser

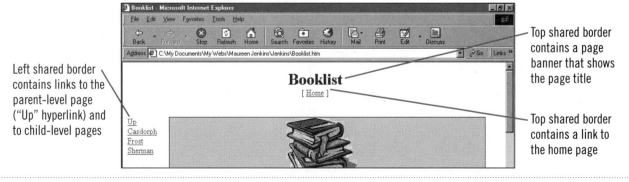

Left shared border contains links to the parent-level page ("Up" hyperlink) and to child-level pages

Top shared border contains a page banner that shows the page title

Top shared border contains a link to the home page

Changing the Content of a Shared Border

After you create shared borders, you can return to the Shared Borders dialog box to make any necessary changes, such as adding or removing navigation buttons or shared borders. You can add text, pictures, or other objects to any shared border to maintain a consistent appearance across the pages of your Web site. For example, you might add a company logo, name, and address to a top shared border to ensure that this information appears in every Web page in the site. ✐ Maureen wants to include the company name and logo in every page of the Web site. She decides to include this information in the site's top shared border.

Steps 1 2 3 4

1. Click the **Microsoft FrontPage program button** on the taskbar
   You return to Page View.

2. Click the text **Home Page** in the top shared border, press **[Home]**, press **[Enter]**, then press the **Up arrow key** to move the insertion point to the new line
   The insertion point appears on a new, blank, centered line above the Home Page heading in the top shared border.

3. Click the **Style list arrow** on the Formatting toolbar, click **Heading 3**, then type **The Jenkins Publishing Company**
   The text that you typed will appear in every Jenkins Web page that uses the top shared border.

4. Press **[Home]** to move the insertion point to the beginning of the line, click the **Insert Picture From File button** 🖼 on the Standard toolbar, double-click the **images folder** (if necessary), then double-click **Books.jpg**
   The picture of the books, which is the Jenkins Publishing Company logo, appears in the top shared border.

5. Click the **picture** to select it, then drag the **lower-right sizing handle** toward the middle of the picture to resize it (see Figure J-8)
   The logo is now appropriately sized for use in the border, as shown in Figure J-8.

6. Click the **Save button** 💾 on the Standard toolbar, click the **Preview in Browser button** 🖼 on the Standard toolbar, then click **Yes** if necessary
   The home page opens in a browser. The logo, the company name, and the page title appear in the top shared border.

7. Click the **Booklist link** in the left shared border
   The Booklist page opens in a browser, as shown in Figure J-9. Because the Booklist page uses the top shared border, it contains the logo and the company name, the page title, and a link to the page's parent page (the home page).

8. Click the **Microsoft FrontPage program button** on the taskbar

FIGURE J-8: Content added to the top shared border

Resized picture of the Jenkins Publishing Company logo

Text with Heading 3 style applied

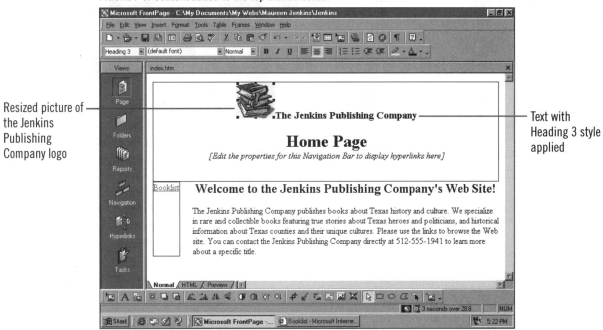

FIGURE J-9: Revised Booklist page in a browser

Top shared border

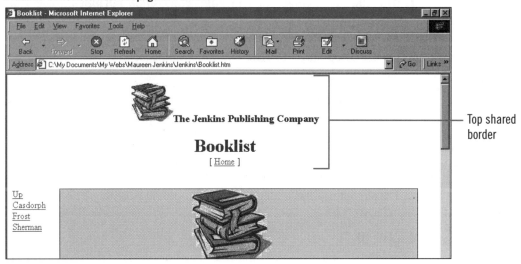

Using FrontPage navigation bars to navigate a Web site

When you use FrontPage to create a navigation bar, you might choose the option in the Navigation Bar Properties dialog box to include the parent page in the Web site's navigation structure. The parent page is the page at the next higher level in the navigation pane. For example, in the Jenkins Web, Home Page is a first-level page (a parent page) and Booklist is a second-level page (a child page). Refer to Figure J-4 to view the hierarchical structure of the pages. The pages Casdorph, Frost, and Sherman are child pages of the Booklist page; the Booklist page is a parent page of these child pages. FrontPage uses the "Up" hyperlink to link a child page to its parent page. For example, if you click an "Up" hyperlink in the Frost page, which is a third-level page, then the parent of that page, Booklist, which is a second-level page, will open in a browser.

Turning Off a Shared Border for a Single Web Page

The Shared Borders dialog box provides the option of creating shared borders for all pages in a Web site, for only the current page, or for pages selected in Folders View. When you need to turn off shared borders for a single page, you simply clear the check boxes in the Shared Borders dialog box for that page. Sometimes the content of a shared border might repeat content that already exists in a home page, such as the company name and address information. In this case, you can turn off the shared border for the home page and then create a page banner and navigation bar to provide page identification and navigation options. ◀━━ Because the heading on the home page already contains the company name, Maureen decides to turn off the top shared border for the home page to avoid duplication of the company name. Instead, she creates a page banner with the page title "Home Page" and a navigation bar with links to child-level pages. She also turns off the left shared border because she wants to move the links that it contained to the top of the home page. Before she creates the page banner and navigation bar, however, she turns off the shared borders.

Steps

1. **With the home page open in Page View, click Format on the menu bar, then click Shared Borders**
   The Shared Borders dialog box opens. The current settings show that all pages in the Web site use a top and a left shared border and that these shared borders contain navigation buttons.

2. **Click the Current page option button to select it**
   Notice that the Reset borders for current page to web default check box becomes active. Selecting this check box restores the shared borders for the selected page to match the shared borders for the Web site.

3. **Click the Top check box to clear it, then click the Left check box to clear it**
   The Shared Borders dialog box shows a sample page that uses no shared borders, as shown in Figure J-10.

4. **Click OK**
   Now the home page does not use shared borders. In the next lesson, you will add a page banner that includes the page title and a navigation bar that includes links.

5. **Click the Save button 🖫 on the Standard toolbar**

6. **Click the Navigation button ◫ on the Views bar, then double-click the Booklist icon**
   The Booklist page opens in Page View, as shown in Figure J-11. Notice that it still uses the shared borders. Even though you turned off shared borders on the home page, other pages in the Web site that appear in Navigation View continue to use the shared borders.

FIGURE J-10: Shared Borders dialog box for the home page

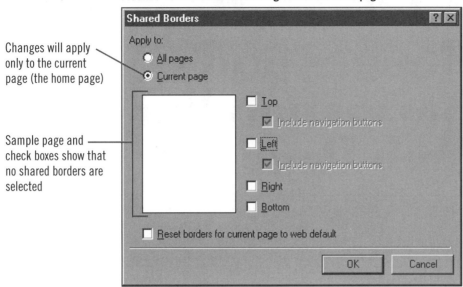

Changes will apply only to the current page (the home page)

Sample page and check boxes show that no shared borders are selected

FIGURE J-11: Booklist page in Page View

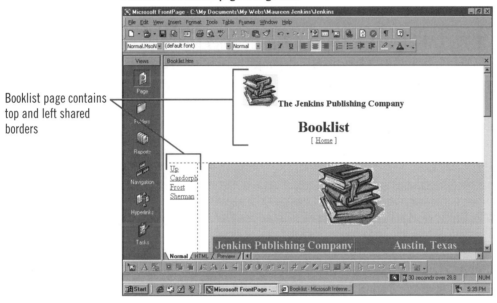

Booklist page contains top and left shared borders

Examining a Web site's shared border files

When you create shared borders in a Web site, FrontPage creates a folder named _borders in the Web site and stores files in it that maintain the shared borders. Every FrontPage folder that begins with an underscore character indicates a hidden folder in the Web site. **Hidden folders** contain files that run your Web site but are not necessary for a browser to display your Web pages. The default in FrontPage is to hide hidden folders from view—even on the machine that created them. The only exception is that the Web site's _private folder is always visible when you work in FrontPage. In FrontPage, to view a Web site's hidden folders, click Tools on the menu bar, click Web Settings, click the Advanced tab, then click the Show documents in hidden directories check box to select it. Click Yes to refresh the Web site, and then the Folder List will show your Web site's hidden folders in Folders View. To hide your Web site's hidden folders, repeat the steps and clear the Show documents in hidden directories check box.

Adding a Page Banner and Navigation Bar to a Web Page

When you turn off the top shared border for a Web page, you can still add the page title and a navigation bar to the page. In this situation, the navigation bar is separate from the one created by FrontPage for use in the top shared border. Because you determine which links to include, the navigation bar may be the same as the one used in the shared border or it may be different. For example, you might remove all shared borders for a home page and replace the top shared border with a page banner and a navigation bar with hyperlinks to child pages. In this situation, the page banner and navigation bar provide the page title and navigation options on the home page. Maureen wants the home page to display the page title and a navigation bar with links to child pages. She adds these features at the top of the page by inserting a page banner and a navigation bar.

Steps

1. Click **Window** on the menu bar, click **index.htm**, click to the left of the Welcome heading to place the insertion point there, press **[Enter]**, press the **Up arrow key**, click **Insert** on the menu bar, then click **Page Banner**

The Page Banner Properties dialog box opens, as shown in Figure J-12. The default settings are to use a picture page banner and the page title (as shown in Navigation View) as the page banner text.

QuickTip

Even though you selected the picture option, the page banner will continue to appear as text until you apply a Web theme. After you apply a Web theme, the page banner text will change to a picture.

2. Click **OK**

FrontPage creates a page banner at the top of the page, where you positioned the insertion point.

3. Press **[Enter]**, click **Insert** on the menu bar, then click **Navigation Bar**

The Navigation Bar Properties dialog box opens.

4. If necessary, click the **Child level option button**, the **Horizontal option button**, and the **Buttons option button**, then click **OK**

A hyperlink to the Booklist page, which is a child page of the home page, appears below the page banner, as shown in Figure J-13. This page now contains a page banner and a hyperlink; it does not use the top or left shared borders.

5. Click the **Save button** on the Standard toolbar, then click the **Preview in Browser button** on the Standard toolbar

The home page does not contain shared borders, but it does contain a page banner and a navigation bar with a link to the Booklist page.

6. Click the **Booklist link**

The Booklist page opens. Notice that the Booklist page still uses the top and left shared borders for the Web site. The top shared border contains the logo, company name, page banner, and navigation bar with a link to the home page. The left shared border contains an "Up" hyperlink to open the parent page (Booklist) and three hyperlinks to open the child pages of the Booklist page.

7. Click the **Microsoft FrontPage program button** on the taskbar

FIGURE J-12: Page Banner Properties dialog box

Page banner will appear as a picture when a theme is applied to the Web page

Page title assigned to index.htm (as seen in Navigation View) is the default text used for the page banner

FIGURE J-13: Revised home page

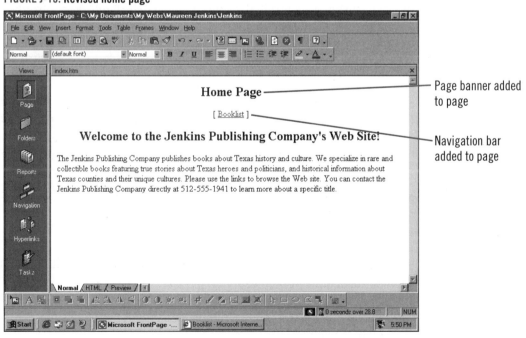

Page banner added to page

Navigation bar added to page

Applying a Web Theme to a Web Site and Changing Its Attributes

When you apply a Web theme to a Web site, you ensure a consistent, professionally designed appearance across every page in the site. FrontPage provides over 50 Web themes from which to select. You can also change a theme's look by changing its **attributes**—active graphics, vivid colors, and a background picture. **Active graphics** are theme elements that become animated in the page, such as a hyperlink button changing color when the pointer moves over it. **Vivid colors** are created by an enhanced color set used by the theme to produce brighter, deeper colors. A **background picture** is a picture that is used as the page's background. Now that Maureen has created some of the pages in the Web site, she wants to work on improving the site's overall appearance by applying a Web theme that conveys a clean, professional image.

Steps

1. With the home page open in Page View, click **Format** on the menu bar, then click **Theme**
   The Themes dialog box opens.

2. Scroll down the Apply Theme to list box, click **Industrial**, then make sure that only the **Active graphics check box** is selected
   A preview of the selected theme appears in the Sample of Theme window, as shown in Figure J-14.

3. Click **OK**, then click **Yes**
   The theme is applied to the entire Web site. The home page now shows the selected theme, as shown in Figure J-15. The page banner appears as a picture. The page banner picture for this theme is a decorative background box with text. Notice also that the Booklist hyperlink changes from text to a button, and the fonts used in the heading and the text change based on the default settings for the theme.

4. Click **Format** on the menu bar, click **Theme**, click the **Vivid colors check box** to select it, click the **Background picture check box** to select it, then click **OK**
   FrontPage changes the theme's properties and applies the theme's vivid color set and background picture to all pages in the Web. If your monitor displays 256 or fewer colors, you might not notice a difference in a theme's regular and vivid color sets.

5. Click the **Save button** 🖫 on the Standard toolbar, then click the **Preview in Browser button** 🔍 on the Standard toolbar
   The home page opens in a browser.

6. Move the pointer back and forth over the **Booklist hyperlink** several times to view the button's active graphics
   Notice that the Booklist hyperlink changes color when you move the pointer over it. When you select the active graphics option for a theme, buttons change their appearance when you move the pointer over them in a browser.

7. Click the **Microsoft FrontPage program button** on the taskbar

FIGURE J-14: Themes dialog box

Industrial theme
selected

Active graphics
enabled

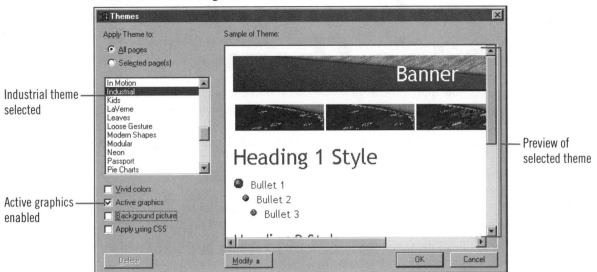

Preview of
selected theme

FIGURE J-15: Theme applied to the home page

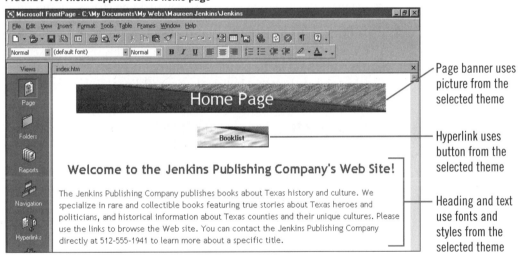

Page banner uses
picture from the
selected theme

Hyperlink uses
button from the
selected theme

Heading and text
use fonts and
styles from the
selected theme

Installing additional Web themes

FrontPage installs only the default themes when you install the program. To install more themes, insert the CD-ROM in the correct drive, click Format on the menu bar, click Theme, click (Install Additional Themes) in the list box, click Yes, then click OK. The new themes will appear in the Themes dialog box.

Customizing a Web Site's Theme

After you apply a theme to a Web site, you might want to change the appearance of text, colors, hyperlinks, backgrounds, and other theme elements to more closely match your needs. Customizing a theme is more efficient than simply using the Formatting toolbar options to create a new look. When you customize a theme to change the style of headings, for example, you ensure that every occurrence of the selected heading has the same appearance in the Web site. Maureen wants to customize the current theme to use a different font for the body text in the Web pages.

1. Click Format on the menu bar, click Theme, then click Modify
The "What would you like to modify?" section of the Themes dialog box appears, as shown in Figure J-16. You decide to preview the various options before making changes.

2. Click Colors
The Modify Theme dialog box opens, showing the Color Schemes tab, as shown in Figure J-17. If you want to change the color set used by a FrontPage theme, clicking each theme color scheme in the list box will show a preview of the new colors in the Sample of Theme box. You decide the colors appear as desired, so you make no changes at this time.

3. Click Cancel to close the Modify Theme dialog box, then click Graphics
The Modify Theme dialog box opens again, but this time it presents the options for changing the fonts used in the picture elements of the theme (the banner, the horizontal navigation bar and its buttons, bullets, horizontal lines, and other hyperlink buttons), and the background picture for the currently applied theme.

4. Click the Font tab, then click the Item list arrow
You can change the selected font used for any text items in the Item list box.

5. Press [Esc] to close the menu, click Cancel, then click Text
The Modify Theme dialog box opens and presents the options for changing the font and style of text used in the Web page.

6. Click the Item list arrow
You can change the style of the body text or any of the headings in the Item list box.

7. Click Body in the Item list, then scroll down the Font list box and click Franklin Gothic Book
The Sample of Theme box shows samples of the text using the Franklin Gothic Book font. Each phrase shows how that element will look on the page.

8. Click OK, click OK in the Themes dialog box, click Yes, then click OK to accept the default theme name of "Copy of Industrial"
The Themes dialog box closes and FrontPage applies the Copy of Industrial theme to the Web site, as shown in Figure J-18. FrontPage also saved the Copy of Industrial theme so that it is available in the Themes dialog box if you wish to apply it to another Web site.

9. Click the Save button 🖫 on the Standard toolbar

QuickTip
Remember that a user's monitor resolution determines how colors will appear when viewed on the Web. Always test your Web pages using different monitor resolution settings, browsers, and operating systems to ensure that your colors appear as desired.

QuickTip
Don't make too many changes to a theme, or you might end up with colors that don't work well together or fonts that aren't readable against the page's background.

Trouble?
If you do not have the Franklin Gothic Book font, select Arial or a similar font.

Trouble?
If the Copy of Industrial theme already exists, change the theme's name to "Copy of Industrial 1" to continue.

FIGURE J-16: Themes dialog box expanded to show Modify options

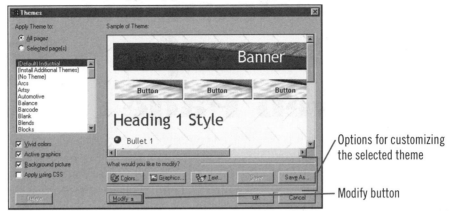

Options for customizing
the selected theme

Modify button

FIGURE J-17: Color Schemes tab

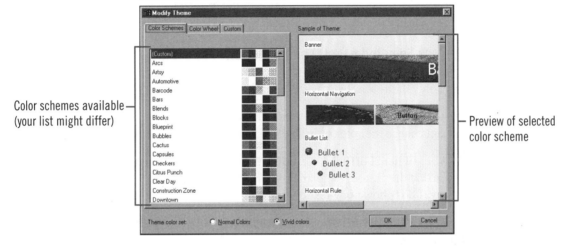

Color schemes available
(your list might differ)

Preview of selected
color scheme

FIGURE J-18: Customized theme applied to the home page

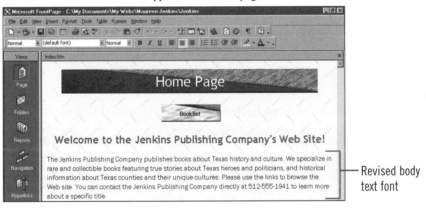

Revised body
text font

Deleting a Web theme

You might need to use a customized Web theme only once. To manage space on your hard drive better, you can delete a Web theme by selecting it in the Themes dialog box, then clicking Delete. Be careful, however, because deleting a Web theme is a permanent action. Deleting a theme means that you can't apply it to future Web sites. Webs that use a deleted theme will still include the theme's elements because the theme's files are stored in the Web site itself in the _themes folder. Make sure that all Webs are closed before deleting any Web themes.

Customizing a Web Theme for a Single Web Page

Although it is best to use a consistent theme across an entire Web site, there are cases in which you might want to create a slightly different appearance to emphasize a single page. You can customize a theme for a single Web page to make that page have a slightly different appearance from other pages in the site. You can also apply a different Web theme to a single page. Maureen decides to customize the theme for the home page by using different colors for the Body and Heading 2 styles.

Steps

1. With the home page open in Page View, click **Format** on the menu bar, then click **Theme**
   The Themes dialog box opens and shows the currently selected site-wide theme.

2. Click the **Selected page(s) option button** to select it
   Now, when you select another theme or customize the existing theme, your changes will apply only to the selected page.

3. Click **Modify**, click **Colors**, then click the **Custom tab**
   You can change the color of individual page elements using the Custom tab.

4. Click the **Item list arrow**, click **Body**, click the **Color list arrow**, then click the **Navy color**
   Notice that the phrase "Regular Text Sample" in the Sample of Theme window changes color to navy. This is how body text on the selected Web page will appear.

5. Click the **Item list arrow**, click **Heading 2**, click the **Color list arrow**, then click the **Purple color**
   Notice that the phrase "Heading 2 style" changes color to purple, as shown in Figure J-19. This is how Heading 2 text on the Web page will appear.

6. Click **OK**, click **OK** in the Themes dialog box, then click **Yes**
   The home page shows the new color settings—the heading is now purple and the text is navy blue, as shown in Figure J-20. Other pages in the Web site, however, will still use the default settings of the selected theme.

7. Click the **Save button** 🖫 on the Standard toolbar

8. Click **File** on the menu bar, click **Close Web**, click **Yes** (if necessary) to save any open Web pages or to replace any shared border files, then close FrontPage and your browser

FIGURE J-19: Theme's font colors customized

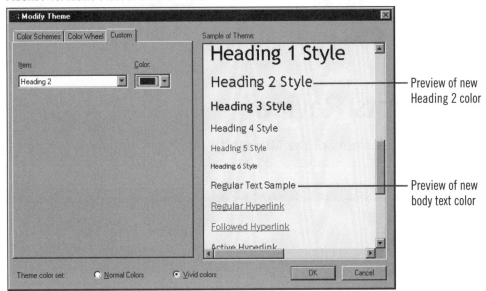

Preview of new Heading 2 color

Preview of new body text color

FIGURE J-20: Home page with revised colors

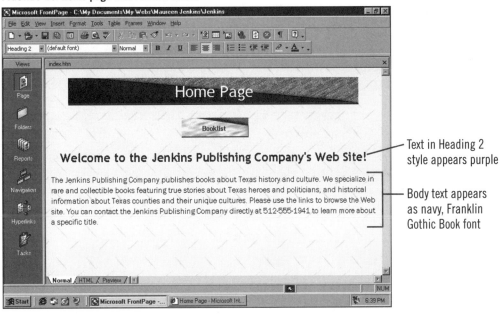

Text in Heading 2 style appears purple

Body text appears as navy, Franklin Gothic Book font

CLUES TO USE

Changing the theme for several pages at once

When you want to apply the same customized theme to several pages in a Web site, you can select those pages in Folders View by selecting the first page, pressing and holding [Ctrl], then selecting the other pages. Click Format on the menu bar, then click Theme. Use the Themes dialog box to customize or change the theme as desired, then save your changes. Each page that you selected in Folders View will use the customized theme. This method saves you some time by applying the customized theme to each selected page simultaneously.

Practice

► Concepts Review

Label each of the elements of the Microsoft FrontPage window shown in Figure J-21.

FIGURE J-21

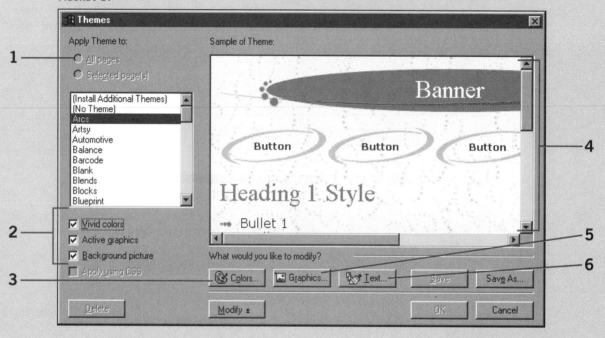

Match each of the terms with the statement that describes it.

7. _borders
8. Include navigation buttons check box
9. Modify
10. Navigation Bar Properties dialog box
11. Shared border
12. Theme
13. Vivid colors

a. A hidden folder in a Web site
b. Used to specify the hyperlinks to include in a shared border and their appearance
c. A predesigned set of fonts, colors, and graphics that you can apply to and customize for a Web site or a single Web page
d. A rich, bright set of colors used in a Web theme
e. Can contain a page banner and navigation bar that appears in every Web page that uses it
f. Specifies to add hyperlinks to a shared border
g. Used to customize a Web theme

Select the best answer from the list of choices.

14. Which shared border(s) can contain navigation buttons?
- **a.** Top and right
- **b.** Top and left
- **c.** Bottom
- **d.** Top

15. What is the first character of a hidden folder's name in a Web site?
- **a.** A dash
- **b.** An underscore
- **c.** A number sign
- **d.** A letter

16. A shared border can contain
- **a.** Text.
- **b.** Pictures.
- **c.** Headings.
- **d.** All of the above.

17. To turn off a shared border for a Web page, change the settings in
- **a.** The Page Banner dialog box.
- **b.** The Navigation Bar Properties dialog box.
- **c.** The Shared Borders dialog box.
- **d.** Navigation View.

18. When you add a picture page banner to a Web page that does not use a theme,
- **a.** The page banner does not appear.
- **b.** The page banner appears as text.
- **c.** The page banner appears as a picture.
- **d.** You cannot add a picture page banner to a Web page that does not use a theme.

19. Which one of the following is NOT an attribute that you can change in a Web theme?
- **a.** Active graphics
- **b.** Vivid colors
- **c.** Shared border
- **d.** Background picture

20. To change the font used for a specific theme's active hyperlinks, click the _____ button in the Themes dialog box.
- **a.** Colors
- **b.** Fonts
- **c.** Text
- **d.** Graphics

► Skills Review

1. Create shared borders in a Web site.
- **a.** Start Microsoft FrontPage and create a new One Page Web named *ECommerce*.
- **b.** Open the home page, type **Using Electronic Commerce Web Sites**, then center this text and apply the Heading 1 style.
- **c.** Press [Enter], then type the following paragraph and left-align it: Electronic commerce allows people to use the Internet to shop for virtually any item or service in the world from the comfort of their computer chair.

d. Save the home page.

e. Add a new page to the Web site in Page View that contains the following content: **Merchants provide many payment options in their electronic commerce sites. You can pay for purchases of goods and services using credit or charge cards, electronic cash, or electronic checks.**

f. Save the new page using the filename *Payment.htm* and the title **Payment Options**.

g. Add a new page to the Web site in Page View that contains the following content: **Web site visitors should look for trustmarks on an electronic commerce Web site to ensure that the Web site is valid and safe.**

h. Save the new Web page using the filename *Security.htm* and the title **Security Issues**.

i. Create top, left, and bottom shared borders for all pages in the Web site. Create navigation buttons in the top and left shared borders.

j. Save your changes.

2. **Add pages to Navigation View.**

a. Change to Navigation View.

b. Add the Payment.htm page to the navigation structure as a child page of the home page.

c. Add the Security.htm page to the navigation structure as a child page of the home page.

d. Add a new page to the navigation structure as a child page of the Security Issues page. (*Hint*: With the Security Issues icon selected in the navigation pane, click the New Page button.)

e. Right-click the new page, click Rename, then rename the page **Encryption**.

f. Add three new child pages to the Payment Options page, then rename them as **Credit**, **Checks**, and **E-Cash**, respectively.

3. **Change the content of a shared border.**

a. Open the home page in Page View.

b. Select the comment in the bottom shared border, press [Enter], type **Copyright 2001**, press [Spacebar], then type your first and last names.

c. Change the hyperlinks in the left shared border to use vertical buttons. (*Note*: You won't see any changes until you apply a theme.)

d. Create a new blank line above the page banner in the top shared border, then insert an appropriate clipart image from the Clip Gallery. Use a picture that represents electronic commerce, such as a computer, a picture of money, or something that shows international business. (If you cannot locate an appropriate picture, select another picture of your choice.)

e. If necessary, resize and resample the picture that you inserted to approximately one inch high.

f. Save the Web page and save the picture that you inserted as *Business.gif* in the Web site's images folder.

4. **Turn off a shared border for a single Web page.**

a. Open the Encryption page in Page View.

b. Turn off the left shared border for this page only.

c. Save the Encryption page, then preview it in a browser.

d. Use the "Up" hyperlink to open the parent page of the Encryption page, which is the Security Issues page.

e. In FrontPage, turn off the left shared border for the Checks, Credit, and E-Cash pages, then save your changes.

f. Turn off the top and left shared borders for the home page, then save it.

5. **Add a page banner and navigation bar to a Web page.**

a. Add a picture page banner on a new line above the heading in the home page with the text **Home Page**. (*Note*: You will see text but not a picture until you apply a theme.)

b. On a new blank line below the page banner, create a navigation bar that includes horizontal, text links to the home page, parent page, and child pages.

c. Save the home page.

d. Change the navigation bar on the home page to use horizontal buttons instead of text hyperlinks, then save the home page. Remember, you will see text but not buttons until you apply a theme.

e. Preview the home page in a browser.

f. Use the links in the shared borders to navigate all the pages in the site.

g. Return to FrontPage.

6. **Apply a Web theme to a Web site and change its attributes.**

a. Apply a theme to the entire Web site that does not use vivid colors, active graphics, or a background picture. Choose a theme that complements the Web's content.

b. Save your changes.

c. Change the Web's theme to use active graphics, vivid colors, and a background picture, then close the Themes dialog box.

d. Save your changes, then preview the home page in a browser.

e. Use the links in the top navigation bar and the shared borders to navigate all the pages in the site.

f. Return to FrontPage.

7. **Customize a Web site's theme.**

a. Change the theme to use another font for the body text, then save the theme using the default name.

b. Change the color of the font used in the body text to another one of your choice, then save your changes.

c. Preview your changes in a browser.

d. Return to FrontPage.

8. **Customize a Web theme for a single Web page.**

a. In Folders View, click the Encryption page to select it, then press and hold [Ctrl] to select the Checks, Credit, and E-Cash pages.

b. Open the Themes dialog box.

c. Customize the Web theme used in the selected pages to use a different color scheme of your choice. Make sure that the color scheme you select maintains the legibility of text in the page.

d. Change the color of the body text for the selected pages to another color. Select a color that ensures legibility against the page background.

e. In the Themes dialog box, click Save As, then save the theme using a new name, such as "Copy of <theme name>2."

f. Open the Payment Options page in Page View, save it, preview the Payment Options page in a browser, then print it. Close your browser.

g. Close the Web, saving any changes to pages and to shared border files.

▶ Independent Challenges

1. You work in the Marketing Department for the All-Season Travel Agency, which is currently promoting special fares on three of its vacation packages. Clients who book their vacations early will receive a 20% discount off the special fares. Because of the high volume of calls generated by radio ads in the area, you decide to create a Web site to provide information about the destinations, fares, and travel dates.

To complete this independent challenge:

a. Start Microsoft FrontPage and use the Import Web Wizard to create a new Web named *Travel*.

b. Select the option to import pages from a file source directory of files on a local computer or network, click Browse, open the UnitJ\Ic1 folder on your Project Disk, then click OK.

c. Click Next, make sure that you see the files Italy.htm, index.htm, Bermuda.htm, and Orlando.htm in the list box, click Next, then click Finish.

d. In Navigation View, add the Italy.htm, Bermuda.htm, and Orlando.htm pages that you imported into the Web as child pages of the home page.

e. Add a top and a bottom shared border to the Web. The top shared border should include navigation buttons.

f. Open the home page in Page View, then check the properties of the navigation bar in the top shared border. Make changes if necessary so the top shared border contains links to the home page, parent page, and child pages. Hyperlinks should appear as horizontal buttons.

g. Select the comment in the bottom shared border, then type **Contact All-Season Travel for departure, upgrade, and airfare information**.

h. Save your changes.

i. Apply the Expedition theme to the entire Web site. Change the theme's attributes to use vivid colors, active graphics, and a background picture. If you don't have the Expedition theme, choose a different theme.

j. Customize the Expedition theme to use Arial Narrow font for the body text, then save the theme using the default name.

k. Save your changes, preview the home page in a browser, use the links to examine each page in the Web site, open the home page again, then print it.

l. Close your browser, close the Web and if prompted to do so, save any Web pages or shared border files, then close FrontPage.

2. Your family is moving to France this summer as part of an employer-sponsored transfer. You are in charge of selling some of your family's assets that you cannot take with you or put in storage. You decide to put an ad in the local newspaper and refer to a URL so interested buyers can view detailed information about the items using the Internet. Because you will update the Web site frequently with new items for sale, you decide to use a shared border to ensure that the correct hyperlinks appear in the Web pages.

To complete this independent challenge:

a. Start Microsoft FrontPage and use the Import Web Wizard to create a new Web named *France*.

b. Select the option to import pages from a file source directory of files on a local computer or network, click Browse, open the UnitJ\Ic2 folder on your Project Disk, click OK, then click Next.

c. Make sure that you see the files index.htm, Honda.htm, Toyota.htm, Table.htm, and Linens.htm in the list box, click Next, then click Finish.

d. Open the pages that you imported and examine their contents. Then change to Navigation View and add the pages to the navigation structure. (*Hint*: Use each page's contents to determine how to arrange the pages in Navigation View.)

e. Add a top and left shared border to all pages in the Web. Both shared borders should include navigation buttons.

f. Open the home page in Page View, then check the properties of the navigation bar in the top shared border. Make changes as necessary so the top shared border contains links to the home page, parent page, and same-level pages. Hyperlinks should appear as horizontal buttons.

g. Add the following text to the top shared border below the page banner: **Everything must go! Please make an offer today**. Format the text using the Heading 4 style.

h. Edit the properties of the left shared border. Be sure it contains links to child-level pages only. Change hyperlinks so they appear as vertical buttons.

i. Save your changes.

j. Apply a theme of your choice to the entire Web site, then change the theme's attributes to use vivid colors, active graphics, and a background picture. Save your changes, preview the home page in a browser, use the links to examine each page in the Web site, open the home page again, then print it. Close your browser.

k. In Folders View, change the Web site to show its hidden folders, open the folder that contains the Web site's shared border files, open the file for the top shared border in Page View and type your first and last names on the first line (under the "Edit the properties" text), then print the top shared border page from FrontPage. Close the top shared border page without saving changes.

l. Close the Web and if prompted to do so, save any Web pages or shared border files, then close FrontPage.

3. You work for the dean of the Business Department at your school. The dean's office wants to create a Web site with information about every business degree it offers. You need to create a Web site to show how the dean's office might structure the site and link its pages together.

To complete this independent challenge:

a. Start Microsoft FrontPage and create a new One Page Web named *Courses*.

b. Open the home page in Page View, enter an appropriate heading on the page using the Heading 1 style, then type a short description of the Web site's contents. See Figure J-22 for the Web's navigation design.

c. Use the navigation structure shown in Figure J-22 to add new pages to the Web site. Rename the pages as indicated in the figure.

FIGURE J-22

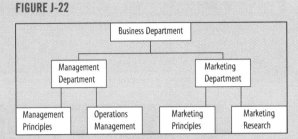

d. Apply a top and left shared border to all pages in the Web. Both shared borders should include navigation buttons.

e. Change the top and left shared border navigation bars to include the correct hyperlinks for your Web site. The top shared border should include horizontal text hyperlinks to child pages. The left shared border should include vertical text hyperlinks to the home page, parent page, and same-level pages.

f. Apply an appropriate theme to your Web.

g. Turn off the top shared border on the home page. Add a centered, picture page banner that contains the text **Business Department**. Then add a centered navigation bar with horizontal text hyperlinks to child pages.

h. Customize the theme for the home page only. Make it compatible with, but more striking than, the rest of the pages in the Web site. Save the customized theme using the default filename, open the home page in Page View, then save your changes.

i. Preview the home page in a browser, then print it. Test the links in your site to make sure they work as expected.

j. Close your browser, close the Web and if prompted to do so, save any Web pages or shared border files, then close FrontPage.

4. As the Webmaster for your company, a not-for-profit organization that provides advice about babies and their health to new parents, you are in charge of managing its Web site. The Web site development team wants to create a new site with a look and feel similar to current Web sites that new parents visit, so they will have an easy time navigating your new site. You decide to visit some of these sites and examine each site's elements and features to determine how effective they are.

To complete this independent challenge:

a. Connect to the Internet.

b. Go to http://www.course.com, navigate to the Student Online Companion for this book, then click the link for Unit J.

c. Follow the links to open the Web sites. For each site, print the home page and one other page that is linked to the home page. (Check with your instructor if you prefer to analyze a group of Web sites focused on a different topic.) On each printed page, identify the type of navigation options that the page uses. For example, does the page use a navigation bar with links to parent-level and child-level pages, or a shared border with navigation buttons?

d. Write a brief report in which you comment on the site's visual appearance. Do you think it uses a theme? Why or why not? Do the pages in the site have a consistent appearance? If yes, what makes the appearance consistent?

e. For each page that you printed, comment on the effectiveness of the page's navigation options and appearance. What changes, if any, would you make? How would you use FrontPage to implement them? Why would you make these changes?

f. Attach your completed report to the top of the printed pages for that site. Complete a report on another Web site.

g. Close your browser and your dial-up connection.

► Visual Workshop

Create a new One Page Web named *Golf*. Add empty pages to the Web site and change the Web site's settings to match the Web page shown in Figure J-23. (*Hint*: The Web site uses the Network Blitz theme. If you do not have this theme, select another one of your choice. The theme's Body font was changed to Arial Black.) Print the Clubs page in a browser, then close your browser, the Web, and FrontPage.

FIGURE J-23

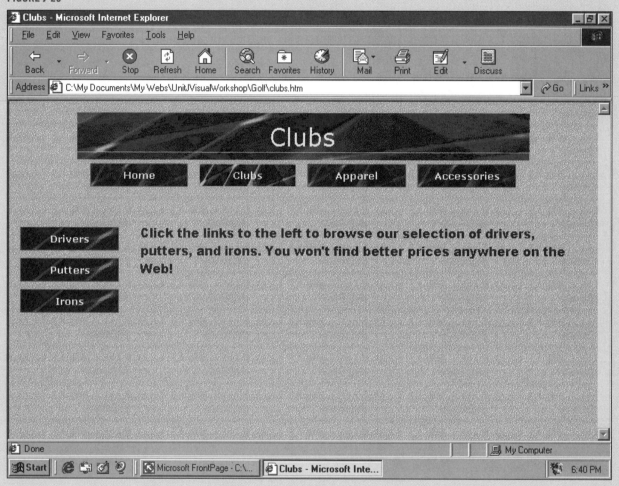

Unit
K

Publishing
a Web Site

Objectives

- [MOUS] ▶ **Position text in a Web page**
- [MOUS] ▶ **Position graphics in a Web page**
- [MOUS] ▶ **Use drag and drop to move files in Folders View**
- [MOUS] ▶ **Change a filename in Folders View**
- [MOUS] ▶ **Find and replace text in a Web site**
- [MOUS] ▶ **Print Navigation and Hyperlinks Views**
- [MOUS] ▶ **Publish a Web site on the PWS**
- [MOUS] ▶ **Open a Web site from the PWS**

Before you publish a Web site, you should review your site's pages to make sure that its files are in the correct folders with the correct filenames, that your Web uses the correct hyperlinks, and that pages are positioned correctly in Navigation View. You can make changes to your disk-based Web after you publish it, but it is usually best to finalize it before publishing it to a Web server. ✐━━ Maureen Jenkins wants to enhance the Jenkins Web before publishing it to the Personal Web Server (PWS). She plans to add new text and pictures to the pages, reorganize the site's folders, rename some files to use more intuitive names, and print Navigation and Hyperlinks Views to verify the site structure. Then she will publish the Web site to the PWS and test its appearance and function. Viewing the Web on the PWS will help Maureen see the Web as it will appear when it is eventually published on a commercial Web server, where it will be available to Internet users.

Positioning Text in a Web Page

Sometimes you might need to place text in a specific location in a Web page to ensure that it always appears in that location. For example, when you insert a picture in a Web page and then wrap text around it, you want to be sure the picture and the text always appear in the same location. When you need to position text in an exact location in a Web page, you use absolute positioning. **Absolute positioning** lets you specify exact coordinates in a page for a selected object. Maureen wants to change the top shared border to delete the company name and logo. Then she wants to add a short phrase to identify the publisher's specialty and a picture of the state of Texas.

Steps 1 2 3 4

QuickTip

If you have saved the Jenkins Web in a different location, enter the path or browse to locate the Web.

1. Start **Microsoft FrontPage**, click **File** on the menu bar, click **Open Web**, click the **[insert your name here] folder**, select the **Jenkins Web** (if necessary), click **Open**, then click the **Folders button** on the Views bar
   The Jenkins Web opens in Folders View.

2. Double-click **Booklist.htm** in the contents pane
   The Booklist Web page opens in Page View. This page uses top and left shared borders. The top shared border includes the company name and logo, a page banner, and a navigation bar. The left shared border includes links to child-level pages and to the parent page.

Trouble?

If a blank line appears above the page banner, select and then delete it. Usually it is easiest to use the pointer to position an object.

3. Click the **logo** (the picture of books) in the top shared border to select it, press **[Delete]**, select the line that contains the text **The Jenkins Publishing Company** in the top shared border, then press **[Delete]**
   The logo and text are deleted from the top shared border. The only elements in the top shared border are the page banner and the hyperlink button to the home page.

4. Click to the right of the Home button in the top shared border, then press **[Enter]**
   A new centered line appears below the navigation bar in the top shared border.

5. Type **Specializing in rare and collectible books about Texas since 1963**

QuickTip

You can position the object by using the pointer or by typing its exact coordinates in the text boxes on the Positioning toolbar.

6. Click **View** on the menu bar, point to **Toolbars**, click **Positioning**, then if necessary, drag the Positioning toolbar to the lower-right area of the window (see Figure K-1)
   The Positioning toolbar (See Figure K-1) lets you select and position an object in a Web page.

7. Select the **text** that you typed in Step 5, then click the **Position Absolutely button** on the Positioning toolbar
   The text is selected and sizing handles appear around the line that contains the text, as shown in Figure K-2. When you resize or move an absolutely positioned object, the object's coordinates change to show the new size or position.

8. Position the pointer over the **middle-right sizing handle** until it changes to ↔, then drag it to the left to resize the positioning text box so that there is no extra white space in the text box (see Figure K-3)
   The positioning text box is resized.

Trouble?

You can type the coordinates shown in Figure K-3 in the appropriate text boxes.

9. Position the pointer over the positioning text box until it changes to ✛, move the positioning text box to the right (see Figure K-3), then click anywhere in the positioning text box to deselect the text
   Figure K-3 shows the positioning text box in the correct position on the page.

10. Click the **Save button** on the Standard toolbar
    Your changes to the top shared border are saved in the Web site.

FIGURE K-1: Positioning toolbar in Page View

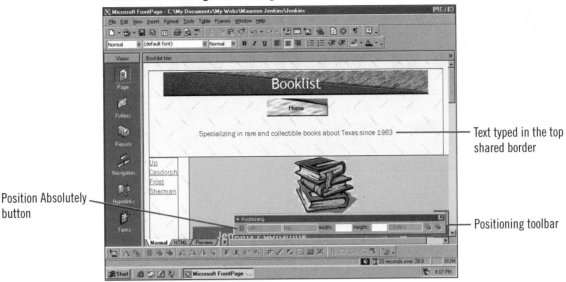

Position Absolutely button

Text typed in the top shared border

Positioning toolbar

FIGURE K-2: Positioning text box created using the Position Absolutely button

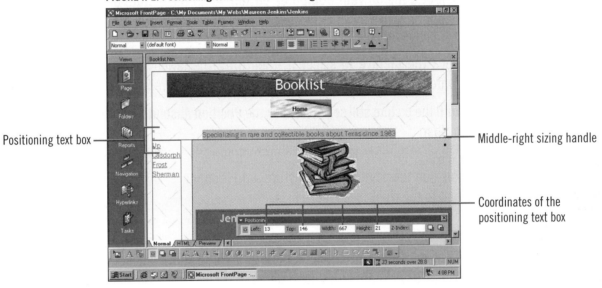

Positioning text box

Middle-right sizing handle

Coordinates of the positioning text box

FIGURE K-3: Revised placement of the positioning text box

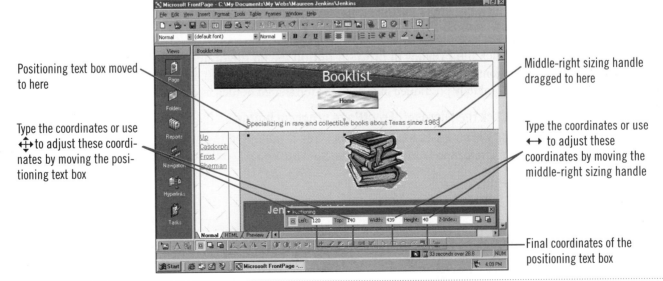

Positioning text box moved to here

Type the coordinates or use ✛ to adjust these coordinates by moving the positioning text box

Middle-right sizing handle dragged to here

Type the coordinates or use ↔ to adjust these coordinates by moving the middle-right sizing handle

Final coordinates of the positioning text box

FrontPage 2000

Positioning Graphics in a Web Page

In the previous lesson, you learned how to use absolute positioning to place text in an exact location in a Web page. You can also use absolute positioning to position other elements, such as pictures. ◤ Maureen wants to include a picture of the state of Texas in the top shared border to further emphasize the publisher's specialty.

Steps 1234

1. Click to the right of the Home button in the top shared border to position the insertion point there

2. Click the **Insert Picture From File button** 📷 on the Standard toolbar, click the **Select a file on your computer button** 🔍 in the Picture dialog box, open the **UnitK folder** on your Project Disk, then double-click **TX053196.gif**
   The picture is inserted to the right of the Home button.

3. Click the **picture** to select it, then drag the lower-right sizing handle toward the center of the picture to resize the picture (see Figure K-4)

4. With the picture still selected, click the **Position Absolutely button** 🔲 on the Positioning toolbar
   The picture blocks part of the Home button, as shown in Figure K-4.

> **Trouble?**
>
> If necessary, type the coordinates shown in Figure K-5 in the appropriate text boxes on the Positioning toolbar so the placement of the picture matches the one in the figure.

5. Position the pointer on the picture until it changes to ✥, then drag the picture down and to the right (see Figure K-5)
   Figure K-5 shows the top shared border, which now contains absolutely positioned text and a picture.

6. Click the **Save button** 💾 on the Standard toolbar, make sure that the TX053196.gif will be saved in the _borders/ folder of the Web site, then click **OK**
   FrontPage saves your changes to the top shared border and saves the picture in the Web's _borders folder.

7. Click the **Close button** on the Positioning toolbar
   The Positioning toolbar closes.

> **Trouble?**
>
> If necessary, click the Maximize button to maximize the browser window.

8. Click the **Preview in Browser button** 🔍 on the Standard toolbar, then click **Yes**
   FrontPage opens a browser and the revised Booklist Web page, which now uses the absolutely positioned objects in the top shared border, as shown in Figure K-6.

9. Click the **Microsoft FrontPage program button** on the taskbar, click the **Close button** on the contents pane, then click **Yes** if prompted to save your changes
   You return to FrontPage, and the Booklist Web page closes.

FIGURE K-4: Picture selected for absolute positioning

Current position of
the picture covers a
portion of the Home
button

FIGURE K-5: Correctly positioned picture

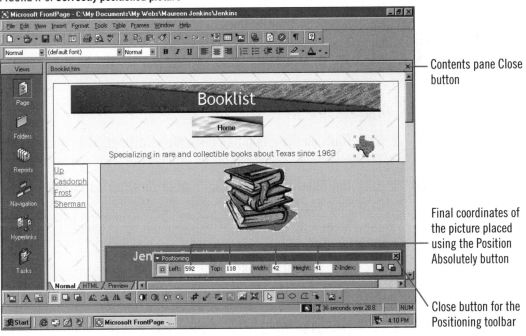

Contents pane Close
button

Final coordinates of
the picture placed
using the Position
Absolutely button

Close button for the
Positioning toolbar

FIGURE K-6: Booklist Web page in a browser

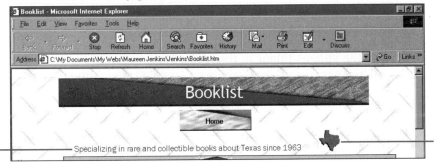

Absolutely
positioned text

Absolutely positioned
picture

CLUES TO USE

Understanding the limitations of absolute positioning

Objects that use absolute positioning will appear in different locations in a Web page, depending on the user's screen settings. For example, an object positioned with the coordinates 503 (left) and 76 (right) will appear in the upper-right corner of a Web page. However, on some monitors, this object might appear farther to the right. When you use absolute positioning, be certain to test your Web pages in different browsers and on different monitors with different screen sizes and resolutions to ensure that your absolutely positioned objects appear as desired.

FrontPage 2000

Using Drag and Drop to Move Files in Folders View

Before publishing your Web site on a Web server, it is a good idea to organize your files into the correct folders. For example, most Web site developers will store all of a Web's picture files in the Web's images folder to make it easy to find picture files, or they will organize pages related to specific topics into folders. ➤ Maureen wants to store all of the Web's picture files in the Web's images folder, so she will move the TX053196.gif file from its current location in the _borders folder to the images folder. To view the _borders folder, Maureen must change the Web's settings to display hidden folders.

Steps

1. Click the **Folders button** on the Views bar
   The Web appears in Folders View.

2. Click **Tools** on the menu bar, click **Web Settings**, then click the **Advanced tab**
   The Web Settings dialog box opens with the Advanced tab in front, as shown in Figure K-7.

Trouble?

If the Folder List is hidden, click the Folder List button on the Standard toolbar.

3. Click the **Show documents in hidden directories check box** to select it, click **OK**, then click **Yes**
   The Web Settings dialog box closes, the Web site is refreshed, and the Web's hidden folders now appear in the Folder List, as shown in Figure K-8.

4. Click the **_borders folder** in the Folder List
   The _borders folder contains three files: left.htm, top.htm, and TX053196.gif. The TX053196.gif file is the picture of the state of Texas that you inserted in the top shared border.

5. Click **TX053196.gif** to select it, then drag it to the images folder in the Folder List and release the mouse button
   The Rename dialog box opens and FrontPage renames the file to show its new location, the images folder. When the file is renamed, the Rename dialog box closes. Now the TX053196.gif file is saved in the Web's images folder.

6. Click the **images folder** in the Folder List
   The file TX053196.gif appears in the images folder. FrontPage automatically updates all Web pages that use this picture so that the link refers to the picture's new location.

7. Click the **Jenkins folder** in the Folder List, then double-click **Booklist.htm** in the contents pane
   The Booklist Web page still uses the state of Texas picture in the top shared border. In the Booklist.htm file, FrontPage correctly changed the picture file link to the images folder.

8. Click the **Close button** in the contents pane, then click **Yes** if prompted to save your changes
   The Booklist Web page closes.

FIGURE K-7: Web Settings dialog box

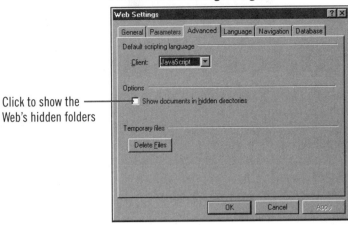

Click to show the
Web's hidden folders

FIGURE K-8: Refreshed Web site shows hidden folders

Jenkins folders

Hidden folder

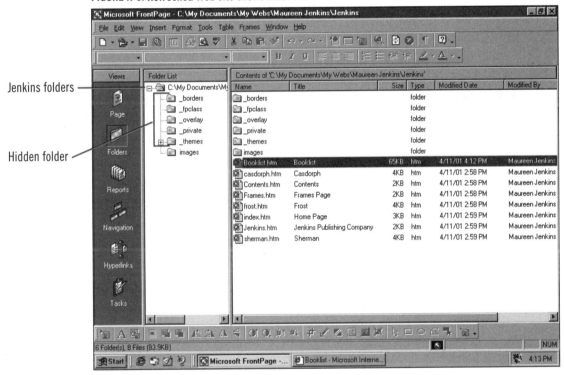

Using FrontPage for all Web site file management tasks

One of the advantages of using FrontPage to create your Web sites is that it also provides you with the capability to manage your files. When you need to move or rename files, you should always use FrontPage for the task, because FrontPage will automatically rename your files and update any hyperlinks to those files within the Web site itself. If you use Windows Explorer to move files from one folder to another or to rename files, the changed files will appear as broken links in your pages.

Changing a Filename in Folders View

After completing your Web pages, it is a good idea to make sure that the filenames and titles of your pages describe their contents. You can change a page's filename or title in Folders View, or change a page's title in Navigation View. Page titles that appear in Navigation View are used in a theme's elements, such as page banners and hyperlink buttons. Page titles used in Folders View appear in the browser's title bar. In some cases, a page might have a different title in Navigation and Folders Views. If you want a page title to be the same in both a browser's title bar and in the theme elements, you must change the page's title in both Folders and Navigation Views. ✎ Maureen wants to rename the picture of the state of Texas to have a more descriptive filename, so it is easy to recognize the contents of this file.

Steps

1. Click the **Folders button** 📁 on the Views bar

2. Click the **images folder** in the Folder List
   The images folder contains three files—Books.gif, Books.jpg, and TX053196.gif.

3. Right-click **TX053196.gif** in the contents pane to select it and to open the pop-up menu, then click **Rename**
   The filename is selected and FrontPage changes to editing mode, as shown in Figure K-9.

4. Type **Texas.gif**, then press **[Enter]**
   The Rename dialog box shown in Figure K-10 opens. FrontPage has identified one hyperlink to this image in the Web site.

5. Click **Yes**
   FrontPage renames the file and also updates the link that uses the original filename TX053196.gif. The picture is used in the top shared border, so the link to this picture in the top shared border is changed to reflect the filename change.

6. Click **Tools** on the menu bar, click **Web Settings**, click the **Advanced tab**, click the **Show documents in hidden directories check box** to clear it, click **OK**, then click **Yes**
   FrontPage refreshes the Web site and hides the site's hidden folders.

FIGURE K-9: File selected to be renamed

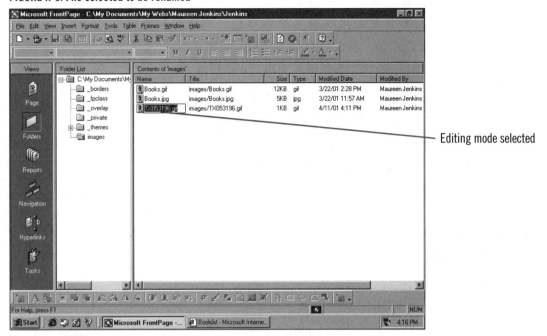

Editing mode selected

FIGURE K-10: Rename dialog box

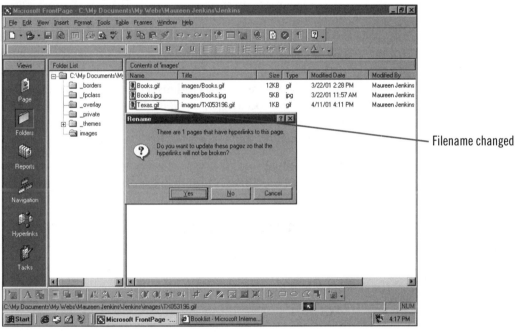

Filename changed

Suggested naming conventions for Web pages

When you add a page to Navigation View, the page title for the page shown in the navigation pane is the same as the one shown in Folders View. When your Web site uses shared borders, FrontPage uses the page title shown in the navigation pane as the page's hyperlink and page banner names. In most FrontPage themes, the sizes of the hyperlink buttons and the page banner pictures used to show page titles are relatively small. If a page title is long or not the exact text that you want to use in a hyperlink or a page banner, you can change the page title in Navigation View by right-clicking its page icon in the navigation pane, clicking Rename on the pop-up menu, typing the new title, then pressing [Enter]. Because this change does not affect the physical filename used for the linking information, the Rename dialog box does not appear and no link information is changed.

Finding and Replacing Text in a Web Site

In other Office programs, the Find and Replace commands search the current document for the requested text. In FrontPage, the Find and Replace commands work the same but provide you with the option of searching one page or every page in the Web. When you select the latter option, you must open and replace the text in each page. ✐ While reviewing the Booklist page, Maureen discovers a missing digit in the ISBN for the book entitled *Basic Texas Books*. She decides to use the Replace command to ensure that all occurrences of the ISBN for this book are changed throughout the Web.

Steps 1 2 3 4

1. **In Folders View, click Edit on the menu bar, then click Replace**
The Replace dialog box opens. See Figure K-11.

2. **Type 0-87611-086-3 in the Find what text box, press [Tab], then type 0-87611-0863-3 in the Replace with text box**
You typed the old ISBN in the Find what text box and the new ISBN in the Replace with text box.

3. **If necessary, click the All pages option button and the Down option button, then make sure that the check boxes in the Options section do not contain check marks**
FrontPage will search all pages in the Web site starting at the beginning and moving down each page. The check boxes in the Options section let you search for text with the same capitalization (finding all occurrences of *Basic* instead of *Basic* and *basic*), to find only whole words (*Basic* but not *Basically*), and to find occurrences of the text in the Web page's HTML code (when you need to find HTML tags).

QuickTip

Instead of immediately finishing your replace action, you can create a task in the tasks list by clicking Add Task.

4. **Click Find In Web**
The Replace dialog box changes to show a list of page(s) that contain the text entered in the Find what text box, as shown in Figure K-12.

5. **Double-click Booklist (Booklist.htm) in the Replace dialog box**
FrontPage opens the Booklist page and selects text that matches the text in the Find what text box, as shown in Figure K-13. You may need to scroll down the page to see the selected text.

6. **Click Replace in the Replace dialog box**
FrontPage replaces the selected text with the text in the Replace with text box and opens the Finished checking documents dialog box.

7. **Make sure that the Save and close the current document check box contains a check mark, then click OK**
FrontPage saves and closes the Booklist page, then opens the Replace dialog box again. Notice that the status for the Booklist page has changed to "Edited" to show that you updated the page.

8. **Click Cancel**
The Replace dialog box closes.

FIGURE K-11: Replace dialog box

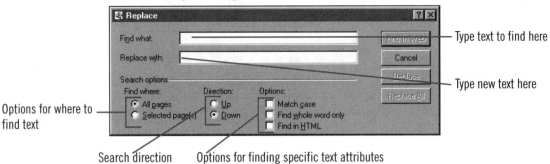

Type text to find here

Type new text here

Options for where to find text

Search direction   Options for finding specific text attributes

FIGURE K-12: Replace dialog box with one Web page located

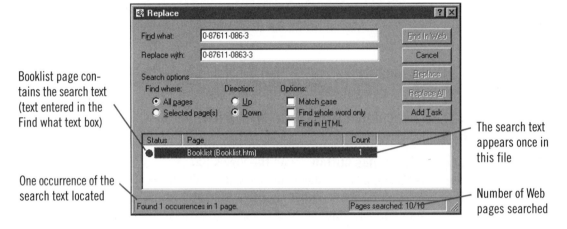

Booklist page contains the search text (text entered in the Find what text box)

One occurrence of the search text located

The search text appears once in this file

Number of Web pages searched

FIGURE K-13: Text in a Web page that matches text in the Find what text box

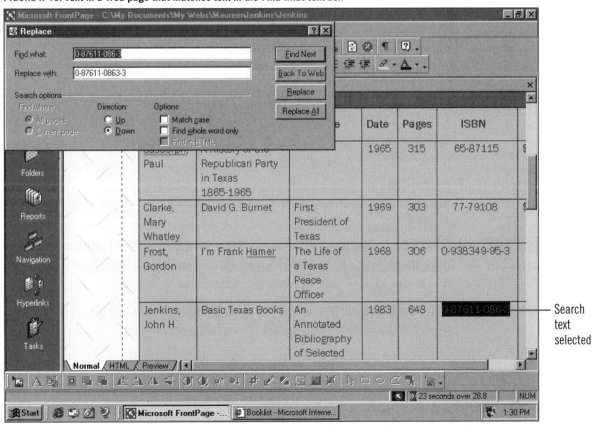

Search text selected

Printing Navigation and Hyperlinks Views

As you create your Web pages, you might want to print Navigation and Hyperlinks Views. You print Navigation View when you want to see the hierarchical structure of Web pages in relation to each other. You print Hyperlinks View when you want to see the hyperlinks to and from a specific Web page. FrontPage does not have a command to print Hyperlinks View, so you must copy the screen's image (called a **screenshot**) to the Windows Clipboard, and then paste the image into a word-processing program, such as WordPad or Microsoft Word. Then you can use that program to print the document that contains the image. Even though the Web site does not contain many pages, Maureen wants to document the Web's navigation and hyperlink structures. She prints Navigation View so she has a printed copy of the Web site's structure. She also uses Hyperlinks View to view the links coming from and going to the home and Booklist pages.

Steps

Trouble?

If the Navigation toolbar is blocking the navigation pane, drag it out of the way.

1. Click the **Navigation button** on the Views bar

There are five pages in the Web's navigation structure.

2. Click the **Print button** on the Standard toolbar

Navigation View prints.

3. Click the **Hyperlinks button** on the Views bar

Hyperlinks View appears, as shown in Figure K-14. The home page is the focus of Hyperlinks View. Pages containing links either to or from the focus page appear in Hyperlinks View with arrows indicating links going to or coming from the focus page. The pages to the left of the index.htm icon include links that open the home page. The home page contains only one link to its right, which opens another page, Booklist.htm.

4. Click **Booklist.htm** in the Folder List

The focus changes from the home page to the Booklist page. Selecting a filename in the Folder List changes the focus of Hyperlinks View to the selected page.

5. Press **[Print Screen]**

A copy of your screen is copied to the Windows Clipboard.

Trouble?

If you cannot find the WordPad command on the Accessories menu, or if WordPad is not installed on your computer, open Word or any other word processor.

6. Click the **Start button** on the taskbar, point to **Programs**, point to **Accessories**, click **WordPad**, then if necessary, click the **Maximize button**

The WordPad program window opens.

7. Press **[Ctrl][V]**

A screenshot of your FrontPage window is pasted into the WordPad document, as shown in Figure K-15.

Trouble?

If the Standard toolbar does not appear, press [Ctrl][P] to print the document.

8. Click **File** on the menu bar, click **Page Setup**, click the **Landscape option button**, click **OK**, then click the **Print button** on the Standard toolbar

The document is printed in landscape orientation.

9. Click the **Close button** on the WordPad title bar, then click **No**

WordPad closes without saving the document, and you return to FrontPage.

FIGURE K-14: Hyperlinks View for the home page

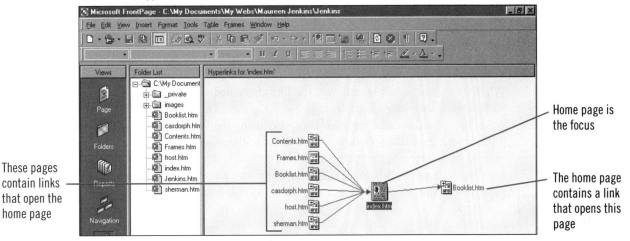

These pages contain links that open the home page

Home page is the focus

The home page contains a link that opens this page

FIGURE K-15: WordPad document after pasting the screenshot

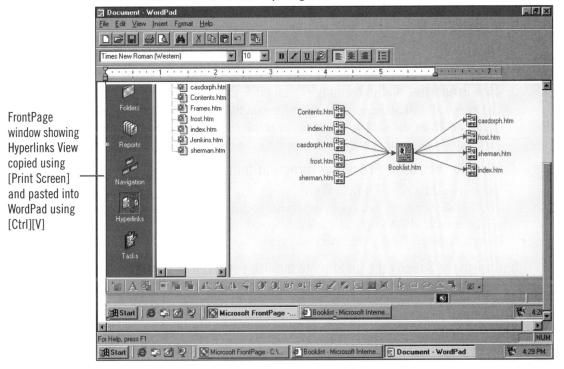

FrontPage window showing Hyperlinks View copied using [Print Screen] and pasted into WordPad using [Ctrl][V]

Customizing Hyperlinks View

You can customize Hyperlinks View to change the appearance of page icons, show repeated hyperlinks, and show hyperlinks to picture files. To show page titles instead of filenames, right-click an empty area in the navigation pane to open the pop-up menu, then click Show Page Titles. To show hyperlinks to picture files, including background pictures, right-click an empty area in the navigation pane, then click

Hyperlinks to Pictures. To show **repeated hyperlinks**, (multiple hyperlinks in one page that all point to the same page, picture, or file), right-click an empty area in the navigation pane, then click Repeated Hyperlinks. When you turn on each of these features, a check mark appears to the left of the command on the pop-up menu. Repeating the steps clears the check mark and turns off the feature.

FrontPage 2000

Publishing a Web Site on the PWS

When you create a disk-based Web, the files contained in the Web site are stored only on a disk, such as your computer's hard disk drive or a Zip disk. The **Personal Web Server (PWS)** is a Web server that you can install on your computer using the Windows 98 CD. The PWS allows you to publish your FrontPage Web to a Web server without needing a network connection to a commercial Web server. Many Web site developers will test their Webs using the PWS to ensure that they function correctly before publishing them on a commercial Web server. ✐✐✐ Maureen is pleased with the current Web and decides to publish it to her computer's PWS.

Steps

Trouble?

If you do not see 🖉, minimize all open programs to show the desktop.

1. Click the **Show Desktop button** 🖉 on the Quick Launch toolbar on the taskbar

2. Double-click the **Publish icon** on the desktop; if necessary, clear the **Show tips at startup check box**, click **Close**, and click **Start** to start the PWS
   The Personal Web Manager dialog box opens, as shown in Figure K-16. In this figure, the Web server is on.

3. Click **Properties** on the menu bar, then click **Exit**
   The Personal Web Manager dialog box closes. PWS is now running on your computer. You might see 🐾 on the taskbar to indicate that it is running. However, because you can set the PWS to hide this icon, it might not appear on the taskbar.

Trouble?

If the Options button has two down arrows on it, click Options to open the rest of the dialog box.

4. Click the **Microsoft FrontPage program button** on the taskbar, click **File** on the menu bar, then click **Publish Web**
   The Publish Web dialog box opens, as shown in Figure K-17. The steps in this lesson assume that you have installed PWS version 4 and configured the FrontPage 2000 Server Extensions. If you have problems publishing your Web, ask your instructor or technical support person for help.

5. Click in the **Specify the location to publish your web to text box**, delete any existing text in the text box, then type **http://localhost/Jenkins[insert your name here]**
   The default name of the computer when you install Windows 98 is **localhost**. Your instructor or technical support person might provide you with a different computer name, in which case you will use that name instead of localhost in the steps.

Trouble?

If a dialog box opens and tells you that it cannot locate a Web server, then you need to start the PWS using Steps 1–3 in this lesson.

6. Make sure that the Specify the location to publish your web to text box contains the text **http://localhost/Jenkins[insert your name here]**, then click **Publish**
   A Microsoft FrontPage dialog box opens and indicates the publish status as the files from your disk-based Web are published to the PWS. The dialog box shown in Figure K-18 opens when the publishing process is complete.

7. Click the link **Click here to view your published web site**
   The home page for the server-based Jenkins Web opens in a browser. Notice that the page's URL in the Address bar now uses http, which is the protocol used on the Internet.

8. Click the **Booklist button**
   The Booklist page opens in a browser. This page uses the top shared border, which includes absolutely positioned text and a graphic.

9. Click the **Microsoft FrontPage program button** on the taskbar, click **Done**, click **File** on the menu bar, then click **Close Web**
   The disk-based Jenkins Web closes, but FrontPage remains open.

FIGURE K-16: Personal Web Manager dialog box

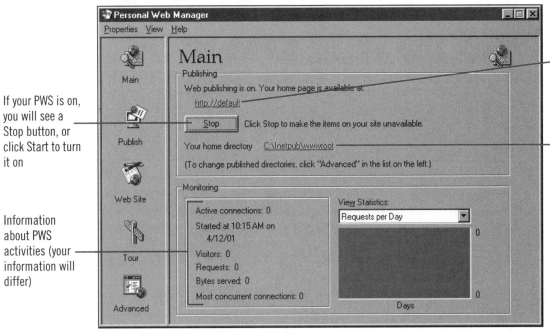

If your PWS is on, you will see a Stop button, or click Start to turn it on

Home page location for your PWS (your location might differ)

Home directory for published Webs (your information might differ)

Information about PWS activities (your information will differ)

FIGURE K-17: Publish Web dialog box

Type Web location and name here (the text in your text box might differ)

FIGURE K-18: Dialog box that opens after publishing a Web

Publishing a Web to a commercial Web server

You can also publish a Web from the PWS to a commercial Web server. For example, after you thoroughly test your Web site on the PWS and are satisfied with its content, you can use the Publish Web command on the File menu to enter the address of the Web server that will host your site. This Web server might be your company's Web server or intranet, or an Internet service provider (ISP) on which you have purchased space to host your Web site. In either case, the Web server must support the FrontPage 2000 Server Extensions for your Web site to function correctly when accessed from the Internet.

Opening a Web Site from the PWS

After you publish a Web to the PWS, you have two copies of the Web—one that is stored on your hard drive (the disk-based Web) and another that is stored on the PWS (the server-based Web). The server-based Web contains the same files as the disk-based Web, but it also includes Server Extensions that run the Web site on the server. You can open the Web site directly from the PWS using FrontPage. Making changes to a server-based Web means that your changes are updated immediately on the server. However, changes you make to your server-based Web are not saved to your disk-based Web. If you want to keep your disk-based Web current after publishing a Web, you must make changes to your disk-based Web, and then use the Publish Web button on the Standard toolbar to update your server-based Web. Omitting this step will result in a server-based Web that does not include the changes that you made in the disk-based Web. Maureen wants to open the server-based Web from her computer's PWS. After thoroughly testing it, she will locate an acceptable ISP so she can publish the Web to make it accessible to Web users. You will learn more about publishing to a commercial Web server in Unit O.

Steps

1. Click **File** on the menu bar, then click **Open Web**
The Open Web dialog box opens.

2. Click the **Web Folders button** on the Places bar
The Open Web dialog box opens, as shown in Figure K-19. The name of your Web server (the default is localhost) appears either in the Look in list box or in the dialog box. Your Web server might have a name different from localhost.

3. If necessary, double-click the **localhost** folder in the window and then click the **Jenkins[insert your name here] Web folder,** or click the **Jenkins on localhost folder** in the window
The Jenkins Web, which has been published to the PWS named localhost, is selected to be opened.

Trouble?
If your home page is not named Default.htm, ask your instructor or technical support person for help.

4. Click **Open**, then click the **Folders button** on the Views bar
The Jenkins Web opens from the PWS in Folders View, as shown in Figure K-20. Notice that the title bar shows that the Web uses the HTTP protocol. Also notice that the home page of your server-based Web is named **Default.htm.** When you publish a FrontPage Web, FrontPage automatically renames the file index.htm to Default.htm, and updates the hyperlinks in the Web to reference the new home page. The content of your home page, however, remains the same.

5. Double-click **Default.htm** in the contents pane
The home page opens in Page View.

6. Click anywhere in the heading that begins **Welcome to the Jenkins**, click the **Style list arrow** on the Formatting toolbar, click **Heading 1**, then click the **Save button** on the Standard toolbar
The page is updated on the PWS. Your disk-based Web remains the same.

Trouble?
If a browser does not open automatically, click its program button on the taskbar. If necessary, refresh or reload the page.

7. Click the **Preview in Browser button** on the Standard toolbar, notice the revised heading style, then click the **Booklist button**
The Booklist Web page opens, as shown in Figure K-21.

8. Close your browser

9. Close the Jenkins Web, then close FrontPage

FIGURE K-19: Open Web dialog box

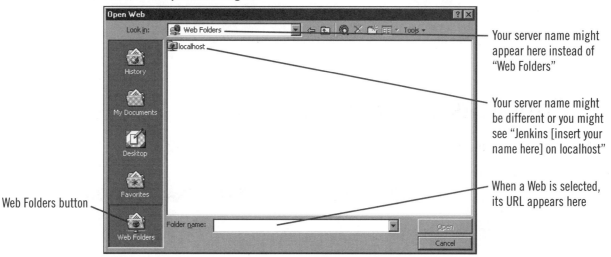

Web Folders button

Your server name might appear here instead of "Web Folders"

Your server name might be different or you might see "Jenkins [insert your name here] on localhost"

When a Web is selected, its URL appears here

FIGURE K-20: Jenkins Web opened from the PWS

Title bar shows http, the server name, and the Web name

Home page is named Default.htm

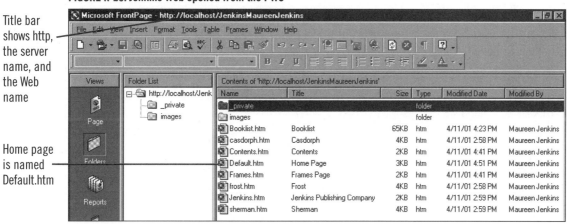

FIGURE K-21: Booklist Web page opened from the PWS

URL of the PWS (yours might be different)

Selecting an ISP to host your Web site

When you are ready to publish your server-based Web from the PWS to a commercial Web server, you need to make sure that the commercial Web server accepts Webs with FrontPage 2000 Server Extensions. If it does not, ask for help to learn how to use a FrontPage Web without the FrontPage 2000 Server Extensions, or find another ISP that will accept them. Some sites, such as Tripod (http://www.tripod.lycos.com/) and Yahoo! GeoCities (http://geocities.yahoo.com/home/), provide free Web space and support for FrontPage Webs. In exchange for free Web space, visitors to your Web site will see advertisements.

FrontPage 2000

Practice

► Concepts Review

Label each of the elements in the dialog box shown in Figure K-22.

FIGURE K-22

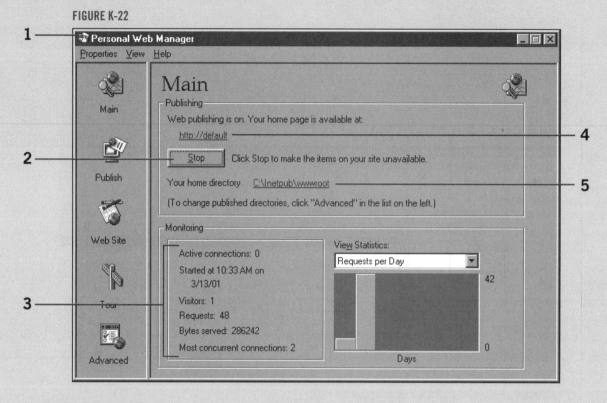

Match each of the terms with the statement that describes it.

6. [Print Screen]
7. _themes
8. Absolute positioning
9. Personal Web Manager
10. PWS
11. Repeated hyperlinks
12. Web Folders button

a. A hidden folder in a Web site
b. A shortcut on your computer to published Web sites
c. A Web server installed by Windows 98 that lets you publish a Web to a server without needing a network connection to a commercial Web server
d. Controls the PWS and provides its activity statistics
e. Copies the current screen image to the Windows Clipboard
f. Lets you specify an exact location in which to place an object
g. Multiple hyperlinks in one page that all point to the same page

Select the best answer from the list of choices.

13. **When you need to place text in an exact location on a Web page, use the**
    a. Alignment buttons on the Formatting toolbar.
    b. Paragraph dialog box.
    c. Position Absolutely button on the Positioning toolbar.
    d. Web Settings dialog box.

14. **To change a positioning text box in a Web page,**
    a. Use a sizing handle to resize it.
    b. Use ✛ to drag it to a new location.
    c. Enter coordinates in the text boxes on the Positioning toolbar.
    d. All of the above.

15. **Absolutely positioned objects in a Web page**
    a. Always appear in the same location, regardless of the user's monitor size.
    b. Appear in the same relative location to other objects in a Web page.
    c. Cannot be resized in a Web page.
    d. None of the above.

16. **To display a Web's hidden folders,**
    a. Click Tools on the menu bar, click Web Settings, then click the Advanced tab.
    b. Click Tools on the menu bar, then click Advanced Settings.
    c. Click Tools on the menu bar, click Page Options, then click the Advanced tab.
    d. Click the Show Hidden Folders button on the Standard toolbar.

17. **The best way to move a file in a Web site from one folder to another is to use**
    a. Windows Explorer.
    b. Folders View.
    c. Navigation View.
    d. Hyperlinks View.

18. **Which one of the following statements about the Replace command is NOT true?**
    a. Click the All pages option button to search for text throughout the Web site.
    b. Click the Up option button to search pages from bottom to top.
    c. Click the Whole words check box to limit your search to whole words (car) instead of words that contain your search text (not carpet or carport).
    d. Click Replace to start the search.

19. **In Hyperlinks View, the page that appears at the center of the Hyperlinks View diagram has the**
    a. Status.
    b. Focus.
    c. Most hyperlinks.
    d. Repeated hyperlinks.

20. **You can customize Hyperlinks View to show**
    a. Repeated hyperlinks.
    b. Hyperlinks to pictures.
    c. Page titles or page filenames.
    d. All of the above.

21. **The default name of the PWS for Windows 98 is**
    a. default.
    b. Inetpub.
    c. wwwroot.
    d. localhost.
22. **To open a published Web from the PWS, click File on the menu bar, click Open Web, then click the**
    a. My Documents button.
    b. Web Folders button.
    c. History button.
    d. Favorites button.

 # Skills Review

1. **Position text in a Web page.**
    a. Start Microsoft FrontPage and create a new One Page Web named *Computer*.
    b. Open the home page in Page View.
    c. Type **Computers are changing the way that people communicate with each other.**
    d. Turn on the Positioning toolbar, then drag it to the lower-right corner of the window, if necessary.
    e. Use absolute positioning to place the text at approximately the following coordinates on the page: Left: 14, Top: 148, Width: 204, and Height: 57.
    f. Save the page.
2. **Position graphics in a Web page.**
    a. Click the line below the positioning text box.
    b. Insert the file *Bd06496_.gif* from the Unit K\Sr folder on your Project Disk on the line you selected in the previous step. (*Note*: The picture might overlap the text.)
    c. Use absolute positioning to place the picture at approximately the following coordinates on the page: Left: 388 and Top: 48. Do not resize the picture.
    d. Save the page, and save the picture file using the default filename in the default folder location. (*Note*: The folder column should be blank; do *not* change the folder.)
    e. Close the Positioning toolbar.
3. **Use drag and drop to move files in Folders View.**
    a. In Folders View, move the Bd06496_.gif file to the Web's images folder.
    b. Click the images folder in the Folder List and verify that the image Bd06496_.gif is in the images folder.
    c. Click the Computer Web folder in the Folder List to view the contents of the Computer Web.
4. **Change a filename in Folders View.**
    a. Open the images folder.
    b. Rename the file Bd06496_.gif to **Internet.gif**.
    c. Update any hyperlinks to this file.
5. **Find and replace text in a Web site.**
    a. Open the Replace dialog box.
    b. Enter **each other** as the text to find.
    c. Enter **other people around the world** as the new text.
    d. Select the option to search all pages in the Web.
    e. Select Up as the search direction.
    f. Run the search and replace the text.
    g. Select the option to save and close the current document.
    h. Close the Replace dialog box.

6. **Print Navigation and Hyperlinks Views.**
   a. Print Navigation View.
   b. Change to Hyperlinks View.
   c. Select the index.htm file as the focus of Hyperlinks View.
   d. Turn on the option to show hyperlinks to pictures. (*Hint*: Right-click an empty area to open the pop-up menu.)
   e. Turn on the option to show page titles instead of page filenames.
   f. Print Hyperlinks View.
   g. Close WordPad without saving changes and return to FrontPage.
   h. Turn off the options to show page titles and hyperlinks to pictures.

7. **Publish a Web site on the PWS.**
   a. If necessary, start the PWS.
   b. Open the Publish Web dialog box.
   c. Type **http://localhost/Computer[insert your name here]** in the Specify the location to publish your web to text box. (*Note*: If your computer uses a different server name, enter that name in the path.)
   d. Publish the Web to the specified location.
   e. Open your published Web site in a browser.
   f. Print the home page.
   g. Close your browser.
   h. Close the dialog box in FrontPage.
   i. Close the disk-based Computer Web.

8. **Open a Web site from the PWS.**
   a. Click File on the menu bar, then click Open Web.
   b. Click the Web Folders button.
   c. If necessary, double-click the folder for your server to open its contents.
   d. Click the Computer[insert your name here] folder, then click Open.
   e. Open the home page in Page View.
   f. Click the HTML tab.
   g. Type your first and last names on the first line of the document, then print the HTML code for the home page.
   h. Close the Web without saving changes, then close FrontPage.

▶ Independent Challenges

1. Amy Gotcher is a registered nurse who soon will relocate to Maui, Hawaii. She does not have a job yet in Maui. Because of the distance between her current residence and Hawaii, she wants to send potential employers the URL to a Web site that includes her résumé, work experience, reference letters, and other information about her that might be relevant. She hopes that her Web site will make it easier to communicate her job potential to the human resource directors at hospitals and doctor's offices. She decides to create a FrontPage Web to store this information.

To complete this independent challenge:

a. Use the Personal Web template to create a new Web named *Nurse*.
b. In Folders View, change the filename of the Favorites page to **resume.htm** and the page title to **Resume**, change the filename of the My Favorite Site 3 page to **references.htm** and the page title to **References**, change the filename of the Photo Album page to **cont_ed.htm** and the page title to **Continuing Education**, and change the page title of the Home Page to **Amy Gotcher, R.N.**
c. Change to Navigation View, update the page titles to reflect the page title changes you made in the previous step, add any missing pages to the navigation structure, then print Navigation View.
d. Print Hyperlinks View for the Web site with the focus on the index.htm page. (*Hint*: Use the vertical scroll bar to scroll the navigation diagram so that all of it appears in the navigation pane before creating a screenshot.)

e. Publish the Nurse Web to your computer's PWS using the Web name *Nurse* plus your first and last names (for example, *NurseJaneDoe*). After FrontPage completes the publishing process, use the hyperlink to open the published Web in a browser.

f. Use the browser to print the home page, then close your browser. Staple your printed pages from Independent Challenge 1 together, with this page on top.

g. Close the dialog box in FrontPage, close the disk-based Nurse Web, then close FrontPage.

2. You work for the manager of the Customer Support Department of a large computer firm. The company has been experiencing higher than normal call volumes, and you want to ensure that all callers receive the answers they need. You decide to create a customer support Web to help your service representatives organize their calls.

To complete this independent challenge:

a. Use the Customer Support Web template to create a new Web named *Support*.

b. In Page View, add a new page to the Web.

c. Turn off all shared borders for the selected page.

d. Type **Customer Support Call Log** on the first line of the document.

e. Use absolute positioning to place the text you typed in the previous step so it appears on three lines and in the upper-right corner of the page.

f. On the next line of the document, insert the *undercon.gif* picture from the Web's images folder.

g. Increase the picture's size by 100% (i.e., make it twice as big).

h. Use absolute positioning to place the picture in the center of the document window, then turn off the Positioning toolbar.

i. Save the page using the filename *support.htm* and the page title **Customer Support Call Log**, then close the page.

j. In Navigation View, add the support.htm page as a child page of the Bugs page, then print Navigation View.

k. In Hyperlinks View, change the focus to the home page by clicking index.htm in the Folder List, then print Hyperlinks View in landscape orientation.

l. Use the Replace command to change all occurrences of **bug report form** in the Web site to **error report form**. Select the option to match the case. Close the Replace dialog box.

m. Publish the Support Web to your computer's PWS using the Web name *Support* plus your first and last names (for example, *SupportJohnDoe*). After FrontPage completes the publishing process, use the hyperlink to open the published Web in a browser.

n. Click the Bugs link, click the Customer Support Call Log link, then print the page. Close your browser.

o. Close the dialog box in FrontPage, close the disk-based Support Web, then close FrontPage.

3. You work for Buck's German Parts House, a local business that specializes in selling hard-to-find parts for older German-manufactured cars. Buck wants to create a Web site to expand his business from its current local retail store to accept orders from people anywhere in the world. Your team has been charged with the task of creating a Web site for the store. To help organize your team's efforts, you decide to use FrontPage to create a Web that lists the team members, production schedule, project status, and other tasks related to completing the Web. Then you will publish the Web on the company's intranet to make it available to all team members so they can easily check the project's overall status at any time.

To complete this independent challenge:

a. Use the Project Web template to create a new Web named *Project*.

b. Open the home page in Page View.

c. Use absolute positioning to place a picture of your choice from the Clip Art Gallery below the text hyperlinks in the left shared border. If necessary, resize and resample the picture. Save the page, and save the picture in the Web's _private folder using the default filename.

d. Select the comment text that appears above the horizontal line in the page, then type your first and last names. Select your names and use absolute positioning to place your names below the picture in the left shared border. (*Hint*: Make sure that your first and last names appear within the border. If necessary, change the font size to make them fit.) Save the page, then turn off the Positioning toolbar.

e. In Folders View, use drag and drop to move the picture that you saved in the _private folder to the images folder.

f. Rename the picture using a more descriptive filename and the default filename extension. Update the hyperlinks in the Web site after renaming the picture file.

g. Find and replace all occurrences of the word **updated** with the word **revised** in the Web site. Select the option to find only lowercase occurrences of the word. (*Hint*: Follow the directions in each dialog box as it appears. If the options Find and Replace are both available, click Replace. If necessary, move the active dialog box so that you can see the text to be replaced.) After replacing all occurrences, make sure that the status of each page is "Edited," then close the Replace dialog box.

h. Print Navigation View for the Project Web.

i. Change the focus of Hyperlinks View to the discuss.htm page.

j. Set Hyperlinks View to show page titles instead of page filenames, then print Hyperlinks View in landscape orientation.

k. Set Hyperlinks View to show page filenames.

l. Publish the Project Web to your computer's PWS using the Web name *Project* plus your first and last names (for example, *ProjectJohnDoe*). After FrontPage completes the publishing process, use the hyperlink to open the published Web in a browser. Use the browser to print the home page, then close your browser.

m. Close the dialog box in FrontPage, close the disk-based Project Web, then close FrontPage.

4. You just returned from a European vacation during which time you took hundreds of pictures with your new digital camera. You want to share your pictures with friends and family members, but the cost of printing the pictures and mailing them out is prohibitive. You decide to use FrontPage to create Web pages with pictures of your trip. Before creating the FrontPage Web, you decide to check out some Web sites that offer free Web space and support FrontPage 2000 Server Extensions. To complete this independent challenge:

a. Connect to the Internet.

b. Go to http://www.course.com, navigate to the Student Online Companion for this book, then click the link for Unit K. Use the links to investigate Web sites that support FrontPage 2000 Server Extensions and provide free server space to registered users.

c. Use the links to find information about using the free Web space at each site. Print one page from each of the sites that you visited. If possible, print a page that shows that the site supports FrontPage Webs.

d. Explore other pages in the sites to get a better understanding of their limitations and services.

e. Close your browser and your dial-up connection.

▶ Visual Workshop

Create a new One Page Web named *Zoo*, then add content and text to the home page as shown in Figure K-23. (*Hint*: The pictures are saved in the VW folder on your Project Disk. After inserting the pictures in your Web page, save them in the Web's images folder.) Publish the Web to the PWS. Print the Zoo page in a browser, then close your browser, the Web, and FrontPage.

FIGURE K-23

FrontPage 2000

Unit L

Creating
a New Web Site on a Web Server

Objectives

- ► Locate a Web presence provider
- ⌐MOUS⌐ ► Use the Import Web Wizard to create a new Web
- ⌐MOUS⌐ ► Set a Web site's page options
- ► Create an executable Web folder
- ⌐MOUS⌐ ► Check out a Web page
- ⌐MOUS⌐ ► Check in a Web page
- ⌐MOUS⌐ ► Open an Office document in a Web
- ► Troubleshoot server problems

In addition to creating disk-based Webs and publishing them to your computer's Personal Web Server (PWS) or a network server, you can also create a Web directly on a server, which eliminates the need to create a disk-based Web and publish it later. When you create a Web on a server, you use the HTTP protocol to access its pages. ◢▬▬ Ariadne McDonald worked for many years as a mortgage broker processing mortgages for individuals buying their first homes. Two years ago, she started her own business, Mortgage Services, Inc., which she has built into a thriving business by developing solid relationships with realtors in the area. As part of her business plan, Ariadne wants to create a Web that will accept online mortgage applications from her clients and provide information about the services she offers to first-time homebuyers.

Locating a Web Presence Provider

Locating a site to host your Web is a critical step in planning a Web. Knowing the terms of service as well as the services provided by the host will help you design a Web that runs efficiently and effectively on the host. When you search for an acceptable **Web presence provider (WPP)**, which might be an Internet service provider (ISP), commerce service provider (CSP), or other Web hosting service, you should ask key questions to make sure that you understand the WPP's terms of service as well as the services it supplies. ▂▂▂ Ariadne wants to find a WPP to host her Web site. She does her research by asking each potential WPP some key questions.

Details

Do you support FrontPage 2000 Server Extensions?
Some WPPs do not accept Webs with the FrontPage 2000 Server Extensions. Microsoft maintains a Web page listing of hosts that do accept FrontPage Webs, as shown in Figure L-1.

If you do not support FrontPage 2000 Server Extensions, do you supply code samples to use for processing FrontPage forms and other objects that require the Server Extensions?
Some FrontPage features that allow you to create dynamic objects in a Web page are not supported by all Web browsers. To create these features so that they are viewable by any Web browser, you must create a script or an applet. Some WPPs will offer to write these programs for you for a fee, whereas others provide code samples that you can use and adapt for your needs. Writing or adapting scripts or applets requires some programming knowledge.

Do you supply a secure server?
If your customers will be providing sensitive or personal information, they will feel more comfortable doing so if you can assure them that the data is transmitted to a secure server. A secure server encrypts data so that unauthorized parties cannot read it.

How much Web space do you provide, can I increase the amount of space needed, and what fees can I expect to incur for creating an account and hosting the site?
Before you inquire about space issues and fees, you need to know approximately how much Web space you will require and how many people will visit your site concurrently. WPPs, in general, can have very different rate structures depending on your anticipated usage.

Do I need to sign a contract, or can I use Web space on a month-to-month basis?
Some WPPs require an annual contract for Web hosting services. Other WPPs let you use the service on a month-to-month basis.

Do you provide domain name registration services?
Many WPPs will register your domain name for a fee and let you use that domain name instead of the WPP's domain name as your URL. For example, instead of using the URL http://geocities.com/mycompany, your customers would use the URL http://www.mycompany.com.

What kind of technical support services do you offer?
When you talk to people at the WPP, try to get a sense of the level of service that you can expect. For example, when you call the technical support number, does a technician answer the phone right away, or are you put on hold for 30 minutes? Remember that a company's Web site can be a vital part of its business. If you need technical support, you will want to make sure that it is easy to reach a support technician.

Word of mouth is an excellent way to get information about Web hosting services. Ask your friends and colleagues for recommendations and review Internet sites that analyze service providers. When searching for an appropriate WPP, keep a worksheet similar to the one shown in Figure L-2. After completing the worksheet, you can compare WPPs and more easily identify the advantages and disadvantages of each.

FIGURE L-1: Microsoft Office Web page for locating a WPP

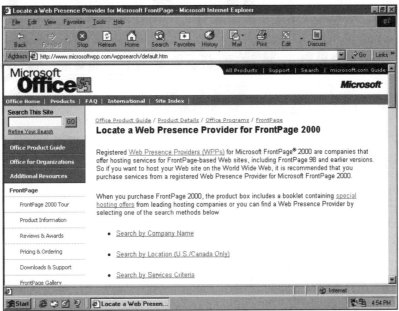

FIGURE L-2: Worksheet for comparing WPPs

	WPP: Phone number: Contact person: Date contacted:	WPP: Phone number: Contact person: Date contacted:	WPP: Phone number: Contact person: Date contacted:
Do you support FrontPage 2000 Server Extensions?			
If no, do you supply code samples to use for processing FrontPage forms and other objects that require the Server Extensions?			
Do you supply a secure server?			
How much Web space do you provide?			
Can I increase the amount of space needed?			
What fees can I expect to incur for creating an account and for hosting a site?			

CLUES TO USE

Registering and using a domain name

If your Web presence provider does not provide domain name registration services, you can still obtain a domain name on your own. To register for a .com, .net, or an .org domain, you can use the official list of ICANN (Internet Corporation for Assigned Names and Numbers) accredited registrars at www.internic.net/reg-ist.htm. ICANN coordinates domain name systems and allocates domain names. To find out if a domain name is available, go to the InterNIC Web site (www.internic.net), which is a U.S. government site that provides public information about domain names through its RegistryWHOIS link. The US DOMAIN Web site (www.nic.us) provides helpful information about the process of registering a domain name.

Using the Import Web Wizard to Create a New Web

When you create a new Web, you can use the Import Web Wizard to create the Web, and at the same time, add existing Web pages to it. Using the Import Web Wizard is especially convenient when you need to use Web pages that you have already created, either in FrontPage or in another program. Imported pages are available immediately in FrontPage and you can edit them just like any Web page created in FrontPage. 　Ariadne has several Web pages that she created earlier. She creates her new FrontPage Web on the PWS using the Import Web Wizard, which allows her to load the Web with her existing pages.

1. If necessary, start the **PWS** or log on to your server

Trouble?

If you forgot how to start the PWS, ask your instructor or technical support person for help.

2. Start **Microsoft FrontPage**, click **File** on the menu bar, point to **New**, then click **Web**
The New dialog box opens.

3. Click the **Import Web Wizard icon**, in the Specify the location of the new web text box type **http://localhost/Mortgage[insert your name here]**, then click **OK**
FrontPage creates the Mortgage Web on the server and opens the Import Web Wizard - Choose Source dialog box.

4. Click the **From a source directory of files on a local computer or network option button**, click **Browse**, open the **UnitL\Lessons folder** on your Project Disk, click **OK**, then click **Next**
The Import Web Wizard - Edit File List dialog box opens, as shown in Figure L-3. Notice that the 12 Web page files from the UnitL\Lessons folder on your Project Disk appear in the Files list box.

Trouble?

If the number of files is not 12, click Back, then make sure that you selected the Lessons folder in the UnitL folder on your Project Disk.

5. Make sure that 12 files will be imported, then click **Next**
The Import Web Wizard - Finish dialog box opens.

6. Click **Finish**, then if necessary click the **Folders button** 📁 on the Views bar
FrontPage imports the requested files into the Mortgage Web. The Web appears in Folders View, as shown in Figure L-4. The Mortgage Web contains nine Web pages and three picture files. The file Default.htm is the Web's home page. FrontPage assigns the name Default.htm to the home page in a server-based Web. Other servers use index or home with the extension .htm or .html as the filename for the Web's home page.

Trouble?

If the images folder does not appear in the Folder List, double click the Mortgage folder.

7. Select the file **background.gif**, press and hold **[Ctrl]**, click the files **collage.gif** and **dotrule.gif**, then release **[Ctrl]** and drag the selected files to the images folder in the Folder List
The picture files are stored in the Web's images folder.

8. Click the **images folder** in the Folder List to confirm that the pictures files have been properly moved
The three picture files appear in the images folder, as shown in the contents pane.

9. Click the **Mortgage folder** in the Folder List
The Mortgage Web page files appear in the contents pane.

FIGURE L-3: Import Web Wizard - Edit File List dialog box

Total number of
files selected
for importing

Files in the
selected folder

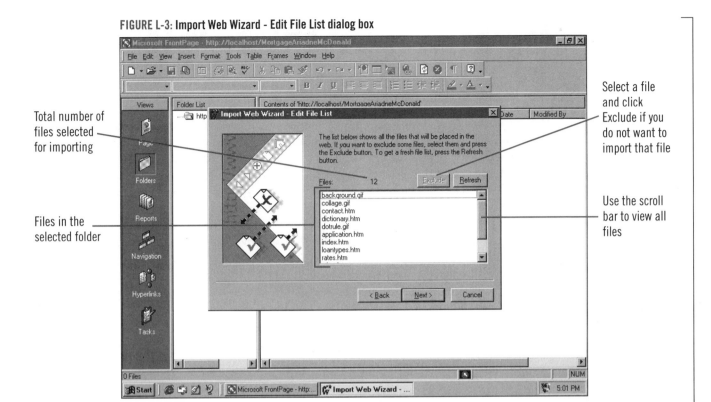

Select a file
and click
Exclude if you
do not want to
import that file

Use the scroll
bar to view all
files

FIGURE L-4: Mortgage Web in Folders View

Server-based
Web address

Main folder of
the Mortgage
Web

Picture files

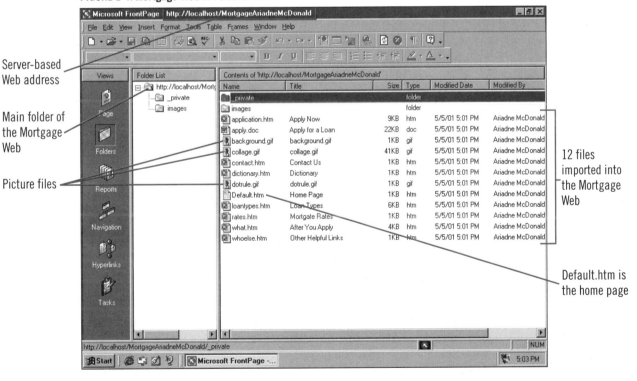

12 files
imported into
the Mortgage
Web

Default.htm is
the home page

FrontPage 2000

Setting a Web Site's Page Options

When you create a Web on a server, you should always consider who will visit your site. Your Web should be viewable by the largest audience possible. Table L-1 describes the different Internet technologies that you can enable or disable in a FrontPage Web. Web programmers with advanced skills can write code to support these Internet technologies in various browsers, and then add that code to a FrontPage Web. In addition, you can enable your Web for a specific server, as well as enable or disable the Web to use the FrontPage 2000 Server Extensions. Disabling the FrontPage Server Extensions from your Web disables some features that require the Server Extensions to function correctly. ⬛⬛⬛ Ariadne's customer research indicates that her audience uses the latest browsers, which support current Internet technologies. Ultimately, she will publish her Web on a Microsoft Internet Information Server that supports the FrontPage 2000 Server Extensions. She sets the Mortgage Web to optimize the features supported by this combination of software and hardware.

Trouble?

FrontPage can be configured in many different ways. Your Compatibility tab might look different.

1. **Click Tools on the menu bar, click Page Options, then click the Compatibility tab**
   The Page Options dialog box opens with the Compatibility tab in front, as shown in Figure L-5.

2. **Click the Browsers list arrow, then click Both Internet Explorer and Navigator**
   This setting enables support for all Web features currently supported by both Internet Explorer and Netscape Navigator.

3. **Click the Browser versions list arrow**
   You can set the browser version to support features for versions 4.0 and later, 3.0 and later, or custom.

4. **Click 4.0 browsers and later**
   This setting enables support for all features of Internet Explorer and Netscape Navigator for versions 4.0 and later. ActiveX controls and VBScript are two Internet technologies that are not supported by the selected browser and browser versions; their check boxes do not contain check marks.

5. **Click the Servers list arrow, then click Microsoft Internet Information Server 3.0 and later**
   Ariadne selected this Microsoft server setting in FrontPage, which will support all of her Web's features, because she knows the ISP that will eventually host the Mortgage Web site has Microsoft Internet Information Server version 5.0.

6. **If necessary, click the Enabled with Microsoft FrontPage Server Extensions check box to select it**
   PWS 4.0 supports the FrontPage 2000 Server Extensions. Your ISP or your Web's administrator can tell you if a different server supports the FrontPage 2000 Server Extensions.

QuickTip

When you change a Web's settings, all future Webs created in FrontPage will use those same settings unless you change them.

7. **Click the ActiveX controls check box to select it, click the VBScript check box to select it, then if necessary, click any empty check box in the Technologies section to select it**
   Compare your screen to Figure L-6. Notice that when you enabled ActiveX controls and VBScript, the Browser versions list box changed to "Custom," as shown in Figure L-6. The default for the 4.0 browsers and later setting does not support these Internet technologies.

8. **Click OK**
   The Page Options dialog box closes and you return to Folders View. Your Web is now enabled for the selected browsers, server, the FrontPage Server Extensions, and all listed Internet technologies.

FIGURE L-5: Compatibility tab in the Page Options dialog box

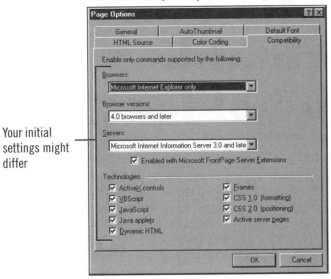

Your initial settings might differ

FIGURE L-6: Completed Compatibility tab

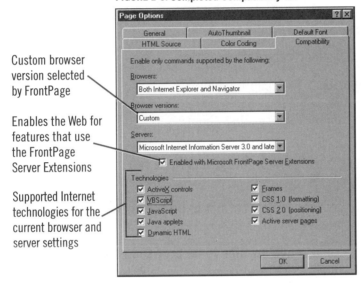

Custom browser version selected by FrontPage

Enables the Web for features that use the FrontPage Server Extensions

Supported Internet technologies for the current browser and server settings

TABLE L-1: Internet technologies that you can set in FrontPage Webs

Internet technology	description
ActiveX control	An application that creates animation, interactive objects, and other multimedia effects in a Web page
VBScript	A Microsoft scripting language used to embed interactive elements in Web pages
JavaScript	A Netscape scripting language used to create dynamic content in Web pages
Java applet	A program written in the Java programming language and run by a browser that adds multimedia effects, interactivity, and other effects to a Web page
Dynamic HTML	Code that lets you create animated effects for text and other objects or respond to user input in a Web page
Frames	A Web page that displays multiple Web pages simultaneously in separate, scrollable windows
CSS 1.0 (formatting)	An HTML specification that lets you apply text attributes, such as color and font size, to a Web page
CSS 2.0 (positioning)	An HTML specification that lets you precisely position objects in a Web page
Active server pages	A dynamic Web page containing scripts that process the page

Creating an Executable Web Folder

Server-based Webs often contain small programs, called scripts, that are displayed by a browser but processed on the server. Usually scripts and other programs are needed to support the Web site. Some Web servers are configured to prevent scripts and programs from running because some scripts and programs can potentially compromise a server by running programs that damage its data. In order to accommodate different server settings, FrontPage lets you set a Web or its folders to permit or prevent the running of scripts and programs. A Web folder that allows scripts and programs to be run is called an **executable** Web folder. ⬤▬▬▬ Ariadne wants to use features in FrontPage that require scripts and programs to execute on the server. For example, Ariadne will use a script to link a Web page that contains a form with a database. She will change the Web's main folder to allow scripts and programs to be run.

Steps

1. If necessary, click the **Mortgage folder** in the Folder List to select it
The Mortgage folder is the Web's main folder.

2. Right-click the **Mortgage folder** to open the pop-up menu

3. Click **Properties** on the pop-up menu
The Properties dialog box for the Mortgage Web opens, as shown in Figure L-7. This dialog box contains information about your Web, including its name, type, location, contents, and size.

4. If necessary, click the **Allow programs to be run check box** to select it
Selecting this option allows the server to run programs.

5. If necessary, click the **Allow scripts to be run check box** to select it
Selecting this option allows the server to run scripts.

6. If necessary, click the **Allow files to be browsed check box** to select it
The default setting for a FrontPage Web is to allow files to be browsed. Figure L-8 shows the completed Properties dialog box.

7. Click **OK**
Now your Web permits programs and scripts to execute on the server and files to be browsed.

FIGURE L-7: Properties dialog box for the Mortgage Web

Your dialog box name will match your Web's name and location

Web's main folder

Initial options for the Web's folder (yours might be different)

Web name

Web location

Web contents and size (your size might be different)

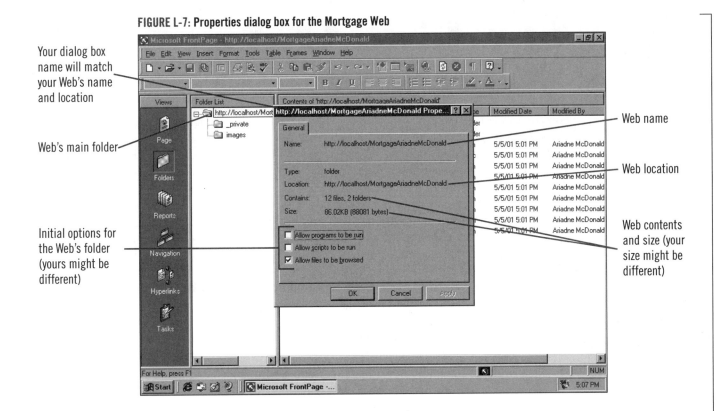

FIGURE L-8: Completed Properties dialog box for the Mortgage Web

Mortgage Web now allows programs and scripts to be run and files to be browsed

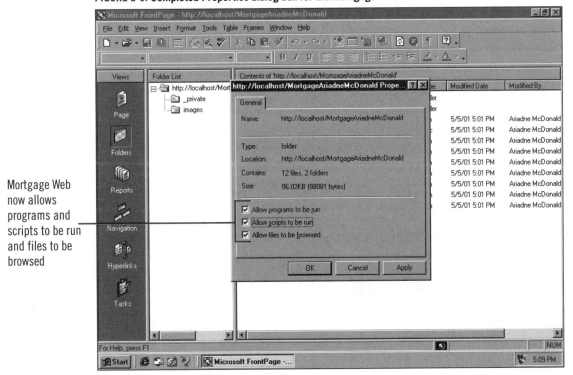

Checking Out a Web Page

Sometimes when a Web is being developed, it is stored on an intranet to allow only authorized users access to its files. These authorized users are usually members of a Web site development team. To ensure that only one person works on a Web page at a time, FrontPage lets you set a Web so that users must check out pages in order to be able to edit them. For example, suppose that Logan and Hannah are members of the same Web site development team. If Hannah checks out a Web page to update its contents, Logan will see a padlock in front of the file in Folders View on his computer, indicating that another author has checked out the page. Logan can still open the locked Web page and view its contents, but he cannot make any changes to it. When Hannah is finished editing the file, she checks in the file, which makes it available to other authors for checking out and editing. When you set a Web to prevent authors from editing files simultaneously, you are enabling the Web to use **source control**. Ariadne is currently the only person working on the Mortgage Web. However, she might ask other people to assist her with its creation in the future and she wants to be sure that only one person can edit a Web page at a time. She enables the Web to use source control to see how this feature works.

Steps

QuickTip

To change a Web's name, type a new Web name in the Web name text box. FrontPage updates a Web's links automatically when you change a Web's name.

1. Click **Tools** on the menu bar, then click **Web Settings**
The Web Settings dialog box opens with the General tab in front, as shown in Figure L-9. The General tab identifies the Web's name, the server in use, the FrontPage Server Extensions version, and the server version. Because you can configure FrontPage in many different ways, your General tab might show different features in use.

2. Click the **Use document check-in and check-out check box** to select it
Selecting this option enables your Web to use source control.

3. Click **OK**
The Web Settings dialog box closes and the Microsoft FrontPage dialog box shown in Figure L-10 opens. FrontPage must recalculate (or refresh) the Web to enable source control.

4. Click **Yes**
FrontPage updates the Web's hyperlinks and text indices and refreshes the Web, as shown in Figure L-11. Notice that a green bullet appears to the left of each Web page in Folders View. These bullets indicate that the files are enabled with source control.

5. Double-click **Default.htm** in the contents pane
The dialog box shown in Figure L-12 opens and tells you that this page is under source control. If you click No, the page opens in Page View with read-only attributes. To open the page for editing in Page View, you must check it out.

6. Click **Yes**
The home page opens in Page View.

7. Click the **Folders button** 📁 on the Views bar
The home page now has a red check mark ✔ to the left of its name. This check mark appears in Folders View on your computer. If your Web was stored on an intranet, other users would see a padlock 🔒 next to the file's name.

FIGURE L-9: Web Settings dialog box

Web name and
location (your server
name might differ)

Webs enabled with
FrontPage Server
Extensions show the
Server Extensions
version here (your
version might differ)

Server version in use
(yours might differ)

Click to enable
source control

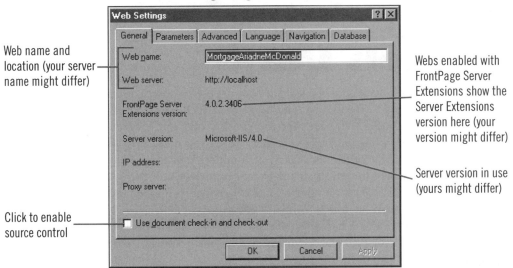

FIGURE L-10: Dialog box that opens after enabling source control

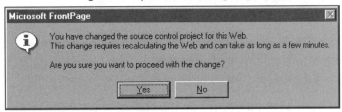

FIGURE L-11: Source control enabled for the Mortgage Web

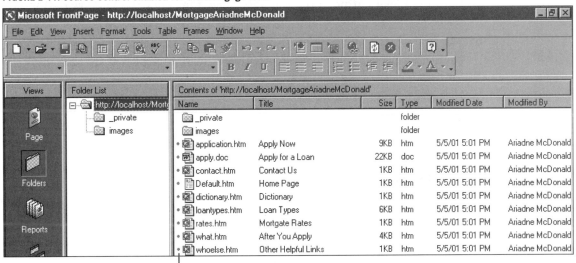

Green bullets indicate
files under source control

FIGURE L-12: Dialog box that opens when you open a file under source control

Click to open the
file for editing

Click to open a
read-only version
of the file

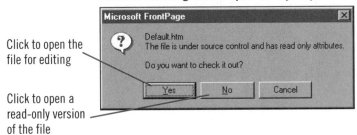

Checking In a Web Page

FrontPage 2000

In the previous lesson, you learned how to enable source control to ensure that only one author can update a Web page at a time. You also learned how to check out a Web page. After you have finished using a Web page that you checked out, you must check in the Web page to make it available to other authors for editing. When you check in a Web page, you have the option of checking in the page or canceling or "undoing" the check out. When you cancel or "undo" the check out, you restore the page to its original version before you edited and saved it. If you decide to disable source control, make sure that all files are **unlocked** (closed and checked in), and then turn off source control. ⬤━━ Ariadne finishes working on the home page. She wants to keep her changes so she will check in the Web page. Because she is the only person working on the Web, she decides to disable source control, so she will not need to check Web files in and out.

1. **Click the Page button 🗐 on the Views bar**
   The home page opens in Page View.

2. **Click the blank, centered line above the table, click the Style list arrow on the Formatting toolbar, click Heading 1, then type Mortgage Services, Inc.**
   Now the page contains a heading.

3. **Click the Save button 🖫 on the Standard toolbar**
   FrontPage saves the Web page.

4. **Click the Close button in the contents pane, then click the Folders button 🗐 on the Views bar**
   FrontPage closes the Web page and you return to Folders View, as shown in Figure L-13. Notice that the Default.htm file shows a check mark to the left of its name, indicating that the page is checked out.

5. **Right-click Default.htm in the contents pane**
   The pop-up menu opens, as shown in Figure L-14. Notice the Undo Check Out option on the pop-up menu. This option lets you restore the page to its original state before you checked it out.

6. **Click Check In**
   FrontPage checks in the home page and releases the lock on the file. Once again, the Default.htm file has a green bullet to the left of its name, indicating that it is under source control and available for checking out and editing by other authors.

7. **Click Tools on the menu bar, then click Web Settings**
   The Web Settings dialog box opens with the General tab in front.

> **QuickTip**
>
> Before turning source control on or off, make sure that all Web pages are closed and checked in.

8. **Click the Use document check-in and check-out check box to clear it, click OK, then click Yes**
   FrontPage refreshes the Web and disables source control. The Web is no longer under source control so the green bullets no longer appear next to the filenames in Folders View.

FIGURE L-13: Folders View shows a file checked out for editing

Red check mark indicates that this file is checked out

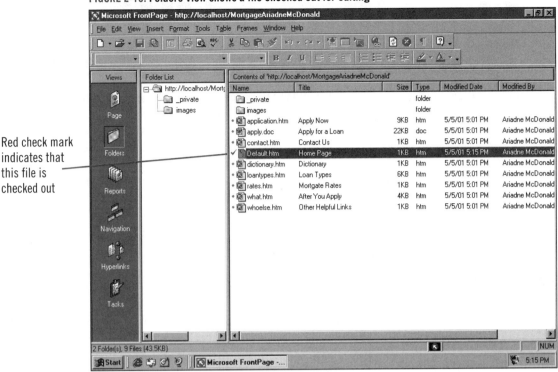

Click to cancel all changes you made to a checked-out page

FIGURE L-14: Pop-up menu for the Default.htm file

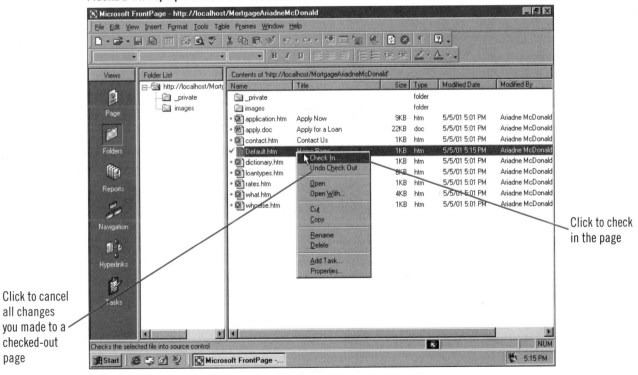

Click to check in the page

Opening an Office Document in a Web

In FrontPage, the default setting is for all HTML pages to open in Page View. When you import files that were created in other programs into your Web, you can set those pages to open in the program that created them. For example, if you import an Excel workbook, a Word document, or a PowerPoint presentation into your Web, you can set that imported file to open on the user's computer in Excel, Word, or PowerPoint. In each of these scenarios, the user must have the program associated with the imported file (Excel, Word, or PowerPoint) on his or her computer to open the file. ➤➤➤ Ariadne is sensitive to the needs of some of her clients, who are cautious about using the Web to send personal information to her. To meet these clients' needs, Ariadne wants her clients to be able to print the loan application form using Word and then mail the completed form to Mortgage Services, Inc.

Steps 1234

1. In Folders View, click **Tools** on the menu bar, click **Options**, then click the **Configure Editors tab**

   The Options dialog box opens with the Configure Editors tab in front, as shown in Figure L-15. This tab shows the editor that is used to open a file of a specified type in FrontPage.

2. If necessary, click the **Open web pages in the Office application that created them check box** to select it, then click **OK**

   Now each file created using an Office program will open in the program that created it.

3. Right-click **apply.doc** in the contents pane to open the pop-up menu

   The pop-up menu has two commands for opening a file, as shown in Figure L-16. The Open command opens the file using the default editor. Because you set FrontPage to open Office files in the Office program that created them, this Word document will open in Word.

4. Click **Open** on the pop-up menu

   The apply document opens in Word. A user can print and fill out this form and then mail it to Mortgage Services, Inc. to submit a mortgage application.

5. Scroll to the bottom of the form, click after the zip code, press [**Spacebar**], type **Attention: [insert your name here]**, click the **Close** button on the Word title bar, then click **Yes** to save your changes

   Word closes and you return to Folders View.

6. Double-click **application.htm** in the contents pane, click the **blank line** that appears after the last bullet in the bulleted list, then type **Click here to complete your application using a Word document that you can submit to [insert your name here] by regular mail.**

7. Use your mouse to select the word **here** in the sentence that you typed in Step 6, click the **Hyperlink button** 🔗 on the Standard toolbar, scroll if necessary and double-click **apply.doc**, then click anywhere in the Web page to deselect the text

   The word "here" is now a hyperlink that opens the Word application form.

8. Click the **Save button** 💾 on the Standard toolbar, click the **Preview in Browser button** 🔍 on the Standard toolbar, then click the **here** hyperlink that you created

   The apply document opens in a browser, as shown in Figure L-17.

9. Use your browser's **Print button** to print the page, close your browser, if necessary click the **Microsoft FrontPage program button** on the taskbar, click **File** on the menu bar, click **Close Web**, then close FrontPage

   The application form prints and your browser and FrontPage close.

FIGURE L-15: Configure Editors tab in the Options dialog box

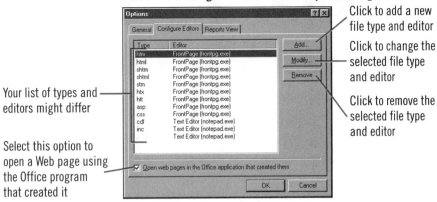

Click to add a new file type and editor

Click to change the selected file type and editor

Click to remove the selected file type and editor

Your list of types and editors might differ

Select this option to open a Web page using the Office program that created it

FIGURE L-16: Pop-up menu for the apply.doc file

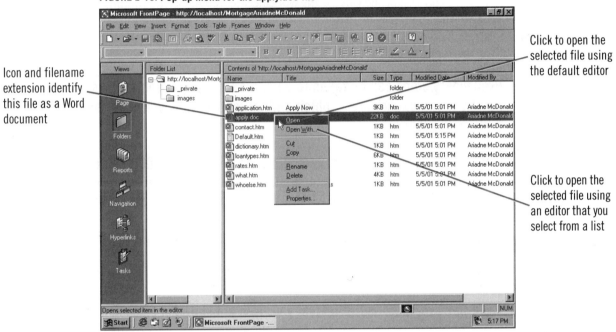

Icon and filename extension identify this file as a Word document

Click to open the selected file using the default editor

Click to open the selected file using an editor that you select from a list

FIGURE L-17: Word document opened in a browser

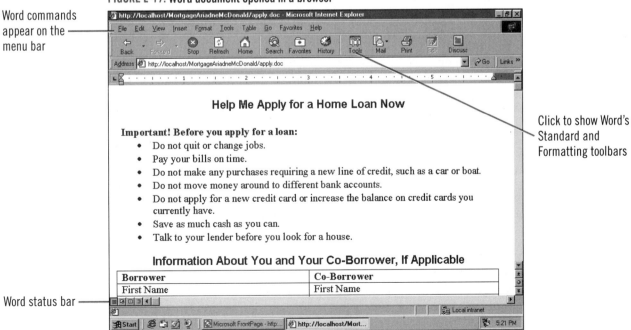

Word commands appear on the menu bar

Click to show Word's Standard and Formatting toolbars

Word status bar

Troubleshooting Server Problems

After you perfect your FrontPage Web, test it thoroughly, and upload its files to your WPP, you should test the site again using different browsers, operating systems, monitors, and monitor resolutions to ensure that your site looks exactly as desired. Keep in mind that when you transfer your Web to a different Web server, the new server might use a different operating system or a different version of the FrontPage Server Extensions. Even though your Web's files might work correctly on your server, you need to make sure that visitors to your site will see things exactly as you intend. ✐ Ariadne knows that she must test her Web using different browsers, operating systems, monitors, and monitor resolutions. Before doing so she creates the worksheet shown in Figure L-18. She will use the worksheet to document her findings and any adjustments she must make to her Web. In addition to her worksheet, Ariadne knows there are some preliminary steps to be taken that will ensure that her FrontPage Web runs properly. She reviews the following tips for troubleshooting server problems.

Preliminary steps can be taken to ensure a FrontPage Web runs as expected on the server. If you experience problems when testing your Web site that is stored on a WPP, do the following:

 Make sure that your WPP accepts Webs with FrontPage 2000 Server Extensions.
Some objects that you include in a FrontPage Web page, such as transitions, animations, hit counters, and forms, will not work if the server on which the Web is stored does not support the FrontPage 2000 Server Extensions.

 Make sure that your WPP uses the latest FrontPage Server Extensions.
Some problems occur when a WPP uses an earlier version of the FrontPage Server Extensions. In most cases, you can ask the WPP to update its Server Extensions to provide support for the latest Internet technologies.

 Make sure programs and scripts for your Web are stored in an executable Web folder.
Some WPPs protect their servers by designating certain folders as executable. You might need to restructure your Web to ensure that certain features requiring programs and scripts are stored in an executable folder.

 Consider choosing another theme or different pictures if your pages take a long time to download the first time you view them.
When you open a Web page for the first time, its graphic objects, such as files required by the theme and pictures, are stored temporarily on your computer's hard drive, usually in a Temporary Internet Files folder. When you open the same Web page again, the browser searches your computer's Temporary Internet Files folder for the same images. If they exist in this folder, then your browser opens them from the hard drive, which is much faster than downloading files from the Web site. One way to make sure that your Web pages download quickly is to avoid using large graphic files. Some Web users lose patience when pages take a long time to download, and they will leave your site before it is fully loaded. You can use Reports View in FrontPage to identify pages that are slow to download. Once identified, you can make adjustments so that the pages download more quickly.

 Consider using Web objects that do not require browser plug-ins if your site's visitors cannot view your Web's dynamic content.
Some animations and other dynamic content require a browser plug-in in order for the browser to show them. Some examples of browser plug-ins are Shockwave and Flash, which both animate Web content. When creating objects that require plug-ins, you can build code into the object that checks for the existence of the required plug-in and a link to download it if necessary.

FIGURE L-18: Worksheet for testing a Web on a server

Web Name: _____

Date Tested: _____

Tester: _____

Browser: _____

Version: _____

Monitor Size: _____

Monitor Resolution: _____

Operating System: _____

Computer: _____

Other: _____

Key
OK = works as expected; NA = not applicable to this page; P [...] = problem and an explanation

of what the problem is

Web Page Filename	Overall Appearance	Download Time	Link Check	Comments
default.htm				
application.htm				
apply.htm				
contact.htm				
dictionary.htm				

Practice

▶ Concepts Review

Label each of the elements of the Microsoft FrontPage window shown in Figure L-19.

FIGURE L-19

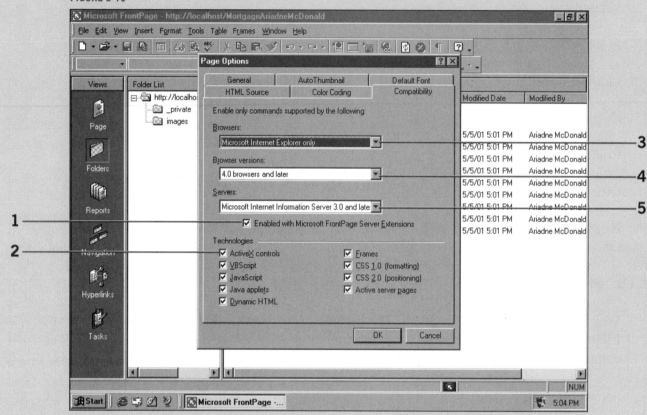

Match each of the terms with the statement that describes it.

6. Check in
7. Web presence provider
8. Default.htm
9. Executable Web folder
10. Check out
11. Source control

a. A business that hosts Web sites for a fee.
b. A feature that ensures that only one author can edit a Web page at a time.
c. A Web folder that allows scripts and programs to be run and files to be browsed.
d. The name of a home page in a FrontPage server-based Web.
e. The process of opening a Web page that is under source control for editing.
f. The process of unlocking a Web page that is under source control.

Select the best answer from the list of choices.

12. **When using the Import Web Wizard to import files into a new Web, you can**
    a. Import files from a disk location.
    b. Import files from a Web address.
    c. Exclude files from the selected disk location.
    d. All of the above.

13. **Which of the following statements is NOT true?**
    a. You can set a Web to enable it for specific browser versions.
    b. You can set a Web to enable it to use FrontPage Server Extensions.
    c. You can set a Web to work with different operating systems.
    d. You can set a Web to create content and objects that use certain Internet technologies.

14. **You can set a Web folder to enable**
    a. Files to be browsed.
    b. Scripts to be run.
    c. Programs to be run.
    d. All of the above.

15. **The process or feature that ensures that only one author can work on a Web page at a time is called**
    a. Creating an executable Web folder.
    b. Internet technology enabling.
    c. Source control.
    d. None of the above.

16. **You can _____ a page that is under source control and that has read-only attributes.**
    a. View
    b. Edit
    c. Save
    d. Lock

17. **The editor associated with the HTM and HTML file types in FrontPage is**
    a. Word.
    b. FrontPage.
    c. Navigator.
    d. Internet Explorer.

18. **A Web presence provider might be**
    a. A commerce service provider.
    b. An Internet service provider.
    c. A Web hosting service.
    d. All of the above.

19. **A Web presence provider might supply**
    a. Services to register your requested domain name.
    b. A secure server.
    c. Support for FrontPage Server Extensions.
    d. All of the above.

20. **Which one of the following statements is NOT true?**
    a. All browsers support animated content and objects, so you are free to create them in any Web page.
    b. You should use large picture files sparingly in your Web pages, as they might require long download times for some users.
    c. A Web presence provider must support the FrontPage 2000 Server Extensions for your FrontPage 2000 Web to work correctly.
    d. Your Web might look different when viewed from the Web by users with older browser versions.

► Skills Review

1. Locate a Web presence provider.

    a. Start your browser and connect to the Internet, if necessary.

    b. Type **http://www.microsoftwpp.com/wppsearch/default.htm** in your browser's address bar, then press [Enter] to open the page.

    c. Use the Search by Location (U.S./Canada Only) link to search for a WPP in your area. (If you do not live in the United States or Canada, click the Locate an International WPP link.)

    d. Select your state from the By State, Province, or Territory list arrow, type your telephone area code in the appropriate text box, then click Go. (If you clicked the Locate an International WPP link, select your country from the list, then follow the on-screen instructions.)

    e. Print a page that shows WPPs in your area. If you cannot locate any WPPs in your area, print the page that includes a message indicating this fact.

    f. Close your browser.

2. Use the Import Web Wizard to create a new Web.

    a. If necessary, start the PWS or log on to your server, and start FrontPage.

    b. Use the Import Web Wizard to create a new Web named *Insurance[insert your name here]*. You will import all seven files located in the UnitL\Sr folder on your Project Disk into the new Web.

    c. If necessary, double-click the Insurance Web folder in the Folder List so the _private and images folders appear in the Folder List. Then move the GIF files into the Web's images folder.

3. Set a Web site's page options.

    a. Set the Insurance Web's main folder to support Netscape Navigator browsers, versions 3.0 and later. (*Note:* You can still complete this Skills Review even if you are not using a Netscape browser.)

    b. Change the server version to Apache server. (*Note:* You can still complete this Skills Review even if you are not using an Apache server.)

    c. Enable the Web for FrontPage Server Extensions.

    d. Which dialog box did you use to set these page options?

    e. Based on these Web page options, which Internet technologies does the Insurance Web support?

    f. Close the dialog box.

4. Create an executable Web folder.

    a. Change the Insurance Web's main folder to an executable folder that allows programs and scripts to be run and files to be browsed.

    b. How much file space does the Insurance Web require? What is the name of the dialog box you used to verify this setting?

    c. Close the dialog box.

5. Check out a Web page.

    a. Open the Web Settings dialog box.

    b. What is the name of your Web server?

    c. What version of the FrontPage Server Extensions does your Web use?

    d. What server version appears in this dialog box?

    e. Change the Insurance Web to use source control.

f. Close the dialog box and refresh the Web.

g. Check out the home page for editing, then change the heading in the home page to centered.

h. Save the page.

6. Check in a Web page.

a. Close the home page.

b. Check in the home page.

c. Disable source control for the Insurance Web, then refresh the Web.

7. Open an Office document in a Web.

a. Open the Options dialog box and select the Configure Editors tab.

b. If necessary, select the option to open Office documents in the Office program that created them.

c. Close the dialog box.

d. In Folders View, right-click the Rates.xls file to open the pop-up menu, then click Open. What program starts and opens the file? Close the program that opens.

e. In Folders View, click the Rates.xls file to select it, then click the Preview in Browser button on the Standard toolbar.

f. If you are using Internet Explorer, click some of the menu commands on the menu bar to investigate their options.

g. Close your browser and FrontPage.

8. Troubleshoot server problems.

a. Create a worksheet you can use to track potential server problems when testing the Insurance Web. Include the name of each file in the Web in your worksheet.

b. Compile a list of questions that might help you troubleshoot potential server problems. Make sure that your questions are specific to the Insurance Web.

► Independent Challenges

1. Glenn Properties is a real-estate brokerage in Portland, Oregon, that specializes in selling residential properties. Riley Glenn manages the firm. Because of rising interest rates, clients have been requesting information about how Portland's mortgage rates compare to the national average, and how the rising rates are affecting the monthly payment amount for an average home in Portland. Riley created pages with rates for adjustable rate mortgages (ARMs), 15-year conventional loans, and 30-year conventional loans. She also created a page that shows the average payment for a home. Riley asks you to create the Web for her. Her market research indicates that most of her clients have older browser versions. The server on which the site will be stored does not accept FrontPage Server Extensions, nor does it permit programs and scripts to run. To ensure that the Web's pages are accessible only to one author at a time, she asks you to enable source control.

To complete this independent challenge:

a. Start the PWS or log on to your server, and then start FrontPage and use the Import Web Wizard to create a new Web named *MoneyRates[insert your name here]*.

b. Import all files from the UnitL\Ic1 folder on your Project Disk into the new Web. (You will import six files.)

c. Change the Web's page options to optimize it to work with Internet Explorer 3.0 and later, Netscape Navigator 3.0 and later, and the Microsoft Internet Information Server, version 3.0 and later. (*Note:* You can still complete this independent challenge even if you are not using these browser and server versions.)

d. Disable the FrontPage Server Extensions for this Web. Do *not* change any of the default Internet technologies. Which Internet technologies are enabled for your Web?

e. Change the MoneyRates folder so that programs and scripts will not run and files can be browsed.

f. Enable source control for the Web, then refresh it.

g. Check out the home page, then add the following on a new line at the bottom of the page: **Last Updated by [insert your name here] on [insert today's date here]**.

h. Save the home page, print it using FrontPage, then close it.

i. Print a screenshot of your Web in Folders View, then close WordPad without saving changes.

j. Check in the home page, then close the MoneyRates Web and FrontPage.

2. Acme Products wants to create a corporate presence Web to include news about the company, press releases, product information pages, and services supplied by the company. Pia Sen is in charge of the Web's development and manages the Web site development team. She wants you to begin work on the project by creating a new Web and setting the Web for current versions of Internet Explorer, Navigator, and Apache server. She also wants the Web enabled with the FrontPage Server Extensions and source control.

To complete this independent challenge:

a. Start the PWS or log on to your server, and then start FrontPage and use the Import Web Wizard to create a new Web named *Acme[insert your name here]*.

b. Import all files from the UnitL\lc2 folder on your Project Disk into the new Web. (You will import 16 files.)

c. Move the two GIF files into the Web's images folder.

d. Change the Web's page options to optimize it to work with Internet Explorer and Navigator browsers versions 4.0 and later, Apache server, and to enable it for the FrontPage Server Extensions. (*Note:* You can still complete this independent challenge even if you are not using these browser and server versions.) Which Internet technologies are enabled for your Web?

e. Enable the Web to use source control, refresh the Web, then check out the home page. Insert the *undercon.gif* file on a new, centered line under the navigation bar in the home page. Press [Enter], then type your first and last names on the new line. Save the home page, print it, then close it.

f. Return to Folders View, then cancel the changes you made to the home page.

g. Check out the home page. Do the picture and your name still appear on the home page? Why or why not? Return to Folders View and check in the home page.

h. Disable source control for the Acme Web, then refresh the Web.

i. Close the Web and FrontPage.

3. You are the human resource director's assistant at WES Consulting, Inc., a company that does consulting work for customers who use Oracle databases. Because many of the company's consultants work in different states, you decide to use a PowerPoint presentation to present the company's employee orientation slide show to newly hired people. You think that a PowerPoint presentation in a Web site, along with a conference call, will make the "virtual" orientations easier to follow. You also want to include a Word document on the site that contains a calendar of events for new employees.

Note: You must have PowerPoint 2000 and Word 2000 installed on your computer and use Internet Explorer to complete this independent challenge.

To complete this independent challenge:

a. Start the PWS or log on to your server, and then start FrontPage and use the Import Web Wizard to create a new Web named *Consulting[insert your name here]*.

b. Import all files from the UnitL\lc3 folder on your Project Disk into the new Web. (You will import three files.)

c. If necessary, set FrontPage to open Office documents in the Office program that created them.

d. Optimize the Web for Internet Explorer and Netscape Navigator browser versions 4.0 and later, Microsoft Internet Information Server versions 3.0 and later, and to use the FrontPage Server Extensions. (*Note:* You can still complete this independent challenge even if you are not using these browsers and server versions.)

e. Open the Welcome.ppt file from FrontPage.

f. Select the text "[type company name here]" in the title slide, type **WES Consulting, Inc.**, press [Enter], then type **Consultant: [insert your name here]**.

g. Select the word "here" on the first slide, click the Hyperlink button on the Standard toolbar, then in the Type the file or Web page name text box type **http://localhost/Consulting[insert your name here]/April.doc**. (If your server and/or Web name is different, type the path to the April.doc file in your Web.)

h. Close PowerPoint and save changes to the presentation.

i. In FrontPage Folders View, select the Default.htm file, then preview the file in Internet Explorer.

j. Click the Orientation Presentation link, then use the Advance command on the Browse menu to examine each slide in the presentation. (There are seven slides.)

k. Advance to the last slide in the presentation, then click the link to return to the beginning of the presentation. Use the Print dialog box to print only the first slide. (*Hint*: With the first slide displayed in the browser window, click File on the menu bar, click Print, then choose the option to print the current slide.)

l. Click the here link on the first slide to open this month's orientation events. Notice that the calendar is a Word document.

m. Turn on the Standard and Formatting toolbars in Word, then use a toolbar button to print the calendar page.

n. Click the Back button to return to the home page of the Consulting Web, then close Internet Explorer.

o. Close the Consulting Web and FrontPage.

4. The school district where you live has asked you to help it decide what type of server to install to run its FrontPage Web. The Web contains over 1,000 pages and receives an average amount of traffic for a Web of this size. The district is considering four different servers: Netscape Enterprise Server, Apache, Microsoft Internet Information Server version 5.0, and Personal Web Server. Your work with FrontPage so far has given you a good understanding of how the Personal Web Server works, but you are not familiar with the other server types, except that you know you can optimize FrontPage for some of these different servers. You decide to learn more about these different server types so you will be prepared to answer the school board members' questions and to provide some guidance to them as they make a decision during their next meeting.

To complete this independent challenge:

a. Connect to the Internet.

b. Go to http://www.course.com, navigate to the Student Online Companion for this book, then click the link for Unit L. Click the link to open a Web page that contains links to different server types.

c. For each server (Netscape Enterprise Server, Apache, Microsoft Internet Information Server version 5.0, and Personal Web Server), print a page that lists its features and reviews. (Click the server name link on the page, such as Microsoft IIS v5.0.) Print the page that opens and lists the primary features of each server that the school board is considering. Note how each server is rated in terms of ease of use, reliability, and cost.

d. For each server, click the Click to Read Our Full Review link at the top of the page (and located below the server's name) to open a page that provides detailed information about the server's features. Read the page that opens.

e. Close your browser and your dial-up connection.

f. Based on the information that you found, which server is the most affordable? Which server is the most reliable? Which server is the easiest to install, use, and maintain? Which server is the most popular, based on its market penetration percentage?

g. Write a short report to the school board in which you recommend one server.

Visual Workshop

Follow the instructions in the document shown in Figure L-20. When you are finished, close your browser and FrontPage. (*Note*: You must use Internet Explorer to complete this Visual Workshop.)

FIGURE L-20

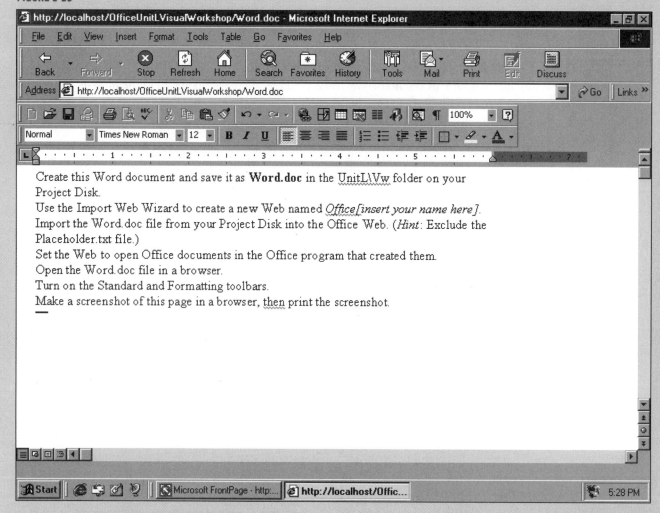

Create this Word document and save it as **Word.doc** in the UnitL\Vw folder on your Project Disk.

Use the Import Web Wizard to create a new Web named *Office[insert your name here]*.

Import the Word.doc file from your Project Disk into the Office Web. (*Hint*: Exclude the Placeholder.txt file.)

Set the Web to open Office documents in the Office program that created them.

Open the Word.doc file in a browser.

Turn on the Standard and Formatting toolbars.

Make a screenshot of this page in a browser, then print the screenshot.

Unit
M

Using
Office Components and Styles

Objectives

► **Understand Office components**
[MOUS] ► **Create a Spreadsheet component**
[MOUS] ► **Import data into a Spreadsheet component**
[MOUS] ► **Create a Chart component**
► **Use a PivotTable List component**
[MOUS] ► **Create special styles in a Web page**
[MOUS] ► **Create a cascading style sheet**
[MOUS] ► **Apply a cascading style sheet**

FrontPage lets you use two features to enhance the usability and appearance of your Webs: Office components and styles. First, FrontPage lets you insert Office components so you can include functional spreadsheets, charts, and pivot tables in your Web pages. Second, when you need to format headings, text and hyperlinks, in special ways, you can create styles to apply to your Web pages, or you can create a style sheet and apply it to one or more pages in your Web. ✎ Ariadne McDonald wants to include Office components in the Mortgage Web in order to create a calculator that computes monthly mortgage payments, a chart of interest rates for last year, and an interactive spreadsheet that shows mortgage data for several mortgage amounts, terms, and rates. In addition, she wants to ensure a consistent appearance for pages in the Web, so she will create styles for certain page elements.

Understanding Office Components

An **Office component** is a self-contained spreadsheet, chart, or pivot table that you include in a Web page. A **Spreadsheet component** is a tool that lets you summarize and analyze data. A **Chart component** displays spreadsheet data as a picture, such as in a pie chart or a bar chart. A **PivotTable List component** is an interactive spreadsheet that lets you quickly summarize, organize, and display spreadsheet data in different ways. Ariadne wants to include two new Web pages in the Mortgage Web. The first page will contain a Spreadsheet component that lets clients calculate their estimated monthly mortgage payments. The second page will contain interest rate information from last year in a Spreadsheet component. This page will also show the data graphically using a line chart. She reads to find out more details about Office components.

Details

Spreadsheet component

Figure M-1 shows a spreadsheet component that computes monthly payments. Notice how a Spreadsheet component in a Web page looks like a small Excel program window. The Spreadsheet component contains many of the same commands found in Excel. You can enter data directly into the Spreadsheet component or import it from a file in the Web or from a file location, such as your hard drive. You use the commands on the Toolbox to format and calculate the data. You use the pointer to change the Spreadsheet component's size and to resize worksheet columns. The Spreadsheet component even contains its own Help system to provide online Help while you're working.

Chart component

Figure M-2 shows a Chart component that graphically illustrates the data in the Spreadsheet component shown in Figure M-1. In order to create a Chart component in a Web page, you must first select or identify the data source you want to use to create the chart. You can create a Chart component from any valid data source, however, a common method of using a Chart component is to create a Spreadsheet component that contains the data source, and then to use that spreadsheet data to create the Chart component.

PivotTable List component

Figure M-3 shows a PivotTable List component with mortgage payment information for different amounts, terms, and rates. Figure M-4 shows the PivotTable List component after user interaction. You can create a PivotTable List component from data stored in a spreadsheet, database, or other program that can create pivot tables. After you create the pivot table, you can place it in a Web page. The primary advantage of using a PivotTable List component in a Web page is that your site's visitors can manipulate the data it contains without needing any special programs on their computers—the browser does all of the work. For example, if you supply data in a PivotTable List component that lists different cities in which you can do business, a user might use the PivotTable List component to identify all cities in a certain state. The user has the power to rearrange the data, but the user cannot change the data stored in your Web. When the user reloads the page that contains the PivotTable List component, the original data that is stored in the Web will appear in the browser.

FIGURE M-1: Office Spreadsheet component

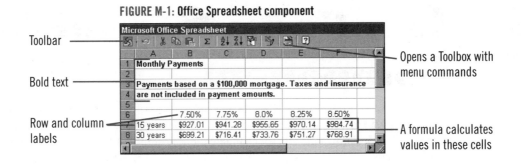

FIGURE M-2: A column chart in an Office Chart component

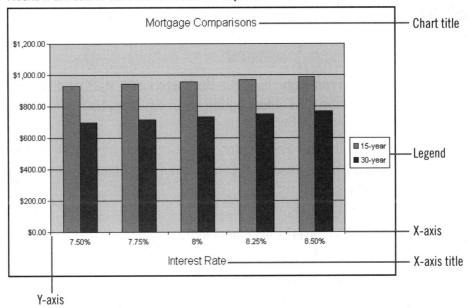

FIGURE M-3: Office PivotTable List component

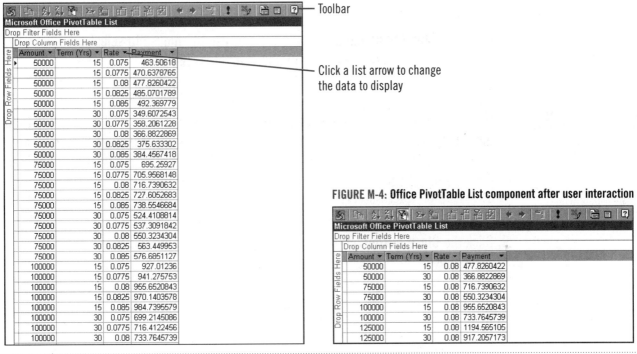

FIGURE M-4: Office PivotTable List component after user interaction

FrontPage 2000

Creating a Spreadsheet Component

A Spreadsheet component is a self-contained spreadsheet in a Web page that is functional when viewed using a browser. The Spreadsheet component contains a Toolbox with commands for formatting and calculating data and for changing the appearance of the Spreadsheet component in the Web page. For example, you can change the name of the Spreadsheet component window, change column widths or turn off the display of the window's scroll bars. ◣▬▬ Ariadne wants to include a spreadsheet in the Web that allows her clients to manipulate its values in order to calculate their estimated mortgage payments by entering the mortgage amount, an interest rate, and the number of years to finance their home. First she creates and formats a Spreadsheet component.

Steps

1. If necessary, start the **PWS** or log on to your server

QuickTip

The http protocol in the Web's folder name indicates this is a server-based Web.

2. Start **FrontPage**, open the **Mortgage[insert your name here] Web** from the server, then click the **Folders button** 🗔 on the Views bar
   The Mortgage Web opens from the server.

3. Click the **New Page button** 🗔 on the Standard toolbar, type **spreadsheet.htm**, press **[Tab]**, type **Spreadsheet Component**, press **[Enter]**, then double-click **spreadsheet.htm** in the contents pane
   FrontPage creates a new Web page and opens it in Page View.

Trouble?

If you do not see the Office Spreadsheet command in the list, then your Web does not support ActiveX controls. Use the Compatibility tab in the Page Options dialog box to enable the Web for ActiveX controls, then repeat Step 4.

4. Click the **Insert Component button** 🖼 on the Standard toolbar
   The Insert Component button list opens, as shown in Figure M-5.

5. Click **Office Spreadsheet** in the Insert Component button list, then click anywhere in the Spreadsheet component to select it
   A Microsoft Office Spreadsheet window appears in your Web page.

6. Click the **Property Toolbox button** 🖼 on the Spreadsheet component toolbar
   The Spreadsheet Property Toolbox opens, as shown in Figure M-6. The Toolbox commands in Figure M-6 are collapsed.

7. Click the **Title Bar command** on the Toolbox, use the mouse to select the text in the Title text box, type **Mortgage Calculator**, then press **[Enter]**
   As shown in Figure M-7, the title bar of the Spreadsheet component changes to "Mortgage Calculator," which better identifies the contents of the Spreadsheet component.

QuickTip

Each Office component has a Help button on the General command menu on the Toolbox so you can get Help while working with that component.

8. If necessary, click the **General command** on the Toolbox to expand it, click the **Help button** 🖼 on the General command menu, if and click the **Maximize button** to maximize the Help window, and click the **Search tab**, then click the **Overview link** and read the Help page
   The Microsoft Spreadsheet Help window opens and displays the Overview page. If you are not familiar with spreadsheets, read this page and use the links to examine additional content.

9. Click the **Close button** on the Microsoft Spreadsheet Help window to close it
   The Toolbox is still open.

FIGURE M-5: Insert Component button list

Commands for creating Office components

Insert Component button

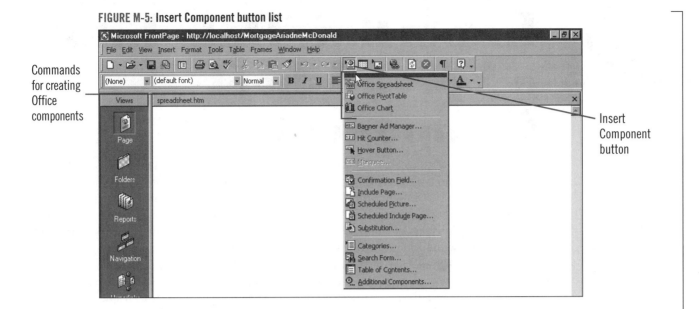

FIGURE M-6: Toolbox for the Spreadsheet component

Property Toolbox button

Cell A1

Sizing handles indicate the component is selected

Toolbox (yours might show expanded menus or appear in a different location)

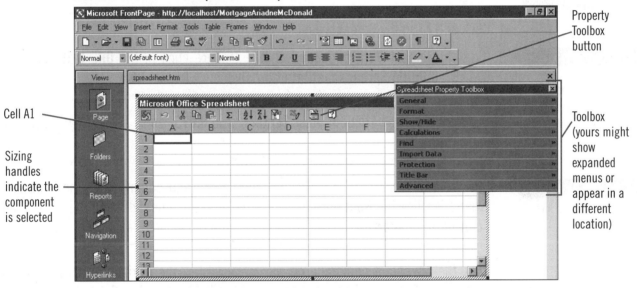

FIGURE M-7: Title on Spreadsheet component title bar changed

New title on title bar

Title for title bar entered here

Other options for formatting the title bar and its title

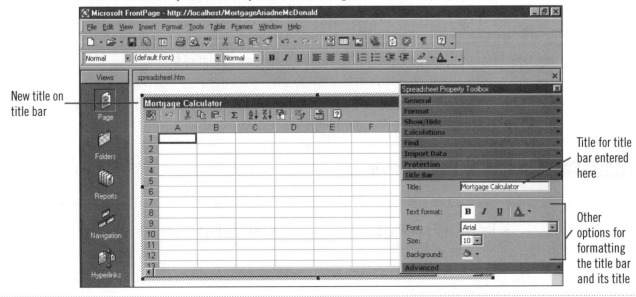

Importing Data Into a Spreadsheet Component

After you create a Spreadsheet component in a Web page, you can either enter data into it by selecting a cell and typing, or you can use the Import Data command on the Toolbox to import data from a file. Data you import from a file must be stored in HTML format. When you import data into a Spreadsheet component from a file, the data is **static**; in other words, the data entered in the Spreadsheet component is not linked to your original file. After you import the data, you can use the Toolbox to format the Spreadsheet component, including its data, in many different ways. ➤ Ariadne already created an HTML document that contains the mortgage calculator text and the function that calculates the monthly mortgage payment. She imports the data into the Spreadsheet component, then formats the Spreadsheet component.

1. Click **cell A1** in the Spreadsheet component to select it

Trouble?
If you are storing your Project Files in a different location, type the path to your file in the URL text box.

2. Click the **Import Data command** on the Toolbox, click in the **URL text box**, type **C:\1767-8\UnitM\SpreadsheetData.htm**, then click **Import Now**
   The contents of the SpreadsheetData.htm file are inserted in the Spreadsheet component.

3. Click **cell D1**, type **100000**, press **[Enter]**, type **0.075**, press **[Enter]**, type **30**, then press **[Enter]**
   The Spreadsheet component calculates a monthly payment, as shown in Figure M-8.

QuickTip
Use the ScreenTips to identify colors by name.

4. Click **cell A5** to select it, if necessary click the **Format command** on the Toolbox to expand it, click the **Bold button** 🅱 on the Format command menu, click the **Font Color button list arrow** 🅰 on the Format command menu, then click the **Blue color**
   The value in the selected cell is changed to blue, bold text.

5. Click the **Advanced command** on the Toolbox, click the **Horizontal scroll bar list arrow**, click **False**, click the **Vertical scroll bar list arrow**, click **False**, then click the **Close button** on the Toolbox title bar
   The Toolbox closes. The Spreadsheet component does not contain scroll bars.

6. Point to the **lower-right sizing handle** until the pointer changes to ↘, then click and drag the **lower-right sizing handle** as shown in Figure M-9
   The Spreadsheet component is resized, as shown in Figure M-9.

7. Click the **Save button** 💾 on the Standard toolbar, then click the **Preview in Browser button** 🔍 on the Standard toolbar
   The Spreadsheet Component Web page opens in a browser.

Trouble?
If you delete the value in cell D5, you will delete the formula that computes the monthly payment. Close your browser and click 🔍 in FrontPage to reload the page.

8. Select cells **D1 through D3**, press **[Delete]**, then repeat Step 3
   Your browser calculates the monthly payment, which is $699.21. You can delete the values in cells D1:D3 and then enter any values you wish to calculate a monthly payment.

9. Return to **FrontPage**, then click the **Folders button** 📁 on the Views bar
   You return to FrontPage and change to Folders View.

FIGURE M-8: Spreadsheet component after calculating a monthly payment

Dark border indicates a selected cell

This cell contains a formula that calculates the payment

Values entered into cells D1:D3

Location from which data was imported

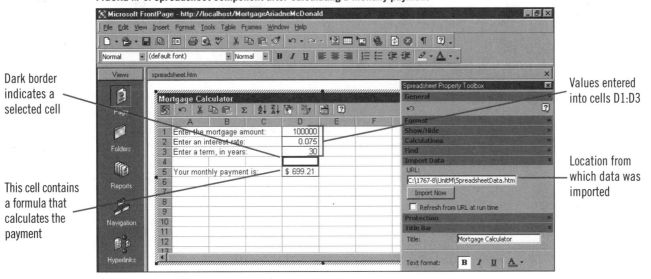

FIGURE M-9: Spreadsheet component after resizing

Blue, bold text

Lower-right sizing handle

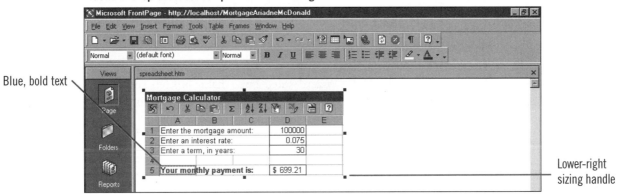

Why use Office components

The advantage of using an Office component in a Web page is that FrontPage contains the tools required to manipulate and format the data in the component so you don't need to have other programs such as Excel installed on your computer.

The only disadvantage of using Office components in a Web page is that some browsers cannot display them or display them differently. Office components are best viewed in Internet Explorer 4.01 or higher.

Creating a Chart Component

When you create a Chart component, a Wizard starts and asks you about the type of chart you want to create and about the data you want to chart. After you create the chart, you can use the Toolbox to change its format and appearance. Ariadne wants to include a chart in a Web page to graphically illustrate the rise and fall of interest rates last year. She already created a Web page that contains a Spreadsheet component with the interest rate data. She uses the data in the Spreadsheet component to create a Chart component in the same Web page.

Steps

1. Click **File** on the menu bar, click **Import**, click **Add File**, open the **UnitM folder** on your Project Disk, double-click **chart**, then click **OK**
   The chart.htm Web page, which contains the data you will use to create the Chart component, is imported into the Mortgage Web and is selected in Folders View.

QuickTip
The easiest way to create a Chart component in a Web page is to first create a Spreadsheet component that holds the data you want to chart. Then you can insert a Chart component that uses that data.

2. Double-click **chart.htm** in the contents pane, then click the line below the Spreadsheet component to position the insertion point so it is centered on the page
   This page contains a Spreadsheet component with mortgage rate data for last year.

3. Click the **Insert Component button** on the Standard toolbar, then click **Office Chart**
   The Microsoft Office Chart Wizard - Step 1 of 3 dialog box opens, as shown in Figure M-10.

4. Click the **Line chart type**, then click the **first chart sub-type** in the second row
   You selected a line chart with markers displayed at each data value.

QuickTip
FrontPage creates an ActiveX control, which appears as an icon, at the top of pages that contain data sources. Don't delete this icon, which does not appear when the page is viewed in a browser, or you will delete the link between the source data and the chart.

5. Click **Next**, then click **Next** again
   The Microsoft Office Chart Wizard - Step 2 of 3 dialog box lets you select the data source on which to base your chart. Because the chart.htm page already contains a Spreadsheet component, FrontPage automatically selects the Spreadsheet component in the chart.htm page as the data source. The Microsoft Office Chart Wizard - Step 3 of 3 dialog box opens.

6. Click the **Set this chart's data in one step button**, select the entry in the Data range text box and type **=B1:B12**, click the **Columns option button** (*even if it is already selected*), then click **OK**
   A line with markers appears in the sample chart, as shown in Figure M-11.

7. Select the text in the Name text box, type **Interest Rates**, in the Category (X) axis labels text box type **=A1:A12**, then click an empty area in the Series box
   The chart now includes a series name for the line ("Interest Rates") and axis labels for the X-axis.

Trouble?
If you need to delete a Chart component, select it, click the HTML tab in Normal Page View, then press [Delete]. Click the Normal tab, then select and delete the ActiveX control at the top of the page.

8. Click **Finish**, click the **Save button** on the Standard toolbar, click the **Preview in Browser button** on the Standard toolbar, then scroll down the page
   The Chart Component Web page opens in a browser, as shown in Figure M-12.

9. Scroll up the page, click **cell B1** in the Spreadsheet component, type **0.09**, then watch the Chart component and press **[Enter]**
   The first line marker in the chart changes to reflect the new value of 0.09. However, you did not change this value in the Spreadsheet component that is stored in the Mortgage Web. When you return to FrontPage, the value in cell B1 will still be 0.0675.

FIGURE M-10: Microsoft Office Chart Wizard - Step 1 of 3 dialog box

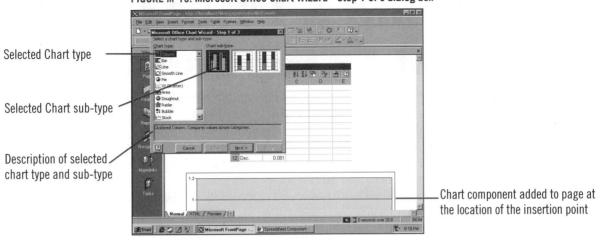

Selected Chart type

Selected Chart sub-type

Description of selected chart type and sub-type

Chart component added to page at the location of the insertion point

FIGURE M-11: Dialog box for selecting the chart's data

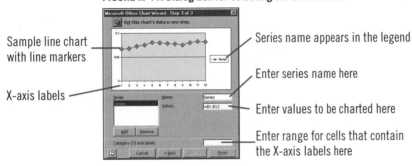

Sample line chart with line markers

X-axis labels

Series name appears in the legend

Enter series name here

Enter values to be charted here

Enter range for cells that contain the X-axis labels here

FIGURE M-12: Chart component in a Web browser

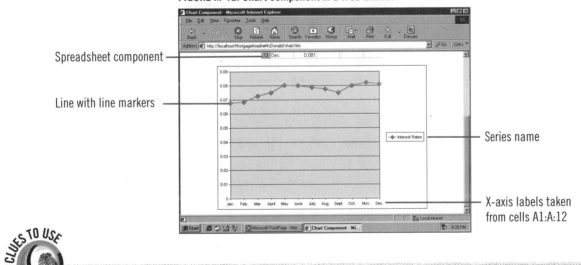

Spreadsheet component

Line with line markers

Series name

X-axis labels taken from cells A1:A:12

Changing a Chart component's appearance

You can change a chart's properties after you create it. However, because the Chart component does not contain a toolbar, you must right-click the selected chart to open the pop-up menu, then click Property Toolbox. The Toolbox commands that appear depend on what part of the chart you right-clicked. For example, to change the name of a series, right-click the line or columns in the chart. To add a title or a label to an axis, right-click an empty area in the component but not the chart or legend. To change the way that gridlines appear, right-click the chart or an existing gridline. When the Toolbox is open, you can change the commands it contains by clicking the chart or its individual elements. If you need help while working with the Chart component, click the Help button on the General command menu to open the Microsoft Office Chart Help window.

Using a PivotTable List Component

You can create a PivotTable List component in a Web page when that page contains a valid data source on which to base the PivotTable List. Unfortunately, the data in a Spreadsheet component is not a valid data source for a PivotTable List, so you need to use a database, spreadsheet, or other program to create your pivot table. One easy way to create a pivot table is to enter the data into Excel, and then use the option in Excel to publish the worksheet with PivotTable interactivity. When you publish an Excel workbook with PivotTable interactivity, Excel automatically creates a Web page with a PivotTable List component. Ariadne used Excel to create a worksheet that includes data about different mortgage amounts, terms, and rates. She published the worksheet with PivotTable interactivity to create a Web page with a PivotTable List component. Now she wants to open the Web page in a browser to test the pivot table's functionality.

1. Select the text in your browser's address field, type **C:\1767-8\UnitM\PivotTable.htm**, then press **[Enter]**
   A Web page that contains a PivotTable List component opens in the browser, as shown in Figure M-13. The pivot table was created using the data shown in Figure M-14.

2. Click the **Amount list arrow**, click the **100000 check box** and the **125000 check box** to clear them, then click **OK**
   The PivotTable List component changes to show only those lines that contain the values 50000 and 75000 in the Amount column. Notice that the list arrow changed color from black to blue, indicating that the data in this column has been manipulated.

3. Click the **Term (Yrs) list arrow**, click the **15 check box** to clear it, then click **OK**
   The PivotTable List component changes again, as shown in Figure M-15, to show only those records with the specified criteria (Amount of 50000 or 75000, and a Term (Yrs) of 30).

4. Click the **Rate list arrow**, click the **(Show All) check box** to clear it, click the **0.08 check box** to select it, then click **OK**
   Now the PivotTable List component only shows the payments for a 50000 or 75000, 30-year mortgage that is financed at an 8% interest rate.

5. Click the **Amount list arrow**, click the **(Show All) check box** to select it, click **OK**, then repeat the steps to show all values for the Term (Yrs) and Rate columns
   The PivotTable List component displays all of its data again.

6. Click the **Microsoft FrontPage program button** on the taskbar to return to FrontPage
   The Chart Component Web page is still open in Page View.

FIGURE M-13: PivotTable List component in a Web browser

Amount list arrow

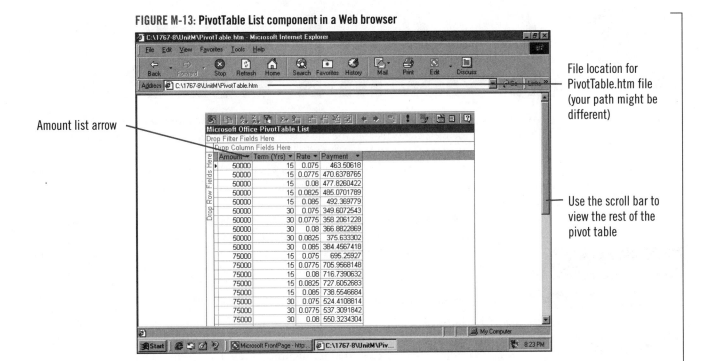

File location for
PivotTable.htm file
(your path might be
different)

Use the scroll bar to
view the rest of the
pivot table

FIGURE M-14: Excel data on which
the PivotTable List component
is based

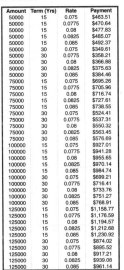

FIGURE M-15: PivotTable List component after selecting amounts and a term to display

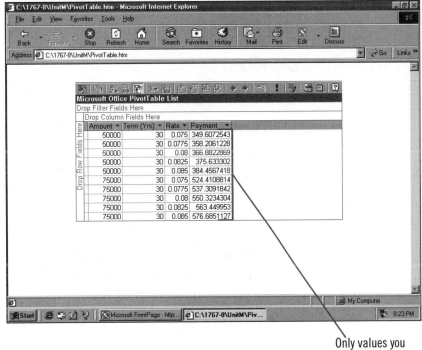

Only values you
specified appear in
the component

Creating Special Styles in a Web Page

When your Web does not use a theme, it is generally the Web site developer's responsibility to format the individual elements used in the site's pages. For example, each page in your site might contain text with the Heading 1 style applied to it. However, if you want these headings to be a certain color and centered, you would need to open every page in the Web and apply the desired formatting options to every text occurrence that uses the Heading 1 style. This task can take a lot of time and it is easy to accidentally omit a page or format one heading differently. You can create styles in a single Web page, or create and apply styles to one or more pages in a Web. It is very easy to create simple styles for fonts, headings, hyperlinks, and other objects to ensure a consistent appearance for those objects. ➤ Ariadne wants the home page to have a different appearance from other pages in the Mortgage Web. She decides to change the style of the heading in the home page.

1. Click the **Folders button** 📁 on the Views bar, then double-click **Default.htm** in the contents pane

   The home page opens in Page View. The home page contains a heading, which uses the default Heading 1 style, except that its alignment was changed to centered.

2. Click **Format** on the menu bar, then click **Style**

   The Style dialog box opens, as shown in Figure M-16. You use this dialog box to change the style associated with any HTML element in a Web page. Because the Heading 1 style uses the h1 tag, you will change the style associated with this tag in the Style dialog box.

3. Scroll down the Styles list, click **h1**, then click **Modify**

   The Modify Style dialog box opens with the h1 tag entered into the Name (selector) text box.

4. Click **Format**

   You can change five aspects of an HTML tag: font, paragraph, border, numbering, and position. These commands open dialog boxes in which you can change the tag's formatting.

5. Click **Font** in the Format button list

   The Font dialog box opens.

6. Scroll down the Font list box and click **Garamond**, in the Font style list box click **Bold**, scroll down the Size list box and click **24pt**, click the **Color list arrow** and click the **Teal color**, then click **OK**

   The Font dialog box closes and the Modify Style dialog box reappears, as shown in Figure M-17.

7. Click **Format** again, click **Paragraph**, in the Paragraph dialog box click the **Alignment list arrow**, click **Center**, click **OK**, click **OK** in the Modify Style dialog box, then click **OK** in the Style dialog box

   As shown in Figure M-18, the existing heading in the home page now uses the style that you defined in the Styles dialog box.

8. Click the **Save button** 💾 on the Standard toolbar, click the **blank line** below the table in the home page, type **This is a Heading**, click the **Style list arrow** on the Formatting toolbar, then click **Heading 1**

   The Heading 1 style that you specified for this page is applied to the text you typed. Any new text that you type and format using the Heading 1 style on this page will immediately use the style you created, which saves you the trouble of changing the font, font size, font color, font style, and alignment of the new text.

9. Click the **Close button** on the contents pane, then click **No**

   FrontPage closes the home page without saving your changes.

FIGURE M-16: Style dialog box

Scrollable list of HTML tags ⎯

Click to change the style of the selected HTML tag

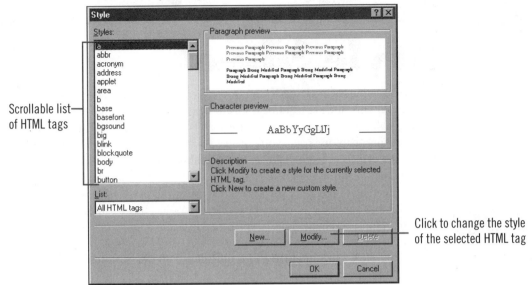

FIGURE M-17: Modify Style dialog box

Sample of selected style for the h1 tag ⎯

Tag being modified

Style description

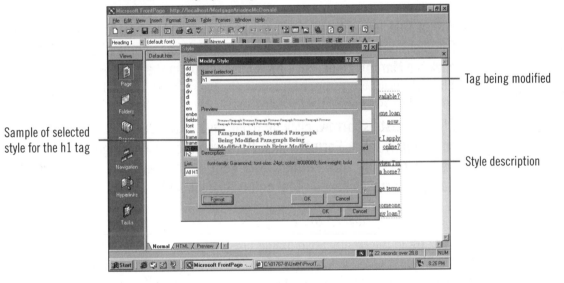

FIGURE M-18: Text uses the user-defined Heading 1 style

Heading's format uses the h1 style you created

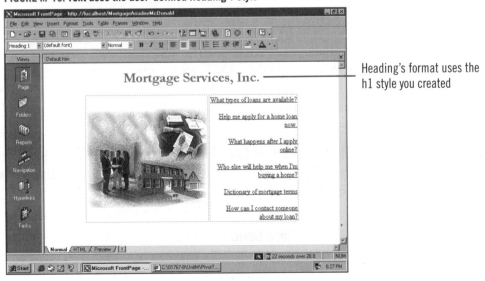

Creating a Cascading Style Sheet

As you learned in the previous lesson, you can create styles for individual Web pages to ensure that specific elements, such as headings, appear consistently within a page. However, the real power of creating styles is to apply consistent formats across selected or all pages in a Web site. To apply styles to more than one page, you create a blank Web page that contains the HTML code for the styles. This page is called a **cascading style sheet** (**CSS**). After creating a cascading style sheet, you can link it—and its defined styles—to every page in a Web site, or to selected individual pages, without needing to re-create the same styles over and over. ⬛ Ariadne creates a cascading style sheet and applies it to selected pages in the Web. The cascading style sheet contains styles for text, paragraphs, and hyperlinks to ensure a consistent appearance of these elements.

Steps

1. In Page View, click the **New Page button** ▢ on the Standard toolbar
   A new, blank page opens in Page View.

2. Click **Format** on the menu bar, then click **Style**
   The Style dialog box opens, with the HTML a tag selected. The HTML a tag is used to create hyperlinks.

3. With **a** selected in the Styles list box, click **Modify**, click **Format**, click **Font**, in the Font list box scroll down if necessary and click **Garamond**, click the **Color list arrow**, click the **Maroon color**, click **OK**, then click **OK** in the Modify Style dialog box
   The Style dialog box reappears, as shown in Figure M-19. The Styles list box shows one style, and the List box shows "User-defined styles."

4. Click the **List list arrow**, click **All HTML tags**, scroll down the Styles list and click **h1**, click **Modify**, click **Format**, click **Paragraph**, click the **Alignment list arrow**, click **Center**, click **OK**, click **Format**, click **Font**, in the Font style list click **Bold**, click the **Color list arrow**, click the **Teal color**, then click **OK**
   A preview and description of the new style for text that uses the Heading 1 style appear in the Modify Style dialog box.

5. Click **OK** in the Modify Style dialog box
   The Modify Style dialog box closes and the Style dialog box reappears. The List list box displays "All HTML tags" so you can continue formatting your styles.

6. Scroll up the Styles list, click **body**, click **Modify**, click **Format**, click **Font**, scroll down the Font list and click **Garamond**, click **OK**, click **OK** in the Modify Style dialog box, then click **OK** in the Style dialog box
   The Style dialog box closes. The Web page shown in Page View does not contain any content. It only contains the HTML code required to create the styles for the a, h1, and body tags.

7. Click the **HTML tab**
   The HTML code required to create the styles for the a, h1, and body tags appears, as shown in Figure M-20.

8. Click the **Normal tab**, click the **Save button** 💾 on the Standard toolbar, in the File name text box type **styles**, click the **Save as type list arrow**, click **HyperText Style Sheet**, then click **Save**
   FrontPage saves the page as a cascading style sheet using the filename styles.css.

9. Click the **Close button** in the contents pane
   The styles.css file closes. In the next lesson, you will apply the cascading style sheet to pages in the Web site.

FIGURE M-19: Style dialog box after creating a user-defined style

The HTML a tag is now a user-defined style

List list arrow

Specifications for the selected HTML tag

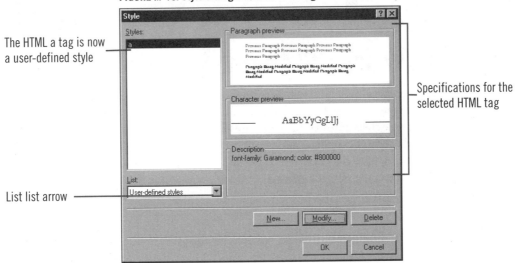

FIGURE M-20: HTML code for a cascading style

HTML tags that have user-defined styles associated with them

HTML code for user-defined styles

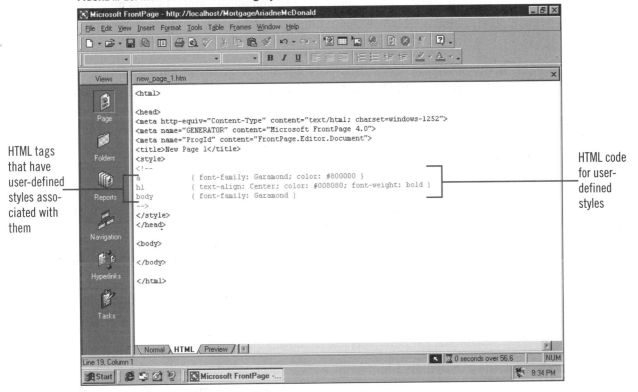

CLUES TO USE

Differences between cascading style sheets and themes

You might wonder how a cascading style sheet is different from a theme. They are actually similar, although they do their work in different ways. A theme is actually just a collection of styles that FrontPage applies to different objects in your Web. The theme's elements are stored in the _themes folder in your Web. For example, by applying the Expedition theme to a Web, you are really applying the styles contained in that theme to the pages. A cascading style sheet, on the other hand, is a document that contains HTML code to specify how to format specific HTML tags, which is then linked to pages in the site. While you can use a cascading style sheet to change the elements in a theme, this feature is for advanced users only. For most people, changing styles is accomplished by applying a Web theme or by applying a cascading style sheet.

Applying a Cascading Style Sheet

After you create a cascading style sheet and save it in a Web, you can use it to change the styles in existing or new Web pages by linking the cascading style sheet to them. The styles defined in your cascading style sheet automatically format the content of your Web page(s). If you update your cascading style sheet, the updated styles will be applied automatically to pages that are linked to it. If your cascading style sheet does not contain a style for an HTML tag, then a browser will format that tag using the default settings. ➤ Ariadne wants to link the cascading style sheet to all pages in the Web, except for the apply.doc file.

1. Click the **Folders button** 📁 on the Views bar

The styles.css file appears in Folders View, along with the other pages in the Mortgage Web.

Trouble?

Your files might be listed in a different order; be sure you select all 10 files.

2. Click **application.htm** in the contents pane, press and hold [**Ctrl**], then click the following files to select them: **contact.htm**, **dictionary.htm**, **Default.htm**, **loantypes.htm**, **rates.htm**, **what.htm**, **whoelse.htm**, **spreadsheet.htm**, and **chart.htm**, then release [**Ctrl**]

Ten Web pages are selected.

3. With the Web pages still selected in Folders View, click **Format** on the menu bar, then click **Style Sheet Links**

The Link Style Sheet dialog box opens.

QuickTip

To apply a cascading style sheet to all pages in a Web, click the All pages option button.

4. Make sure that the **Selected page(s) option button** is selected, then click **Add**

The Select Hyperlink dialog box opens, as shown in Figure M-21. The styles.css file is the cascading style sheet you created previously.

5. Click **styles.css**, then click **OK**

The Link Style Sheet dialog box reappears, as shown in Figure M-22. Now the URL text box shows "styles.css" as the selected style sheet.

QuickTip

The time it takes to refresh the pages varies. The pages are refreshed when the ⧖ pointer changes to ⬚.

6. Click **OK**, wait for FrontPage to refresh the pages, then double-click **loantypes.htm** in the contents pane

FrontPage applies the cascading style sheet to the 10 selected pages and opens the Loan Types Web page in Page View. As shown in Figure M-23, this page now uses the styles you created in the styles.css file. The hyperlinks use maroon, Garamond font; the heading is Garamond, teal, bold, centered, text; and the body text in the page uses Garamond font.

7. Click the **Folders button** 📁 on the Views bar, double-click **spreadsheet.htm** in the contents pane, press the **Left arrow key**, press [**Enter**], then press the **Up arrow key**

The insertion point appears on a blank line above the Spreadsheet component that you created in this page.

8. Click the **Style list arrow** on the Formatting toolbar, click **Heading 1**, then type **Mortgage Calculator**

The text that you typed automatically uses the Heading 1 style you defined in the cascading style sheet, because you linked this page to the cascading style sheet.

9. Click the **Save button** 💾 on the Standard toolbar, then close the Mortgage Web, FrontPage, and your browser

FIGURE M-21: Select Hyperlink dialog box

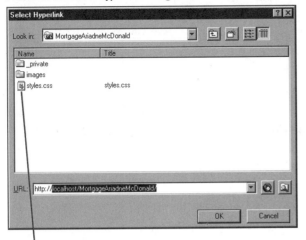

Cascading style sheet

FIGURE M-22: Link Style Sheet dialog box

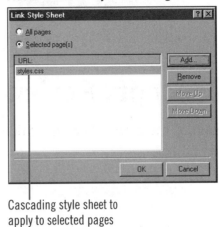

Cascading style sheet to
apply to selected pages

FIGURE M-23: Web page after applying the cascading style sheet

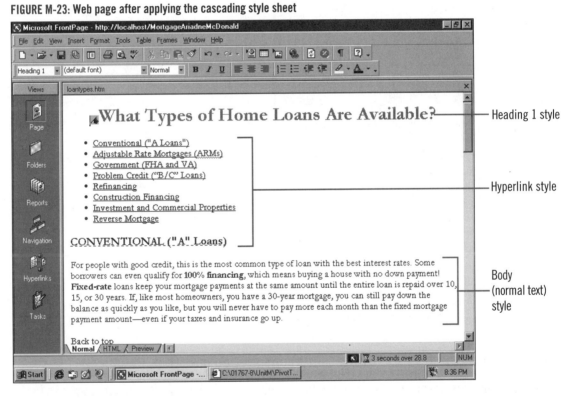

Heading 1 style

Hyperlink style

Body
(normal text)
style

Cascading style sheets and browsers

Before using styles and cascading style sheets in your Webs, make sure that the people who will visit your site are using browsers that can display styles. Internet Explorer 3.01 and higher and Netscape Navigator 4.0 and higher *generally* can display pages that use styles. However, some versions of some browsers cannot read some code generated by styles, or the code is read unpredictably. As with all Webs, make sure to test

your pages carefully using different browsers, browser versions, operating systems, and monitors to ensure that your content appears as desired. If you know that some of your site's visitors are using older browser versions, use the Compatibility tab in the Page Options dialog box to deselect CSS support so FrontPage will disable CSS commands in your Web.

Practice

► Concepts Review

Label each of the elements of the Microsoft FrontPage window shown in Figure M-24.

FIGURE M-24

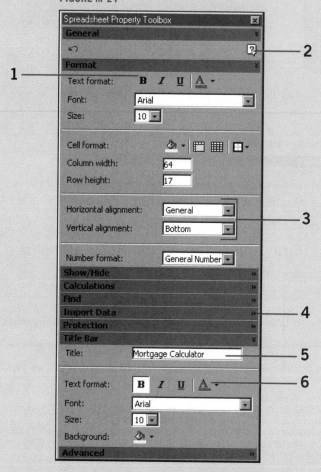

Match each of the terms with the statement that describes it.

7. Cascading style sheet
8. Chart
9. Office component
10. Pivot table
11. Spreadsheet
12. Style
13. Toolbox

a. A file that contains HTML codes with styles that you can link to Web pages
b. A format that you create for an HTML tag in a Web page
c. A self-contained spreadsheet, chart, or pivot table in a Web page
d. A tool that lets you summarize and analyze data
e. An interactive spreadsheet that lets you quickly summarize, organize, and display data
f. An Office component feature that contains menu commands for working with that component
g. A graphic depiction of data in a Web page

Select the best answer from the list of choices.

14. Which one of the following statements is TRUE?
a. Using an Office component is the same as importing an Excel workbook into a Web.
b. To use the Office Spreadsheet component, you must first create the spreadsheet data using Excel.
c. A Spreadsheet component might be a data source for a Chart component.
d. To use the Spreadsheet component, you must have Excel installed on your computer.

15. If the Office Spreadsheet command does not appear on the Insert Component button list,
a. Excel is not installed on your computer.
b. Your Web does not support ActiveX controls.
c. The PWS is not running.
d. All of the above.

16. To import data into a Spreadsheet component, the data must be in _____ format.
a. Text
b. Excel
c. HTML
d. Word

17. To add a title to an existing Chart component, right-click _____ to open the pop-up menu, then click Property Toolbox.
a. The chart
b. The legend
c. An empty area in the component, but not the chart or legend
d. The gridlines

18. The HTML tag for a hyperlink is
a. a.
b. alt.
c. href.
d. None of the above.

19. When viewed in Normal Page View, a cascading style sheet contains
a. HTML code.
b. Sample text with the applied styles.
c. No content.
d. The names of the tags that have styles defined for them.

▶ Skills Review

1. Understand Office components.
   a. Identify one advantage and one disadvantage of using a Spreadsheet component in a Web page.
   b. Why would you use a Chart component in a Web page instead of a static chart that you create using another program, such as Excel?

2. Create a Spreadsheet component in a Web page.
   a. If necessary, turn on the PWS or log on to your server. Start FrontPage.
   b. Use the Import Web Wizard to create a new server-based Web named *Budget[insert your name here]*. Import all files from the UnitM\Sr folder on your Project Disk into the new Web. Click the Include subfolders check box in the first dialog box before clicking the Next button. (You will import five files.) If necessary, enable your Web to support cascading style sheets, ActiveX controls, and the FrontPage Server Extensions.
   c. In Folders View, create a new Web page using the filename *budget.htm* and the title **Monthly Budget**. Open the Monthly Budget page in Page View.
   d. Type **Monthly Budget for [insert your name here]**, then format this text using the Heading 2 style.
   e. On the next line, insert a centered Spreadsheet component. (*Hint*: Click the Center button before inserting the component to center it.)
   f. Select the component, open on the Toolbox, then change the title bar text to **Monthly Budget**.
   g. Open the Help window. On the Search tab and in the Type in the keyword to find text box, type **formulas**, then click List Topics. In the Select Topic to display list box, double-click About using formulas in a spreadsheet. Read the page that opens. Click any hyperlinks that will help you to understand more about using formulas. Close the Help window.

3. Import data into and format a Spreadsheet component.

   a. If necessary, click cell A1 in the Spreadsheet component to select it.

   b. Use the Import Data command on the Toolbox to import the file BudgetData.htm into the Spreadsheet component. (*Hint*: The BudgetData.htm file is located in the Budget Web. In the URL text box, type the path to the Budget Web. For example, http://localhost/Budget[insert your name here]/BudgetData.htm.)

   c. In cell A8, type **Total**, press [Tab] to move to cell B8, type **=sum(B1:B7)**, then press [Enter]. The formula adds the values in cells B1 through B7 and displays the results in cell B8.

   d. Use the mouse to select cells A1 through A8, then use the Format command on the Toolbox to change the color of the text in these cells to violet. Change cell A8 to bold.

   e. Turn off the vertical and horizontal scroll bars in the Spreadsheet component, then close the Toolbox.

   f. Resize the component so its bottom edge is under row 8 and its right edge is to the right of column E. Save the page.

4. Create a Chart component in a Web page.

   a. Click the blank line below the Spreadsheet component, then insert a centered Chart component.

   b. Select the Pie Chart type and the first Chart sub-type in the first row.

   c. In the Step 2 of 3 dialog box, accept the default data source (the Spreadsheet component).

   d. In the Step 3 of 3 dialog box, click the Set this chart's data in one step button, then enter **=B1:B7** in the Data range text box. Click the Columns option button—even if it is already selected—to select it, then click OK.

   e. Click in the Category (X) axis labels text box, type **=A1:A7**, then click a blank area in the Series box. A legend is added to the sample chart area. The legend uses the values in cells A1:A7. Click Finish.

   f. Right-click the pie chart in the Chart component to open the pop-up menu, then click Property Toolbox. Wait a moment for the Toolbox to appear, click the Series command on the Toolbox, then click the Add Data Labels button. (*Hint*: Use the ScreenTip to find this button.)

   g. Click any white area in the Chart component, wait a moment for the Toolbox to change the available commands, click the Chart command, then click the Show title check box to select it. Click the title that was added in the Chart component (it is a text box with the label "Series"), then click the Title command. Select the value in the Caption text box, then type **Monthly Budget**.

   h. Close the Toolbox, save the page, then preview the page in a browser. Change the value in cell B3 to **400**, press [Enter] to update the components, then use your browser's Print button to print the page.

5. Use a PivotTable List component in a Web page.

   a. Return to FrontPage and use Folders View to open the Regions.htm file in Page View.

   b. Change the heading at the top of the page to **Sales by Region, [insert your name here]**.

   c. Save the page, then preview it in a browser.

   d. Use the PivotTable List component to display sales for stores in Chicago and Nashville.

   e. Restore the PivotTable List component to display data for all stores.

   f. Use the PivotTable List component to display the only line for the store that has Q3 Sales of 14419, then use your browser's Print button to print the page.

   g. Close your browser.

6. Create special styles in a Web page.

   a. Modify the h2 style in the Regions.htm page so it uses Century Schoolbook, bold, 18pt, maroon font.

   b. Change the h2 style to center alignment. Close the Styles dialog box.

   c. Save and preview the page in a browser, then use your browser's Print command to print the page.

7. Create a cascading style sheet.

   a. In Page View, create a new Web page. Define the following styles in the page:

      h1 tag: Arial Black, Bold, 24pt, and navy font; center alignment

      h2 tag: Arial Black, Bold, 18pt, and teal font; left alignment

      body tag: Arial, Regular, 12pt, and black font

   b. Save the page as a HyperText Style Sheet using the filename *BudgetStyles*, then close the page.

8. **Apply a cascading style sheet.**
   a. Apply the BudgetStyles cascading style sheet to the budget.htm page.
   b. Open the budget.htm page in Page View, then create a new line below the heading. On the new line, type **The Spreadsheet component contains data that you can change using a browser. The Chart component will be updated automatically when you make changes to the Spreadsheet component.**
   c. Create a new line above the Monthly Budget heading, type **Budget Analysis**, then apply the Heading 1 style to the text.
   d. Save the page, preview it in a browser, use your browser's Print button to print the page, then close your browser.
   e. Close the Budget Web and FrontPage.

► Independent Challenges

1. You run the Student Help Center at a local community college. Many students seek the center's help to get control of their finances. Most students have two things in common: They buy lunch everyday and they go to a theater to watch a movie once a week. You decide to add a new page to the Center's Web site that uses a Spreadsheet component. Students can enter amounts for these categories (lunch and movies) into a Web page to view the potential savings.

   To complete this independent challenge:

   a. If necessary, start the PWS or log on to your server. Start FrontPage and create a new server-based Web using the Empty Web template and the name *HelpCenter[insert your name here]*.
   b. If necessary, enable the Web to support ActiveX controls and FrontPage Server Extensions.
   c. In Folders View, create a new Web page using the filename *savings.htm* and the title **Savings**, then open the page in Page View.
   d. At the top of the page, type **Savings Calculator**, then format this text using the Heading 1 style.
   e. On the next line, type a short paragraph that describes how to use the Spreadsheet component that you will create. For example, tell users how to enter numbers into it and not to delete cells that contain formulas. (Refer to Figure M-25 when writing this paragraph.)
   f. On the next line, insert a centered Spreadsheet component. Then enter the data shown in Figure M-25 into the correct cells. Enter the formula **=B2+B3** into cell B4, the formula **=D2+D3** into cell D4, and the formula **=D4-B4** into cell B5.
   g. Use the Spreadsheet component's Help system as needed to learn how to format elements in the Spreadsheet component to match Figure M-25. Then make these changes.
   h. Change the text in the title bar of the Spreadsheet component to **Savings Calculator**, then change the color of the title bar to green.
   i. Turn off the scroll bars in the Spreadsheet component, then reduce its size (see Figure M-25).

FIGURE M-25

	A	B	C	D
	Savings Calculator			
1		Cost		Cost
2	Bring Lunch (5 times/wk)	$0.00	Buy Lunch (5 times/wk)	$0.00
3	Rent Movie (once/wk)	$0.00	Go to Theater (once/wk)	$0.00
4	Totals	$0.00		$0.00
5	Weekly Savings	$0.00		

   j. On a blank line below the Spreadsheet component, type **Spreadsheet calculator designed by [insert your name here]**. Then left-align the text.
   k. Save the page, then preview it in a browser. Test the Spreadsheet component to make sure that your calculator is working correctly. If necessary, return to FrontPage and make any corrections. After using the calculator, use your browser's Print command to print the page.
   l. Close your browser, the HelpCenter Web, and FrontPage.

2. You are a legislative aide to Senator Chase Brummerhop. Who is proposing a new bill he will propose during the next legislative session, which will limit the amount of interest that a company can charge for short-term loans. He wants to add a page to his Web site that demonstrates the impact of high interest rates on consumer loans.

To complete this independent challenge:

a. If necessary, start the PWS or log on to your server. Start FrontPage and create a new server-based Web using the Empty Web template and the name *Loans[insert your name here]*.

b. Enable the Web to support ActiveX controls and FrontPage Server Extensions.

c. In Folders View, create a new Web page using the filename *loan.htm* and the title **Short-Term Loan Page**, then open the page in Page View.

d. On the first line, type **Understanding Short-Term Loans**, then format this text using the Heading 1 style.

e. Create a user-defined style in the loan.htm page for the Heading 1 style. The new style should use Arial, bold, 24pt, blue font, and a center alignment.

f. On a new, left-aligned line, type **A $100 loan with a term of two weeks and a fee of $15 will cost the consumer a total of $115, or the equivalent of an annual interest rate of 390%. Compare this to charging the same amount on a credit card with an annual interest rate of 21%.**

g. On a new, centered line, create a Spreadsheet component. Enter the following data: cell B1: **Rate**; cell C1: **Total**; cell A2: **$100.00**; cell B2: **21%**; cell C2: **$111.72**; cell A3: **$100.00**; cell B3: **390%**; and cell C3: **$403.80**. Resize the Spreadsheet component.

h. On a new, centered line, create a Clustered Bar chart that uses the data in the Spreadsheet component. The Series data appears in the column that contains cells C2:C3. Change the Series name to **Loan Amounts**. The Y-axis labels appear in columns in cells B2:B3.

i. Change the Chart component to include the title **One-Year Loan Payment Amounts**, add a Y-axis title of **Annual Interest Rate**, and add data labels to the series data. Use the Help system for the Chart component as needed to learn how to change the Chart component's properties.

j. On a blank, left-aligned line under the Chart component, type **Page designed by [insert your name here]**.

k. Save the page, preview the page in a browser, print the page using the browser's Print button, then close the browser.

l. Close the Loans Web and FrontPage.

3. You are the Webmaster for Newberry Products, an office supply store located in Newberry, Connecticut. The president of Newberry Products, Travis Moseley, wants to compete with online office supply stores by creating a Web presence. In a few months, Travis will add functionality to the Web to allow customers to purchase products online. For now, he wants to concentrate on the site's content and appearance. He asks you to create a style sheet for the Web and apply it to the existing pages.

To complete this independent challenge:

a. If necessary, start the PWS or log on to your server. Start FrontPage and use the Import Web Wizard to create a new server-based Web named *Newberry[insert your name here]*. Import the files from the UnitM\Ic3 folder on your Project Disk into the new Web. (You will import eight files.)

b. In Page View, create a new Web page. Use the table that follows to define the styles in the new page.

tag	style description
h1	Tahoma font, bold, 24pt, maroon, center alignment
h2	Tahoma font, bold, 18pt, navy, left alignment
body	Tahoma regular font, 12pt, black, justify alignment
a	Arial Narrow regular font, 12pt, blue

c. Save the page as a cascading style sheet using the filename *Nstyles*, then close it.

d. In Folders View, apply the cascading style sheet to every page in the Web, except for the Nstyles.css page

e. Open the home page (Default.htm) in Page View. Use the Link Style Sheet dialog box to remove the cascading style sheet link to this page. Then, use the table that follows to define the styles in the home page.

tag	style description
h1	Arial Black regular font, 24pt, blue, center alignment
body	Arial regular font, 12pt, navy, justify alignment

f. On a new line below the paragraph in the home page, type **For more information contact [insert your name here] at 1-800-555-1289.** Save the home page.

g. Print the HTML code for the home page, then print the Nstyles.css page. (*Hint*: With the home page open in Page View, click the HTML tab, then click the Print button. To print the HTML code for the Nstyles.css page, open it in Page View, then click the Print button.) Staple the pages together with the home page on top.

h. Close the Newberry Web and FrontPage.

4. You are the Webmaster for the Hudson Bend Fire Department. The fire department's marketing director wants you to create a cascading style sheet to apply to the site's pages, however, she wants to make sure that all site visitors will be able to view and read the pages. She asks you to do some research about cascading style sheets and report back to her on your findings. To complete this independent challenge:

a. Connect to the Internet.

b. Go to http://www.course.com, navigate to the Student Online Companion for this book, then click the link for Unit M. Click the links and use the pages at the sites that open to find out about browser compatibility with cascading style sheets. Conduct your research to answer the following questions.

c. What was the first browser and version to support cascading style sheets?

d. What are the four main features that cascading style sheets provide as a means of complementing HTML?

e. What are the four methods you can use to create a style sheet?

f. What organization sets the standards for cascading style sheets?

g. How many levels of cascading style sheets are there, and what are they?

h. Close your browser and your dial-up connection.

▶ Visual Workshop

Create a new server-based Web using the One Page Web template and the name *Spreadsheet[insert your name here]*, then add content and text to the home page as shown in Figure M-26. (*Hint*: Create a Spreadsheet component to hold the data shown in Figure M-26, then create the Chart component. When you type the numbers in the Spreadsheet component, type the commas as shown in the figure.) On a blank, left-aligned line below the Chart component, type **Created by [insert your name here].** Save the home page, print it in a browser, then close your browser, the Web, and FrontPage.

FIGURE M-26

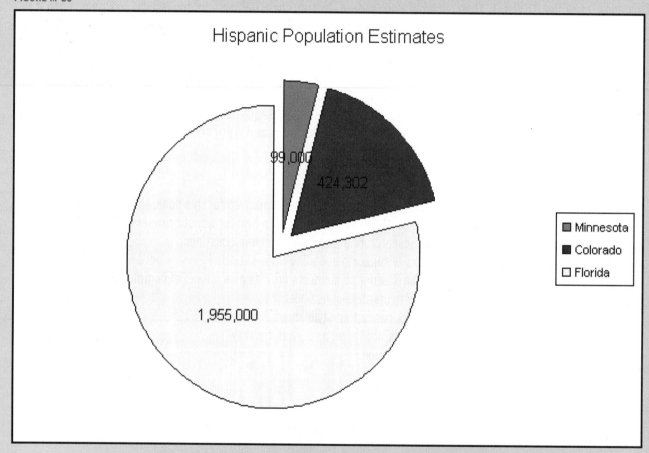

Integrating
a Database with a FrontPage Web

Objectives

- ▶ **Review database concepts**
- [MOUS] ▶ **Import a database into a FrontPage Web**
- [MOUS] ▶ **Create a data access page**
- ▶ **Use a data access page**
- [MOUS] ▶ **Send form results to a database**
- ▶ **Use an Active Server Page**
- [MOUS] ▶ **Create a Database Results region**
- [MOUS] ▶ **Create a search form in a Web page**

When you create a Web that contains a page with a form, you can send the form results to one of many places. You might choose to store the form results in a text file, as an HTML page, or in a database. When you create a page that displays database data, FrontPage saves it as an Active Server Page and with an .asp filename extension. An **Active Server Page** is a dynamic Web page whose contents change as required, based on either a user request or a change in the data on which the Active Server Page is based. ✒ Ariadne McDonald expects many of her clients to use the Apply Now page in the Mortgage Web to submit their loan application forms. Ariadne decides to use a Microsoft Access database to collect data from the Apply Now page. She also maintains a database with information about the lenders with which she does business. She wants to include this information in a Web page that is updated as new lenders are added to the list, so she creates an Active Server Page to display the database information.

Reviewing Database Concepts

A **database** is a collection of related tables that stores data about an entity. An **entity** is a person, place, thing, or idea. A **table** contains fields (or columns) that describe the characteristics of the entity. For example, in the Mortgage Web, the Apply Now page contains a form that collects information about a person who is borrowing money to purchase a home. The **fields** in the form store data about the person's first and last names, Social Security number, employer, and income. The data stored in the fields for one form create a **record** for one person in the database. In any table, one field must contain a value that uniquely identifies each record in the table. This field is called the table's **primary key**. Because no two people can have the same Social Security number, this number is a good value to use as a table's primary key. If your table doesn't contain a field that stores unique values, you can create an **AutoNumber field** in the table, which automatically numbers records in sequential order, thereby creating a primary key. ✎ Ariadne wants to incorporate two databases into the Mortgage Web. The first database, named Lenders, stores information about the financial institutions with which she does business. The second database, named Mortgage, stores data about clients who use the Web's Apply Now page to submit loan applications. She examines these databases to ensure that their structures are correct.

Steps

Trouble?

If Access is not installed on your computer, ask your instructor or technical support person for help.

1. Click the **Start button** 🔲Start on the taskbar, point to **Programs**, then click **Microsoft Access**
   Microsoft Access starts and opens the Microsoft Access dialog box.

2. If necessary, click the **Open an existing file option button** to select it and click the **More Files option** in the list box, then click **OK**
   The Open dialog box opens.

Trouble?

If the Tables object is not selected, click it on the Objects bar.

3. Open the **UnitN folder** on your Project Disk, then double-click **Lenders**
   The Lenders database opens in the Database window, as shown in Figure N-1, with the Tables object and the Lenders table selected.

4. Double-click **Lenders** in the Database window
   The Lenders table opens in Table Datasheet View, as shown in Figure N-2. (Your Lenders table might open with a different window size, or as a maximized window.) The Lenders table contains six records and five fields. The LenderID field is the table's primary key—each lender has a unique lender ID number. In another lesson, you will create a Web page that displays data from this table.

5. Click the **Close button** on the Table Datasheet View window, click the **Close button** on the Database window, click the **Open button** 📂 on the Standard toolbar, then double-click **Mortgage**
   The Lenders database closes and the Mortgage database opens in the Database window with the Tables object and the Borrower table selected.

6. Double-click **Borrower**
   The Borrower table opens in Table Datasheet View. This table contains two records and 14 fields. The BorSocSecNum is the table's primary key—this number uniquely identifies each record in the table. You can use the scroll bar to scroll the table's contents to the right to see all of the fields. In another lesson, you will set a Web page form to store its data in this table.

7. Click the **Close button** on the Microsoft Access title bar to close Access
   The Borrower table and Access close.

FIGURE N-1: Lenders database in the Access program window

Database window

Tables object selected on the Objects bar

Lenders table selected

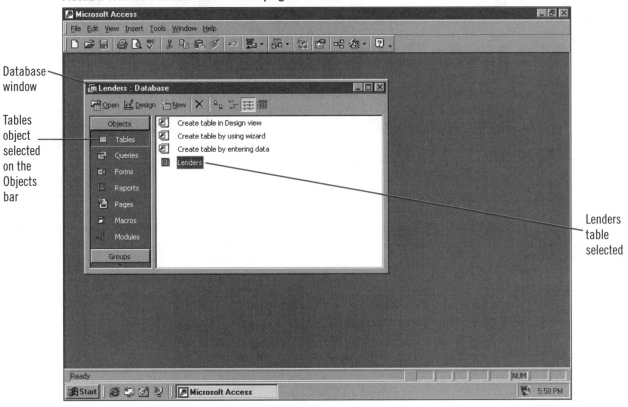

FIGURE N-2: Lenders table in Table Datasheet View

Records in the table

Fields in the table

Record 1 is the currently selected record

Six records are stored in the table

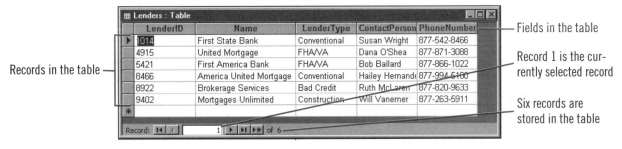

More about database objects

In addition to tables, a database contains other objects that you use to organize and arrange the data stored in its tables. A **form** shows table data in a way similar to how you might show data in a paper form. You can use a form to enter, delete, and sort data. A **query** is a question that you ask of the database in order to view records that answer your question. For example, you might query a database to retrieve all records for clients who live in a certain zip code. A **report** retrieves data from the database and arranges it in a specified format.

Importing a Database into a FrontPage Web

There are two ways to incorporate a database into a FrontPage Web. The first way is to create the database in Access and then copy and paste the database file into the Web. The second way is to create a form in a Web page, and then to use FrontPage to create a database or a database connection using Access or another supported database program in which to store the form's data. In either case, FrontPage automatically adds the database file into the Web, creates a folder named **fpdb** (for **FrontPage database**) in which to store the database file, and creates a connection to the database. A **database connection** specifies the name, location, and type of database that you want to access from a Web. Without a database connection, the Web's pages would not be able to interact with the database. ✎ Because the Lenders database is already created, Ariadne will copy and paste it into FrontPage and let FrontPage create the database connection.

1. If necessary, start the **PWS** or log on to your server, start **Microsoft FrontPage** and open the **Mortgage[insert your name here] Web** from the PWS, then if necessary click the **Folders button** 📁 on the Views bar
   The Mortgage Web opens from the server in Folders View.

2. Click the **Start button** 🏁 Start on the taskbar, point to **Programs**, then click **Windows Explorer**

3. Browse to the drive or folder that contains your Project Disk, open the **UnitN folder**, then click **Lenders** to select it

Trouble?

If Windows is configured to show filename extensions, you will see Lenders.mdb in Windows Explorer. This is the same file.

4. Click the **Copy button** 📋 on the toolbar, then click the **Close button** on the Windows Explorer title bar
   A copy of the Lenders database is placed on the Windows Clipboard and Windows Explorer closes.

5. If necessary, return to FrontPage, right-click any white area in the Folder List to open the pop-up menu, then click **Paste**
   The Importing Files dialog box opens, and then the Add Database Connection dialog box opens, as shown in Figure N-3.

QuickTip

It is a good idea to provide descriptive database connection names because a Web can have more than one database connection. However, it is not a requirement to use the database filename as the database connection name.

6. Be sure the text in the Name text box is selected, type **Lenders**, then click **Yes**
   You created a database connection named Lenders. The Importing Files dialog box appears again, and then a dialog box opens as shown in Figure N-4.

7. Click **Yes**
   FrontPage finishes creating the database connection, stores the Lenders database in the new fpdb folder, and creates a new page in the Web named global.asa, as shown in Figure N-5. The global.asa file contains a VBScript that maintains and runs the database connection.

8. Click **Tools** on the menu bar, click **Web Settings**, then click the **Database tab**
   The Database tab shows that there is one database connection in the Web. The Status column contains a question mark, which indicates that the connection has not been verified.

9. Click **Lenders** in the Connection column, then click **Verify**
   The Status changes to a check mark, as shown in Figure N-6.

10. Click **OK**
    The Web Settings dialog box closes.

FIGURE N-3: Add Database Connection dialog box

Database file
to import

Default database
connection name

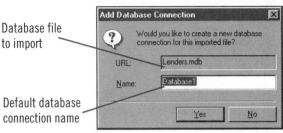

FIGURE N-4: Dialog box with message about where to store the imported database

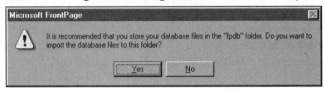

FIGURE N-5: Web after importing the database

fpdb
folder
created

global.asa
file
created

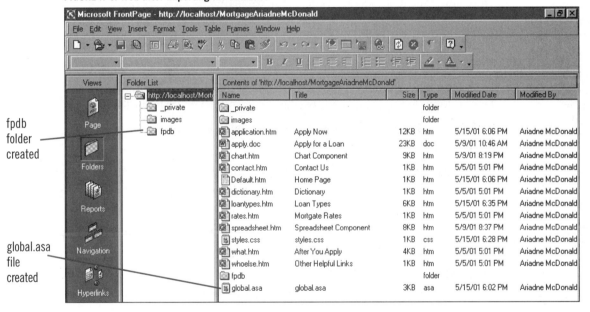

FIGURE N-6: Database tab after verifying the Lenders database connection

Check mark indicates
a verified database
connection

Connection name

Click to create a new
database connection

Click to change the selected
database connection

Click to delete the
selected database
connection

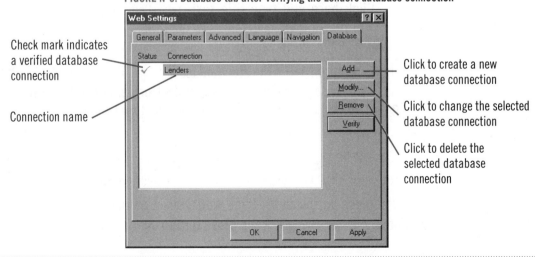

Creating a Data Access Page

In the previous lesson, you imported the Lenders database into the Mortgage Web and verified the database connection. The Lenders database that exists in the fpdb folder of the Mortgage Web is a copy of the file that exists on your Project Disk, however, the two files are *not* linked. In this lesson, you will create a data access page that displays data from the Lenders database in a Web page. A **data access page** is a Web page that shows data from the database table on which the page is based. You can use a data access page to view, add, delete, and sort database table records. You must use a database program that supports data access pages, such as Access, to create a data access page object in the database and an HTML page that you can save in a Web. ✏️ Ariadne wants to incorporate a data access page in the Mortgage Web to display data about the lenders with which she does business. She opens the Lenders database stored in the Web's fpdb folder, uses Access to create the data access page, and saves the related Web page in the Mortgage Web.

Steps

1. In Folders View, click the **fpdb folder** in the Folder List
   The contents pane shows the Lenders.mdb database.

Trouble?

When you open a database file from a Web, the database that opens in Access might be the database name plus a digit, such as Lenders1. This is the file stored in the Web.

2. Double-click **Lenders.mdb** in the contents pane
   Access starts and opens the Lenders database in the Database window. The Tables object is selected.

3. Click the **Pages object** on the Objects bar of the Database window
   Three options for creating or editing data access pages appear in the list box.

4. Double-click **Create data access page by using wizard**
   The Page Wizard starts, as shown in Figure N-7.

5. Make sure that the Tables/Queries list box displays "Table: Lenders," click 	≫ 	 to move all available fields to the Selected Fields list box, then click **Next**
   The data access page will contain all of the fields in the Lenders table.

QuickTip

A grouping level arranges records by a certain field. A sort order arranges records in ascending or descending order based on a selected field.

6. Click **Next** to omit adding a grouping level, click **Next** to omit adding a sort order, be sure the text in the What title do you want for your page? text box is selected and type **LendersDAP**, then click **Finish**
   Access creates the LendersDAP data access page in the Lenders database that is stored in the fpdb folder, and then opens it in Page View.

Trouble?

If you see one or more floating toolbars on your screen, close them or drag them out of the way.

7. If necessary, use the scroll box to scroll to the top of the page, click anywhere in the heading **Click here and type title text**, type **Lender Information**, then click any white area of the page to finish creating the title
   A title is added to the data access page, as shown in Figure N-8.

QuickTip

If you need to modify a data access page, open it in Access Page View, then save your changes to update the data access page object and its related HTML file.

8. Click the **Save button** 💾 on the Standard toolbar, click the **Web Folders button** 🗐 in the Save As Data Access Page dialog box, select the **Mortgage[insert your name here] Web**, click **Open**, select the text in the File name text box, type **LendersDAP**, then click **Save**
   The Save As Data Access Page dialog box closes and the Transferring File dialog box opens for a moment as Access saves the HTML file (the Web page) for the LendersDAP data access page in the Mortgage Web. Now the LendersDAP object is stored in the Lenders database, and the LendersDAP Web page is stored in the Mortgage Web.

9. Click the **Close button** on the Page View window, notice the LendersDAP object in the Database window, then click the **Close button** on the Microsoft Access title bar
   Access closes.

FIGURE N-7: Page Wizard dialog box

The data access page will be based on the Lenders table

Fields in the Lenders table

Click to remove all Selected Fields from the Selected Fields list box

Click to move a selected field from the Available Fields list box to the Selected Fields list box

Click to move all fields in the Available Fields list box to the Selected Fields list box

Click to delete a selected field from the Selected Fields list box

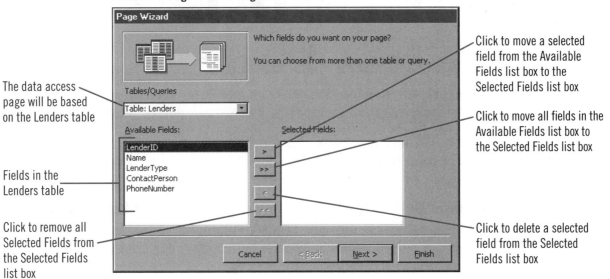

FIGURE N-8: Data access page in Access Page View

Title added to the data access page

Fields from the Lenders table

Access creates a data access page toolbar for the page

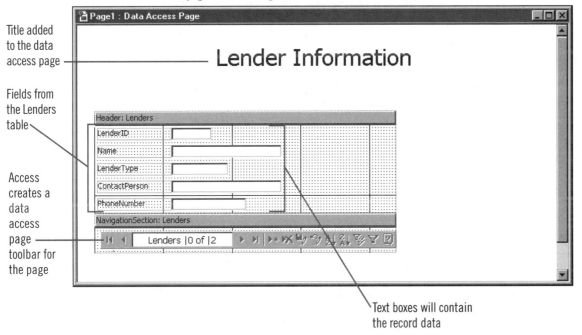

Text boxes will contain the record data

Setting a Web page so it is not published with a Web site

Some data access pages and other types of dynamic Web pages might contain sensitive information that you do not want to make public to all of your Web site's visitors, yet you might want to view the information using a Web page. You can create a Web page but prevent it from being published with the Web. For example, if you create a Web page on the PWS, you might set the page so it does not get published on a commercial Web server. To prevent FrontPage from publishing a Web page, select the page in Folders View, click File on the menu bar, click Properties, click the Workgroup tab, then click the Exclude this file when publishing the rest of the Web check box to select it. Click OK, then click Yes to refresh the Web.

Using a Data Access Page

In the previous lesson, you created a data access page in the Lenders database and saved its related Web page in the Mortgage Web. The Web page displays the current data in the Lenders table; any changes made to the table are immediately reflected in it. The opposite is also true: if you make changes using the Web page, those changes are reflected immediately in the Lenders table. ➤➤➤ Ariadne opens the data access page in a browser and navigates the records for the available lenders. She also adds a record for a new lender that she is using.

Steps

1. Click the **Mortgage folder** in the Folder List, click the **Refresh button** 🔄 on the Standard toolbar, click the **LendersDAP.htm** file in the contents pane to select it, then click the **Preview in Browser button** 🔍 on the Standard toolbar; if the dialog box shown in Figure N-9 opens, click **Yes**

   The Lender Information page opens in a browser, as shown in Figure N-10, and displays the first record in the Lenders table. When you created the related Web page, Access automatically created the data access page toolbar that appears below the table's fields. The data access page toolbar buttons and their descriptions appear in Table N-1.

2. Click the **Next Record button** ▶ on the data access page toolbar

   The data access page displays the second record in the Lenders table, which is the record for United Mortgage.

   > **QuickTip**
   >
   > You can sort records in ascending or descending order by clicking in the text box for the field you want to sort, then clicking the appropriate toolbar button.

3. Click in the **Name text box**, click the **Sort Ascending button** ↕ on the data access page toolbar, then click the **Next Record button** ▶ on the data access page toolbar to view each of the six records

   The insertion point appears in the LenderID text box, and the records in the data access page now appear in alphabetical order based on the data in the Name field.

4. Click the **New Record button** ▶* on the data access page toolbar

   The fields in the data access page are cleared and the insertion point appears in the LenderID text box. Notice that the data access toolbar now shows that there are seven records.

5. Enter the information shown in Figure N-11 into the text boxes, pressing [Tab] to move to the next text box, but do not press [Tab] after entering the PhoneNumber value

   You entered the data for all five fields into the data access page. The record is 5 of 7 because the sort you applied in Step 3 is still in effect; this record appears fifth alphabetically. The record is not permanently saved in the Lenders table until you intentionally save it.

   > **QuickTip**
   >
   > If you want the records sorted by default using a field other than the primary key field, you must specify the sort order when you create the data access page in Access.

6. Click the **Save Record button** 💾 on the data access page toolbar

   The record is saved in the Lenders table. When you add new records to the data access page and save the file, the records are sorted based on the primary key, unless you specified another sort order when creating or using the data access page.

7. Close your browser, return to FrontPage (if necessary), in the Confirm Save dialog box click **Yes**, click the **fpdb folder** in the Folder List, then double-click **Lenders.mdb** in the contents pane

   Access starts and opens the Lenders database.

   > **QuickTip**
   >
   > The record is second in the table because the records are sorted using the primary key (the LenderID field).

8. Click the **Tables object** on the Objects bar, then double-click **Lenders**

   The Lenders table opens in Table Datasheet View. The record that you added using the data access page—LenderID 1996 for First United Mortgage—appears in the table.

9. Close Access, and if necessary, return to FrontPage

FIGURE N-9: Microsoft Data Access Components dialog box

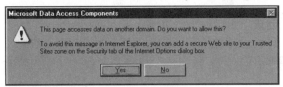

FIGURE N-10: Lender Information page in a browser

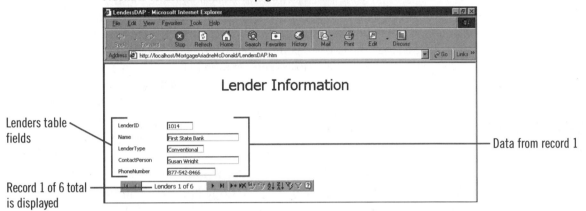

Lenders table fields

Data from record 1

Record 1 of 6 total is displayed

FIGURE N-11: New records in the data access page

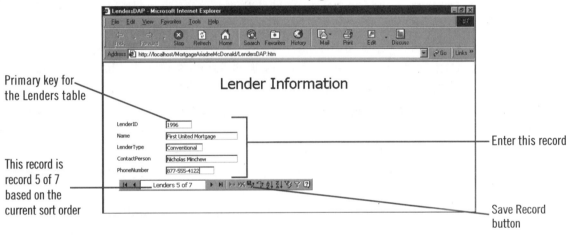

Primary key for the Lenders table

Enter this record

This record is record 5 of 7 based on the current sort order

Save Record button

TABLE N-1: Data access page toolbar buttons and their descriptions

button	description	button	description
First Record	Displays the first record	**Previous Record**	Displays the previous record
Next Record	Displays the next record	**Last Record**	Displays the last record
New Record	Clears the fields so you can enter a new record	**Delete Record**	Deletes the currently displayed record
Save Record	Saves the current record in the table	**Undo Last Change**	Restores the previous action to its original state
Sort Ascending	Sorts the records in ascending order based on the field that contains the insertion point	**Sort Descending**	Sorts the records in descending order based on the field that contains the insertion point
Help	Opens the Microsoft Access Data Pages Help window	**Remove Filter**	Removes an applied filter
Filter By Selection	Lets you display a subset of records that match the value in the field that contains the insertion point		

FrontPage 2000

Sending Form Results to a Database

You can use a form in a Web page to send data to a database table. The main difference between using a data access page and using a Web form is that you can only use a form to add records to the database; you cannot use a form to view or change database data. Before the form can send data to a database, you must identify the database connection to use as well as the name of each form field in the form on the Web page and its corresponding field name in the database. The form field names in the form and the field names in the database do not need to have the same names, but using the same names does make it easier to identify corresponding fields. ⟶ Ariadne wants to store the data collected by the form on the Apply Now Web page in the Borrower table in the Mortgage database. She imports the Mortgage database into the Mortgage Web, verifies the database connection, and sets the form to store its data in the Borrower table in the Mortgage database.

1. Start **Windows Explorer**, open the **UnitN folder** on your Project Disk, select the Mortgage database file, then click the **Copy button** 🗎 on the toolbar

Trouble?

If a dialog box opens and asks if you want to store the database file in the fpdb folder, click Yes.

2. Close Windows Explorer, return to FrontPage, right-click any white area in the Folder List to open the pop-up menu, click **Paste**, in the Name text box of the Add Database Connection dialog box type **Mortgage**, then click **Yes**
   FrontPage automatically stored the database file in the Web's fpdb folder.

3. Click **Tools** on the menu bar, click **Web Settings**, click the **Database tab**, select the **Mortgage** connection, click **Verify**, then click **OK**

4. Click the **Mortgage folder** in the Folder List, then double-click **application.htm** in the contents pane
   The application.htm file opens in Page View. The dotted line indicates the contents of the form.

5. Right-click anywhere in the form to open the pop-up menu, then click **Form Properties**
   The Form Properties dialog box opens, as shown in Figure N-12.

6. Click the **Send to database option button**, then click **Options**
   The Options for Saving Results to Database dialog box opens, as shown in Figure N-13.

7. Click the **Database Connection to Use list arrow**, click **Mortgage**, then make sure that the Table to hold form results list box contains the text "Borrower"
   The database connection is Mortgage and the data will be stored in the Borrower table.

QuickTip

To select a different corresponding database column, click the Save to database column list arrow, then click the corresponding database column name in the list.

8. Click the **Saved Fields tab**, then in the Form Fields to Save list box, double-click **BorEmployer**
   The Modify Field dialog box opens, as shown in Figure N-14. You selected the BorEmployer form field and FrontPage selected the corresponding database column name "BorEmployer" from the Borrower table.

9. Click **OK**, repeat Step 8 to select the corresponding database column for each form field, scroll to the top of the Form Fields to Save list box, click **Authorize**, then click **Remove**
   The Authorize field is an Access control object that does not appear in the form on the Apply Now Web page. The completed Saved Fields tab appears in Figure N-15.

10. Click **OK**, click **OK** in the Form Properties dialog box, read the message about saving a page that contains a component, then click **OK**
    In the next lesson, you will save this page as an Active Server Page.

FIGURE N-12: **Form Properties dialog box**

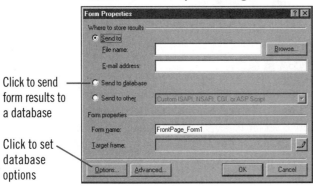

Click to send form results to a database

Click to set database options

FIGURE N-13: **Options for Saving Results to Database dialog box**

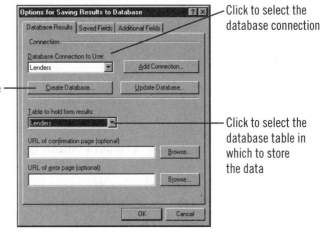

Click to select the database connection

Click to create a new database and database connection

Click to select the database table in which to store the data

FIGURE N-14: **Modify Field dialog box**

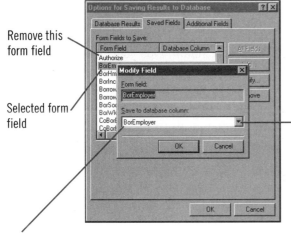

Remove this form field

Selected form field

Matching database column in the Borrower table

Click to select another database column name, if necessary

FIGURE N-15: **Completed Saved Fields tab**

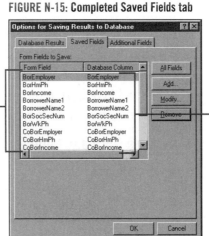

Scrollable list of form fields in the application.htm Web page

Scrollable list of corresponding fields from the Borrower table in the Mortgage database

Using an Active Server Page

When you set the form in the application.htm page to send its results to the Borrower table in the Mortgage database, you received a message in FrontPage that the page must be saved with the filename extension .asp, which stands for Active Server Page. An Active Server Page is a dynamic Web page that contains scripts to process the page. Active Server Pages contain data that is generated when the page is viewed using a Web browser. When an Active Server Page is used to display database data, the scripts in the page ensure that the data is current. ◄▬▬▬ Ariadne changes the filename of the Apply Now page to application.asp, previews it in a browser, and uses it to store a record in the Borrower table in the Mortgage database.

Steps 1 2 3 4

1. Click the **Close button** on the contents pane, click **Yes** to save the page, then click **OK** to close the dialog box

2. Click the **Folders button** 🗀 on the Views bar, right-click **application.htm** in the contents pane to open the pop-up menu, click **Rename**, type **application.asp**, press **[Enter]**, click **Yes** to rename the page, then click **Yes** to update the hyperlinks
   The Apply Now page now has an .asp filename extension.

3. With the application.asp file still selected, click the **Preview in Browser button** 🔍 on the Standard toolbar
   The Apply Now page opens in a browser.

4. Click in the **First Name text box** in the Borrower column, type your first name, press **[Tab]**, type your last name, press **[Tab]**, type **555-00-1234**, then scroll to the bottom of the page and click **Submit Form**; if necessary, click **Yes** to close the alert dialog box
   A Form Confirmation page opens. The information that you entered into the First Name, Last Name, and Social Security Number text boxes appears in the confirmation page, as shown in Figure N-16.

5. Click the **Return to the form. link**, close your browser, return to FrontPage (if necessary), click the **fpdb folder** in the Folder List, then double-click **Mortgage.mdb** in the contents pane
   Access starts and opens the Mortgage database.

6. Click the **Tables object** on the Objects bar, then double-click **Borrower**
   The Borrower table opens in Table Datasheet View. The record that you entered using the Apply Now Web page appears in the table, as shown in Figure N-17.

7. Click the **Close button** on the Microsoft Access title bar to close Access, then if necessary, return to FrontPage

8. Click the **Mortgage folder** in the Folder List
   The Web's contents appear in the contents pane.

FIGURE N-16: Form Confirmation page

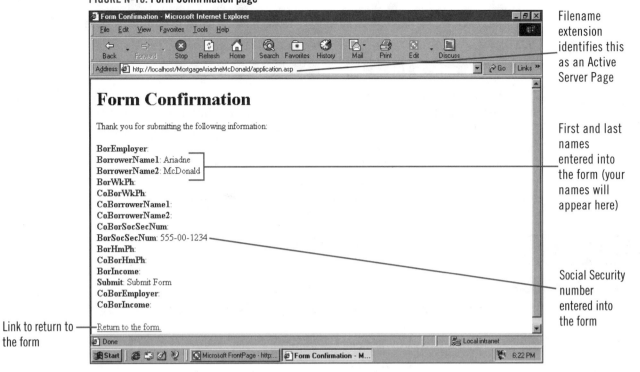

Filename extension identifies this as an Active Server Page

First and last names entered into the form (your names will appear here)

Social Security number entered into the form

Link to return to the form

FIGURE N-17: Borrower table after adding a record

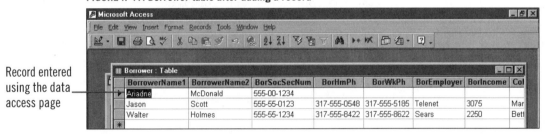

Record entered using the data access page

Creating a Database Results Region

When you need to display database data in a Web page, you can create a FrontPage component called a Database Results region in the Web page. The **Database Results region** displays data from the database table on which it is based. The Database Results region lets you examine the data contained in the database table, but unlike a data access page, you cannot add, delete, or change the data that appears in a Database Results region. A Database Results region is for viewing purposes only. Just like any other Web page that contains a component, you can use FrontPage to format the Web page in many ways. ➤ Ariadne wants to include a Web page in the Mortgage Web that displays data from the Lenders table. Because she does not want her Web's visitors to be able to enter, change, or delete records from the database table, she uses the Database Results Wizard to create a Database Results region in the Web page.

Steps 123 4

Trouble?

If you do not see the styles.css file, navigate to the root folder of the Mortgage Web.

1. In Folders View, click the **New Page button** ▢ on the Standard toolbar, type **lenders.asp**, press **[Tab]**, click **Yes**, type **Lender List**, then press **[Enter]**
Because a Web page that contains a Database Results region displays dynamic data, the page must have an .asp filename extension.

2. Double-click **lenders.asp** in the contents pane
The lenders.asp page opens in Page View.

3. Click **Insert** on the menu bar, point to **Database**, then click **Results**
The Database Results Wizard starts and opens the first of five dialog boxes, as shown in Figure N-18. The Lenders database connection is already selected for you.

4. Click **Next**, make sure that the **Record source option button** is selected and the **Lenders** table appears in the Record source list box, then click **Next**
You selected the Lenders table as the data source for the Web page and the Database Results Wizard - Step 3 of 5 dialog box opens. You use this dialog box to change the fields to display in the Web page or to filter them in a predefined way. You will skip this option for now.

QuickTip

If you create a Database Results region in a Web page that has an .htm or .html filename extension, a message appears in the yellow shaded area reminding you to change the filename extension to .asp.

5. Click **Next**, click **Next** again, click the **Display all records together option button**, then click **Finish**
You accepted the default formatting option, which determines how the Database Results region appears in the Web page, and selected the option to display all records together. A Database Results region appears in the lenders.asp Web page, as shown in Figure N-19. The fields in the Database Results region are the same ones used in the Lenders table in the Lenders database.

6. Press **[Ctrl][Home]**, press **[Enter]**, type **Lender List**, click the **Style list arrow** on the Formatting toolbar, then click **Heading 1**
You added a heading to the Web page.

7. Click **Format** on the menu bar, click **Style Sheet Links**, if necessary click the **Selected page(s) option button**, click **Add**, double-click **styles.css**, then click **OK**
The lenders.asp page now uses the cascading style sheet that you created for the Web.

8. Click the **Save button** 💾 on the Standard toolbar, then click the **Preview in Browser button** 🔍 on the Standard toolbar
The Lender List page opens in a browser, as shown in Figure N-20, and displays all of the records from the Lenders table in the Lenders database.

9. Close your browser, then if necessary, return to FrontPage
The lenders.asp page appears in Page View.

FIGURE N-18: Database Results Wizard dialog box

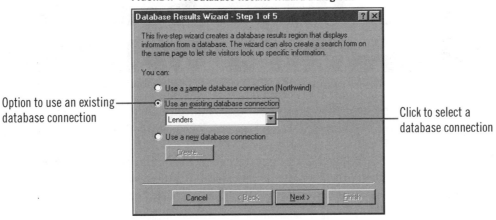

Option to use an existing database connection

Click to select a database connection

FIGURE N-19: Database Results region in a Web page

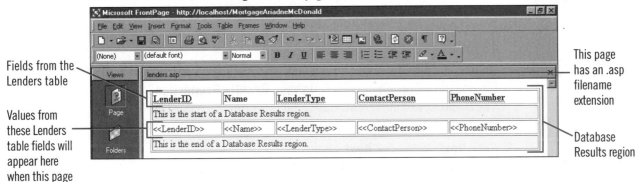

Fields from the Lenders table

Values from these Lenders table fields will appear here when this page is viewed in a browser

This page has an .asp filename extension

Database Results region

FIGURE N-20: Lender List page in a browser

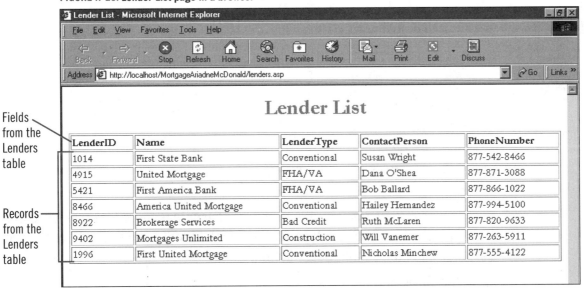

Fields from the Lenders table

Records from the Lenders table

Creating a Search Form in a Web Page

A query is a question that you ask a database, which returns records that answer your question. For example, you might want to know which mortgage companies specialize in processing a certain loan type. You can add a search form to a Web page that contains a Database Results region that lets the user query the table on which the Database Results region is based. The user can query the database table, but the user still cannot change the table data. ◢◣ Ariadne expects the list of lenders with which she does business to grow. She realizes that visitors to her site will find it more useful to see lenders that provide services for specific loan types (conventional, FHA/VA, and bad credit) rather than to see the entire list of vendors. To accomplish this objective, she adds a criterion to the LoanType field. After a visitor submits a query, only those record(s) in the Lenders table that answer the query will appear in the Database Results region.

Steps

1. **With the insertion point blinking at the end of the Lender List heading, press [Enter]**
   The search form will appear on the new line.

2. **Right-click either of the shaded yellow rows in the Database Results region to open the pop-up menu, then click Database Results Properties**
   The Database Results Wizard starts. You must run the Wizard again to change the Database Results region.

3. **Click Next, then click Next again**
   The Database Results Wizard - Step 3 of 5 dialog box opens.

4. **Click More Options, then in the More Options dialog box click Criteria**
   The More Options dialog box opens and the Criteria dialog box opens on top of it.

5. **Click Add**
   The Add Criteria dialog box opens.

6. **Click the Field Name list arrow, then click LenderType**
   The Add Criteria dialog box opens, as shown in Figure N-21. To create the search form, you must tell FrontPage that *LenderType Equals LenderType*, which means that any LenderType value entered by the user into the search text box will retrieve and display records in the Database Results region having the same LenderType value. In other words, if the user enters "Conventional," all records with "Conventional" in the LenderType field will appear in the Database Results region.

7. **Click OK, click OK in the Criteria dialog box, click OK in the More Options dialog box, click Next, click Next, then click Finish**
   A search form is added to the lenders.asp page.

8. **Click the blank line below the title, then type To locate lenders that specialize in a loan type of interest to you, type Conventional, FHA/VA, or Bad Credit in the text box, then click the Submit Query button.**

9. **Click the Save button 🔲 on the Standard toolbar, then click the Preview in Browser button 🔍 on the Standard toolbar**
   The Lender List page opens in a browser, as shown in Figure N-22.

10. **Click in the LenderType text box, type Conventional, then click Submit Query**
    The records that match the query are displayed, as shown in Figure N-23.

11. **Close your browser, then close FrontPage**

FIGURE N-21: Add Criteria dialog box

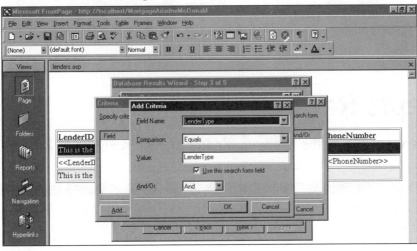

FIGURE N-22: Lender List page with search form added

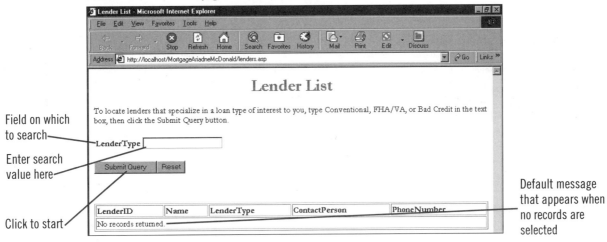

Field on which to search

Enter search value here

Click to start

Default message that appears when no records are selected

FIGURE N-23: Lender List page after executing a search

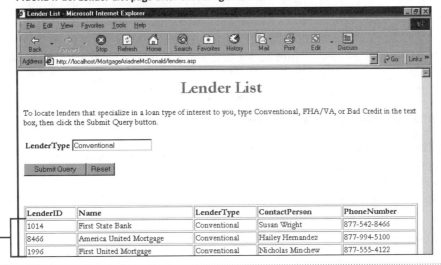

Records from the Lenders table matching the search request

Practice

▶ Concepts Review

Label each of the elements of the Browser window shown in Figure N-24.

FIGURE N-24

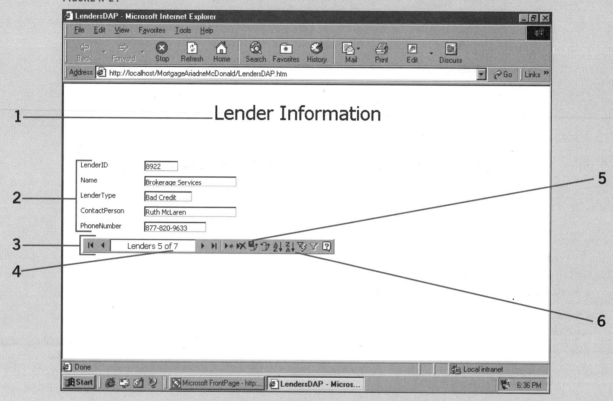

Match each of the terms with the statement that describes it.

7. Active Server Page
8. Data access page
9. Database
10. Database connection
11. fpdb
12. Table

a. A collection of related tables that store data about an entity
b. A Web page that shows data from the database table on which the page is based
c. A Web page with an .asp filename extension that contains scripts to process the page
d. Contains fields that describe the characteristics of an entity
e. Specifies the name, location, and type of database that you want to access from a Web
f. The default FrontPage folder that stores database files

Select the best answer from the list of choices.

13. Which of the following is an entity?
   a. The governor of the state of Kansas
   b. A tax regulation
   c. Dallas, Texas
   d. All of the above

14. Which of the following is NOT a database object?
   a. Query
   b. Database window
   c. Form
   d. Data access page

15. The default FrontPage folder that stores database files is
    a. Created when you save a Web.
    b. Created when you import a database into a Web.
    c. Named _fpdb.
    d. Created when you import a data access page into a Web.

16. **You can use a data access page to**
    a. View database data.
    b. Enter, delete, and change records in the database.
    c. Sort records.
    d. All of the above.

17. **The main difference between a data access page and a Database Results region in a Web page is that**
    a. You can view records in a data access page, but not in a Web page that contains a Database Results region.
    b. You can change records using a Database Results region, but not using a data access page.
    c. You can view, add, delete, and change database records in a data access page, but you can only view and query database records using a Database Results region.
    d. A data access page is an Active Server Page.

18. **For every form field in a Web page that contains a form, there must be a corresponding _____ the database table that will store that data.**
    a. database connection to
    b. ActiveX control in
    c. database column in
    d. primary key in

19. **After entering information in a form in a Web page that sends its data to a database table,**
    a. Your browser closes automatically.
    b. A Form Confirmation page opens and displays your entries.
    c. The form automatically resets and clears all fields.
    d. The form closes.

► Skills Review

1. **Review database concepts.**
   a. What is the relationship between an entity, a table, a field, and a record?
   b. How are tables related to each other in a database?
   c. In a database table that stores information about cars of the same make and model, which field might contain values that could serve as the table's primary key? Why?

2. **Import a database into a FrontPage Web.**
   a. If necessary, start the PWS or log on to your server. Start FrontPage and use the Import Web Wizard to create a new server-based Web named *Dorm[insert your name here]*. Import the files from the UnitN\Sr folder on your Project Disk into the new Web. (You will import two files.)
   b. Start Windows Explorer and open the UnitN folder on your Project Disk. Select and copy the Dorm database file, then close Windows Explorer.
   c. Paste the Dorm database into the Dorm Web. Use the database connection name **Dorm** and store the database file in the Web's fpdb folder.
   d. Open the fpdb folder to make sure that the Dorm.mdb file was imported into it.

3. **Create a data access page.**
   a. Double-click the Dorm.mdb file in the fpdb folder to start Access and open the Dorm database.
   b. Double-click the Census table in the Database window to open it in Table Datasheet View. If necessary, scroll the table to the right to view its contents, then close the Table Datasheet View window.
   c. Click the Pages object on the Objects bar of the Database window.
   d. Use the Wizard to create a new data access page with the following requirements: use the Census table and all available fields, do not specify a grouping level, do not specify a sort order, and use the page title **CensusDAP**. Click the Finish button to create the page.
   e. Replace the "Click here and type title text" heading in the data access page with the title **Dorm Census Data**.

f. Save the data access page as *CensusDAP* in the Dorm Web on the server.

g. Close Access.

4. Use a data access page.

a. Click the Dorm folder in the Folder List, then refresh the Web.

b. Preview the CensusDAP page in a browser.

c. Use the Dorm Census Data page to create a new record. Enter your first and last names and fictitious information to complete the form, then save the record. (*Hint*: Type dashes in the SocSecNum text box (e.g., 555-11-1234). Do *not* type a dollar sign in the Rent text box.)

d. Add a second record using data that you make up, then save it.

e. Use the navigation buttons on the data access page toolbar to display your record.

f. Close your browser. If necessary, click Yes to save the database file.

g. Open the Dorm.mdb file from the fpdb folder, click the Tables object on the Objects bar of the Database window, then double-click the Census table to open it. Confirm that the records you entered using the data access page appear in the table, use the Print button on the Standard toolbar to print the database table, then close Access.

5. Send form results to a database.

a. Click the Dorm folder in the Folder List, then open the census.htm page in Page View. This page contains a form with form fields to collect data.

b. Open the Form Properties dialog box, click the Send to database option button, then click Options.

c. Make sure that the Dorm database connection and the Census table are selected, then click the Saved Fields tab.

d. For each form field in the Web page form, select the matching database column. (*Hint*: The form field and database column names for each field have the same names.) If necessary, delete any form fields that do not have a corresponding database column name.

e. Click OK to accept the information in the Options for Saving Results to Database dialog box, then click OK in the Form Properties dialog box.

f. Save and close the page, rename the page in Folders View to use the correct filename extension, and update any hyperlinks.

6. Use an Active Server Page.

a. Preview the census.asp page in a browser.

b. Use the Census Form page to enter a record for Chris Williams with fictitious data for the rest of the fields, then click the Send Form button.

c. Print the Form Confirmation page that opens, click the link to return to the Census Form page, then close your browser.

d. Open the Dorm.mdb file from the fpdb folder and verify that the record you added appears in the Census table.

e. Close Access.

7. Create a Database Results region.

a. Click the Dorm folder in the Folder List.

b. Change to Page View, then create a new Web page.

c. Type **Dorm Census Data** on the first line, change this text to centered and the Heading 1 style, press [Enter], then left-align the new line.

d. Insert a Database Results region on the new line. Use the Dorm database connection, the Census table as the record source, and accept the default options in the third and fourth dialog boxes. In the fifth dialog box, click the Display all records together option button, then click Finish.

e. Save the page using the default filename (*dorm_census_data*) and file type (Active Server Pages) in the Dorm Web.

f. Preview the page in a browser, then use your browser's Print button to print the page.

g. Close your browser.

8. Create a search form in a Web page.

a. Create a new, left-aligned, blank line below the heading, then use the Database Results Wizard - Step 3 of 5 dialog box to create a search form that queries the Age field. (*Hint*: Use the Add Criteria dialog box to set the comparison *Age Equals Age*.)

b. Accept the settings in the remaining dialog boxes of the Database Results Wizard, then save the page.

c. On a new, blank line below the heading, enter some descriptive text to tell visitors how to use this page. Save the page.

d. Preview the Dorm Census Data page in a browser.

e. In the Age text box, type the age that you entered into your record. Print the page that appears, then close your browser.

f. Close the Dorm Web and FrontPage.

► Independent Challenges

1. You work for the donations coordinator of your local children's hospital. As part of a campaign to honor the hospital's generous donors, the board voted unanimously to add a page to the Web site that lists the donors' names and the amounts contributed. The board hopes that the Web page will encourage donors' employers, family members, and friends to match existing donations as part of a campaign to increase the overall donation amounts. As a member of the Web site development team, you are assigned the task of linking the database of donor names with a new Web page in the Web site.

To complete this independent challenge:

a. If necessary, start the PWS or log on to your server. Start FrontPage and create a new server-based Web using the One Page Web template and the name *Hospital[insert your name here]*.

b. Start Windows Explorer, open the UnitN folder on your Project Disk, select and copy the Hospital database file, then close Windows Explorer.

c. Import the Hospital database file into the Hospital Web. Use the database connection name **Hospital** and store the database file in the Web's fpdb folder. Verify the Hospital database connection.

d. Open the Hospital.mdb database file from the Web's fpdb folder. Use a wizard to create a new data access page based on the Donors table. Select all fields to appear in the page, then click Next.

e. Click Next to omit adding a grouping level, click Next again to omit adding a sort order, change the page title to **DonorsDAP**, then click Finish.

f. If necessary, scroll to the top of the page, then change the heading to **Honoring Our Donors**.

g. Save the data access page as *DonorsDAP* in the Hospital Web on the server, then close Access.

h. Return to FrontPage, click the Hospital folder in the Folder List, then refresh the Web. Preview the DonorsDAP.htm page in a browser.

i. Use the buttons on the data access page toolbar to browse the records in the Donors table. With record 1 displayed (DonorID 1001), click in the DonationAmount text box, then click the Filter By Selection button on the data access page toolbar. Browse to the second record.

j. Use a button on the data access page toolbar to remove the filter that you applied in the previous step.

k. Browse to the record with the DonorID 1004, then use a button on the data access page toolbar to delete it.

l. Change the DonationAmount for the record with DonorID 1005 to **$10,000**, then save the record. (*Hint*: Do not type the dollar sign or the comma.)

m. Sort the records in descending order by LastName.

n. Close your browser, if necessary click Yes to replace the Hospital.mdb file, then close the Hospital Web and FrontPage.

2. The registrar's office at your school is changing its registration system from a paper catalog to a Web site. The registrar's office wants you to create a sample site that shows the staff how to enter course data using a Web page. After analyzing your sample site and working out any problems, the registrar's office will input all of the course data using the Web page.

To complete this independent challenge:

a. If necessary, start the PWS or log on to your server. Start FrontPage and create a new server-based Web using the Import Web Wizard and the name *Courses[insert your name here]*. Import the files from the UnitN\Ic2 folder on your Project Disk into the new Web. (You will import two files.)

b. Start Windows Explorer, open the UnitN folder on your Project Disk, select and copy the Courses database file, then close Windows Explorer.

c. Import the Courses database file into the Courses Web. Use the database connection name **Courses** and store the database file in the Web's fpdb folder. Verify the Courses database connection.

d. Open the courses.htm file in Page View.

e. Set the form to send its results to the Courses table in the Courses database.

f. Select the database column name in the Courses table that corresponds to each form field in the Course Web page. (*Hint*: The form fields and the database columns have the same names.)

g. Close the courses.htm page, then use Folders View to rename the page to **courses.asp**.

h. Preview the courses.asp page in a browser, then use the page to enter the following new record: Course ID: **CS100**, Course Name: **Introduction to Computer Science**, Instructor: **[insert your last name here]**, Number of Credits: **3**, and Class Location: **COM 5.22**.

i. Submit the record, then use your browser's Print button to print the Form Confirmation page. Close your browser.

j. Open the Courses.mdb file from the Web's fpdb folder, then open the Courses table in Table Datasheet View. Confirm that the new record for the CS100 course has been added to the database, then close Access.

k. In Folders View, add a new page to the Web using the filename *search.asp* and the title **Courses Search Page**. Open the search.asp page in Page View.

l. Insert a Database Results region in the page using the Courses database connection. Specify the Courses table as the record source. Create a criterion that selects the Credits field from the database. Use the default formatting options and display all records together.

m. In Page View, click the text Credits in the search form, press [Home], then press [Enter] to create a new line above it. Enter some explanatory text to describe to site visitors how to use this page. For example, you might identify the values that a user can enter into the Credits text box and how to submit the query. (*Hint*: Open the Courses.mdb database and the Courses table to identify the values that users can enter into the Credits text box.)

n. Save the page, then preview it in a browser. Enter **3** in the Credits text box, then submit the query. Use your browser's Print button to print the page that appears, then close your browser.

o. Close the Courses Web and FrontPage.

3. As the information systems specialist at your local library, you are in charge of ensuring that computer operations are up and running. For many years, the library has taken book requests from its patrons. These book requests were paper forms that patrons completed and left in a basket on the main counter. Unfortunately, some patrons thought that these forms were scrap paper and took them to write notes while in the library. In many cases, patrons requested duplicate books and too many books were ordered. In addition, patrons have no way to check and make sure that their books were requested. To address all of the problems associated with paper forms, you created a Web page that contains an electronic version of the paper form. You need to create the database in which to store the data and a data access page to make the information available to patrons over the Internet. Because the form is already created, you will use FrontPage to create the database in which to store its data and the database connection.

To complete this independent challenge:

a. If necessary, start the PWS or log on to your server. Start FrontPage and create a new server-based Web using the Import Web Wizard and the name *Library[insert your name here]*. Import the file from the UnitN\lc3 folder on your Project Disk into the new Web. (You will import one file.)

b. Open the book.htm file in Page View and examine the form. Open the Form Properties dialog box.

c. Select the option to send the form's results to a database, then click Options.

d. On the Database Results tab of the Options for Saving Results to Database dialog box, click Create Database. FrontPage creates a new database and assigns it a database connection name. Accept the default database connection name.

e. Click the Saved Fields tab, then notice that each form field name in the Web page form is matched to its corresponding database column name.

f. Click OK to close each dialog box, close and save the book.htm page, then use Folders View to rename the page as directed.

g. Preview the Book Request Form page in a Web browser. Use the page to enter your information and information about any book into the text boxes. Submit the form, then print the Form Confirmation page that opens. Close your browser.

h. Open the database file from the Web's fpdb folder, click the Tables object on the Objects bar of the Database window (if necessary), then open the Results table in Table Datasheet View and verify that your record was stored in the table. Click the Design View button  on the Standard toolbar, click in the ID column, then click the Primary Key button on the toolbar. (*Note*: The primary key for this database is an AutoNumber field that assigns each record in the table a unique value. You must assign a primary key in order to continue adding new records to the table.) Close the Results table and save your changes.

i. Use a wizard to create a data access page using all fields of the Results table, *except* for Remote_computer_name, User_name, Browser_type, and Timestamp. (*Hint*: To remove these fields, select all available fields, then select these field names in the Selected Fields list box and click .) Do not specify a grouping level or a sort order. Enter the page title **ResultsDAP**, then click Finish.

j. Add the page title **Book Requests** at the top of the data access page, then save it as *ResultsDAP* in the Library Web on the server.

k. Close Access, click the Library folder in the Folder List in Folders View, refresh the Web, then preview the ResultsDAP.htm page in a browser. Use the page to add and save a new record to the database. (*Hint*: Do not enter a value in the ID text box; Access creates this value automatically using the AutoNumber field.) Close your browser.

l. In Folders View, create a new Web page with the filename *book_search.asp* and the title **Book Search Form**. Then open the page in Page View.

m. Create a Database Results region in the page that uses the book database connection and the Results table. Add a search criterion for the Author field where *Author Equals Author*. Accept the default formatting options, select the option to display all records together, then click Finish.

n. Use the pointer to select the last four columns in the Database Results region, which collect data about the user's computer name, user name, browser type, and the date and time the page was accessed. Click Table on the menu bar, then click Delete Cells. Save the page, then preview it in a browser.

o. Type an author's name that you entered into the table in a previous step in the Author text box, then submit the query. (*Hint*: You must enter the author's name *exactly* as you typed it when you created the record.) Close your browser.

p. Close the Library Web and FrontPage.

4. You are the Webmaster for a company that processes student loans. One page in the Web site contains a form that collects information about each student, including the student's name, address, phone number, and e-mail address. You are considering changing the form to store its data in an Access database, instead of as a text file on the server. In addition, you want to create a page that allows authorized users to view the records contained in the database that stores the student data. As part of your research, you decide to examine forms and Web pages that use these features.

To complete this independent challenge:

a. Connect to the Internet.

b. Go to http://www.course.com, navigate to the Student Online Companion for this book, then click the link for Unit N.

c. Click the first link to open a page that displays information from a database, then use the Print command on your browser's File menu to print the first page. This page is based on a database. Use the page to answer the following questions. What are the field names? Do you think that this page is an Active Server Page or a data access page? Why?

d. Click your browser's Back button, then click the second link to open a page that contains a form. Print one page of the form. On the printout, identify the different types of form fields used in the form, how to submit the form to the server for processing, and the total number of database fields in the form. What filename extension does this page use?

e. Close your browser and your dial-up connection, if necessary.

► Visual Workshop

If necessary, start the PWS or log on to your server. Start FrontPage and create a new server-based Web using the Import Web Wizard and the name *Registration[insert your name here]*. Import the file from the UnitN\Vw folder on your Project Disk into the new Web. (You will import one file.) Import the *Registration* database file from the UnitN folder on your Project Disk into the Web. Use the database connection name **Registration**. Set the Form Submission page to send its results to the Registration database. Enter a record into the form, using your first and last names as the user name. Print the page that appears, which is similar to the one that appears in Figure N-25. (Your data will be different.) Close your browser, the Registration Web, and FrontPage. 23

FIGURE N-25

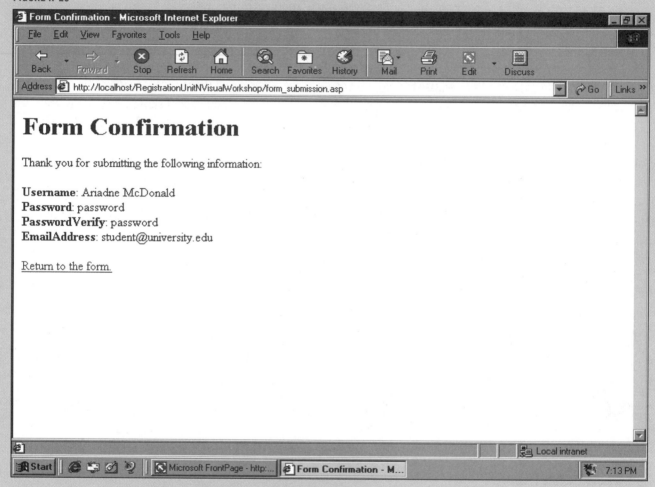

Publishing

a Web on a Web Server

Objectives

► **Assess a Web's overall function and appearance**

⌐MOUS⌐ ► **Add content from an Office document**

► **Create navigation options in a Web**

⌐MOUS⌐ ► **Recalculate and verify hyperlinks**

► **Customize a Site Summary report**

⌐MOUS⌐ ► **Publish a Web to another server**

⌐MOUS⌐ ► **Secure a Web**

► **Use a Web's usage logs**

As soon as you finish creating the content of your Web, you will need to make sure that the Web works as expected. FrontPage includes several commands that automate the process for you. Reports View, for example, lets you view a **Site Summary report**, which provides information about every aspect of your Web, including broken hyperlinks, unlinked files, pages that are slow to download, and pages that contain component errors. You can use this report interactively to identify and correct your Web's mechanical problems. After you have finalized your Web's content and function, you are ready to publish it to another server. After publishing your site to a commercial server, you can set permissions that specify how authorized users will access and/or change the Web. Ariadne McDonald is ready to finalize the Mortgage Web before publishing it from the PWS to the Web Presence Provider (WPP) that will host it. She assesses the Web's content and function, adds navigation links, fixes problems in the site, publishes the Web, and finally sets the Web's security on the server.

Assessing a Web's Overall Function and Appearance

The final step in creating a Web is publishing it to a WPP to make it available to the public. As part of your preparation for publishing a Web to a Web server, you will test its function using different browsers, browser versions, monitors, monitor resolutions, and operating systems. However, another part of your testing is to make sure that you have addressed the tasks shown in Figure O-1. When you are satisfied with your Web's overall function and appearance, you can publish it to the WPP that will host it, and then repeat your testing using different browsers, systems, and monitors. This process ensures that your site functions and looks as expected. Even after a Web is published, you are not really "done" with the Web. As you add new pages to your site and update older pages, it is a good idea to return to your worksheet as needed to assess the current Web's function and content. Good maintenance of a Web is as critical as good design. ✏️ Ariadne is pleased with the site's content. She decides to test each page to ensure that the necessary content is included and that the site's appearance is suitable. Then she imports previously created Word files to provide the missing content in three pages.

Steps 1 2 3 4

If you have saved the Mortgage Web in a different location, enter the path or browse to locate the Web.

1. If necessary, start the **PWS** or log on to your server, start **Microsoft FrontPage**, open the **Mortgage[insert your name here] Web** from the server, then if necessary click the **Folders button** 📁 on the Views bar
The Mortgage Web opens from the server in Folders View.

2. Click **Default.htm** in the contents pane, then click the **Preview in Browser button** 🔍 on the Standard toolbar

3. Click the **What types of loans are available? link** on the home page
The Loan Types page opens. Notice that this page does not use shared borders or a navigation bar.

4. Click your browser's **Back button**, then click the **Help me apply for a home loan now. link**
The Apply Now page opens, and it does not have any navigation options.

5. Click your browser's **Back button**, then continue clicking the hyperlinks on the home page and clicking the **Back button** until you have examined each linked page
Figure O-2 shows some problems associated with the Mortgage Web and their solutions.

6. Close your browser, if necessary return to FrontPage, click **File** on the menu bar, click **Import**, click **Add File**, open the **UnitO folder** on your Project Disk, click **contact**, press and hold [Ctrl], click **rates**, click **whoelse**, release [Ctrl], click **Open**, then click **OK**
The Confirm Save dialog box opens, as shown in Figure O-3, because you are importing files that already exist into the Web.

7. Click **Yes to All**
The new contact.htm, rates.htm, and whoelse.htm pages are imported into the Web.

8. Make sure that **Default.htm** is selected in the contents pane, click 🔍, click the **Who else will help me when I'm buying a home? link**, examine the page that opens, click the **Back button**, click the **How can I contact someone about my loan? link**, then examine the page that opens
The problem of pages with no content, as noted in Figure O-2, is corrected.

9. Close your browser

FIGURE O-1: General tasks for preparing a Web for publication

Tasks:
- Finalize the content in each page
- Apply a Web theme or format pages as necessary to enhance their appearance
- Spell check the entire site
- Complete any outstanding tasks in Tasks View
- Make sure that all pages are linked as expected
- Add any missing pages or page content as necessary
- Verify that all image files are present in the Web
- Verify hyperlinks in the entire site
- Recalculate hyperlinks in the entire site
- After publication, set security for the site and its pages as necessary

FIGURE O-2: Problems identified in the Mortgage Web

Problem	Solution/Task	Completed?
Web pages do not contain navigation options to other pages in the Web.	Add top shared border with navigation links.	
Pages including the Other Helpful Links page (whoelse.htm) and the Contact Us page (contact.htm) contain headings, but no content.	Import completed whoelse.htm page, contact.htm page, and rates.htm page into the Web.	
The Dictionary page (dictionary.htm) does not contain any content other than the heading.	Copy and paste content from the completed Word document.	
The home page does not contain links to every page in the Web site.	Add top shared border with navigation links.	
The Mortgage Rates page will need to be updated to reflect current rates as soon as the site is published to the WPP.	Import revised rates.htm page into the Web. Add content using current mortgage rates.	

FIGURE O-3: Confirm Save dialog box

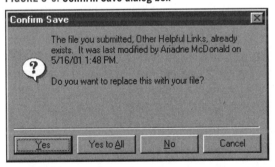

```
Confirm Save                                    ☒

      The file you submitted, Other Helpful Links, already
      exists.  It was last modified by Ariadne McDonald on
  ?   5/16/01 1:48 PM.

      Do you want to replace this with your file?


    Yes        Yes to All        No         Cancel
```

Checking the spelling across a Web

You can check the spelling in an individual Web page by clicking the Spelling button ⬛ on the Standard toolbar. When you want to check the spelling in all pages in a Web, change to Folders View, then click ⬛. The Spelling dialog box opens. Click the Selected page(s) option button to check the spelling in pages selected in Folders View, or click the Entire web option button to check the spelling in all Web pages.

After you click Start, FrontPage will check the Web's pages for spelling errors and identify them in the Spelling dialog box. To correct an error, double-click the page, use the Spelling dialog box that opens to correct or ignore the error, then click Next Document to correct spelling errors in the remaining pages. When you are finished, click OK, then click Cancel.

Adding Content from an Office Document

The next problem that you need to fix in the Mortgage Web is to add the content to the Dictionary Web page. When content that you need to insert into a Web page exists in a document created in another program, such as Word, you can use the Copy and Paste commands in Word and FrontPage to insert the data into a Web page. After you copy selected text or other objects in a program, they are stored temporarily on the Windows Clipboard. When you paste content into a Web page, FrontPage automatically copies it from the Windows Clipboard, converts it to HTML format, and preserves any of the document's original formatting that HTML supports. ◢━━ Ariadne used Word to create the dictionary of mortgage terms. She wants this page to open as a Web page and not as a Word document. She starts Word and opens the document that contains the dictionary terms. She copies the entire page's contents to the Clipboard and closes Word. Then she opens the dictionary.htm page in Page View and pastes the content from the Clipboard into the Web page.

Trouble?
If Microsoft Word is not installed on your computer, ask your instructor or technical support person for help.

Trouble?
Word might be configured to open the Office Clipboard, which is a temporary storage area for Office documents. If it opens, click the Close button on its title bar.

QuickTip
You can select text to copy in Word and drag it to the FrontPage program button on the taskbar. When the Web page appears in Page View, drop the text to the desired location in the Web page—thus copying text from Word and pasting it into FrontPage.

1. Click the **Start button** ▣Start on the taskbar, point to **Programs**, then click **Microsoft Word**
   Microsoft Word starts and opens a blank document.

2. Click the **Open button** 🖝 on the Standard toolbar, open the **UnitO folder** on your Project Disk, then double-click **dictionary**
   The dictionary document opens in the Word program window.

3. Press **[Ctrl][A]** to select the entire document, then click the **Copy button** 🖺 on the Standard toolbar
   The entire document is selected and copied to the Windows Clipboard.

4. Close Word, if necessary return to FrontPage, double-click **dictionary.htm** in the contents pane, then click the **blank line** below the heading in the page
   The dictionary.htm page opens in Page View and the insertion point is blinking in the location where you will paste the contents of the Word document.

5. Click the **Paste button** 🖺 on the Standard toolbar
   The content of the Word document is pasted into the Web page, as shown in Figure O-4. The cascading style sheet that is linked to this page automatically formatted the normal text using the font specified in the style sheet. Because HTML supports bold text, words formatted as bold text in the original Word document also appear as bold text in the Web page.

6. Click the **Save button** 🖫 on the Standard toolbar, then click the **Preview in Browser button** 🖳 on the Standard toolbar
   FrontPage saves the dictionary.htm page and opens it in a browser.

7. Close your browser, return to FrontPage if necessary, then click the **Close button** on the contents pane
   Your browser and the dictionary page close.

FIGURE O-4: Web page after pasting Word document contents

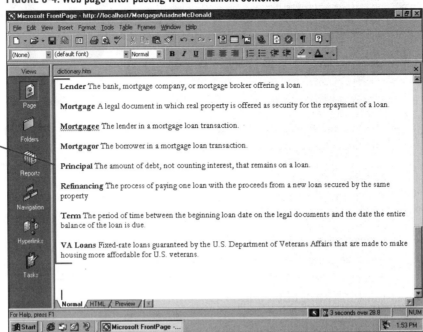

Text uses Word formatting and the fonts specified in the cascading style sheet that is linked to this page

Using Word to create a Web page

You can use Word to create a Web page. After creating your document's content and formatting it as desired in Word, click File on the menu bar, then click Save as Web Page to open the dialog box shown in Figure O-5. In the Save As dialog box, click Change Title and type a Web page title in the Page title text box, then click OK. Type the desired filename in the File name text box, make sure that the file will be saved in the correct location, then click Save. (You can save a document in a Web on a server or in any file location.) The Transferring File dialog box opens temporarily as Word converts the content of your document to HTML, then the Web page opens in the Word program window. You can use Word's menus and toolbars to edit the page as necessary. Any picture or theme files that are used in the document are saved in a folder that uses the document's filename plus "_files". For example, a Word document named Pets.doc might be saved as Pets.htm and picture and theme files associated with Pets.htm would be saved in the folder named Pets_files in the same folder as the Pets.htm file.

FIGURE O-5: Save As dialog box in Word

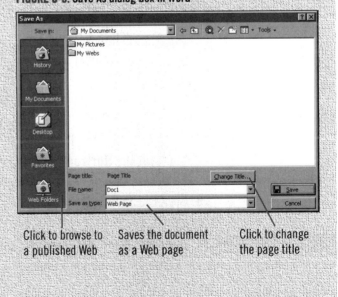

Click to browse to a published Web

Saves the document as a Web page

Click to change the page title

Creating Navigation Options in a Web

The next problem that you need to correct in the Web is to link its pages. Shared borders are easy to create and maintain. Before creating shared borders, you must add pages as necessary to the Web's navigation structure and decide how you want the pages to be related to each other. After adding pages to Navigation View and creating the shared borders, you must determine which hyperlinks to place on each page. ✎ Ariadne wants to include a navigation bar on every page in the Web that contains links to child-level pages and to the home and parent pages. She adds the Web's pages to the navigation structure, then creates a top shared border with navigation links. Because many of the pages already include headings, she will delete the page banner from the top shared border.

Steps 1 2 3 4

Trouble?

If necessary, drag the Navigation toolbar to the top of the navigation pane.

QuickTip

The page title associated with each file is shown in the navigation pane. Use Figure O-6 as needed to associate a page title with its file.

1. **Click the Folders button** 📁 **on the Views bar**
   The Mortgage Web appears in Folders View, as shown in Figure O-6.

2. **Click the Navigation button** 📊 **on the Views bar**
   The home page already appears in the navigation pane.

3. **Drag the loantypes.htm file from the Folder List to below the Home Page icon in the navigation pane, then release the mouse button**
   The Loan Types page appears in the navigation pane as a child page of the home page.

4. **Continue dragging the files from the Folder List into the navigation pane, being sure to position the files exactly as shown in Figure O-7**
   The Web's navigation structure is complete.

5. **Click** 📁, **click Format on the menu bar, click Shared Borders, if necessary click the All pages option button, click the Top check box to select it, if necessary click the Include navigation buttons check box to select it, then click OK**
   FrontPage creates the top shared border and applies it to all pages in the Mortgage Web.

6. **Double-click Default.htm in the contents page**
   The top shared border contains a page banner and a navigation bar.

7. **Right-click Home Page in the top shared border to open the pop-up menu, click Cut, then press [Delete]**
   The top shared border does not contain a page banner or the extra blank line.

8. **Right-click the navigation bar placeholder text in the top shared border to open the pop-up menu, click Navigation Bar Properties, click the Child level option button, make sure that the Home page and Parent page check boxes contain check marks and that the Horizontal and Text option buttons are selected, then click OK**
   The top shared border contains a navigation bar, as shown in Figure O-8.

9. **Click the Save button** 💾 **on the Standard toolbar, click the Preview in Browser button** 🔍 **on the Standard toolbar, then if necessary click Yes**

Trouble?

If the LendersDAP.htm and lenders.asp pages are not working correctly, ask your instructor or technical support person for help.

10. **Use the links in the top shared border of each Web page to navigate the Web**
   Each Web page contains links to child-level pages, the home page, and to the parent page, when appropriate.

FIGURE O-6: Mortgage Web in Folders View

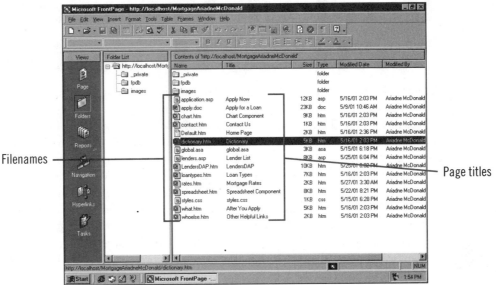

Filenames

Page titles

FIGURE O-7: Navigation structure of the Mortgage Web

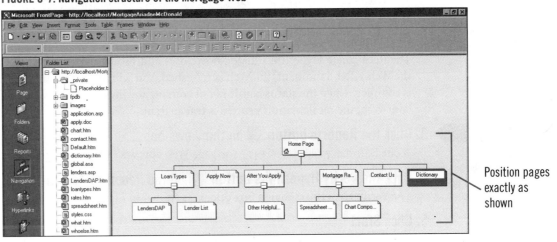

Position pages
exactly as
shown

FIGURE O-8: Top shared border after making changes

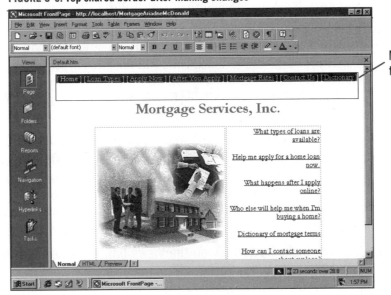

Navigation bar with links
to child-level pages

FrontPage 2000

Recalculating and Verifying Hyperlinks

Before finalizing your Web, it is a good idea to repair any broken hyperlinks, update the shared border and navigation files, update all FrontPage components, update data on the server, and delete any unused theme files. This process is known as **recalculating** the hyperlinks in a Web. You can recalculate the hyperlinks in a Web at any time during its development. It is a good practice to recalculate the hyperlinks before publishing a Web on a Web server. You can also **verify** the hyperlinks in a Web, which causes FrontPage to examine each hyperlink in the Web to check its validity. You must recalculate and verify hyperlinks to test your Web. Recalculating hyperlinks ensures that the Web's links *exist*; verifying hyperlinks ensures that the Web's links are *valid*. The Broken Hyperlinks report in Reports View identifies each link that is broken or cannot be verified. ◄━━━ Ariadne recalculates the hyperlinks in the Mortgage Web to update the shared borders and navigation bars and to delete any unnecessary files. Then she verifies the hyperlinks, correcting as many broken links as possible.

Steps

1. **Close your browser and if necessary return to FrontPage, click Tools on the menu bar, then click Recalculate Hyperlinks**
   The Recalculate Hyperlinks dialog box opens, as shown in Figure O-9. Depending on the size of the Web, the recalculation process can take several minutes.

2. **Click Yes**
   The Recalculate Hyperlinks dialog box closes and FrontPage recalculates the hyperlinks in the Web. After a moment, the Web is refreshed. You will know that the recalculation process is complete when the status bar does not contain any messages. You won't see any changes to your Web; the recalculation process is transparent.

> **Trouble?**
> If necessary, drag the Reporting toolbar to the bottom of the screen so it is not blocking the report.

3. **Click the Reports button 🗔 on the Views bar**
   A Site Summary report for the Mortgage Web appears in Reports View.

4. **Click the Verify Hyperlinks button 🖳 on the Reporting toolbar**
   The Verify Hyperlinks dialog box opens, as shown in Figure O-10.

5. **Click Start**
   Reports View changes to show the Broken Hyperlinks report for the Mortgage Web, as shown in Figure O-11. The status of each hyperlink is listed in the Status column. A broken hyperlink appears with a broken link icon; a verified hyperlink appears with a green check mark; and other messages, such as Unknown or Edited, might appear in the Status column, as well.

> **QuickTip**
> As you gain experience working with FrontPage, you will find that you won't need to fix every broken link identified by FrontPage. However, you must fix broken hyperlinks to missing pages in the Web or to pages that have had filename changes. Use the Help system to learn more about identifying and fixing broken links.

6. **Double-click the Status column for the LendersDAP_files/filelist.xml hyperlink**
   The Edit Hyperlink dialog box opens, as shown in Figure O-12. Notice the file listed in the Replace hyperlink with text box. This is the file that a hyperlink in the LendersDAP.htm page is linked to. When you created the LendersDAP.htm file, Access created the LendersDAP_files folder, which contains an XML file (extensible markup language). You decide to fix this broken link later.

7. **Click Cancel, right-click the Status column for the LendersDAP_files/filelist.xml link to open the pop-up menu, click Add Task, then click OK**
   The Status for the LendersDAP_files/filelist.xml link changes to a question mark because this link has not been repaired, and the Status column now displays the text "Added task." This task now appears in Tasks View to remind you to complete the process of verifying the broken link.

8. **Click the Tasks button 🗏 on the Views bar, examine the task that you just added, then click the Reports button 🗔 on the Views bar**

FIGURE O-9: Recalculate Hyperlinks dialog box

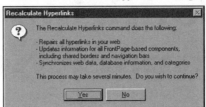

FIGURE O-10: Verify Hyperlinks dialog box

Broken, unverified hyperlinks

Report list arrow

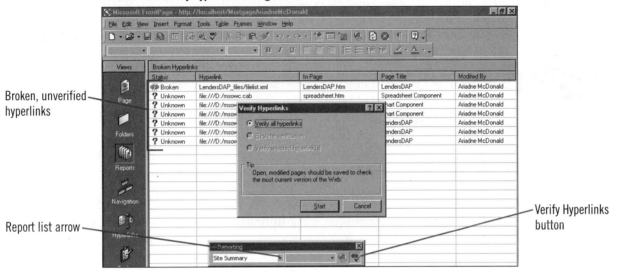

Verify Hyperlinks button

FIGURE O-11: Broken Hyperlinks report after verifying hyperlinks

Broken hyperlink

Verified hyperlinks (your hyperlinks to .cab files might remain broken; these broken links will not affect your Web's function)

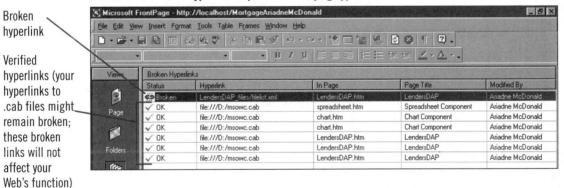

FIGURE O-12: Edit Hyperlink dialog box

When the broken link occurs in multiple places, use these options to fix the broken link in all pages or in selected pages

Page that contains the broken link may or may not be the page you want to associate with the hyperlink file

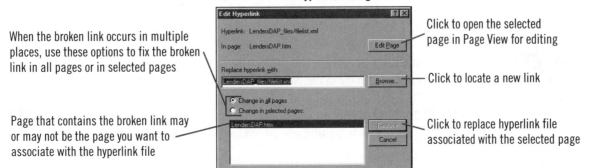

Click to open the selected page in Page View for editing

Click to locate a new link

Click to replace hyperlink file associated with the selected page

FrontPage 2000

Customizing a Site Summary Report

After examining the content of your Web and recalculating and verifying your Web's hyperlinks, you can use a Site Summary report to search for other potential problems, such as pages that are slow to download, component errors, and uncompleted tasks. Table O-1 describes the different reports available in a Site Summary report. Three of the reports—Recently Added Files, Older Files, and Slow Pages—use a day or time value to list pages that were recently added to the Web, pages that were added to the Web within a number of days, and pages that take a preset number of seconds to download. One report—Slow Pages—also uses an Internet connection speed to determine pages that are slow to download. You can change the default values for these report settings using the Reports View tab in the Options dialog box. Ariadne uses Reports View to search for possible problems within the Mortgage Web. She also wants to change the Slow Pages, Older Files, and Recently Added Files reports to change the amount of time used as the benchmark for each page.

Steps

1. Click the **Report list arrow** on the Reporting toolbar, scroll up the list, then click **Site Summary**

   The Site Summary report for the Mortgage Web appears in Reports View. Notice the number of pages for the Slow pages, Older files, and Recently added files reports. The number of pages listed for each of these reports depends on the settings used by your copy of FrontPage.

2. Click **Tools** on the menu bar, click **Options**, then click the **Reports View tab**

   The Options dialog box opens with the Reports View tab in front, as shown in Figure O-13. Your settings might be different, depending on whether you or another user has changed them. Figure O-13 shows the default settings.

QuickTip

Changes that you make in the Options dialog box are not saved with the Web. If you change the defaults, they will apply to all Webs that you open.

3. Be sure the value in the "Recent" files are less than text box is selected, type **10**, press **[Tab]**, type **20** in the "Older" files are more than text box, press **[Tab]**, type **30** in the "Slow pages" take at least text box, click the **Assume connection speed of list arrow**, then click **56.6**

4. Click **OK**

   The Options dialog box closes and the Site Summary report appears in Reports View. The different reports are updated to display the number of pages that meet the criteria you specified in the Options dialog box.

QuickTip

If your pages take a long time to download, resample any pictures or edit longer pages to create multiple short pages.

5. Double-click the **Slow pages report**

   There are no pages in the Web that require more than 30 seconds to download at a connection speed of 56.6 baud.

6. Click the **Report Setting list arrow** on the Reporting toolbar, then click **5 seconds**

   Only one page has a download time that exceeds five seconds. The home page has a download time of 12 seconds at 56.6 baud, which is acceptable.

QuickTip

You can use the Report Setting list arrow on the Reporting toolbar to change the number of days to use as your criteria.

7. Click the **Report list arrow** on the Reporting toolbar, then click **Older Files**

   This report identifies each file in the Web that was last created or updated within the past 20 days.

8. Click the **Report list arrow** on the Reporting toolbar, then click **Recently Added Files**

   This report identifies each file that was added to the Web within the last 10 days.

FIGURE O-13: Reports View tab in the Options dialog box

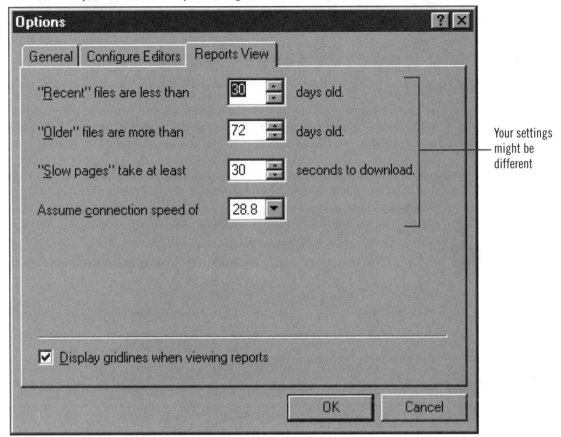

Your settings might be different

TABLE O-1: Reports available in a Site Summary report

report name	description
All Files	The total number of files in the Web and their cumulative file size in kilobytes
Pictures	The total number of pictures in the Web and their cumulative file size in kilobytes
Unlinked Files	The number of files in the Web and their cumulative file size that are *not* linked to the home page
Linked Files	The number of files in the Web and their cumulative file size that are linked to the home page
Slow Pages	The number of files in the Web and their cumulative file size that exceed a specific download time and connection rate
Older Files	The number of files in the Web and their cumulative file size that have not been updated in a specific number of days
Recently Added Files	The number of files in the Web and their cumulative file size that have been created within a specific number of days
Hyperlinks	The number of hyperlinks, both internal and external, in the Web
Unverified Hyperlinks	The number of hyperlinks in the Web that have not been confirmed using the Verify Hyperlinks command
Broken Hyperlinks	The number of hyperlinks in the Web that are broken
External Hyperlinks	The number of hyperlinks in the Web that connect to files or locations outside the Web
Internal Hyperlinks	The number of hyperlinks in the Web that connect to files or locations within the Web
Component Errors	The number of files in the Web that have component errors, such as errors in shared borders or navigation bar files
Uncompleted Tasks	The number of uncompleted tasks in Tasks View
Unused Themes	The number of theme files in the Web that are not used with any file

Publishing a Web to Another Server

After finalizing the content of your Web and thoroughly testing it on the PWS or a local server, you are ready to move the Web's files to the server at the Web presence provider (WPP) that will host your site. You publish the Web from the PWS or a local server using the same steps that you use to publish a disk-based Web to the PWS or a local server. The only difference is that you are publishing to a server's URL, and not to the server on your computer or local network. After you publish your Web from the PWS or a local server to a commercial Web server, you can open the Web from the commercial server by entering its URL in the Folder name text box in the Open Web dialog box. After clicking Open, you will be prompted for your user name and password. If you have the proper permission for opening the site, the Web opens in FrontPage just like any other server-based Web. ✐ Ariadne is satisfied with the content and appearance of the Mortgage Web. She publishes the Web to the WPP that she selected to host her site.

Steps

1. **Click the Folders button ▢ on the Views bar**
   To publish a Web, the Web must be open in FrontPage.

2. **Click File on the menu bar, then click Publish Web**
   The Publish Web dialog box opens.

Trouble?
If your instructor provides you with a URL, complete the steps. Otherwise, read the steps so you know how to publish a Web to another server.

3. **Select the text in the Specify the location to publish your web to text box, then type the URL for the WPP**
   The URL must include the HTTP protocol, the Web server name, and if applicable, the folder name in which to store your pages.

4. **Click the Publish all pages, overwriting any already on the destination option button to select it, then click Publish**
   If necessary, FrontPage starts your Internet connection, contacts the server that you specified in Step 3, then opens a dialog box similar to the one shown in Figure O-14.

5. **Type your user name and password in the appropriate text boxes, then click OK**
   Depending on your Internet connection speed, it might take several minutes to upload your Web's files.

6. **When the dialog box shown in Figure O-15 opens, click the Click here to view your published web site link**
   The Mortgage Web that you published on the commercial Web server opens in a browser.

7. **Close your browser, if necessary return to FrontPage, click Done in the dialog box, click File on the menu bar, then click Close Web**
   The Mortgage Web that is stored on the PWS or on a local server closes.

8. **Click File on the menu bar, click Open Web, select any text that appears in the Folder name text box, type http://[insert your URL here], then click Open**

9. **Type your user name and password in the appropriate text boxes, then click OK**
   Depending on your Internet connection speed, it might take a few minutes for the Mortgage Web that is stored on the commercial Web server to open in FrontPage. After the Web opens, if you have permission to do so, you can add and delete pages, update page content, and format the Web exactly like you would in a Web that is stored on the PWS or on a local server.

FIGURE O-14: Name and Password Required dialog box

Your Web's URL appears here

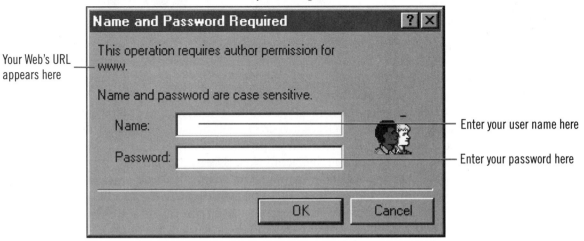

Enter your user name here

Enter your password here

FIGURE O-15: Dialog box that opens after publishing a Web

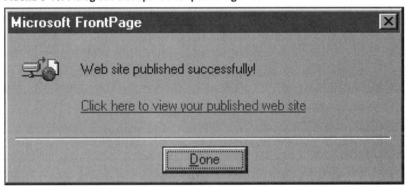

Checking your Web after publishing it

After you publish your Web to a WPP, it is important to continue maintaining it. On a regular basis, use a browser to view your Web by typing its URL in the browser's address field. If you included a link on the home page that allows visitors to report problems by sending an e-mail message to the Webmaster, be sure to check that e-mail address regularly and to respond to users' comments. If you need to make any corrections, open the Web in FrontPage, make your changes, then save the pages to update them on the server.

FrontPage 2000

Securing a Web

You can use FrontPage to secure a published Web. As the **administrator** of a Web, you can give users different types of permission for accessing a Web. **Browsing permission** lets a user open a Web and view it after it has been published. This permission is basically the same as what a user would see if he or she opened the Web in a Web browser using the Web's URL, except the user does the browsing from FrontPage and has access to Reports View and the Web's hidden folders. **Authoring permission** lets a user create and edit pages in the Web. **Administering permission** lets a user create new Webs and set permissions for other users. Usually, only the administrator of the Web has administering permission. ▬▬▬ Ariadne is the Mortgage Web's administrator and as such, she has administering permission. She wants to set the permissions for another user. Amanda Baran will have authoring permission so she can edit Web pages. Ariadne also verifies that all other users will have browsing permission. *Note*: If you are not the administrator of the Web that you published in the previous lesson, you will not be able to change the Web's security. Read the following steps without completing them at the computer.

Steps

Trouble?
If the Security command on the Tools menu is dimmed, then the server on which your Web is published does not support security.

1. Click **Tools** on the menu bar, point to **Security**, then click **Permissions**
The Permissions - <Root Web> dialog box opens, as shown in Figure O-16.

2. Click **Add**
The Add Users dialog box opens, as shown in Figure O-17.

QuickTip
The most secure passwords are ones that contain letters and digits. Don't use obvious or easily guessed information. Most passwords are case-sensitive, which means that uppercase and lowercase letters are different characters.

3. Type **Amanda Baran** in the Name text box, press **[Tab]**, type a password of your choice in the Password text box, press **[Tab]**, type the same password in the Confirm Password text box, then click the **Author and Browse this Web option button** to select it
You set authoring and browsing permissions for Amanda and created her user name and password. Amanda will use this user name and password to open the Web on the server using FrontPage.

4. Click **OK**
Amanda Baran's permission is set.

5. On the Users tab in the Permissions - <Root Web> dialog box, make sure that the **Everyone has browse access option button** is selected
This option ensures that all registered users can browse the Web in FrontPage. If you select the Only registered users have browse access option button, then the Web's administrator must create the registered users' accounts and set their accounts to assign browsing permission to selected users.

6. Click **OK**
The Permissions - <Root Web> dialog box closes.

7. Close the Web and FrontPage

FIGURE O-16: Permissions dialog box

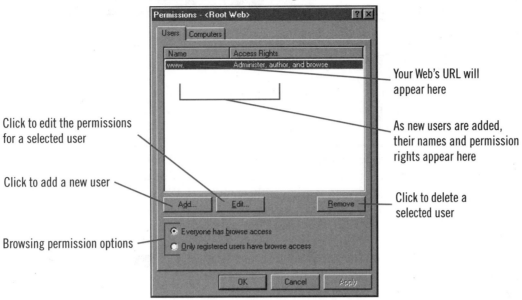

Click to edit the permissions for a selected user

Click to add a new user

Browsing permission options

Your Web's URL will appear here

As new users are added, their names and permission rights appear here

Click to delete a selected user

FIGURE O-17: Add Users dialog box

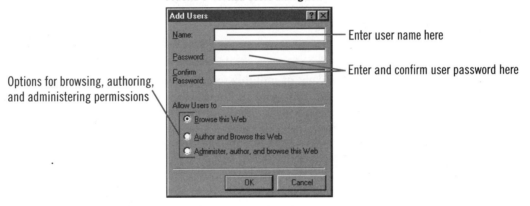

Options for browsing, authoring, and administering permissions

Enter user name here

Enter and confirm user password here

Changing your Web's password on the server

When you create an account with a WPP, the WPP provides you with a user name and password for accessing your account. If you want to change your Web's password after publishing your Web, open the Web in FrontPage, click Tools on the menu bar, point to Security, then click Change Password. The Change Password dialog box opens, as shown in Figure O-18. Type your old password and your new password in the appropriate text boxes, then click OK. The next time you open your Web in FrontPage, you will enter your user name and your new password. If you want to change your user name, you must contact the WPP. Some WPPs do not allow you to change your user name. If this is

the situation and you want to change your user name, then you must cancel your current account and open a new account with a new user name.

FIGURE O-18: Change Password dialog box for a Web

Change Password for www.

Old password:

New password:

Confirm password:

OK   Cancel

Your Web's URL will appear here

FrontPage 2000

Using a Web's Usage Logs

Depending on which WPP is hosting your Web, you might see new folders in the Folder List when you open your Web in FrontPage that you did not see when you opened your Web from the PWS or your local server. Some WPPs create a Logs, Data, or similarly named folder that stores Web pages created by the server and that contain data about the Web. For example, your WPP might create a **usage log**, which is a page containing information about the number of times your home page has been opened, the number of times various pages were opened each day or each hour during the day, or the total number of times a Web page was refreshed during a single session. The information provided about your Web varies based on the WPP that hosts it. Some WPPs only provide usage information if you purchase additional services. Depending on your WPP, you can open your logs either from FrontPage or using a browser. Check with your WPP about where the Web's usage files are stored. After publishing the Mortgage Web to the WPP, Ariadne examines some of the pages that provide usage data.

Details

Some common reports about your Web's usage include the following:

Traffic reports

Traffic reports provide data about the number of visitors to your Web, page views, hits, and the total number of bytes transferred from the server to a browser. This information might be summarized in an hourly, daily, or monthly report. Figure O-19 shows a traffic report for one week that provides data on such categories as the number of visitors, page views, or hits for a Web site.

Page reports

Page reports provide data about the number of page views for each page in the Web. One page report might show the number of hits based on the different types of files included in the Web (JPEG, GIF, HTML, etc.). Another page report might show the status of pages that were opened based on an HTTP code that represents a normal page view, a partial page view, a page forbidden error, or a page not found error. This information can help you to determine if your site's pages are opening normally and whether visitors have attempted to open pages that they did not have permission to view, such as a text file that contains data.

Domain reports

Domain reports provide data about the number of visitors from each domain name (such as aol.com) that used a browser to access the site. This report might also list domains from countries outside the United States separately, to help you assess your site's international traffic.

Browser reports

Browser reports identify the different browsers used to access your site and the number of visitors using each browser. This report also might show the different operating systems on which the browser is used, such as Windows 98 or Macintosh. Figure O-20 shows a browser report that lists the different browsers used to access the site.

FIGURE O-19: Sample usage report about Web site traffic

FIGURE O-20: Sample report about the browsers used to access a Web site

Submitting your Web to search engines

Normally, people don't just stumble into your Web site after you publish it. A few days to a few weeks after you publish your Web site, a search engine will index your site's URL and keywords in its database for users to see when they run a search. For example, the Mortgage Web's keywords might be "home ownership," "financing a home," "mortgage," and "home loans," among others. Instead of waiting for the various Web search engines,

such as Yahoo!, AltaVista, HotBot, and Excite to find your site, you can submit your site's URL to the search engines individually by following the instructions listed at their Web sites. If you don't have time to submit your URL to individual search engines, you can use a specialized Web site, such as Submit It!, to submit your site's URL to multiple search engines simultaneously.

Practice

▶ Concepts Review

Label each of the elements of the Microsoft FrontPage window shown in Figure O-21.

FIGURE O-21

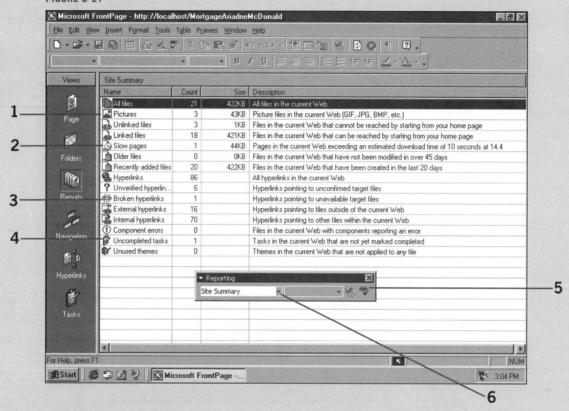

Match each of the terms with the statement that describes it.

7. Administrator
8. Authoring permission
9. Document_files folder
10. Page report
11. Recalculate hyperlinks
12. Site Summary report
13. Slow Pages report
14. Verify hyperlinks

a. A folder created by Word that stores Web-related files for a Web page named Document.htm
b. A process that checks each hyperlink in a Web to ensure that it is valid
c. A process that repairs any broken hyperlinks, updates shared border and navigation files and data on the server, and deletes any unused theme files in a Web
d. A type of usage report about a Web's page views
e. Lists information about your Web's size, features, and potential problems
f. Lists pages in the Web that are slow to download using specific time and download values
g. The person who is responsible for assigning users different levels of permissions for accessing a Web
h. The specified user can create and edit pages in the Web

Select the best answer from the list of choices.

15. Which one of the following statements about creating a Web is TRUE?
   a. At some point, your work is complete.
   b. If your site's objectives change, you should create a new Web to address them.
   c. Your work is never really "done."
   d. After publishing a Web with a WPP, you cannot edit or add pages to the Web.

16. The easiest way to check the spelling in all pages in a Web is to
   a. Open each page in the site in Page View, then click the Spelling button.
   b. Click the Spelling button in Folders View, click the Entire web option button, then click Start.
   c. Use the All pages report in Reports View.
   d. None of the above.

17. When you create a Web page using Word, the
   a. Page is saved with a .doc filename extension.
   b. Files that support the Web page are saved in the Web page.
   c. Files that support the Web page are saved in a folder that includes the HTML filename plus "_files".
   d. Page is automatically saved in a Web on a server.

18. Detailed information about the broken hyperlinks in a Web appear in the
   a. Recalculate Hyperlinks dialog box.
   b. Broken Hyperlinks report.
   c. Verify Hyperlinks dialog box.
   d. Site Summary report.

19. Which of the following reports in Reports View can you customize using the Options dialog box?
   a. Slow Pages
   b. Recently Added Files
   c. Older Files
   d. All of the above

20. When you open a secured Web in FrontPage, you must have
   a. Authoring permission.
   b. Browsing permission.
   c. Administering permission.
   d. Any of the above.

► Skills Review

1. Assess a Web's overall function and appearance.
a. If necessary, start the PWS or log on to your server. Start FrontPage and create a new server-based Web using the Import Web Wizard and the name *Rates[insert your name here]*. Import the files from the Unit0\Sr folder on your Project Disk into the new Web. (You will import nine files.)

b. Use Page View to assess each page's content and function. Prepare a worksheet similar to the one shown in Figure O-2 to identify any problems and their possible solutions. (*Hint*: The Underwriting.doc file in the Unit0 folder on your Project Disk contains the content for one of the Web pages.)

2. Add content from an Office document.
a. If necessary, open the conventional.htm file in Page View.

b. Start Word, then open the Underwriting file from the Unit0 folder.

c. Select all of the text in the document. Drag the selected text to the Microsoft FrontPage program button on the taskbar, wait for FrontPage to open the conventional.htm file in Page View, then move the pointer into the document so it changes to and release the mouse button.

d. Save the conventional.htm page.

3. Create navigation options in a Web.
a. In Navigation View, add the following pages as child pages of the home page: ARMs.htm, conventional.htm, and payment.htm. Then add the pages 15yr.htm and 30yr.htm as child pages of the conventional.htm page.

b. Change to Folders View, then add top and left shared borders to all pages in the Web. Both shared borders should contain navigation buttons.

c. Open the home page in Page View, then set the navigation bar in the top shared border to contain horizontal, text links to same-level pages and to the home page.

d. Set the navigation bar in the left shared border to contain vertical, text links to child-level pages only.

e. Save your changes, test the Web's links in a browser, then close the browser.

4. Recalculate and verify hyperlinks.
a. In FrontPage Folders View, recalculate the hyperlinks in the Web.

b. Change to Reports View and, if necessary, turn on the Reporting toolbar and display the Site Summary report.

c. Verify all hyperlinks in the Web.

d. Open the Edit Hyperlink dialog box for the first broken link (to the sunset.gif file).

e. Click Edit Page, right-click the broken icon link for the picture to open the pop-up menu, click Picture Properties, click Browse, double-click sunset.gif, then click OK. Save the page, then return to Reports View.

f. Right-click the broken link to the URL http://www.toaks.tothe.net/ to open the pop-up menu, then add this link to Tasks View using the default settings. (*Hint*: If you are connected to the Internet when you run the Site Summary report, FrontPage will verify the URL as a valid link and the URL will not appear as a broken link. Continue with the next step.)

g. Display the Web's Site Summary report again.

5. Customize a Site Summary report.
a. Use the Reports View tab in the Options dialog box to customize Reports View as follows: recent files should be less than 20 days old, older files should be more than 45 days old, slow pages should take at least 10 seconds to download at 14.4 baud.

b. Click OK to close the dialog box. Which pages are slow to download using these settings?

c. Use Reports View tab in the Options dialog box to change the connection speed in the Slow Pages report to 56.6 baud. What pages, if any, are still listed in the Slow Pages report?

d. Use the information shown in the Site Summary report and a blank sheet of paper to create a list of problems that you need to fix in this Web, such as files that aren't linked to the home page, broken hyperlinks, or any other potential problems. If you cannot identify any problems, state this fact on your paper.

6. Publish a Web to another server.

a. If your instructor asks you to complete this section of the Skills Review and provides you with a URL, use the Publish Web command on the File menu to publish all pages in your Rates Web to another server.

b. After the publishing process is complete, use the link in the dialog box that opens to view your published Web. Use the hyperlinks in the site to examine its pages.

c. Close your browser, then open the published Web in FrontPage using your user name and password. (*Note*: Depending on your Internet connection speed, it might take several minutes to open the Web in FrontPage. Be patient.)

7. Secure a Web.

a. If your instructor assigns this section of the Skills Review, use the open Web in FrontPage to create a user account for a classmate or an individual as specified by your instructor. Assign the new user a user name and a password.

b. Give the new user authoring and browsing permissions in the Web.

c. Close the Permissions dialog box.

8. Use a Web's usage logs.

a. If your published Web includes folders or links that report the Web's usage statistics, locate and open the page that shows the Web's activity by hour, day, or month. Print the page that opens.

b. Locate and find a page that identifies the browsers that were used to open your site's pages, then print it.

c. Close the Web, FrontPage, Word, and your browser.

▶ Independent Challenges

1. You work for the Garden Café, a small bistro-style family restaurant. The restaurant is creating a Web site that will feature different menu item descriptions and pictures, along with pages that feature daily specials. The Web site is a mess because different people have contributed to it with no general direction provided by any one manager. As a result, most of the Web's hyperlinks are broken. Your manager, Susan Baukus, has asked you to take charge of the project and to review the site's contents, to identify and fix as many of the problems as possible, and to provide a report of what you have done and what still needs to be done.

To complete this independent challenge:

a. If necessary, start the PWS or log on to your server. Start FrontPage and create a new server-based Web using the Import Web Wizard and the name *Cafe[insert your name here]*. Import the files from the Unit0\Ic1 folder on your Project Disk into the new Web. (You will import 27 files.)

b. Preview some of the pages in Page View to get an overall understanding of the Web.

c. Run a Site Summary report. If necessary, drag the Reporting toolbar out of the way so it is not covering any text in the report. Use [Print Screen] and WordPad to print a copy of the Site Summary report in Reports View. Close WordPad without saving changes.

d. Recalculate the hyperlinks in the Web site.

e. Verify all hyperlinks in the Web site. Correct as many of the problems as possible. (*Hint*: To correct some of the broken hyperlinks to images, use Folders View to move all of the Web's picture files into the images folder.)

f. Return to the Broken Hyperlinks report to correct other broken hyperlinks. (*Hint*: Some of the remaining broken hyperlinks are due to filename changes. Double-click the status column of a broken hyperlink. Browse the Web's folders to find the file associated with the broken link. Most of the files that are identified as broken links will be in the images folder.)

g. The Garden.gif file is missing from the Web. Add a task for fixing broken links to this file.

h. Change the settings for the Slow Pages report to use five seconds as the download time and 28.8 baud as the connection speed. How many pages meet these criteria?

i. In Navigation View, add the following pages as child pages of the home page: AboutUs.htm, Employment.htm, Feedback.htm, Menu.htm, Search.htm, franchise.htm, and Specials.htm. Then add the following pages as child pages of the Specials page: AngelCake.htm, Pasta.htm, Pecan.htm, and Pudding.htm.

j. Create a top shared border on all pages. Open the home page in Page View, then set the navigation bar to use horizontal, text hyperlinks to child-level pages and a link to the home page and the parent page.

k. Save your changes, preview the home page in a browser, then use the links to navigate the entire site. Print the home page in the browser. If you notice any pages with problems, print them and describe the problem that you find. Close your browser.

l. Close the Web and FrontPage.

2. TAPPO is a not-for-profit association that represents health insurance companies before the state legislature. As part of the association's start-up tasks, it wants to create a Web site that lists the association's goals, objectives, and legislative agenda. Richard Wayne is the association's executive director and you are his assistant. Richard has all of the pages that were created and edited by staff members. He needs you to examine the pages to identify any missing content or potential errors. As the association grows over time, he will continue adding pages to its Web site.

To complete this independent challenge:

a. If necessary, start the PWS or log on to your server. Start FrontPage and create a new server-based Web using the Import Web Wizard and the name *TAPPO[insert your name here]*. Import the files from the Unit0\Ic2 folder on your Project Disk into the new Web. (You will import three files.)

b. Open each page in the Web site in Page View and examine its contents using the guidelines shown in Figure O-1. Close each page after you review it, without making any changes. Create a worksheet similar to the one shown in Figure O-2 in which you list the problems that you find in the pages. Do *not* make any corrections, but list some possible solutions. If you are unsure about the solution to a problem, state a possible solution in your worksheet. If you do not know the solution, state this fact.

c. Use your worksheet to fix as many of the problems as possible. If you are unable to fix a problem giving the existing resources that you have, state this in the Solution column. In the Completed? column, indicate that you cannot fix the problem and state the reason why.

d. Save all pages as you change them, then preview the pages in a browser. If necessary, return to Page View and make any necessary corrections. Close your browser and FrontPage.

e. In a report addressed to your instructor, describe the problems that you found and the tasks that Richard and his staff must complete to finalize the Web site for publication. For example, list any missing pages, content, etc., using only the information provided in the introduction to this independent challenge and in the Web pages.

f. Submit your report and your completed worksheets to your instructor.

3. Use your knowledge of FrontPage to create a Web site that features content related to a subject that you enjoy, such as a sport, hobby, or other interest, or about yourself or a business (real or fictitious).
To complete this independent challenge:

a. If necessary, start the PWS or log on to your server. Start FrontPage and create a One Page Web named *Web[insert your name here]*.

b. Create at least five Web pages related to your topic. Save the pages with appropriate filenames and titles.

c. On at least two of the pages, include pictures that you have available (such as digital or scanned picture files) or from the Clip Art Gallery. Resize and resample the pictures as necessary to make them the appropriate size in your pages, then save them with the default filenames in the Web's images folder.

d. Add your site's pages to Navigation View.

e. Use one or more shared borders to add navigation options to the Web as appropriate.

f. Recalculate and then verify the hyperlinks in your site. If necessary, fix any broken hyperlinks. If you cannot fix a broken hyperlink, add it to Tasks View.

g. Use the information contained in the Site Summary report to identify any potential problems, then fix them.

h. Save and close all pages in the Web. If your instructor asks you to publish your Web from your server to another server, use the Publish Web command on the File menu to publish your Web.

i. Open your published Web from the server in Reports View. If necessary, make any changes as indicated by the report. Save your changes.

j. Set the Web's security to add at least one user who has authoring permission and one user who has browsing permission.

k. Close the Web, FrontPage, your browser, and your dial-up connection, if necessary.

4. You are the Web administrator for Anna's Logos, a retail store that creates digital logos for small businesses. Anna just moved her operations from a physical store location to an electronic commerce site in order to expand her business reach. You are responsible for ensuring the security of the Web site and server. You decide to use the Web to learn more about permissions that you can set in a FrontPage Web as you create new user accounts for different staff members. In addition, you want to learn about different security measures that you can implement to ensure that sample logos (pictures) that Anna places are traceable if they are reproduced elsewhere on the Web without her permission.
To complete this independent challenge:

a. Connect to the Internet.

b. Go to http://www.course.com, navigate to the Student Online Companion for this book, then click the link for Unit O.

c. Click the first link, then read the page that opens. On a blank sheet of paper, answer the following questions. How can you assign the same permission to more than one person at a time? How would you accomplish this objective in FrontPage?

d. Click the second link, then read the page that opens. Use the hyperlinks in the page that opens to learn more about digital watermarks. What is a digital watermark? Could Anna use a digital watermark to protect her logos from being copied? Why or why not?

e. Click the third link, then read the page that opens. Use the hyperlinks in the page that opens to learn more about steganography. What is steganography? Could Anna use steganography to protect her logos from being copied? Why or why not?

f. Which data protection method—digital watermark or steganography—should Anna use? Support your recommendation.

g. Close your browser and your dial-up connection, if necessary.

▶ Visual Workshop

Examine the Site Summary report shown in Figure O-22. What problems do you expect this Web to have? How would you fix these problems? After you analyze the Site Summary report, write a report detailing the problems and possible solutions you would expect to find if you were asked to test this Web.

FIGURE O-22

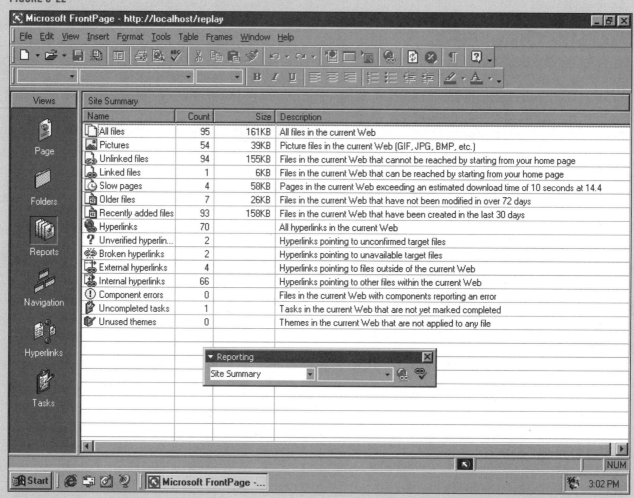

Microsoft FrontPage - http://localhost/replay

File Edit View Insert Format Tools Table Frames Window Help

Site Summary

Name	Count	Size	Description
All files	95	161KB	All files in the current Web
Pictures	54	39KB	Picture files in the current Web (GIF, JPG, BMP, etc.)
Unlinked files	94	155KB	Files in the current Web that cannot be reached by starting from your home page
Linked files	1	6KB	Files in the current Web that can be reached by starting from your home page
Slow pages	4	58KB	Pages in the current Web exceeding an estimated download time of 10 seconds at 14.4
Older files	7	26KB	Files in the current Web that have not been modified in over 72 days
Recently added files	93	158KB	Files in the current Web that have been created in the last 30 days
Hyperlinks	70		All hyperlinks in the current Web
Unverified hyperlin...	2		Hyperlinks pointing to unconfirmed target files
Broken hyperlinks	2		Hyperlinks pointing to unavailable target files
External hyperlinks	4		Hyperlinks pointing to files outside of the current Web
Internal hyperlinks	66		Hyperlinks pointing to other files within the current Web
Component errors	0		Files in the current Web with components reporting an error
Uncompleted tasks	1		Tasks in the current Web that are not yet marked completed
Unused themes	0		Themes in the current Web that are not applied to any file

Views: Page, Folders, Reports, Navigation, Hyperlinks, Tasks

Reporting — Site Summary

Start | Microsoft FrontPage -... | 3:02 PM

Unit
P

Working

with HTML Code

Objectives

- ► **Understand HTML**
- MOUS ► **Use Reveal Tags to show HTML code**
- MOUS ► **Work in HTML Page View**
- ► **Edit a Web page in HTML Page View**
- MOUS ► **Nest HTML code**
- ► **Create a hyperlink**
- ► **Insert a horizontal line and a picture**
- ► **Insert a background picture**

When you use a Web browser to open a page on a Web server, the browser interprets the page's contents and displays it on your computer. A Web page is really just a document that contains programming code written in a markup language. A **markup language** is a set of codes in a file that a computer uses to format and display the file. The most common markup language used on the Web is **HTML**, which stands for **Hypertext Markup Language**. HTML makes it possible for computers with different browsers, operating systems, and monitors to display pages that are stored on different types of servers with different operating systems. HTML is readable by almost any computer, which lessens the burden on Web site developers to ensure that their pages are viewable by the maximum number of people possible. And because a browser *interprets* HTML, it is entirely possible for different browsers to display HTML code in different ways; however, the *content* of the page is the same. Sharon Curtis is a Web site developer who teaches students how to use FrontPage 2000 to create Web sites and pages. She also teaches her students about HTML to enhance their understanding of creating Web pages.

Understanding HTML

To create a Web page, you can use the toolbars and menu commands in FrontPage or any other Web page creation program to issue commands about how you want your Web pages to appear and function. When you click the New button on the Standard toolbar in FrontPage, FrontPage automatically creates a new page that contains the required HTML tags for a Web page. Because a Web page contains HTML code, a Web page is also known as an **HTML document**. Sharon used HTML to create a Web page shown in Figure P-1. She explains the code shown in Figure P-2 and some rules for writing HTML code.

Details

HTML tags contain instructions for displaying content in an HTML document

An HTML **tag** is a container that tells the browser how to display the content that either follows the tag or is enclosed by the tags. Tags are enclosed in brackets. For example, a browser will display the HTML code <b>Hello</b> as **Hello** because in HTML, a browser displays the text enclosed by the <b> and </b> tags as bold.

Most HTML tags are two-sided, but some tags are one-sided

Tags usually come in pairs. The first tag, or the **opening tag**, tells the browser to turn on a certain feature or format and apply it to the content contained within the tags. The second tag, or the **closing tag**, tells the browser to turn off the feature or format. A closing tag always contains a slash character. When a tag appears as a pair, it is called a **two-sided tag**. Some HTML tags require only one tag, in which case there is no closing tag. When only one tag is required, it is called a **one-sided tag**.

HTML tags can contain properties that further describe a tag

Sometimes a tag will contain additional code to identify certain properties of the content enclosed by the tag. For example, when you align a heading in a Web page, the code will include the HTML align property to describe how to align the text enclosed by the heading tags, <h1> and </h1>. For example, a browser will display the HTML code <h1 align="center">Hello</h1> as the text "Hello" with the Heading 1 style and centered on the page, or the code <p align="right">Welcome!</p> as the text "Welcome!" on a new right-aligned line.

An HTML document must contain several tags to identify and display it as a Web page

The <html> and </html> tags at the beginning and end of a document identify a file as an HTML document. These tags must enclose all of the code and content within the HTML document. The <body> and </body> tags enclose all content that users see when they open the file using a Web browser. Some other tags that are not required, but that are usually added, are the <title> and </title> tags, which identify the file's title that appears in the browser's title bar, and the <head> and </head> tags, which identify information about the Web page. Figure P-2 shows the information added by FrontPage in all FrontPage-created pages.

You can nest HTML tags inside other HTML tags to apply several formats or features to text

A **nested tag** is an HTML tag that appears within another set of HTML tags. For example, you might create a numbered list within a bulleted list.

Pictures and other objects that appear in a Web page are not part of an HTML document

When you insert a picture in a Web page, you really aren't saving the picture *in* the Web page; you are just adding code to the page indicating how and where a browser should display the picture. For example, the HTML code <img src="picture.gif"> tells a browser to display a picture named picture.gif in the location where the code appears. The HTML code <body background="picture.jpg"> tells the browser to display the picture named picture.jpg as a background picture. (The img src and body background tags are one-sided.)

FIGURE P-1: Web page in a browser

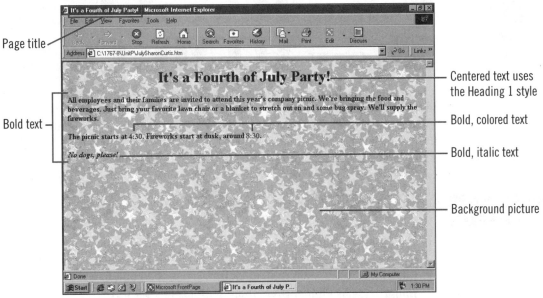

Page title

Centered text uses the Heading 1 style

Bold text

Bold, colored text

Bold, italic text

Background picture

FIGURE P-2: HTML code for the Web page shown in Figure P-1

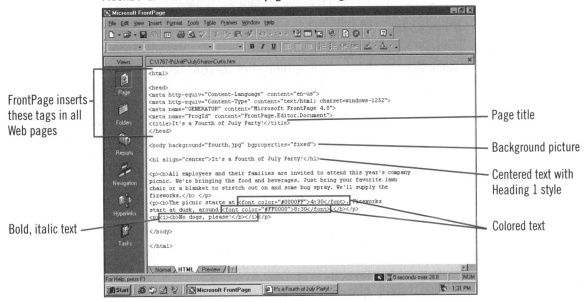

FrontPage inserts these tags in all Web pages

Page title

Background picture

Centered text with Heading 1 style

Colored text

Bold, italic text

Using HTML to create Web pages

To become proficient in creating Web pages by writing HTML code, you must learn about the different tags and how to use them. As you are working, it is important to preview your Web pages periodically in a browser to ensure that they appear as desired. If your pages don't look right, check your typing carefully. Some common mistakes are forgetting to type the closing tag of a two-sided tag and omitting the slash character in the closing tag of a two-sided tag. For example, if you omit the closing </h1> tag at the end of a line of text that you want to use the Heading 1 style, all of the text that follows the opening <h1> tag will use the Heading 1 style because you never provided an instruction to the browser to turn off the Heading 1 style. It is also helpful to check your problematic code against similar code that you know works to help you find your mistake.

Using Reveal Tags to Show HTML Code

You can open the Web page that you examined in the previous lesson in HTML Page View to see the HTML code that creates it. Another way to see HTML code is to use the Reveal Tags command in Normal Page View. When you turn on this feature, you do not see all the HTML tags that create a page. The nice thing about revealing the tags in Normal Page View is that you can still see the document's basic formatting, instead of looking at just the code. Table P-1 lists some common HTML tags and their descriptions. The ellipsis (…) in the tags indicates the placement of content entered by the developer. Sharon shows her students how to display the HTML tags for a Web page in Normal Page View.

1. Start **FrontPage** and if necessary change to Page View

2. Click **File** on the menu bar, click **Open**, use the **Look in list arrow** and open the **UnitP folder** on your Project Disk, then double-click **FP P-1**
   The FP P-1 Web page opens in Normal Page View.

3. Click **File** on the menu bar, click **Save As**, if necessary select the text in the File name text box and type **July[insert your name here]**, then click **Save**
   You created a copy of the page, in case you need to start over.

4. Click **View** on the menu bar, then click **Reveal Tags**
   FrontPage displays the HTML tags in the document, as shown in Figure P-3. Notice that the body tags enclose all of the text in the document. Tags that contain properties do not appear, such as the align property that centers the heading. In addition, you cannot see the HTML tags that identify this file as an HTML document or that apply the background picture to the Web page.

5. Click anywhere in the heading **It's a Fourth of July Party!**, click the **Style list arrow** on the Formatting toolbar, then click **Heading 2**
   The tags that enclose the heading change to <h2> and </h2>, which are the HTML tags for the Heading 2 style; the "It's a Fourth of July Party!" text now uses the Heading 2 style. In HTML, there are six levels of headings that you can apply to text. The h1 tag applies the largest font size, and the h6 tag applies the smallest font size.

6. Click the **Undo button** on the Standard toolbar
   The heading now uses the Heading 1 style again.

7. Click after the ! in the heading, then press **[Enter]**
   FrontPage creates a new blank line below the heading. The new line uses the <p> and </p> tags; the "p" stands for paragraph. In HTML, even one line is a paragraph.

8. Click the **Save button** on the Standard toolbar
   FrontPage saves the page.

9. Click **View** on the menu bar, then click **Reveal Tags**
   The Reveal Tags feature is turned off and your page appears in Normal Page View without the HTML tags displayed.

FIGURE P-3: Web page with HTML tags revealed

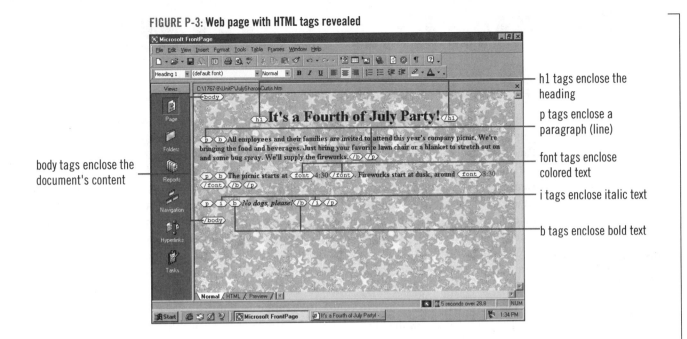

body tags enclose the document's content

h1 tags enclose the heading

p tags enclose a paragraph (line)

font tags enclose colored text

i tags enclose italic text

b tags enclose bold text

TABLE P-1: Common HTML tags and their descriptions

HTML tag	description
<a href="filename.xxx">...</a> or <a href="URL">...</a>	Creates a hyperlink to a file named *filename.xxx* or to a URL
<a name="location">...</a>	Creates a hyperlink in a Web page to a bookmark named *location*
...	Creates bold text
<body background="filename.xxx">	Inserts a background picture named *filename.xxx* in the Web page
<body>...</body>	Encloses the content of the Web page
 	Creates a line break in a page
<font color="#000000">...</font>	Creates colored text using the specified HTML code for the desired color
<h1>...</h1>	Creates a heading with the largest font size
<head>...</head>	Encloses the HTML document header, which includes information about the character set and editor used in the page
<hr>	Creates a horizontal line in a Web page
<html>....</html>	Encloses the entire HTML document and identifies the file as a Web page
<i>...</i>	Creates italic text
<img src="filename.xxx">	Inserts a picture named *filename.xxx* in a Web page
<li>...</li>	Creates one item in a list
<ol/>...</ol>	Creates a numbered list
<p>...</p>	Creates a new paragraph (line)
<title>...</title>	Creates the text that appears in the browser's title bar
<u>...</u>	Creates underlined text
<ul>...</ul>	Creates a bulleted list

FrontPage 2000

Working in HTML Page View

Using the Reveal Tags command doesn't give you a complete view of the HTML tags for a Web page. To see all of an HTML document's HTML code in FrontPage, you must change to HTML Page View. If something is selected in Normal Page View when you change to HTML Page View, the same text is selected in HTML Page View. Any changes that you make in Normal or HTML Page View are automatically updated in the other Page View. While you are working in HTML Page View, you can use some of the toolbar buttons and menu commands to format text and objects and to insert components. However, most FrontPage toolbar buttons and menu commands are dimmed in HTML Page View. ▰▰▰▰ Sharon shows her students how to work with HTML code in HTML Page View by entering and formatting text and inserting a FrontPage component. She then previews the page to show her students the results of the inserted code.

Steps 1234

QuickTip
You can set FrontPage to display HTML tags and user-supplied content in different colors; your colors might be different.

QuickTip
You can type HTML tags using uppercase or lower-case letters; the tags <b> and <B> are the same.

QuickTip
You do not need to retype the entire line of code; you need to type only the information that has changed.

1. **Click the HTML tab, then examine the code in the page**
   The HTML code for the July Web page appears in HTML Page View, as shown in Figure P-4. The HTML tags appear in blue text, and the document's content appears in black text. Notice the status bar in the lower-left corner of the FrontPage program window. In HTML Page View, the status bar shows the line and column number of the position of the insertion point. Use the line numbers to complete the steps in this lesson.

2. **Locate the line of code that formats the heading using the Heading 1 style (line 13), then edit the code to <h2 align="left">It's a Fourth of July Party!</h2>**

3. **Click the Normal tab**
   The changes that you made in HTML Page View are reflected in Normal Page View. The heading is now left-aligned and uses the Heading 2 style.

4. **Click the Undo button [icon] on the Standard toolbar, then click HTML tab**
   The heading uses the Heading 1 style and is centered.

5. **Click line 24 (the blank line above the </body> tag), click the Insert Component button [icon] on the Standard toolbar, then click Hover Button**
   The Hover Button Properties dialog box opens, as shown in Figure P-5. A hover button is a button in a Web page that animates when the pointer moves over it and that usually opens another file or URL when clicked. (You will not link this hover button to a file.)

6. **Type See You There! in the Button text text box, then click OK**
   As shown in Figure P-6, a Java applet that creates the hover button is added to the HTML document.

7. **Click the Save button [icon] on the Standard toolbar, click the Preview tab, then point to the hover button**
   The hover button uses the text you added and the default settings.

8. **Click the HTML tab, change line 29 to <param name="effect" value="reverseGlow">, click [icon], click the Preview tab, then point to the hover button**
   Now the hover button uses the reverse glow effect based on the changes that you made to the HTML code.

9. **Click the HTML tab, then click the Close button on the contents pane to close the page**

FIGURE P-4: HTML code for the July page

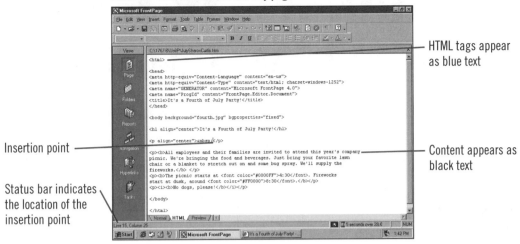

Insertion point

Status bar indicates the location of the insertion point

HTML tags appear as blue text

Content appears as black text

FIGURE P-5: Hover Button Properties dialog box

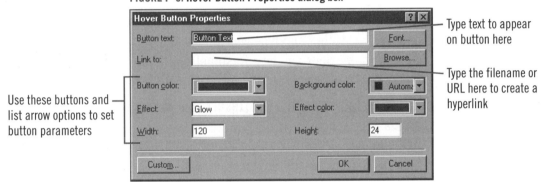

Type text to appear on button here

Type the filename or URL here to create a hyperlink

Use these buttons and list arrow options to set button parameters

FIGURE P-6: Java applet added to the July page

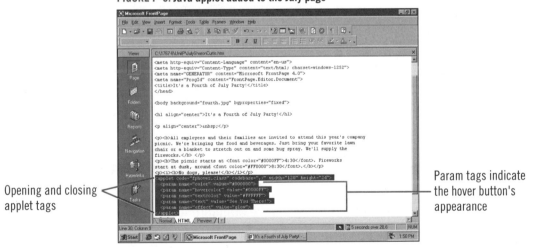

Opening and closing applet tags

Param tags indicate the hover button's appearance

Viewing HTML code using a browser

You can enhance your understanding of HTML code by viewing the code used to create Web pages on the Internet. In Internet Explorer, click View on the menu bar, then click Source. A Notepad program window opens and displays the HTML code that creates the page. In Navigator, click View on the menu bar, then click Page Source. A Netscape window opens and displays the HTML code. If you have permission to do so, you can make changes to the HTML code displayed by the browser and save your code changes to update the page.

Editing a Web Page in HTML Page View

Throughout this book, you have used Normal Page View to edit your Web pages. In the previous lesson, you learned how to edit Web pages in HTML Page View. Of course, you need to be very familiar with HTML and its programming rules to be able to write HTML code from scratch. However, even as a novice programmer, you will find it easy to insert tags that format your document's contents. ✎ Sharon wants her students to create a document that they will need in the future: a resume. She asks them to open an existing Web page in HTML Page View and then to format its contents.

Steps 1 2 3 4

1. Click **File** on the menu bar, click **Open**, then double-click **FP P-2**
   The FP P-2 Web page opens in Normal Page View.

2. Click **File** on the menu bar, click **Save As**, click **Change**, be sure the text in the Page title text box is selected and type your first and last names, click **OK**, select the text in the File name text box and type **Resume[insert your name here]**, then click **Save**
   You created a copy of the page, in case you need to start over.

QuickTip
Use the line numbers displayed on the status bar to complete the steps in this lesson.

3. Click the **HTML tab**, select the text **[Insert Your Name Here]** in line 11, then type your first and last names
   The Web page now uses a new title, filename, and your name in the document. Refer to Figures P-7 and P-8 as you edit and add the HTML code to format the page.

4. In line 11, change the <p> tag to **<h3 align="center">**, then in line 14, change the </p> tag to **</h3>**
   The name and address information now uses the Heading 3 style and is centered in the page.

5. Change the <p> and </p> tags in lines 17 and 24 to **<h3>** and **</h3>** in both lines
   The "Education" and "Experience" text now uses the Heading 3 style.

6. Scroll down the page as necessary, click to the right of the <p> tag in line 25, type ****, click to the right of the "t" in Assistant in line 25, then type ****
   The text "Computer Services Lab Assistant" changes to bold.

7. Scroll down the page as necessary, click to the right of the <p> tag in line 28, type ****, click to the right of the "r" in Director in line 28, then type ****
   The text "Student Computer Services Assistant Director" changes to bold.

8. Click the **Save button** 🖫 on the Standard toolbar, then click the **Preview in Browser button** 🔍 on the Standard toolbar
   The page opens in a browser, as shown in Figure P-8.

9. Scroll down the page, if necessary, to examine its contents

FIGURE P-7: HTML code for the Resume page

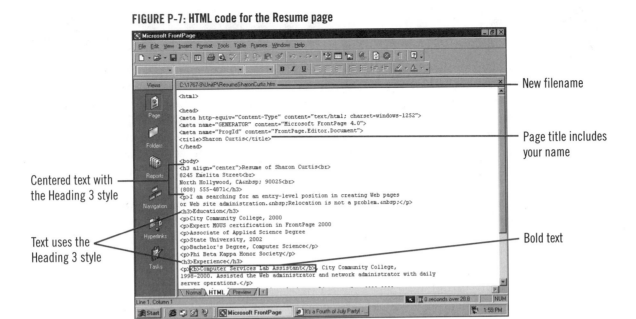

New filename

Page title includes your name

Centered text with the Heading 3 style

Text uses the Heading 3 style

Bold text

FIGURE P-8: Resume page in a browser

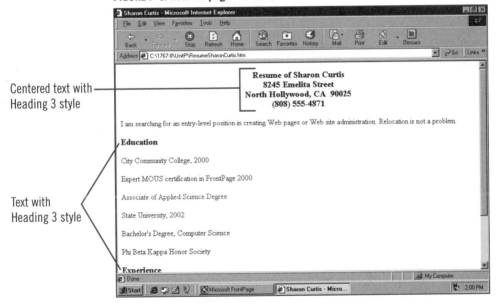

Centered text with Heading 3 style

Text with Heading 3 style

HTML tags that must appear in all Web pages

When you create a new Web page in Normal Page View, the page does not appear to have any content—you create a blank Web page. However, that "blank" Web page actually contains HTML code that identifies the file as an HTML document, describes the character set used by the page, and identifies the beginning and end of the HTML document as well as the beginning and end of the body of the page.

FrontPage automatically includes this code for you when you create a new Web page. Where you go from there is up to you—the only requirement is for you to enter the content of the Web page within the body tags. In Web pages created in FrontPage, a line of code is added to identify the editor that created the page. The editor for FrontPage 2000 is called Microsoft FrontPage 4.0.

FrontPage 2000

FrontPage 2000

Nesting HTML Code

In addition to changing the properties of a tag, you can also add HTML tags inside other HTML tags. These tags are called nested tags. For example, you can use nested tags to nest a table within another table or to nest a list within another list. In FrontPage, you can create bulleted and numbered lists. A bulleted list is also called an **unordered list**; the HTML tags that create an unordered list are <ul> and </ul>. Each bullet in the list uses the <li> and </li> tags to indicate one line. A numbered list is also called an **ordered list**; the HTML tags that create an ordered list are <ol> and </ol>. The nested tags are called the **inner tags** and they are nested within the **outer tags**. The browser reads the outer tags first, and then it reads the inner tags. Sharon shows her students the code for a bulleted list with nested numbered lists, as shown in Figure P-9. Sharon asks her students to create a bulleted list in the Web page and to nest a numbered list within that bulleted list.

1. Return to FrontPage

The Resume page appears in HTML Page View. Use Figures P-9, P-10, and P-11 and the line numbers on the status bar to complete the steps in this lesson.

2. Click after the </h3> tag in line 17, press **[Enter]**, then type <ul>

The <ul> tag is the opening tag for the bulleted (unordered) list.

3. Replace the <p> tag at the beginning of line 19 with <li>, press **[End]**, then type </li>

The <li> and </li> tags enclose each item in the list. When the <li> and </li> tags appear within the <ul> and </ul> tags, the browser creates a bullet character at the beginning of each line.

4. Press **[Enter]**, type <ol>, replace the <p> tag at the beginning of line 21 with <li>, press **[End]**, type </li>, then replace the <p> tag at the beginning of line 22 with <li>, press **[End]**, type </li>, press **[Enter]**, then type </ol>

The HTML code now contains the opening tag for the bulleted (unordered) list, one item in the bulleted list, the opening and closing tags for the first nested numbered list, and two items in the nested numbered list. When the <li> and </li> tags appear within the <ol> and </ol> tags, the browser automatically adds numbers to the beginning of each line, beginning with the number 1 and continuing sequentially.

QuickTip

The HTML tags
<ul>...</ul>,
<ol>...</ol>, and
<li>...</li> are two-sided
tags. Make sure that you
type the opening and closing
tags for each.

5. Continue to change your HTML code to match the bracketed code shown in Figure P-10

The HTML code now contains the second item in the bulleted list, the opening and closing tags for the second nested numbered list, two items in the second nested numbered list, and the closing tags for the second nested numbered list and the bulleted list.

6. Click the **Save button** 🖫 on the Standard toolbar, then click the **Preview in Browser button** 🖫 on the Standard toolbar

The Web page appears in Figure P-11. You created two nested numbered lists within a bulleted list.

7. Return to FrontPage

FIGURE P-9: **HTML code and browser output for a bulleted list with nested numbered lists**

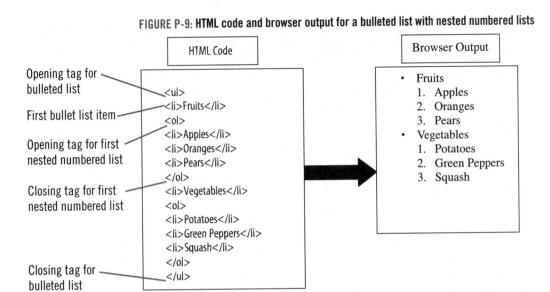

Opening tag for bulleted list

First bullet list item

Opening tag for first nested numbered list

Closing tag for first nested numbered list

Closing tag for bulleted list

HTML Code

```
<ul>
<li>Fruits</li>
<ol>
<li>Apples</li>
<li>Oranges</li>
<li>Pears</li>
</ol>
<li>Vegetables</li>
<ol>
<li>Potatoes</li>
<li>Green Peppers</li>
<li>Squash</li>
</ol>
</ul>
```

Browser Output

- Fruits
  1. Apples
  2. Oranges
  3. Pears
- Vegetables
  1. Potatoes
  2. Green Peppers
  3. Squash

FIGURE P-10: **HTML code for the Resume page**

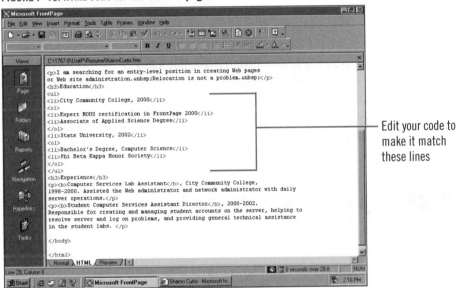

Edit your code to make it match these lines

FIGURE P-11: **Resume page with nested lists**

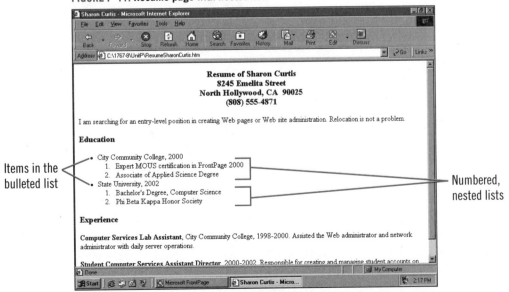

Items in the bulleted list

Numbered, nested lists

Creating a Hyperlink

When you use FrontPage to create a hyperlink, the Web page that contains the hyperlink is a **source document** and the target of the hyperlink is a **destination**. For example, if a link on a Web site's home page opens a page named Search.htm, then the home page is the source document and Search.htm is the destination. The HTML tag that creates a hyperlink is the **a** tag, where the "a" stands for anchor. When a hyperlink opens a destination outside of the current Web page, the HTML code is <a href="filename.gif">Hyperlink Name</a>, where *filename.gif* is the destination of the hyperlink and *Hyperlink Name* is the text in the Web page that contains the hyperlink. A hyperlink that uses the <a href=""> tag can include a URL as its destination of the hyperlink. You can also create a hyperlink to an anchor within a Web page or to another Web page. A hyperlink that appears in the same Web page is called a **bookmark**. The HTML code for a bookmark is <a name="location">Hyperlink Name</a>, where *location* is the name of the anchor and *Hyperlink Name* is the text in the Web page that contains the hyperlink. ✐ Sharon asks her students to create a hyperlink using the "MOUS certification" text in the numbered list to link this text to the Web site for the Microsoft Office User Specialist exam so prospective employers can learn about the MOUS program.

Steps

1. Locate the text **MOUS certification** in line 21, then click the insertion point to the left of the "M" in MOUS

2. Type **<a href="http://www.mous.net">**
   The opening tag for the hyperlink is inserted to the left of the "MOUS" text. The text in quotation marks is the URL for the MOUS Web site.

3. Click the insertion point after the "n" in certification, then type **</a>**
   The closing tag for the hyperlink, as shown in Figure P-12, appears to the right of the "certification" text. The hyperlink is complete. The text between the <a href="URL"> and </a> tags is the hyperlink's name in the Web page.

QuickTip
The browser changes the hyperlink's color to blue (or to whatever color it is configured to change it to) automatically. You do not need to do anything to the HTML code to make this color change.

4. Click the **Save button** 🖫 on the Standard toolbar, then click the **Preview in Browser button** 🔍 on the Standard toolbar
   The hyperlink appears in the Web page as blue, underlined text, which indicates that it is a hyperlink.

5. Point to the **hyperlink** that you just created
   The URL for the hyperlink appears in the status bar, as shown in Figure P-13. Clicking this hyperlink opens the MOUS home page.

6. Return to FrontPage

FIGURE P-12: HTML code to create a hyperlink to a Web site

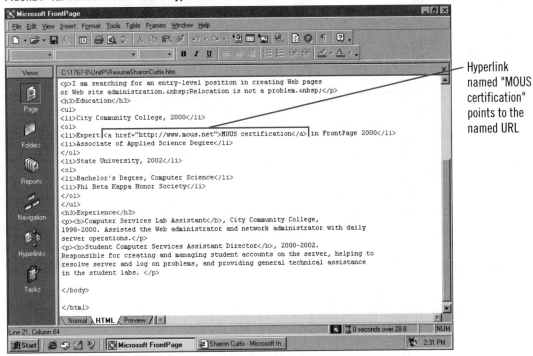

Hyperlink named "MOUS certification" points to the named URL

FIGURE P-13: Resume page with a hyperlink added

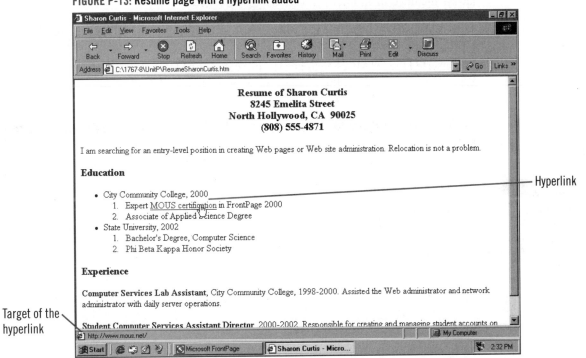

Hyperlink

Target of the hyperlink

FrontPage 2000

Inserting a Horizontal Line and a Picture

When you need to create sections in a Web page, you can use the <hr> tag to create a horizontal line (or horizontal rule) in a page. The <hr> tag is a one-sided tag. You can also insert a picture in an HTML document using the <img src> tag. The <img src> tag can contain just the file-name of the picture that you want to insert, or it can contain properties to describe the width and height of the picture (in pixels), an alternative tag (which displays the picture's name when the pointer points to it), an align property to indicate its alignment on the page (left, right, or centered), and any special effects (such as a washed out appearance). If the file for the picture is saved in the same folder as the Web page in which it will be displayed, you don't need to indicate a path to the file. However, if the picture is saved in a different folder, you need to specify the complete path to the file. A **broken link**, which is an empty box with a small red "x" icon in it, appears on a Web page when the browser cannot locate a picture. Sharon asks her students to insert a horizontal line and a picture in the Web page.

Steps

QuickTip

To create a new line in a Web page, you must enter tags such as <p> and </p> or <h1> and </h1>. Pressing [Enter] in HTML Page View does not create a new line in the Web page; it only creates a new line in the code, which make the code easier to read.

1. Click at the end of line 14 in the HTML code (this line contains the phone number), then press **[Enter]**

A new, blank line is created in the HTML document.

2. Type **<hr>**, then click the **Preview tab**

A horizontal line appears below the heading.

3. Click the **HTML tab**, press **[Enter]**, then on line 16 type ** **

The picture will be centered on a new line below the horizontal line. Notice that the code to align the picture is included in the opening tag for a new paragraph. The align property is always included in another tag, such as <p> or <h1>.

4. Type **<img src="Internet.gif" alt="Web site administration and creation"> ** on the same line (line 16)

You inserted the HTML code to insert a picture named Internet.gif, as shown in Figure P-14. When the user points to the picture, the alternative text "Web site administration and creation" will appear as a ScreenTip.

5. Click the **Save button** 🖫 on the Standard toolbar, then click the **Preview in Browser button** 🔍 on the Standard toolbar

The page opens in a browser.

Trouble?

If the picture or ScreenTip does not appear as expected, change your HTML code so it matches the same lines of code in Figure P-14.

6. Point to the picture

The text that you entered using the alt property of the <img src> tag appears as a ScreenTip, as shown in Figure P-15.

7. Return to FrontPage

FIGURE P-14: **HTML code to add a horizontal line and picture**

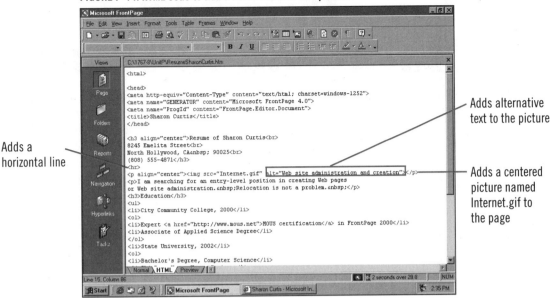

Adds a
horizontal line

Adds alternative
text to the picture

Adds a centered
picture named
Internet.gif to
the page

FIGURE P-15: **Resume page after adding a horizontal line and picture**

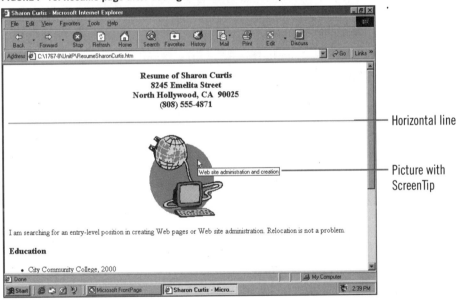

Horizontal line

Picture with
ScreenTip

Reusing code from Web pages on the Internet

Anyone with a browser can view the HTML code in a Web page. When you view the HTML code, you are opening a text file, which can be easily copied and pasted into another document. However, U.S. Copyright laws prohibit people from copying and pasting—or even copying and adapting—content from a Web page and reproducing it on their own Web sites. Even if you do not see a "Copyright 2001" or a similar statement on a Web page, you still cannot reproduce or adapt content, pictures, or a specific design from a Web page without the express written permission of the site's owner. You can, however, copy code to create a specific element in a Web page, such as an animated transition, because the HTML code that you would write to create the same animated transition would be exactly the same as what you might find in another Web page.

FrontPage 2000

Inserting a Background Picture

A background picture is a picture file that the browser applies to the background of a Web page. You can use a background color in a Web page, as well, by specifying the HTML code for a color. When you use a background picture or color in a Web page, make sure that the readability of the text is maintained. Sometimes after applying a background picture or color to a Web page, you will need to adjust the colors of the fonts used in the page to make them lighter or darker, depending on the appearance of the background picture or color. When using a background picture in a Web page, you must specify a path to the picture if it is not stored in the same folder as the HTML document. ✎ Sharon asks her students to insert a background picture in the HTML code for the Resume page.

Steps

1. Scroll up the page as necessary, click the insertion point on line 9 (the blank line under the </head> tag), then press **[Enter]**

   A new, blank line is created in the code.

2. Type **<body background="background.gif">**

   The HTML code that inserts a background picture appears as the first item after the </head> tag. This HTML code, as shown in Figure P-16, identifies the background picture as background.gif in the current folder.

3. Click the **Save button** 🖫 on the Standard toolbar, then click the **Preview in Browser button** 🔍 on the Standard toolbar

   The page opens in a browser, as shown in Figure P-17. The background picture is light in color and the text in the page is easy to read.

4. Close your browser

5. Close FrontPage

FIGURE P-16: HTML code to add a background picture

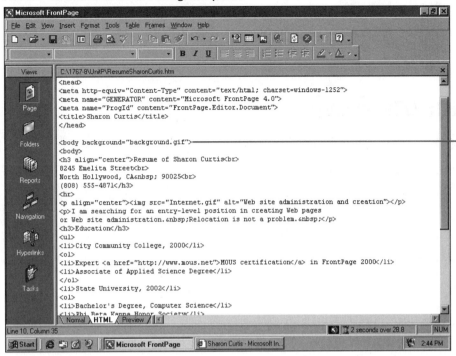

Adds a background picture named background.gif to the page

FIGURE P-17: Resume page after adding a background picture

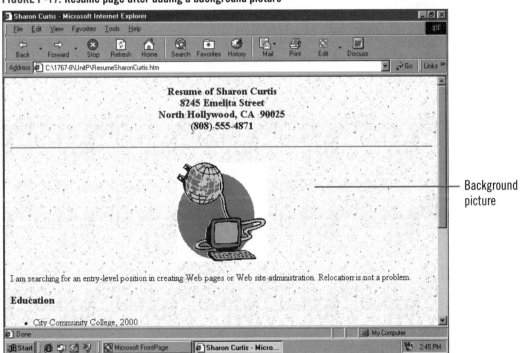

Background picture

Practice

► Concepts Review

Label each of the elements of the Microsoft FrontPage window shown in Figure P-18.

FIGURE P-18

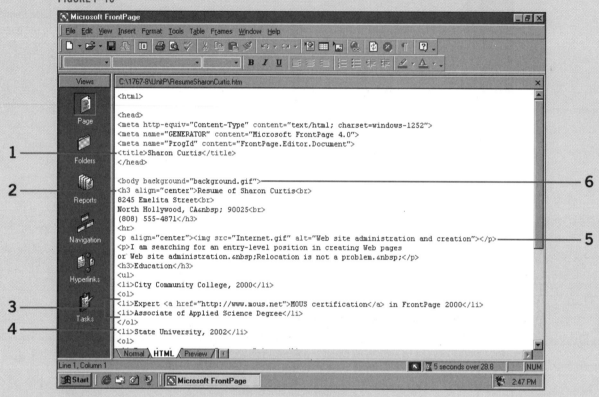

Match each of the terms with the statement that describes it.

7. ...
8. <body>...</body>
9.
10. <hr>
11. <ol>...</ol>
12. <ul>...</ul>

a. Creates a bulleted list
b. Creates a horizontal line in a Web page
c. Creates a line break in a Web page
d. Creates a numbered list
e. Creates bold text
f. Encloses the content of the Web page

Select the best answer from the list of choices.

13. **An HTML tag is**
    a. A container that tells a browser how to display text that follows it.
    b. A container that tells a browser how to display text that appears within it.
    c. Both a and b are correct.
    d. None of the above.

14. **The HTML tag that creates bold text in a Web page is a**
    a. One-sided tag.
    b. Two-sided tag.
    c. Property of the font tag.
    d. Property of the body tag.

15. **In the HTML code <h3 align="right">Whimsey Company</h3>, "right" is a(n) _____ of the h3 tag.**
    a. characteristic
    b. function
    c. opening tag
    d. property

16. **The HTML code to apply a background picture to a Web page is**
    a. <img src="picture.gif">.
    b. <body="picture.gif">.
    c. <body background="picture.gif">.
    d. None of the above.

17. **The HTML code to display the text "Hello World!" as a left-aligned heading with the Heading 4 style is**
    a. <h4 align="left"Hello World!>.
    b. <p align="left">Hello World!</p>.
    c. <h4><align="left">Hello World!</align></h4>.
    d. <h4 align="left">Hello World!</h4>.

▶ Skills Review

1. **Understand HTML.**
    a. Start FrontPage, create a new Web page, then change to HTML Page View.
    b. On the first line after the <body> tag, type the <p> tag, your first and last names, and then type the </p> tag.
    c. On the next line, type the following line of text and then change it to bold and underlined: **Microsoft FrontPage 2000 Illustrated Complete**. (*Hint*: Make sure that you type the <p> and </p> tags so the text appears on a new line.)
    d. On the next line, type the HTML code to create a hyperlink named "Click here" that opens a file named *here.htm*. This file is non-existent. Assume it is stored in the same folder as the source document.
    e. On the next line, type the HTML code to create the text "This is a Heading" in a Web page that is right-aligned and uses the Heading 2 style.
    f. On the next line, type the HTML code to create the following list and nested lists:
       - Unit 1
         1. Lesson 1
         2. Lesson 2
       - Unit 2
         1. Lesson 1
         2. Lesson 2
    g. Save the page using the filename *Practice[insert your name here]* and the title **This is my practice document** in the UnitP folder on your Project Disk. Preview the page in a browser. If necessary, return to FrontPage and make any necessary corrections. Use FrontPage to print the HTML code for the document and use a browser to print the Web page.
    h. Close your browser, return to FrontPage, and then close the Practice page.

2. **Use Reveal Tags to show HTML code.**
    a. In FrontPage, open the FP P-3 file from the UnitP folder on your Project Disk.
    b. Use the Save As command on the File menu to save the file as *Events[insert your name here]* in the UnitP folder.
    c. Reveal the HTML tags for the Web page using Normal Page View. Which tags appear in the page?
    d. Turn off the display of the tags in Normal Page View.

3. Work in HTML Page View.
   a. Change to HTML Page View.
   b. Change the Web page's title to your first and last names.
   c. Edit the HTML code in line 13 so the text "Join our Kids' Club" is centered and uses the Heading 1 style.
   d. Click line 30 (the blank line above the </body> tag at the bottom of the page). Create a new paragraph using the <p> and </p> tags. On the new line use the Insert Component button on the Standard toolbar to add a hover button to the page. Enter the button text **Kids' Club** and use the default settings.
   e. Save the page, then preview the page using the Preview tab. (*Note*: When previewing your pages, return to HTML Page View and correct any problems, then save and preview the page again.)

4. Edit a Web page in HTML Page View.
   a. Return to HTML Page View.
   b. Change the HTML code in line 14 to format the word "free" as bold, italic text.
   c. Change the HTML code in line 16 to format the word "each" as italic text.
   d. Change the HTML code for the text "Membership is free." so it appears on its own line and uses the Heading 2 style. (*Hint*: Click to the right of the ending period, press [Enter], then change the text to use the <h2> and </h2> tags. Delete the extra space created at the beginning of the next line to the left of the word "To".)
   e. Change the HTML code for the "As a Kids' Club member" line (line 26) so it uses the Heading 3 style.
   f. Change the HTML code for the four lines under the heading that you just created so they appear as a bulleted list.
   g. Save the page, then preview the page using the Preview tab.

5. Nest HTML code.
   a. Return to HTML Page View.
   b. Change the HTML code for the lines that contain the text "Name," "Address," "Date of birth," "General information," and "Parents' names and phone numbers" to appear as items in a bulleted list. (*Hint*: Add the opening and closing tags for the bulleted list on new lines above and below the first and last items in the list. Then add the tags for each item in the bulleted list.)
   c. Change the HTML code for the lines that contain the text "Emergency contact name and phone number," "Any known food, plant, or insect allergies," and "Restricted activities" to appear as items in a nested, numbered list. (*Hint*: Add the opening and closing tags for the numbered list on new lines above and below the first and last item in the list. Then add the tags for each item in the numbered list.)
   d. Save the page, then preview the page using the Preview tab.

6. Create a hyperlink.
   a. Edit the HTML code for the word "store" (in line 32; the first item in the bulleted list under the heading that uses the Heading 3 style) to create a hyperlink that points to the URL http://www.course.com/illustrated/MediaLoft/storese.html.
   b. Save the page, then preview the page using the Preview tab.

7. Insert a horizontal line and a picture.
   a. Insert a horizontal line below the centered heading at the top of the page.
   b. Insert a horizontal line above the heading "As a Kids' Club member…" in the middle of the page.
   c. Create a new, centered line between the heading and horizontal line at the top of the page.
   d. Insert the picture Logo.gif from the UnitP folder on your Project Disk on the new centered line. (*Hint*: Because the Logo.gif file is stored in the same folder as the Events page, you do not need to specify a path for the file.)
   e. Save the page, then preview the page using the Preview tab.

8. Insert a background picture.
   a. On the line below the </head> tag at the top of the page, create the HTML code to insert a background picture named Hands.gif in the Web page. (*Hint*: Because the Hands.gif file is stored in the same folder as the Events page, you do not need to specify a path for the file.)
   b. Save the page, then preview it in a browser.

c. Return to FrontPage HTML View and make whatever changes are necessary. Save your changes, then preview the page in a browser again. Use your browser to print the page. Close your browser.

d. Return to FrontPage HTML Page View, print the HTML code, then close FrontPage.

▶ Independent Challenges

1. The city of Nassau Bay needs to add a page to its Web site that identifies the materials that the city's sanitation department can recycle from the curbside. The Marketing Department will advertise the new recycling program and provide the URL to the page to help residential customers know which materials they can recycle. They ask you to create the Web page shown in Figure P-19.

To complete this independent challenge:

a. Start FrontPage, then open the FP P-4 file from the UnitP folder on your Project Disk.

b. Use the Save As command on the File menu to save the file as *Nassau[insert your name here]* in the UnitP folder.

c. Change to HTML Page View.

d. Change the HTML code for the text that will appear at the top of the Web page to centered and the Heading 1 style.

e. Change the HTML code to create the bold text in the first paragraph.

f. Change the HTML code for the text "Need a container" to left-aligned and the Heading 2 style.

g. Create the fire station hyperlink shown in Figure P-19 to the file stations.htm. (*Hint*: Assume that the file is in the same folder. This file does not actually exist.)

FIGURE P-19

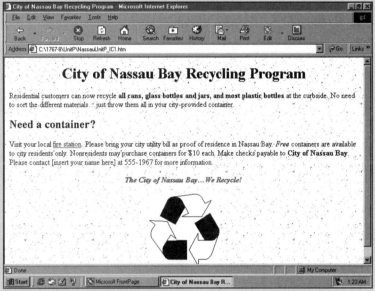

h. Change the HTML code for the word "Free" in the second paragraph to italic.

i. Change the HTML code for the text "City of Nassau Bay" in the second paragraph to bold.

j. Change the text "[insert your name here]" in the second paragraph to your first and last names.

k. Change the HTML code for the text "The City of Nassau Bay…We Recycle!" to bold, italic, blue, and centered. (*Hint*: Use the align property to change the line to centered. The align property should appear in the opening <p> tag. Nest the tags to change the text to bold, blue, and italics within the <p> and </p> tags. The color code for blue text is "#0000FF".)

l. Create the HTML code to insert the Recycle.gif picture in the correct position. Add your first and last names as alternative text for this picture.

m. Create the HTML code to insert the Speckles.gif file as the background picture.

n. Save the page, then preview it in a browser. If necessary, return to FrontPage and make any necessary corrections. Save your changes and then preview the page in a browser again.

o. Use your browser to print the page, then close your browser.

p. Use FrontPage to print the HTML code, then close FrontPage.

2. Your dog Scout has several canine pals who play together in the park. Every time you visit the park, someone asks you about having a Boxer and where to find one. You decide to create a Boxer enthusiast Web page, which you plan to post to the Web. In the future, you hope to collect information from other Boxer owners in the country in order to create a site that addresses topics such as breeding, health conditions, training, feeding, and general hints for raising a Boxer.

To complete this independent challenge:

a. Start FrontPage, then open the FP P-5 file from the UnitP folder on your Project Disk.

b. Use the Save As command on the File menu to save the file as *Boxer[insert your name here]* in the UnitP folder.

c. Change to HTML Page View.

d. Change the HTML code for the "Welcome to the Boxer Web Site!" text to the Heading 1 style and centered.

e. On a new, centered line below the heading that you just created, insert the picture Scout.jpg from the UnitP folder.

f. Change the HTML code for lines that contain the text "Boxers and Your Family," "Healthcare," "Breed Specifications," and "Character and Temperament" to items in a bulleted list.

g. Change the HTML code for the lines that contain the text "Relationships with children," "Meeting strangers," "Grooming and bathing," "Nutrition," and "Exercise" to be items in two separate numbered, nested lists under the bulleted item above them.

h. Change the HTML code for the hyperlinks in the chart to point to the hyperlinked file indicated (these files do not actually exist; create the hyperlinks as if the files are stored in the same directory as the Boxer.htm file).

i. As the last line before the </body> tag, type **Web page prepared by [insert your name here]**.

j. Save the page, then preview it in a browser. If necessary, return to FrontPage and make any necessary corrections.

k. Use your browser to print the page, then close your browser.

l. Use FrontPage to print the HTML code, then close FrontPage.

hyperlink name	linked file
Relationships with children	children.htm
Meeting strangers	strangers.htm
Grooming and bathing	grooming.htm
Nutrition	nutrition.htm
Exercise	exercise.htm
Breed Specifications	http://www.akc.org/breeds/recbreeds/boxer.cfm
Character and Temperament	character.htm

3. You work for a company that provides health insurance. Many patients suffer from common, chronic conditions. Research has shown that patients are better able to care for themselves when they are properly and thoroughly educated in how to care for themselves. You decide to add a Web page to the company's Web site that lists hyperlinks to Web sites that provide information about the following chronic conditions: seasonal allergies, cholesterol management, and childhood ear infections. You will create the links for the Seasonal Allergies topic and insert "under construction" icons for the other two topics so they will be ready to go when you complete your research.

To complete this independent challenge:

a. Start FrontPage, open a new, blank page in Page View, then save it using the filename *Health[insert your name here]* and the page title **Common Health Conditions** in the UnitP folder on your Project Disk.

b. Change to HTML Page View, then change the page title to your first and last names.

c. Within the <body> and </body> tags, type **Common Health Conditions**. Change the HTML code for this text to centered and the Heading 1 style.

d. On a new line below the heading that you just created, enter one or two sentences to describe the purpose of this page and to inform readers that the page will be updated frequently. (*Note*: In HTML Page View, as you type text it might cause the window to scroll to the right instead of wrapping text to the next line. Your text will appear correctly in a browser.)

e. On a new line, type the text **Seasonal Allergies** and change it to the Heading 2 style.

f. On a new line, type the text **Treatment and Management**, then change it to a hyperlink with the URL http://drkoop.com/conditions/allergies/page_5_352.asp.

g. On a new line, type the text **About Allergies**, then change it to a hyperlink with the URL http://www.saonet.ucla.edu/health/healthed/handouts/alergy.htm.

h. On a new line, type the text **National Institutes of Health**, then change it to a hyperlink with the URL http://www.hoptechno.com/book46.htm.

i. Change the code for the three lines that contain hyperlinks to a bulleted list.

j. On a new line, type **Cholesterol Management**, then change this text to the Heading 2 style. On the next line, insert the undercon.gif file from the UnitP folder. Add the alternative text **Coming Soon!** to the picture.

k. On a new line, type **Childhood Ear Infections**, then change this text to the Heading 2 style. Create a new line under the heading, select the HTML code that creates the under construction picture that you just inserted, click the Copy button on the toolbar, then paste this text on the new line below the Childhood Ear Infections heading.

l. On a new line below the picture, insert a hover button with the text **Home Page** and the default properties.

m. Change the hover button effect to use the fill effect. (*Hint*: Edit the <param> tag to change the value property to "fill.")

n. On a new line below the picture that you inserted below the Childhood Ear Infections picture, type **Web page prepared by [insert your name here]**. Change this text to bold.

o. Save the page, then preview it in a browser. If necessary, return to FrontPage and make any necessary corrections. Save your changes and then preview the page in a browser again.

p. Use your browser to print the page, then close your browser.

q. Use FrontPage to print the HTML code, then close FrontPage.

4. One of the best ways to expand your knowledge of HTML code is to look at the code another Web developer used to create a page or an element in a page. In Microsoft Internet Explorer and Netscape Navigator, you can use a menu command to open a separate window that displays the code for the page. If you examine the code for a page in a commercial Web site, you will find many HTML tags with which you are familiar. You will also find the code for scripts and Java applets. It takes many lines of code to animate content in a Web page or to create a form that accepts user input.

To complete this independent challenge:

a. Connect to the Internet.

b. Go to http://www.course.com, navigate to the Student Online Companion for this book, then click the link for Unit P.

c. Click the link to open the Web page. If you are using Internet Explorer, click View on the menu bar, then click Source. A Notepad program window opens and displays the HTML code for the Web page that appears in the browser. (*Note*: If you are using Netscape Navigator, click View on the menu bar, then click Page Source. Press [Ctrl][A] to select the HTML code, press [Ctrl][C] to copy it to the Clipboard, then close the Source window. Start Word, WordPad, or Notepad, then press [Ctrl][V] to paste the code into the document.)

d. Click the first line of the document, type your first and last names, then press [Enter]. Click File on the menu bar, then click Print to print the HTML code, then close the window that contains the HTML code without saving changes.

e. Close your browser and close your dial-up connection, if necessary.

f. On the printout, circle the different HTML tags that you recognize and indicate their functions in the page margins.

g. When you are finished, hand in your printout.

▶ Visual Workshop

Use HTML Page View in FrontPage to create the Web page shown in Figure P-20. Save it using the filename *Golf[insert your name here]* and the title **Pee-Wee Golf Academy** in the UnitP folder on your Project Disk. The pictures and background picture are saved as Driving.jpg, Putting.jpg, and Confetti.gif, respectively, in the UnitP folder on your Project Disk. The color for the heading is "#000080". When you are finished, use FrontPage to print the HTML code for the page, preview the page in a browser and print it, then close your browser and FrontPage.

FIGURE P-20

Centered Heading 1 style

Centered Heading 2 style

Centered Heading 3 style

FrontPage 2000 MOUS Certification Objectives

Below is a list of the Microsoft Office User Specialist program objectives for Core FrontPage 2000 skills showing where each MOUS objective is covered in the Lessons and the Practice. This table lists the Core MOUS certification skills covered in the units in this book. For more information on which Illustrated titles meet MOUS certification, please see the inside cover of this book.

Standardized Coding Number	Activity	Lesson page where skill is covered	Location in lesson where skill is covered	Practice
FP2000.1	Create a new Web site			
FP2000.1.1	Save a FrontPage Web	FRONTPAGE A-8	Step 1	Skills Review 2
FP2000.1.2	Create a Web site using a Web wizard	FRONTPAGE A-8	Step 1	Skills Review 2
FP2000.1.3	Create a Web site using a Web template	FRONTPAGE A-9		Independent Challenges 3 and 4 Visual Workshop
FP2000.2	Open and edit an existing FrontPage-based Web site			
FP2000.2.1	Open an existing FrontPage Web	FRONTPAGE B-4	Step 2	This skill is practiced in every unit.
FP2000.2.2	Modify and save changes to the Web site	FRONTPAGE B-6	Steps 1–8	Skills Review 2, 5–7 Independent Challenges 1–3 Visual Workshop
FP2000.3	Apply and edit a Theme across the entire Web site			
FP2000.3.1	Apply a Theme to entire Web site	FRONTPAGE J-12	Steps 1–6	Skills Review 6 Independent Challenges 1–4
FP2000.3.2	Apply a custom Theme across entire Web site	FRONTPAGE J-12 FRONTPAGE J-14	Steps 1–6 Steps 1–9	Skills Review 7 Independent Challenges 1 and 3 Visual Workshop
FP2000.4	Add a new Web page			
FP2000.4.1	Create and Preview a new Web page using a FrontPage page template or wizard	FRONTPAGE B-10	Steps 1–10	Skills Review 4 Visual Workshop
FP2000.4.2	Create a new page within Page View	FRONTPAGE B-10	Steps 1–5	Skills Review 4 Visual Workshop
FP2000.5	Open, view and rename Web page			
FP2000.5.1	View a Web document in Normal, HTML and Preview view	FRONTPAGE B-9	Clues To Use	Independent Challenges 1 and 3
FP2000.5.2	Open an Office document in a FrontPage Web	FRONTPAGE L-14	Steps 1–7	Skills Review 7 Independent Challenge 3 Visual Workshop

Standardized Coding Number	Activity	Lesson page where skill is covered	Location in lesson where skill is covered	Practice
FP2000.5.3	Rename page title and change page URL	FRONTPAGE C-2 FRONTPAGE N-12	Steps 3–4 Step 2	Unit C: No practice Unit N: Independent Challenge 2 Visual Workshop
FP2000.6	**Import text and images onto Web page**			
FP2000.6.1	Add or import images into a Web page (automatically converted to GIF/JPEG)	FRONTPAGE D-2 FRONTPAGE D-3	Steps 3–8 Clues To Use	Skills Review 1 Independent Challenges 1, 3, and 4 Visual Workshop
FP2000.6.2	Add or import text to a Web page (automatically converted to HTML)	FRONTPAGE I-2 FRONTPAGE O-4	Steps 1–7 Steps 1–6	Unit I: Skills Review 1 Independent Challenges 1 and 4 Unit O: Skills Review 2
FP2000.6.3	Add or import elements from a Web site to a FrontPage Web	FRONTPAGE C-14	Steps 1–9	Skills Review 6
FP2000.7	**Type and format text and paragraphs and create hyperlinks**			
FP2000.7.1	Type and format text/fonts on a Web page	FRONTPAGE C-8	Steps 1–7	Skills Review 3 Independent Challenges 1–3 Visual Workshop
FP2000.7.2	Add multi-level bulleted or numbered lists to Web page	FRONTPAGE P-10	Steps 2–6	Skills Review 1, 5 Independent Challenges 2 and 3
FP2000.7.3	Format bulleted or numbered lists	FRONTPAGE C-10	Steps 4–7	Skills Review 4 Independent Challenges 1–3 Visual Workshop
FP2000.7.4	Add hyperlinks pointing to: an existing page in the current site, the WWW, or a brand new page	FRONTPAGE D-8	Steps 2–4	Skills Review 3–8 Independent Challenges 1, 2, and 4
FP2000.7.5	Use the Format Painter to apply formats	FRONTPAGE I-9	Clues To Use	No practice
FP2000.7.6	Use the Clipboard	FRONTPAGE I-2 FRONTPAGE O-4	Steps 1–7 Steps 1–6	Unit I: Skills Review 1 Independent Challenges 1 and 4 Unit O: Skills Review 2
FP2000.8	**Edit images, apply image effects; create hotspots**			
FP2000.8.1	Rotate, flip, bevel, or resize images on a Web page	FRONTPAGE E-8	Steps 1–8	Skills Review 4
FP2000.8.2	Add text over image	FRONTPAGE E-16	Steps 2–3	No practice
FP2000.8.3	Create a hotspot (clickable imagemap)	FRONTPAGE E-12	Steps 1–8	Skills Review 6

Standardized Coding Number	Activity	Lesson page where skill is covered	Location in lesson where skill is covered	Practice
FP2000.9	**Create and edit tables on a Web page**			
FP2000.9.1	Create tables on a Web page	FRONTPAGE F-2	Steps 7–11	Skills Review 1 Independent Challenge 1 Visual Workshop
FP2000.9.2	Erase or delete table rows or columns	FRONTPAGE F-8	Steps 1–4	No practice
FP2000.9.3	Draw or add table rows or columns	FRONTPAGE F-6	Steps 1–5	Skills Review 3 Independent Challenge 1 Visual Workshop
FP2000.9.4	Resize tables and cells	FRONTPAGE I-2 FRONTPAGE I-4	Steps 7–9 Steps 1–8	Skills Review 1, 2 Independent Challenges 1, 3, and 4 Visual Workshop
FP2000.9.5	Select and merge table cells	FRONTPAGE F-8	Steps 5–6	Skills Review 4 Independent Challenge 1
FP2000.10	**Insert dynamic, Active Elements and FrontPage components on a Web page**			
FP2000.10.1	Add a Hit Counter to Web page	FRONTPAGE H-2	Steps 4–6	Skills Review 1 Independent Challenge 3
FP2000.10.2	Format Page Transition for Web page	FRONTPAGE E-16	Steps 4–5	Skills Review 8
FP2000.10.3	Add or edit scrolling Marquee text on a Web page	FRONTPAGE E-14	Steps 2–7	Skills Review 7 Independent Challenge 3 Visual Workshop
FP2000.10.4	Add a Search Form to Web page	FRONTPAGE H-4 FRONTPAGE N-16	Steps 1–8 Steps 1–9	Unit H: Skills Review 2 Independent Challenge 2 Visual Workshop Unit N: Skills Review 8 Independent Challenge 2
FP2000.11	**View and organize Web site documents**			
FP2000.11.1	View a Web site in Reports View, Hyperlinks View, or Folders View	FRONTPAGE A-12	Steps 1–5	Skills Review 4 Independent Challenge 3
FP2000.11.2	View your Web site structure and print it from Navigation View	FRONTPAGE K-12	Steps 1–2	Skills Review 6 Independent Challenges 1–3
FP2000.11.3	Move and organize files using drag and drop in Folders View and Navigation View	FRONTPAGE B-14 FRONTPAGE K-6	Steps 1–3 Steps 1–8	Unit B: Skills Review 5 Independent Challenges 2 and 3 Unit K: Skills Review 3 Independent Challenges 1–3

Standardized Coding Number	Activity	Lesson page where skill is covered	Location in lesson where skill is covered	Practice
FP2000.12	**Manage a Web site (including all files, pages and hyperlinks) and automatically keep contents up-to-date**			
FP2000.12.1	Check spelling on a page or across a Web site	FRONTPAGE B-6 FRONTPAGE O-3	Steps 5–8 Clues To Use	Unit B: No practice Unit O: Skills Review 1
FP2000.12.2	Change file name in Folders View and update its hyperlinks	FRONTPAGE K-8	Steps 1–6	Skills Review 4 Independent Challenges 1 and 3
FP2000.12.3	Verify hyperlinks	FRONTPAGE O-8	Steps 1–5	Skills Review 4 Independent Challenges 1–3
FP2000.12.4	Use Global Find and Replace across a Web site	FRONTPAGE K-10	Steps 1–8	Skills Review 5 Independent Challenges 2 and 3
FP2000.13	**Manage tasks**			
FP2000.13.1	View task history	FRONTPAGE A-10	Clues To Use	Skills Review 3
FP2000.13.2	View and sort tasks in Tasks View	FRONTPAGE A-10	Steps 1–8	Skills Review 3 Independent Challenge 4

FrontPage 2000 Expert MOUS Certification Objectives

Below is a list of the Microsoft Office User Specialist program objectives for Expert FrontPage 2000 skills showing where each MOUS objective is covered in the Lessons and the Practice. This table lists the Expert MOUS certification skills covered in the units in this book. For more information on which Illustrated titles meet MOUS certification, please see the inside cover of this book.

Standardized Coding Number	Activity	Lesson page where skill is covered	Location in lesson where skill is covered	Practice
FP2000E.1	**Create a FrontPage Web using existing resources**			
FP2000E.1.1	Use Import Wizard to import an existing Web site from a file into FrontPage	FRONTPAGE L-4	Steps 2–6	Skills Review 2 Independent Challenges 1–3 Visual Workshop
FP2000E.1.2	Use Import Wizard to import an existing Web site from a URL into FrontPage	FRONTPAGE C-14	Steps 1–9	Skills Review 6
FP2000E.1.3	Modify HTML tags and verify results using Reveal Tags	FRONTPAGE P-4	Steps 4–9	Skills Review 2
FP2000E.1.4	Use buttons and drop-down menus to insert code directly in HTML View	FRONTPAGE P-6	Steps 5–8	Skills Review 3 Independent Challenge 3
FP2000E.2	**Apply and change Themes for an entire Web site and individual Web pages**			
FP2000E.2.1	Select a new Theme and apply to an individual Web page	FRONTPAGE J-16	Steps 1–5	Skills Review 8 Independent Challenges 1–3 Visual Workshop
FP2000E.2.2	Change attributes (Vivid Colors, Active Graphics, Background Image) for a currently selected site-wide Theme	FRONTPAGE J-12	Steps 1–5	Skills Review 6 Independent Challenges 1–3 Visual Workshop
FP2000E.2.3	Create a custom Theme and apply it to an individual Web page	FRONTPAGE J-14	Steps 1–9	Skills Review 8 Independent Challenges 1–3 Visual Workshop

Standardized Coding Number	Activity	Lesson page where skill is covered	Location in lesson where skill is covered	Practice
FP2000E.3	**Create and organize navigational structure for entire Web site**			
FP2000E.3.1	Rename new pages in Navigation View	FRONTPAGE B-14 FRONTPAGE J-4	Step 2 Steps 2–3	Unit B: Skills Review 6 Independent Challenges 1–3 Unit J: Skills Review 2 Independent Challenge 3 Visual Workshop
FP2000E.3.2	Add new pages to Navigation View	FRONTPAGE J-4	Steps 1–3	Skills Review 2 Independent Challenge 3 Visual Workshop
FP2000E.3.3	Add existing pages to Navigation View	FRONTPAGE F-2 FRONTPAGE J-4	Step 4 Step 1	Unit F: No practice Unit J: Skills Review 2 Independent Challenges 1 and 2
FP2000E.3.4	Use drag and drop to organize/re-structure pages in Navigation View	FRONTPAGE F-2 FRONTPAGE J-4	Steps 3–4 Step 1	Unit F: No practice. Unit J: Skills Review 2 Independent Challenges 1–3 Visual Workshop
FP2000E.4	**Modify the Web page layout**			
FP2000E.4.1	Position graphics on a page	FRONTPAGE K-4	Steps 1–7	Skills Review 2 Independent Challenges 2 and 3 Visual Workshop
FP2000E.4.2	Position text on a page	FRONTPAGE K-2	Steps 2–9	Skills Review 1 Independent Challenges 2 and 3 Visual Workshop
FP2000E.5	**Add or edit Shared Borders across entire site and on individual Web pages**			
FP2000E.5.1	Turn off (deselect) site-wide Shared Borders for the current Web page	FRONTPAGE B-16 FRONTPAGE H-8 FRONTPAGE J-8	Step 8 Step 1 Steps 1–5	Unit B: Skills Review 7 Independent Challenges 2 and 3 Unit J: Skills Review 4 Independent Challenge 3 Unit H: Independent Challenge 1
FP2000E.5.2	Edit content within Shared Borders for an entire Web site	FRONTPAGE B-16 FRONTPAGE J-6	Steps 1–4 Steps 1–7	Unit B: Skills Review 7 Independent Challenges 2 and 3 Unit J: Skills Review 3 Independent Challenges 1–3 Visual Workshop

Standardized Coding Number	Activity	Lesson page where skill is covered	Location in lesson where skill is covered	Practice
FP2000E.5.3	Edit content within Shared Borders for current Web page	FRONTPAGE J-8	Steps 1–6	Independent Challenge 3
FP2000E.5.4	Turn on (set) alternate Shared Borders for the current Web page	FRONTPAGE B-16 FRONTPAGE J-8	Steps 1–2 Steps 1–5	Unit B: Skills Review 7 Independent Challenges 2 and 3 Unit J: Independent Challenge 3
FP2000E.6	**Automatically add navigation bars and page banners to Web pages**			
FP2000E.6.1	Add Navigation Bar to the top of a Web page	FRONTPAGE B-12 FRONTPAGE J-10	Steps 6–7, Clues To Use Steps 3–4	Unit B: Skills Review 5 Independent Challenge 2 Unit J: Skills Review 5 Independent Challenge 3
FP2000E.6.2	Add Page Banner to the top of a Web page	FRONTPAGE J-10	Steps 1–2	Skills Review 5 Independent Challenge 3
FP2000E.6.3	Select/change levels of navigational buttons to include in navigation bar on Web page	FRONTPAGE B-12 FRONTPAGE J-10	Clues To Use Step 4	Unit B: Skills Review 5 Independent Challenge 2 Unit J: Skills Review 5 Independent Challenges 1–3 Visual Workshop
FP2000E.7	**Add background elements to Web pages**			
FP2000E.7.1	Add a background image on a Web Page	FRONTPAGE E-4	Steps 1–8	Skills Review 2 Independent Challenge 3 Visual Workshop
FP2000E.8	**Manipulate table contents on a Web page**			
FP2000E.8.1	Center image or text within a table cell	FRONTPAGE I-6	Step 6	Skills Review 3 Independent Challenges 1 and 3
FP2000E.8.2	Add a custom background color or image to an entire table and to individual table cells	FRONTPAGE I-8 FRONTPAGE I-10	Steps 1–8 Step 4	Skills Review 4 Independent Challenges 1 and 3
FP2000E.8.3	Add a table within a table	FRONTPAGE I-10	Steps 1–2	Skills Review 5 Independent Challenge 1

Standardized Coding Number	Activity	Lesson page where skill is covered	Location in lesson where skill is covered	Practice
FP2000E.9	**Enhance or edit a Web page with custom text/hyperlink styles and formatting**			
FP2000E.9.1	View page Estimated Time to Download	FRONTPAGE H-14	Step 4	Skills Review 7
FP2000E.9.2	Resample/ Restore image on Web page	FRONTPAGE I-6	Step 5	Skills Review 3 Independent Challenges 1 and 3
FP2000E.9.3	Format special styles for fonts, paragraphs, and hyperlinks	FRONTPAGE M-12 FRONTPAGE M-14 FRONTPAGE M-16	Steps 1–7 Steps 1–9 Steps 1–9	Skills Review 6–8 Independent Challenges 2 and 3
FP2000E.10	**Customize a Web page with dynamic, Active Elements and FrontPage components**			
FP2000E.10.1	Add Hover Button to Web page	FRONTPAGE H-8	Steps 2–8	Skills Review 4 Independent Challenge 1
FP2000E.10.2	Edit Hover Button transitional effect	FRONTPAGE P-6	Steps 8–9	Independent Challenge 3
FP2000E.10.3	Change FrontPage component properties	FRONTPAGE P-6	Steps 8–9	Independent Challenge 3
FP2000E.10.4	Insert pre-built and Office Web components into a page	FRONTPAGE M-4 FRONTPAGE M-6 FRONTPAGE M-8 FRONTPAGE M-10	Steps 3–9 Steps 1–8 Steps 3–9 Steps 1–6	Skills Review 1–5 Independent Challenges 1 and 2 Visual Workshop
FP2000E11	**Build a Web site for user input**			
FP2000E.11.1	Add text boxes, check boxes, radio buttons, drop down pick lists, and push buttons	FRONTPAGE G-8 FRONTPAGE G-12 FRONTPAGE G-14 FRONTPAGE G-16	Steps 1–6 Steps 1–9 Steps 1–7 Steps 1–8	Skills Review 3–7 Independent Challenges 1–3 Visual Workshop
FP2000E.11.2	Save form to file	FRONTPAGE G-6	Steps 1–5	Skills Review 1–2
FP2000E.11.3	Add Search Form to a Web page	FRONTPAGE H-4	Steps 1–8	Skills Review 1 Independent Challenge 2 Visual Workshop
FP2000E.11.4	Save form to email	FRONTPAGE G-6	Step 6	No practice
FP2000E.11.5	Create a custom form on a Web page	FRONTPAGE G-8 FRONTPAGE G-10 FRONTPAGE G-12 FRONTPAGE G-14 FRONTPAGE G-16	Steps 1–6 Steps 1–8 Steps 1–9 Steps 1–7 Steps 1–8	Skills Review 1–7 Independent Challenges 1–3 Visual Workshop

Standardized Coding Number	Activity	Lesson page where skill is covered	Location in lesson where skill is covered	Practice
FP2000E.12	**Integrate databases**			
FP2000E.12.1	Create a form that sends data to an Access database	FRONTPAGE N-10	Steps 1–10	Skills Review 5 Independent Challenges 2 and 3 Visual Workshop
FP2000E.12.2	Incorporate data access pages into a Web page	FRONTPAGE N-6 FRONTPAGE N-8	Steps 1–9 Steps 1–8	Skills Review 3–4 Independent Challenges 1 and 3
FP2000E.12.3	Incorporate database queries using the Database Results Wizard	FRONTPAGE N-14 FRONTPAGE N-16	Steps 1–7 Steps 1–10	Skills Review 7–8 Independent Challenges 1 and 2
FP2000E.13	**Use collaboration features**			
FP2000E.13.1	Check in and check out FrontPage files	FRONTPAGE L-10 FRONTPAGE L-12	Steps 1–7 Steps 1–8	Skills Review 5–6 Independent Challenges 1 and 2
FP2000E.13.2	Set rights to a FrontPage Web and sub-Webs	FRONTPAGE H-16 FRONTPAGE O-14	Clues To Use Steps 1–6	Unit H: No practice Unit O: Skills Review 7 Independent Challenge 3
FP2000E.14	**Create and edit a Frames Web page**			
FP2000E.14.1	Edit size of existing frames in Frames page using drag and drop of border lines	FRONTPAGE I-14	Step 4	Skills Review 6 Independent Challenge 2 Visual Workshop
FP2000E.14.2	Edit actual content within a frame on the Frames page	FRONTPAGE I-12	Step 2	Skills Review 6 Independent Challenge 2 Visual Workshop
FP2000E.14.3	Create a new Frames page from template or using Frames Wizard	FRONTPAGE F-10 FRONTPAGE I-12	Steps 1–9 Step 1	Unit F: Skills Review 5 Independent Challenges 2 and 3 Unit I: Skills Review 6 Independent Challenge 2 Visual Workshop
FP2000E.14.4	Add target content within a frame	FRONTPAGE F-12	Steps 1–12	Skills Review 6 Independent Challenges 2 and 3

Standardized Coding Number	Activity	Lesson page where skill is covered	Location in lesson where skill is covered	Practice
FP2000E.15	**Publish a Web site**			
FP2000E.15.1	Publish a Web from one server to another	FRONTPAGE O-12	Steps 2–8	Skills Review 6 Independent Challenge 3
FP2000E.15.2	Use FrontPage or Microsoft Personal Web Server as appropriate	FRONTPAGE K-14 FRONTPAGE K-16	Steps 1–9 Steps 1–6	Skills Review 7–8 Independent Challenges 1–3
FP2000E.15.3	Set FrontPage/server permissions as appropriate	FRONTPAGE O-14	Steps 1–6	Skills Review 7 Independent Challenge 3

Project Files List

To complete many of the lessons and practice exercises in this book, students need to use a Project File that is supplied by Course Technology and stored on a Project Disk. Below is a list of the files that are supplied, and the unit or practice exercise to which the files correspond. For information on how to obtain Project Files, please see the inside cover of this book. The following list only includes Project Files that are supplied; it does not include the files students create from scratch or the files students create by revising the supplied files.

Unit	File supplied on Project Disk	Location file is used in unit
Unit A	No files supplied.	
Unit B	No files supplied.	
Unit C	No files supplied.	
Unit D	No files supplied.	
Unit E	No files supplied.	
Unit F	No files supplied.	
Unit G	No files supplied.	
Unit H	No files supplied.	
Unit I	**UnitI folder:**	
	BMW.doc	Lessons
	Books.doc	Skills Review
	Zones.doc	Independent Challenge 1
Unit J	**UnitJ\Ic1 folder:**	Independent Challenge 1
	Bermuda.htm	
	index.htm	
	Italy.htm	
	Orlando.htm	
	UnitJ\Ic2 folder:	Independent Challenge 2
	Honda.htm	
	index.htm	
	Linens.htm	
	Table.htm	
	Toyota.htm	
Unit K	**UnitK folder:**	Lessons
	TX053196.gif	
	UnitK\Sr folder:	Skills Review
	Bd06496_.gif	
	UnitK\Vw folder:	Visual Workshop
	Chicken.gif	
	Frog.gif	
	Lion.gif	

Unit	File supplied on Project Disk	Location file is used in unit
Unit L	**UnitL\Lessons folder:** application.htm apply.doc background.gif collage.gif contact.htm dictionary.htm dotrule.gif index.htm index.htm loantypes.htm rates.htm what.htm whoelse.htm	Lessons
	UnitL/Sr folder: Default.htm Paper.gif Pen.gif Rates.xls request_info.htm rolodex.gif states.htm	Skills Review
	UnitL\Ic1 folder: 15year.htm 30year.htm ARMs.htm conventional.htm Default.htm payment.htm	Independent Challenge 1
	UnitL\Ic2 folder: Default.htm news.htm pr01.htm pr02.htm pr03.htm prod01.htm prod.02.htm prod03.htm products.htm serv01.htm serv02.htm serv03.htm services.htm smallnew.gif toc.htm undercon.gif	Independent Challenge 2

Unit	File supplied on Project Disk	Location file is used in unit
Unit L (cont)	**UnitL\lc3 folder:** April.doc Default.htm Welcome.ppt	Independent Challenge 3
Unit M	**UnitM folder:** chart.htm ChartData.htm Payments.htm Payments.xls PivotTable.htm PivotTable_files folder (includes the files filelist.xml and PivotTable_12850_cachedata.xml) PivotTable.xls SpreadsheetData.htm	Lessons
	UnitM\Sr folder: BudgetData.htm Regions.htm Regions_files folder (includes the files Book3_16515_cachedata.xml and filelist.xml) RegionsData.xls	Skills Review
	UnitM\lc3 folder: Default.htm news.htm pr01.htm pr02.htm pr03.htm serv01.htm serv02.htm services.htm	Independent Challenge 3
Unit N	**UnitN folder:** Lenders.mdb Mortgage.mdb	Lessons Lessons
	Dorm.mdb	Skills Review
	Hospital.mdb	Independent Challenge 1
	Courses.mdb	Independent Challenge 2
	Registration.mdb	Visual Workshop
	UnitN\Sr folder: census.htm Default.htm	Skills Review
	UnitN\lc2 folder: courses.htm Default.htm	Independent Challenge 2

Unit	File supplied on Project Disk	Location file is used in unit
Unit N (cont)	**UnitN\Ic3 folder:** book.htm	Independent Challenge 3
	UnitN\Vw folder: form_submission.htm	Visual Workshop
Unit O	**UnitO folder:** contact.htm dictionary.doc rates.htm Underwriting.doc whoelse.htm	Lessons
	UnitO\Sr folder: 15yr.htm 30yr.htm ARMs.htm city.gif conventional.gif Default.htm frontpag.gif payment.htm sunset.gif	Skills Review
	UnitO\Ic1 folder: AboutUs.htm AngelCake.htm AngelPict.jpg appetizer.htm bd14579_1.gif bd21295_.gif Contact.htm contents.htm Default.htm desserts.htm Employment.htm entrees.htm Feedback.htm fphover.class fphoverx.class franchise.htm Menu.htm Pasta.htm PastaPict.jpg Pecan.htm PecanPict.jpg Pudding.htm PuddingPict.jpg sandwich.htm Search.htm Specials.htm Up.gif	Independent Challenge 1

Unit	File supplied on Project Disk	Location file is used in unit
Unit O (cont)	**UnitO\Ic2 folder:** index.htm legislative_issues.htm tappo.htm	Independent Challenge 2
Unit P	**UnitP folder:** background.gif fireworks.jpg fourth.jpg FP P-1.htm FP P-2.htm Internet.gif	Lessons
	FP P-3.htm Hands.gif Logo.gif	Skills Review
	FP P-4.htm Recycle.gif Speckles.gif	Independent Challenge 1
	FP P-5.htm Scout.jpg	Independent Challenge 2
	Undercon.gif	Independent Challenge 3
	Confetti.gif Driving.jpg Putting.jpg	Visual Workshop

Glossary

a tag The HTML tag that creates a hyperlink.

Absolute positioning A feature that lets you position text, a picture, or another page element in a specific position in a Web page by specifying exact page coordinates.

Active elements FrontPage components, HTML forms, or Java applets that represent powerful features on a Web page.

Active graphics Theme elements that become animated in a Web page, such as a hyperlink button that changes color when the pointer moves over it.

Active server page A dynamic Web page containing scripts that process a Web page.

ActiveX control An application that creates animation, interactive objects, and other multimedia effects in a Web page.

Administering permission Lets a user create new Webs and set permissions for other Webs.

Administrator The person in charge of assigning users different types of permission for accessing a Web.

Alignment (text to image) Specifies how the text is placed in relation to the image.

Animations Movement of an object or text on a page, such as zooming or flying from the left.

Attributes Elements of a theme that produce active graphics, vivid colors, or a background picture in the Web's pages.

Authoring permission Lets a user create and edit pages in a Web.

AutoNumber field In a database table, a field that automatically numbers records in sequential order to create a primary key.

Background picture A graphic that is tiled to fill the background of a page, table, or table cell.

Banner ad manager Displays alternating banner images on a Web page.

Bookmark A hyperlink whose target appears in the same Web page as the hyperlink.

Bottom alignment Aligns the top row of text with the bottom edge of the image.

Browser A program that lets you view Web pages on your computer. A browser can request a Web page from a Web server.

Browser report A report that identifies the different browsers used to access a Web and the number of visitors using each browser.

Browsing permission Lets a user open a Web and view it after it has been published.

Caption A title for a table.

Cascading style sheet (CSS) A Web page that contains HTML code that specifies the appearance and format of different tags included in the Web page.

Categories Lets you group your files, images, and folders into categories for easier management.

Cell The intersection of a vertical column and a horizontal row in a table.

Cell padding The number of pixels between a cell's contents and the cell border.

Cell properties Options such as alignment of text in the cells, the width and color of the cells, and the cell span.

Cell spacing The number of pixels between cells in the table.

Cell span The number of rows or columns covered by a cell.

Change Style list A list on the Formatting toolbar that contains six levels of preformatted headings for Web page text.

Chart component A tool that displays spreadsheet data as a picture in a Web page.

Check boxes Let visitors make multiple choices in a form group.

Check in The process of opening a Web page that uses source control for editing.

Check out The process of closing a Web page that uses source control to make it available to other authors for editing.

Child page A page below another page in the Web hierarchy.

Closing tag The second tag in a two-sided tag that tells the browser to turn off the specified feature or format. A closing tag always contains a slash character.

Color values Combinations of red, green, and blue that determine the color of an object on the screen.

Command tag Symbols (< >) used in HTML to indicate the beginning and end of commands. For example, the command <B>My sentence is formatted as bold.</B> would display the following in a Web browser: **My sentence is formatted as bold.**

Comment component Lets the Web developer insert comments that can be viewed only in FrontPage.

Common Gateway Interface (CGI) Provides one method for Web clients and servers to communicate. FrontPage Server Extensions eliminate the need for CGI scripts in Web communication.

Common targets Frame settings recognized by all Web browsers.

Confirmation Field component Creates a personalized feedback page.

Create Hyperlink dialog box The dialog box used to specify the URL for a text or image hyperlink.

Custom color A color created by a user of FrontPage. Custom colors can be used in the same way that default colors are.

Dark border color In a table, the color that you can apply to a cell's top and left borders.

Data access page A Web page that shows data from the database table on which the page is based. You can use a data access page to view, add, delete, and sort table records.

Database A collection of related tables that stores data about an entity.

Database connection Specifies the name, location, and type of database that you want to access from a Web.

Database Results region An area in a Web page that displays data from the database table on which it is based. The Database Results region lets you examine the data contained in the database table, but you cannot add, delete, or change its data.

Default.htm The default filename of the home page in a FrontPage server-based Web.

Delete command In Navigation View, lets you permanently remove unneeded files from your Web or remove files from the Web structure but not the Web.

Destination The target of a hyperlink.

Dial-up connection A service that lets you dial into the Internet whenever you choose.

Direct connection A connection to the Internet that is available each time you turn on your computer.

Domain report A report that provides data about the number of visitors from each domain name that used a browser to access a Web.

Download time The time it takes to fully display a Web page in a browser. Pages with large graphics files often have a long download time.

Drag and drop method The process of dragging files from one location to another in Folders and Navigation Views.

Drop-down menu On a form, allows visitors to make a single selection or multiple selections from a menu containing multiple choices.

Dynamic HTML Code that lets you create animated effects for text and other objects or respond to user input in a Web page.

E-mail A way to send messages from one computer to another.

E-mail hyperlink Lets users send e-mail messages from a Web page.

Entity A person, place, thing, or idea.

Executable Web folder A folder in a Web that allows scripts and programs to be run.

FAQ (Frequently Asked Questions) A template designed to answer common questions about your business or service. FAQs are often seen on the World Wide Web.

Field In a database table, a column that describes one characteristic about an entity.

Find Setup Wizard Appears when you use FrontPage Help for the first time. You can then choose the Help database size that suits your needs.

Folders View Displays the folder hierarchy of the entire Web site.

Form (database) A database object that shows table data in a way similar to how you might show data in a paper form. You can use a form to enter, delete, and sort data.

Form (HTML) An interactive area of a Web page used to collect data from a visitor to a Web site.

Form fields Data collection areas on a form.

Form Page Wizard Lets you create a custom form by answering a series of questions.

Format Painter A tool that lets you copy the format from existing formatted text and apply it to new text.

Formatting toolbar Provides buttons that allow you quick access to formatting changes.

fpdb (FrontPage database folder) The folder automatically created by FrontPage in which to store database files in a Web.

Frame properties Options such as whether the user can resize the frames or whether a scroll bar will appear on the frames.

Frames page A Web page that displays multiple Web pages simultaneously in separate, scrollable windows.

FrontPage components Software modules that you can easily insert into Web pages, which allow you to include features that would otherwise require advanced programming skills.

GIF format A graphics file format commonly used for line drawings, such as bar charts. Graphics files on Web pages must be in either GIF or JPEG format.

Gradient A color scale used to create custom colors.

Hidden folder A folder in a Web site that contains files that run the site but that are not necessary for a browser to use to display the Web's pages. The first character of a hidden folder is an underscore.

Hit Counter component Inserts a counter to tally all visits to your Web page.

Home page The first page that a visitor to a Web site usually sees. The home page usually links to other main pages and might include a mission statement for an organization, as well as an index or a table of contents. The home page (usually designated as index.htm or default.htm) typically resides in the root folder.

Horizontal lines Lines that appear on a Web page to help divide the content.

Horizontal line properties Settings including the color of the line, its width, height, and alignment.

Hotspot An area on an image that contains a hyperlink.

Hover button A button that becomes highlighted when a mouse is positioned over it. A hover button is usually linked to another Web page.

HTML (Hypertext Markup Language) The programming language used to create Web pages. FrontPage uses HTML to create Web pages based on the commands you give.

HTML document A Web page.

HTML form An interactive area of a Web page used to collect data from a visitor to a Web site.

HTML tab A page view that shows the HTML code for a Web page.

HTML tag A container that tells the browser how to display the content that either follows a tag or is enclosed by a pair of tags.

Hue A color's value. On the color matrix, red is 0; green is 80; blue is 160.

Hyperlink A highlighted word, phrase, or graphic that opens another Web page when a user clicks it. Hyperlinks can link to pages within a Web site, to e-mail addresses, or to remote Web sites.

Hyperlink dialog box Provides options for hyperlinks, such as destinations.

Hyperlinks View Displays an overview of the site and the existing hyperlinks between Web pages.

Hypertext Transfer Protocol (HTTP) A language used by Web clients and servers to communicate.

Import command Lets you copy external files, such as graphics and text files, to your Web site. You can import files from the hard drive, the floppy drive, or any network drives to which you are connected.

Include Page component Includes the contents of one Web page in other Web pages.

Inner tags In a nested list, the inner tags are the second set of tags that appear within the opening tag of the outer set of tags.

Interlaced image An image that appears gradually on a Web page, starting with a poor resolution and then sharpening.

Internet A worldwide communication network.

Internet service provider (ISP) A supplier of two basic types of Internet connection service: direct and dial-up.

Java applet A program written in the Java programming language and run by a browser that adds multimedia effects, interactivity, and other effects to a Web page.

JavaScript A Netscape scripting language used to create dynamic content in a Web page.

JPG (or JPEG) format A graphics file format typically used for photographic images. Graphics files on Web pages are usually in either GIF or JPEG format.

Left alignment The image appears at the left margin and the text wraps on the right.

Light border color In a table, the color that you can apply to a cell's bottom and right borders.

Luminosity The amount of white added to a color.

Marquee Words that move across a Web page when it is viewed in a browser.

Menu bar Contains the menu options for FrontPage.

Middle alignment Aligns the top row of text with the middle of the image.

Name/value pair An HTML form sends data to a Web server for processing by pairing the form field name with the value entered into the form field by the user.

Navigation bar Displays buttons that link to other Web pages.

Navigation button A button with a hyperlink to a Web page.

Navigation View Shows the navigation structure of the Web.

Nested table A table that appears in one cell of another table.

Nested tag An HTML tag that appears within another set of HTML tags.

Network Two or more computers that can share information. The Internet connects computer networks from all over the world.

No Frames page HTML code in a frames page that displays a message when the frames page is opened by a browser that does not support frames.

Normal tab Displays a Web page in Normal view, which is the view you use to edit Web pages in FrontPage.

Office component An object created in and by FrontPage that contains the necessary tools for entering and formatting spreadsheet, chart, or pivot table data.

One-line text box Provides space on a form for one line of data entry.

One-sided tag An HTML container that contains only an opening tag.

Opening tag The first tag in a two-sided tag that tells the browser to turn on a certain feature or format and apply it to the content contained within the tags.

Ordered list A numbered list in a Web page.

Orphan file A file not linked in the Web hierarchy.

Outer tags In a nested list, the outer tags are the first set of tags.

Page Banner component Inserts specially formatted text or images into a Web page.

Page properties Settings for the Web page title, background and text color, and margins, among other things. You set page properties in the Page Properties dialog box.

Page report A report that provides data about the number of page views for each page in a Web.

Page transition A special effect that appears when a page is displayed.

Page View Displays the contents of a page, along with tools for editing.

Parent page Any page in the Web that has links to child pages that are below the parent in the Web's hierarchy.

Personal Web Server (PWS) A Web server that you can install on your computer using the Windows 98 CD and that runs your Webs using the HTTP protocol.

Pictures toolbar Contains editing tools that can be used along with tools on the Format toolbar to alter the color, size, or placement of a picture or to select a transparent color, etc.

Preview tab A feature that lets you see how the Web page will look in a Web browser. You can preview pages by clicking the Preview tab on the Views bar.

PivotTable List component An interactive spreadsheet that lets you quickly summarize, organize, and display spreadsheet data in different ways in a Web page.

Print Preview A feature that lets you see how a Web page will look when it is printed.

Primary key In a database table, the field that contains a value to uniquely identify each record in the table.

Property Additional information supplied to an HTML tag.

Protocol A language used by the Web client and the Web server software to communicate. For example, clients and servers use a protocol called HTTP (Hypertext Transfer Protocol) to send and receive documents.

Publish The process of transferring your Web files to the URL of your Web site.

Push buttons Allow the user to submit form data for processing or to clear a form.

Query A database object that is a question that you ask of the database in order to view records that answer your question.

Radio buttons On a form, allow visitors to make a single choice from multiple entries in a group.

Recalculating hyperlinks A process that repairs any broken hyperlinks, updates the shared border and navigation files, updates all FrontPage components, updates data on the server, and deletes any unused theme files.

Record One item in a database table.

Repeated hyperlink A hyperlink in a single Web page that points to the same page, picture, or file and that appears in more than one location in the Web page.

Remote Web pages Pages located at other Web sites.

Report A database object that retrieves data from the database and arranges it in a specified format.

Reports View Allows for easier Web management by providing multiple reports about files, components, download times, hyperlinks, update information, etc.

Results file A database file containing form results.

Reveal Tags A feature that lets you view the HTML tags in a Web document in Normal Page View.

Right alignment The image appears at the right margin and the text wraps on the left.

Root folder The main folder in a Web server's folder hierarchy.

Saturation The amount of color used.

Save As Allows you to save the current document in a different location or with a different name.

Scheduled Picture component Displays a designated image for a specified amount of time.

Screenshot A picture of the image displayed on a computer's monitor. You press [Print Screen] to capture the picture.

ScreenTip A description of a toolbar button's function that appears when you place the mouse pointer over that button. The status bar simultaneously displays an expanded version of the ScreenTip information.

Script A small program that is displayed by a browser and processed on a server.

Scrolling text box Provides space on a form for multiple lines of data entry.

Search Form A FrontPage component that can be inserted into any page and provides text searching capabilities for the user.

Search Page A FrontPage template that creates a page that automatically includes a search form for text searching capabilities.

Secure server A Web server that encrypts data so that unauthorized parties cannot read it.

Server Extensions Let you develop your Web pages on a local computer or server and then publish them on a remote server.

Server permissions Security properties that determine who can view or modify your Web pages.

Shared border An area that appears on every page in a Web site that uses it. Shared borders often include navigation bars or page banners.

Site Summary report A report available in Reports View that lists information about a Web.

Size handles Small squares that appear on an object when it is selected. You can drag a size handle to resize the object. Dragging a corner size handle resizes the object uniformly in all directions.

Source control A Web feature that ensures that only one author can edit a Web page at a time.

Source document A Web page that contains a hyperlink.

Split The process of creating a new frame by dividing an existing frame in a frames page.

Spreadsheet component A tool that lets you summarize and analyze data in a Web page.

Static data Data that is imported into a Web page but not linked to the spreadsheet that created it.

Status bar Conveys messages pertaining to FrontPage operations and displays descriptions of toolbar buttons.

Style A combination of settings, such as font size.

Substitution component Inserts the value of a parameter into a Web page.

Tab order The order in which fields are activated on a form when the user presses [Tab].

Table The database object that contains fields (or columns) to describe the characteristics of an entity.

Table of Contents page A FrontPage template that creates a page that automatically lists all the pages within the Web as a table of contents.

Table properties Let you control the appearance of a table.

Tables Let you organize text, hyperlinks, and graphics into columns and rows to improve the design of your Web pages.

Target The page to which a hyperlink in one frame page links.

Task History A list of all tasks added to the Tasks list since the Web was created, including all completed and uncompleted tasks.

Taskbar A feature of Windows 98 that displays buttons for open applications as well as the Start button, which you can use to start a program or open a document.

Tasks list A list generated by a FrontPage wizard, the spell checker, or a user that defines the unfinished jobs needed to complete a Web site.

Tasks View Provides access to the FrontPage Tasks list feature.

Templates Ready-made frameworks that you can customize to create Webs and Web pages.

Theme A collection of coordinated graphics, colors, and fonts that you can apply to individual Web pages or to an entire Web site.

Tile An image that is repeated over and over again until it fills a page.

Title bar Shows the program name and the URL of the open FrontPage Web.

Traffic report A report that provides data about the number of visitors to a Web, page views, hits, and the total number of bytes transferred from the server to a browser.

Toolbars Contain buttons to carry out common tasks.

Top alignment Aligns the top row of text to the top edge of the image.

Transparent A setting used to make an image color blend into the background color of a page.

Two-sided tag An HTML container that contains an opening and closing tag.

Under construction icon An icon that tells visitors to a Web site that the current Web page is not yet finished.

Unlocked A file that uses source control and that is available for editing.

Unordered list A bulleted list in a Web page.

Up hyperlink A hyperlink created by FrontPage in a shared border that, when clicked, opens the parent of the currently displayed Web page.

URL (Uniform Resource Locator) A server's network address, typically taking the following form: *http://www.myaddress.com*

Usage log A Web page containing information about the number of times a Web's home page has been opened, the number of times various pages were opened each day or each hour during the day, or the total number of times a Web page was refreshed during a single session.

VBScript A Microsoft scripting language used to embed interactive elements in a Web page.

Verifying hyperlinks A process that examines each hyperlink in a Web to check its validity.

Video active element Inserts a video clip into a Web page.

Views bar Contains buttons for displaying different views of the open FrontPage Web.

Vivid colors An enhanced color set that creates brighter, deeper colors in a Web's theme.

Watermark A background image that does not scroll when the user scrolls the Web page.

Web client A browser, such as Netscape Navigator or Microsoft Internet Explorer.

Web pages Individual documents within a Web site.

Web presence provider (WPP) An Internet service provider (ISP), commerce server provider (CSP), or other Web hosting service that provides space on a Web server for a fee.

Web server A remote computer running Web server software.

Web site A collection of documents that can be published via the Internet.

Window panes Enable you to view the hyperlinks or folders contained in your Web site.

Wizards Let you create Webs or Web pages by answering a series of questions in dialog boxes.

WYSIWYG (What You See Is What You Get) A program that displays text on the screen as it will appear on the printed page, with all of the same formatting.

Zoom In Magnifies the current view.

Zoom Out Reduces the current view.

Index

A

absolute positioning, K-2–5

    limitations, K-5

active graphics, J-12

Active Server Pages, L-7, N-1, N-12–13

activeX controls, L-7

Add Choice dialog box, G-16, G-17

Add Criteria dialog box, N-16, N-17

Add Database Connection dialog box, N-4, N-5

Add Users dialog box, O-14, O-15

administering permission, O-14

administrators of Web sites, O-14

aligning text to images, E-10–11

Alignment property, tables, F-4

All Files report, O-11

Alternate property, marquees, E-15

animations, E-16, E-17

attributes of themes, J-12, J-13

authoring permission, O-14

AutoNumber fields, N-2

B

background(s), images, E-4–5

background colors

    contrast with text color, C-5

    custom, in tables, I-8–9

background pictures, J-12

    background, J-12

    inserting, P-16–17

backups for Web pages, C-17

banner ad manager(s), H-10–11

Banner Ad Manager Properties dialog box, H-11–12

bookmarks, P-12

    inserting, D-16

    inserting hyperlinks to, D-16–17

borders

    color, tables and cells, I-11

    shared. *See* shared borders

Border size property, tables, F-4

bottom alignment, E-10

broken hyperlinks, O-8, O-9, P-14

Broken Hyperlinks report, O-8, O-9, O-11

browser(s), A-2, A-3

    inserting pictures, text, or hyperlinks, D-3

    styles, M-17

    unable to display frames, I-15

    viewing HTML code, P-7

browser reports, O-16, O-17

browsing permission, O-14

buttons. *See also specific buttons*

    hover, H-8–9

    navigation, B-12

    push, G-4, G-5

    radio. *See* radio button(s)

C

captions, tables, F-6–7

cascading style sheets (CSSs), M-14–17

    applying, M-16–17

    browser display of styles, M-17

    creating, M-14–15

    themes compared, M-15

cell(s), tables, F-2

    border colors, I-11

    centering pictures, I-6–7

    formatting using Format painter, I-9

    modifying properties, F-8–9

    resizing, I-4–5

    spacing versus padding, F-5

Cell padding property, tables, F-4

Cell Properties dialog box, F-8–9

Cell spacing property, tables, F-4

cell span, F-8

centering

    pictures in table cells, I-6–7

    tables on Web pages, I-7

CGI (Common Gateway Interface), G-7

Change Password dialog box, O-15

Chart components, M-2, M-3, M-8–9

    changing appearance, M-9

    creating, M-8–9

check boxes, G-5

    adding to HTML forms, G-14–15

Check Box Properties dialog box, G-14, G-15

checking in Web pages, L-12–13

checking out Web pages, L-10–11

child pages, B-12

clip art, downloading, E-6, E-7

Clip Art Gallery, D-2, D-3

Close option, Print Preview window, C-12

closing

    Web pages, B-8, B-9

    Web sites, A-18, A-19

closing tags, P-2

color(s)

    background. *See* background colors

    border, tables and cells, I-11

    custom, images, E-2–3

    individual page elements, changing, J-16

    text and background, contrast between, C-5

    values, E-3

    vivid, J-12

Color dialog box, E-2, E-3

Color Schemes tab, Theme dialog box, J-14, J-15

columns, tables, F-6—7

   resizing, I-5

commerce service providers (CSPs), L-2

commercial Web servers, publishing Web sites, K-15

Common Gateway Interface (CGI), G-7

Component Errors report, O-11

Confirm Delete dialog box, C-16, C-17

Confirm Save dialog box, O-2, O-3

Connect to Web for More Clip Art dialog box, E-6, E-7

content listings, H-6—7

contrast, text and background colors, C-5

copying HTML code from Internet, P-15

correcting hyperlinks, D-11

Create E-mail Hyperlink dialog box, D-14—15

Create Hyperlink dialog box, D-9, D-12, D-13, D-16, D-17

creating Web sites on Web servers, L-1—24

   checking in pages, L-12—13

   checking out pages, L-10—11

   executable Web folders, L-8—9

   Import Web Wizard, L-4—5

   locating Web presence providers, L-2—3

   opening Office documents in Web pages, L-14—15

   setting page options, L-6—7

   troubleshooting server problems, L-16—17

CSPs (commerce service providers), L-2

CSS(s). See cascading style sheets (CSSs)

CSS 1.0, L-7

CSS 2.0, L-7

Custom background color property

   cells, F-9

   tables, F-4

Custom background image property

   cells, F-9

   tables, F-4

Custom border color property

   cells, F-9

   tables, F-4

custom colors

   images, E-2—3

   table backgrounds, I-8—9

Custom dark border color property, tables, F-4

custom forms, G-2

customizing

   Hyperlinks View, K-13

   Site Summary reports, O-10—11

   themes, J-14—15

   themes for single pages, J-16—17

Custom light border color property, tables, F-4

►D

dark border color, I-11

data, static, M-6

data access pages, N-6—9

   creating, N-6—7

   toolbar buttons, N-9

   using, N-8—9

database(s)

   basic concepts, N-2—3

   integrating with Web pages. See integrating databases with Web pages

database connections, N-4

database objects, N-3

Database Results regions, N-14—15

Database Results Wizard, N-14, N-15

Delete Record button, N-9

deleting

   themes, J-15

   Web pages, C-16, C-17

descriptive titles, C-3

destinations, hyperlinks, P-12

DHTML Effects dialog box, E-16, E-17

dial-up connections, H-16

direct connections, H-16

displaying. See viewing

documents

   HTML. See Web pages

   Office. See Office documents

   source, hyperlinks, P-12

domain names, L-3

domain reports, O-16, O-17

downloading

   clip art, E-6, E-7

   pictures, D-5

download limit, C-14

drag and drop, moving files in Folders View, K-6—7

drop-down menus, G-5

   inserting in HTML forms, G-16—17

Drop-Down Menus Properties dialog box, G-16, G-17

dynamic HTML, L-7

►E

Edit Hyperlinks dialog box, D-11, O-8, O-9

editing

   hotspots, E-13

   pictures, D-4—5

   Web pages, B-6—7, P-8—9

e-mail addresses, D-15

   linking to, D-14—15

entering text, C-6—7

entities, N-2

executable Web folders, L-8—9

exiting FrontPage, A-18, A-19

exporting Web pages, C-16, C-17

External Hyperlinks report, O-11

►F

feedback forms, G-2

fields, N-2

file(s)

   shared borders, J-9

   unlocked, L-12

file formats, G-7

file hyperlinks, D-13

file management, K-7

filenames

   changing in Folders View, K-8—9

   naming conventions, K-9

File Properties dialog box, H-7, H-8

Filter by Selection button, N-9

finding text in Web sites, K-10, K-11

First Record button, N-9

Index

Float property, tables, F-4

folders

    creating, A-14—15

    executable, L-8—9

    hidden, J-9

    hierarchies, A-7

Folders button, A-12, A-13

Folders View, A-12, A-14—15, L-12, L-13

    changing filenames, K-8—9

    moving files, K-6—7

font(s), changing in picture elements, J-14

Font dialog box, C-9, E-14, E-15

form(s), N-3

    HTML. See HTML forms

    search, creating in Web pages, N-16—17

    sending results to databases, N-10—11

format(s), files, G-7

Format Painter, formatting table cells, I-9

formatted text file format, G-7

formatted text with HTML file format, G-7

formatting

    paragraph styles, C-10—11

    text, C-8—9

Formatting toolbar, C-8, C-9

form fields, G-4, G-5

    properties, G-10—11

Form Page Wizard, G-4—5

Form Properties dialog box, G-6, G-7, N-10, N-11

frame(s), F-1, F-10—17, L-7

    creating in frames pages, I-12—13

    creating Web pages with frames, F-10—11

    deleting from frames pages, I-14—15

    exiting frame pages, F-16—17

    modifying properties, F-14—15

    setting targets, F-12—13

    splitting, I-12

Frame Properties dialog box, F-14—15

frames pages

    creating new frames, I-12—13

    deleting frames, I-14—15

    printing in, I-16—17

FrontPage

    exiting, A-18, A-19

    starting, A-4—5

FrontPage components, H-2, H-3

FrontPage Server Extensions, A-2, G-7

FrontPage window, viewing, A-12—13

fttp hyperlinks, D-13

▶G

graphics, E-1—17. See also picture(s)

    active, J-12

    aligning text to images, E-10—11

    custom colors, E-2—3

    downloading clip art, E-6—7

    hotspots, E-12—13

    images as backgrounds, E-4—5

    marquees, E-1, E-14—15

    modifying images using Pictures toolbar, E-8—9

    page transitions and animations, E-16—17

    positioning in Web pages, K-4—5

guest book forms, G-2

▶H

Header cell property, F-9

Help button, data access toolbar, N-9

Help system, A-16—17

hidden folders, J-9

hit counters, H-2, H-3

home pages, A-8

Horizontal alignment property, cells, F-9

horizontal line(s), inserting, D-6—7

    HTML code, P-14, P-15

Horizontal Line Properties dialog box, D-6, D-7

hotspots, E-12—13

    editing, E-13

hover button(s), H-8—9

Hover Button Properties dialog box, H-8, H-9, P-6, P-7

HTML (Hypertext Markup Language), A-2, A-3, B-2, P-1—24

    cascading styles, M-14, M-15

    creating hyperlinks, P-12—13

    creating Web pages, P-3

    displaying code, P-4—5

    dynamic, L-7

    HTML Page View. See HTML Page View

    inserting horizontal lines, P-14, P-15

    inserting pictures, P-14, P-15, P-16—17

    nesting HTML code, P-10—11

    reusing code from Internet, P-15

    tags. See HTML tags

    viewing, P-7

HTML bulleted list file format, G-7

HTML definition list file format, G-7

HTML documents. See Web pages

HTML file format, G-7

HTML forms, G-1—17

    adding check boxes, G-14—15

    adding text boxes, G-8—9

    creating using Form Page Wizard, G-4—5

    inserting drop-down menus, G-16—17

    inserting radio buttons, G-12—13

    overview, G-2—3

    setting form field properties, G-10—11

    setting properties, G-6—7

HTML Page View, P-6—9

    editing Web pages, P-8—9

    working in, P-6—7

HTML tab, Page View, B-9

HTML tags, P-2

    closing, P-2

    common, list, P-5

    inner and outer, P-10

    nested, P-2, P-10—11

    one-sided and two-sided, P-2

    opening, P-2

    required, P-9

HTTP (Hypertext Transfer Protocol), A-2

http hyperlinks, D-13

hue, E-3

hyperlink(s), A-12

    to bookmarks, inserting, D-16—17

    broken, O-8, O-9, P-14

correcting, D-11

creating, P-12–13

creating simultaneously with Web page, D-12

to e-mail addresses, D-14–15

hotspots, E-12–13

inserting from Web browser, D-3

to local Web pages, inserting, D-8–9

pictures used as, D-18–19

recalculating, O-8, O-9

to remote Web pages, creating, D-12–13

repeated, K-13

testing, D-10–11

types, D-13

verifying, H-12, H-13, O-8, O-9

viewing, H-12, H-13

Hyperlink dialog box, D-8

Hyperlinks button, A-12, A-13

Hyperlinks report, O-11

Hyperlinks View, A-12, H-12, H-13

    customizing, K-13

    printing, K-12, K-13

Hypertext Markup Language. *See* HTML *entries*

Hypertext Transfer Protocol (HTTP), A-2

▶ I

ICANN (Internet Corporation for Assigned Names and
    Numbers), L-3

images, sizing, E-9

Import dialog box, C-14, C-15

importing

    databases into Web pages, N-4–5

    data into Spreadsheet components, M-6–7

    Web pages, C-14–15

Import Web Wizard, L-4–5

inner tags, P-10

Insert Component button list, M-4, M-5

inserting

    bookmarks, D-16

    captions in tables, F-6, F-7

check boxes in HTML forms, G-14–15

drop-down menus in HTML forms, G-16–17

horizontal lines, D-6–7, P-14, P-15

hyperlinks. *See* inserting hyperlinks

pictures, D-2–3, P-14, P-15, P-16–17

radio buttons in HTML forms, G-12–13

rows and columns in tables, F-6, F-7

search forms, H-4–5

tables, F-2–3

inserting hyperlinks

    to bookmarks, D-16–17

    to local Web pages, D-8–9

    to remote Web pages, D-12–13

Insert Rows or Columns dialog box, F-6, F-7

Insert Table dialog box, F-2, F-3

integrating databases with Web pages, N-1–24

    Active Server Pages, N-1, N-12–13

    data access pages. *See* data access pages

    database concept review, N-2–3

    Database Results regions, N-14–15

    importing databases, N-4–5

    search forms in Web pages, N-16–17

    sending form results to databases, N-10–11

integration, FrontPage features, B-2

interlaced pictures, D-4

Internal Hyperlinks report, O-11

Internet, A-1

Internet Corporation for Assigned Names and Numbers
    (ICANN), L-3

Internet Explorer, printing options, I-17

Internet Service Providers (ISPs), H-16, L-2

    selecting to host Web sites, K-17

Internet technologies, setting in pages, L-7

ISPs. *See* Internet Service Providers (ISPs)

▶ J

Java applets, H-8, L-7

JavaScript, L-7

▶ L

Last Record button, N-9

left alignment, E-10

light border color, I-11

lines, horizontal

    HTML code for inserting, P-14, P-15

    inserting, D-6–7

link(s). *See* hyperlink(s)

Linked Files report, O-11

Link Style Sheet dialog box, M-16, M-17

lists, ordered and unordered, P-10

local Web pages, inserting hyperlinks to, D-8–9

luminosity, E-3

▶ M

markup languages, P-1. *See also* HTML (Hypertext
    Markup Language)

marquee(s), E-1, E-14–15

Marquee component, H-2, H-3

Marquee Properties dialog box, E-14, E-15, H-2, H-3

menu(s), drop-down. *See* drop-down menus

menu bar, A-13

Microsoft Clip Art Gallery, E-6, E-7

Microsoft Clip Gallery Live site, E-6, E-7

Microsoft Office Chart Wizard, M-8, M-9

middle alignment, E-10

Minimum size Width/height property, tables, F-4

Modify Field dialog box, N-10, N-11

Modify Style dialog box, M-12, M-13

More Colors dialog box, E-2, E-3, I-8

Movement Speed: Amount property, marquees, E-15

Movement Speed: Delay property, marquees, E-15

moving. *See also* navigating Web sites; navigation
    entries; positioning

    files in Folders View, K-6–7

▶ N

Name and Password Required dialog box, O-13

name/value pairs, G-10

Index

navigating Web sites, J-7

  creating options, O-6–7

Navigation Bar Properties dialog box, J-4, J-5

navigation bars, B-12, J-7

  adding, B-12

  adding to pages, J-10, J-11

  setting properties, B-12

Navigation button, A-12, A-13

navigation buttons, B-12

Navigation View, A-12

  adding banners and navigation bars, B-12, B-13

  adding pages, J-4–5

  creating new pages, B-14–15

  inserting tables, F-2, F-3

  printing, K-12, K-13

nested HTML tags, P-10–11

nested tables, I-10–11

nested tags, P-2

networks, A-2

New dialog box, F-10, F-11

New Message dialog box, D-14–15

New Record button, N-8, N-9

news hyperlinks, D-13

Next Record button, N-8, N-9

No Frames pages, I-15

Normal tab, Page View, B-9

No wrap property, cells, F-9

Number of columns spanned property, cells, F-9

Number of rows spanned property, cells, F-9

▶ O

Office Chart Wizard, M-8, M-9

Office components, M-1–11

  Chart components, M-2, M-3, M-8–9

  PivotTable List components, M-2, M-3, M-10–11

  reasons for using, M-7

  Spreadsheet components. *See* Spreadsheet components

Office documents

  adding content to Web sites, O-4–5

  opening in Webs, L-14–15

Office styles, M-12–17

  cascading style sheets. *See* cascading style sheets (CSSs)

  creating in Web pages, M-12–13

Older Files report, O-11

one-line text boxes, G-5, G-8

opening

  Office documents in Webs, L-14–15

  Web pages, B-4–5

  Web sites, A-19, K-16–17

opening tags, P-2

Open Web dialog box, K-16, K-17

Options dialog box, L-14, L-15, O-10, O-11

Options for Saving Results to Database dialog box, N-10, N-11

ordered lists, P-10

order forms, G-2

outer tags, P-10

▶ P

padding, cells, spacing versus, F-5

Page Banner Properties dialog box, J-10, J-11

page banners, adding to pages, J-10, J-11

Page button, A-12, A-13

page options, setting, L-6–7

Page Options dialog box, L-6, L-7

Page Properties dialog box, C-3, C-4–5, D-8, D-9

page reports, O-16, O-17

page transitions, E-16, E-17

Page Transitions dialog box, E-16, E-17

Page View, A-12, B-9, J-8, J-9. *See also* HTML Page View

paragraph styles, formatting, C-10–11

parent pages, B-12

passwords, changing, O-15

permissions, servers, H-16

Permissions dialog box, O-14, O-15

Personal Web Manager dialog box, K-14, K-15

Personal Web Server (PWS)

  opening Web sites, K-16–17

  publishing Web sites, K-14–15

picture(s). *See also* graphics

  background. *See* background pictures

  centering in table cells, I-6–7

  changing fonts, J-14

  downloading, D-5

  editing, D-4–5

  HTML code for inserting, P-14, P-15

  as hyperlinks, D-18–19

  inserting, D-2–3

  interlaced, D-4

  transparent, D-4, D-5

Picture dialog box, D-2, D-3

Picture Properties dialog box, D-4, D-5

Pictures File report, O-11

Pictures toolbar, D-4, D-5, E-8–9

PivotTable List components, M-2, M-3, M-10–11

planning

  Web pages, B-3

  Web sites, A-6–7

positioning. *See also* moving

  absolute, K-2–5

  graphics in Web pages, K-4–5

  text in Web pages, K-2–3

Positioning toolbar, K-2, K-3

Preview in Browser dialog box, B-8, B-9

previewing Web pages, B-2, B-8, B-9

Preview tab, Page View, B-9

Preview View, frame pages, F-13

Previous Record button, N-9

primary keys, N-2

Print dialog box, I-16, I-17

printing

in frames pages, I-16–17

options in Internet Explorer, I-17

Web pages, C-12–13

Print option, Print Preview window, C-12

Print Page Setup dialog box, C-12, C-13

Print Preview window, C-12, C-13

Print Properties dialog box, C-12, C-13

Programs menu, A-4, A-5

properties

cells, modifying, F-8–9

forms, setting, G-6–7

frames, F-14–15

setting, C-4–5

Properties dialog box, L-8, L-9

protocols, A-2

publishing Web sites, H-16–17, K-1–24, O-1–24

adding content from Office documents, O-4–5

assessing sites' function and appearance, O-2–3

changing filenames in Folders View, K-8–9

checking site after publishing, O-13

commercial Web servers, K-15

creating navigation options, O-6–7

customizing Site Summary reports, O-10–11

finding and replacing text in Web sites, K-10–11

Hyperlinks View, K-12, K-13

moving files in Folders View, K-6–7

Navigation View, K-12, K-13

to other servers, O-12–13

positioning graphics in Web pages, K-4–5

positioning text in Web pages, K-2–3

preventing publishing of specific pages, N-7

PWS. See Personal Web Server (PWS)

recalculating and verifying hyperlinks, O-8–9

securing site, O-14–15

spell checking site, O-3

usage logs, O-16–17

Publish Web dialog box, H-16, H-17, K-14, K-15

Publish Web feature, A-2

push buttons, G-4, G-5

PWS. See Personal Web Server (PWS)

▶ Q

queries, N-3

▶ R

radio button(s), G-5

inserting in HTML forms, G-12–13

Radio Button Properties dialog box, G-2, G-13

Recalculate Hyperlinks dialog box, O-8, O-9

recalculating hyperlinks, O-8, O-9

Recently Added Files report, O-11

records, N-2

registering domain names, L-3

registration forms, G-2, G-3

remote Web pages, inserting hyperlinks to, D-12–13

Remove Filter button, N-9

Rename dialog box, K-8, K-9

repeated hyperlinks, K-13

Replace dialog box, K-10, K-11

replacing text, Web sites, K-10, K-11

reports

Broken Hyperlinks, O-8, O-9

databases, N-3

Site Summary, O-1, O-10–11

usage logs, O-16–17

Reports button, A-12, A-13

Reports View, A-12, H-14–15

Reports View tab, Options dialog box, O-10, O-11

results files, viewing, G-17

Reveal tags command, P-4–5

right alignment, E-10

rows, tables, F-6–7

resizing, I-5

▶ S

saturation, E-3

Save As dialog box, C-16, C-17, F-10, F-11, I-12, I-13

Save Record button, N-8, N-9

saving Web pages, B-8, B-9

screenshots, K-12, K-13

ScreenTips, A-12

scrolling text boxes, G-5, G-8

Scroll property, marquees, E-15

search engines, submitting Web site, O-17

search form(s), G-2, H-4–5

creating in Web pages, N-16–17

Web pages, N-16–17

Search Form Properties dialog box, H-5

search pages, H-4, H-5

security, O-14–15

Select Background Picture dialog box, E-4, E-5

Select Hyperlink dialog box, M-16, M-17

server extensions, H-16

server permissions, H-16

Set Page Title dialog box, C-16, C-17

shared borders, J-1

adding, B-12

changing content, J-6–7

creating in Web sites, J-2–3

files maintaining, J-9

removing, C-2, C-3

turning off, for single Web page, J-8–9

using, B-16–17

Shared Borders dialog box, B-16, B-17, J-2, J-3, J-8, J-9

Site Summary reports, O-1

customizing, O-10–11

sizing

cells in tables, I-4–5

images, E-9

tables, I-2–3

sizing handles, D-4

Slide property, marquees, E-15

Slow pages report, O-11

Sort Ascending button, N-8, N-9

Sort Descending button, N-9

source control, L-10, L-11

Index

source documents, hyperlinks, P-12

spacing, cells, padding versus, F-5

Specify height property, cells, F-9

Specify width property, cells, F-9

spell checking, Web sites, O-3

Spelling dialog box, B-6, B-7

splitting frames, I-12

Spreadsheet components, M-2, M-3, M-4—7

   creating, M-4—5

   importing data into, M-6—7

Spreadsheet Property Toolbox, M-4, M-5

Standard toolbar, A-13

starting, FrontPage, A-4—5

Start menu, A-4, A-5

static data, M-6

status bar, A-13

style(s), C-10. *See also* cascading style sheets (CSSs)

   paragraph, C-10—11

Style dialog box, M-12, M-13, M-14, M-15

Style list, C-10

► T

table(s), F-1

   border colors, I-11

   captions, F-6—7

   cells. *See* cell(s), tables

   centering on Web pages, I-7

   columns. *See* columns, tables

   custom background colors, I-8—9

   databases, N-2

   inserting, F-2—3

   modifying properties, F-3, F-4—5

   nested, I-10—11

   resizing, I-2—3

   rows. *See* rows, tables

   setting width, F-3

Table of Contents pages, H-6—7

Table Properties dialog box, F-3, F-4—5, I-2, I-3, I-8

Tables toolbar, F-8, F-9

target(s), frames, F-12—13

Target Frame dialog box, F-12, F-13, F-16, F-17

task(s), viewing history, A-10

taskbar, A-4, A-5, A-13

Tasks lists, A-2, A-10—11

Tasks View, A-10—11

telnet hyperlinks, D-13

templates, B-1, B-10—11

testing hyperlinks, D-10—11, H-12, H-13

text

   aligning to images, E-10—11

   color, contrast with background color, C-5

   entering, C-6—7

   finding and replacing in Web sites, K-10—11

   formatting, C-8—9

   inserting from Web browser, D-3

   positioning in Web pages, K-2—3

text boxes, adding to HTML forms, G-8—9

Text Box Properties dialog box, G-10, G-11

text database file format, G-7

theme(s). *See* Web themes

Themes dialog box, J-13, J-14, J-15, J-17

Thesaurus dialog box, C-6, C-7

title(s), descriptive, C-3

title bar, A-13

top alignment, E-10

traffic reports, O-16, O-17

transparent pictures, D-4, D-5

troubleshooting, servers problems, L-16—17

► U

Uncompleted Tasks report, O-11

Undo Last Change button, N-9

Universal Resource Locators (URLs), A-2, D-12

Unlinked Files report, O-11

unlocked files, L-12

unordered lists, P-10

Unused Themes report, O-11

Unverified Hyperlinks report, O-11

URLs (Universal Resource Locators), A-2, D-12

usage logs, O-16—17

► V

values, colors, E-3

VBScript, L-7

Verify Hyperlinks dialog box, O-8, O-9

verifying hyperlinks, H-12, H-13, O-8, O-9

Vertical alignment property, cells, F-9

viewing

   FrontPage window, A-12—13

   HTML code, P-7

   HTML tags, P-4—5

   hyperlinks, H-12, H-13

   previewing Web pages, B-2, B-8, B-9

   results files, G-17

   task history, A-10

Views bar, A-13

visual interface, B-2

vivid colors, J-12

► W

Web, A-2

Web browsers. *See* browser(s)

Web clients, A-2, A-3

Web folders, executable, L-8—9

Web pages, B-1

   adding to Navigation View, J-4—5

   centering tables, I-7

   checking in, L-12—13

   checking out, L-10—11

   closing, B-8, B-9

   creating from templates, B-10—11

creating in Navigation View, B-14—15

creating using HTML, P-3

creating using Word, O-5

descriptive titles, C-3

editing, B-6—7, P-8—9

frames pages. *See* frames pages

No Frames, I-15

opening, B-4—5

planning, B-3

preventing publishing, N-7

previewing, B-2, B-8, B-9

remote, inserting hyperlinks to, D-12—13

saving, B-8, B-9

setting page options, L-6—7

setting properties, C-4—5

Web Presence Providers (WPPs)

locating, L-2—3

publishing Web sites. *See* publishing Web sites

worksheet for comparing, L-3

Web servers, A-2, A-3

creating Web sites. *See* creating Web sites on
Web servers

troubleshooting, L-16—17

Web Settings dialog box, K-6, K-7, L-10, L-11

Web sites, A-1

administrators, O-14

closing, A-18, A-19

creating on Web servers. *See* creating Web sites on
Web servers

navigating, J-7

opening, A-19

planning, A-6—7

publishing. *See* publishing Web sites

setting Web pages to prevent printing, N-7

submitting to search engines, O-17

Web themes, J-1

additional, installing, J-13

applying to Web sites, J-12, J-13

attributes, J-12, J-13

cascading style sheets compared, M-15

changing, B-15

customizing, J-14—15

deleting, J-15

for multiple pages, changing simultaneously, J-17

removing, C-2, C-3

for single pages, customizing, J-16—17

Web wizards, A-8—9

What You See Is What You Get (WYSIWYG), A-2

width, tables, setting, F-3

Word, creating Web pages, O-5

WPPs. *See* Web Presence Providers (WPPs)

WYSIWYG (What You See Is What You Get), A-2

▶ Z

Zoom In option, Print Preview window, C-12

Zoom Out option, Print Preview window, C-12